# GERMAN WARSHIPS
of the Second World War

*H. T. Lenton*

# GERMAN WARSHIPS
of the Second World War

ARCO PUBLISHING COMPANY, INC.
NEW YORK

Published 1976 by Arco Publishing Company, Inc.
219 Park Avenue South, New York, N.Y. 10003

Copyright © by H. T. Lenton 1975

Printed in Great Britain

Library of Congress Cataloging in Publication Data
  Bibliography:  p.
  1.  Warships.  2.  Germany.  Kriegsmarine.
3.  World War, 1939–1945—Germany.    I.  Title.
V767.L46  1976    940.54′59′43    76–13609
ISBN 0–668–04037–8

# Contents

# FOREWORD

No study of the naval history of the Second World War can be complete without a comprehensive list of the warships of the various combatant navies that participated. A list of only the vessels that were actually completed is not enough in itself. For the whole picture to be appreciated the unfulfilled and projected programmes are equally important in denoting the effort detailed to securing victory at sea, and with it complete victory.

Even the study of one particular navy cannot be viewed objectively unless the composition of the navy, or navies, it was built against is known in some depth. Briefly, in 1939, the Anglo-French alliance was opposed to that of Germany and Italy, while the United States of America, not formally aligned with any European country, nevertheless countered the growing military might of Japan in the Far East. For the preservation of its world-wide trade, and the defence of its dispersed Dominion and Colonial territories, the United Kingdom was confronted with the heavy responsibility of maintaining three widely separated fleets in Home waters, in the Mediterranean, and in the Far East. The last was no more than a token force being quite devoid of a battlefleet and generally weak in all other categories.

On the outbreak of war the Royal and French Navies were not greatly extended in curbing the German Navy but in 1940, following the surrender of France and the entry of Italy into the Second World War, the Royal Navy was stretched to the limit to retain its command of the seas. This acute situation was worsened late in 1941 following the Japanese attack on Pearl Harbor when, with the American battle fleet temporarily out of action, the Japanese swept the Far Eastern oceans clear of Allied naval opposition. Such reinforcements as the Royal Navy was able to send to the Far Eastern theatre were both inadequate and unbalanced and only added to the list of losses.

[1] Such as France and Italy and Japan and the United States.

The Allied command of the seas was now threatened by a combination of German submarines in the Atlantic, the Italian fleet and German and Italian aircraft in the Mediterranean, and the air and sea power of Japan in the Far East. Whereas the Pacific war was almost exclusively waged between America and Japan, the Royal Navy was the dominant Allied partner in the Mediterranean, and the major partner in the Atlantic in conjunction with American and Canadian naval forces. It was against this harsh background at the beginning of 1942 that the Allied navies by uniform agreement systematically set out to re-establish their dominance at sea by vast naval construction programmes which could not be matched by Germany, Italy, and Japan except in the matter of submarines; and then only by Germany.

Acknowledgments are due particularly to the Admiralty for submarine plans; to Mr. J. F. Golding and the staff of the Imperial War Museum for photographs; to Deutsche Werft A.G. (Hamburg), Howaldtswerke Hamburg A.G., and A.G. Weser (Bremen) for information on the submarines they built, and to Hr. Karl-Wilhelm Grutzemacher who assisted in many ways. Without their kind assistance this book would have been lacking in many details.

H.T.L.

# ABBREVIATIONS

| | | | |
|---|---|---|---|
| A.A. | anti-aircraft | O.F. | oil fuel |
| AR | air ranging (radar) | (pp) | perpendicular length |
| A/S | anti-submarine | RAF | Royal Air Force |
| ATW | ahead throwing weapon | RAN | Royal Australian Navy |
| AW | air warning | RCN | Royal Canadian Navy |
| B.H.P. | brake horse power | RDF | radar |
| C.T. | conning tower | RDN | Royal Danish Navy |
| cyl. | cylinder | R/F | rangefinder |
| d. | depth (of hull) | RHN | Royal Hellenic Navy |
| DCT | director control tower | RIN | Royal Indian Navy |
| D/F | direction finder | RIt.N | Royal Italian Navy |
| D/G | de-gaussing | RN | Royal Navy |
| D.P. | dual-purpose | RNN | Royal Norwegian Navy |
| d.w. | deadweight (tons) | | |
| GW | general warning | RNeth.N | Royal Netherlands Navy |
| HA.DCT | high-angle director control tower | RNZN | Royal New Zealand Navy |
| HA/LA | combined high- and low-angle | RYN | Royal Yugoslavian Navy |
| IFF | identify friend or foe (radar) | R/T | radio telephony |
| I.H.P. | indicated horse power | SAN | South African Navy |
| IJN | Imperial Japanese Navy | SB | surface bearing |
| | | S.H.P. | shaft horse power |
| LA.DCT | low-angle director control tower | S/L | searchlight |
| | | Sqn. | Squadron |
| lb. | pound (avoirdupois) | SR | surface ranging |
| lb/in$^2$ | pounds per square inch | SW | surface warning |
| | | t. | ton (avoirdupois) |
| m | mile (sea) | T.T. | torpedo tube |
| m$^3$ | cubic metres | USAF | United States Air Force |
| MA/SB | motor anti-submarine boat | USCG | United States Coast Guard |
| MFV | motor fishing vessel | | |
| MGB | motor gunboat | USN | United States Navy |
| ML | motor launch | (VC) | vertical compound |
| M/L | minelayer, -ing | (VQE) | vertical quadruple expansion |
| mm | millimetre | | |
| MMS | motor minesweeper | (VTE) | vertical triple expansion |
| M/S | minesweeper, -ing | | |
| MTB | motor torpedo boat | (wl) | waterline length |
| (oa) | overall length | W/T | wireless telegraphy |

# INTRODUCTION

The Second World War started five years too early for the German Navy. They had planned to build up a balanced navy which, by 1944, would be strong enough to challenge the Royal Navy's command of the seas, but not by outright conflict. It was to be a corsair navy, composed of strong surface groups and a powerful submarine arm, with which depredations on British trade could be made on an unprecedented scale. Fortunately, the plan never materialised, nor was it certain of success, but the challenge would have been a strong one with the issue contested to the bitter end.

Maritime trade was the lifeblood of the dispersed British Empire and its Dominions, and it was both the strength and weakness of the British position. With her sea communications secure Great Britain could resist aggression, and wage war all round the world using the ocean highways as a flexible and economic means of transport. But the trade routes were long and vulnerable and none realised this better than the British themselves. Despite, one may say in spite of, successive British Governments preoccupied with disarmament and appeasement, the semblance of a large and powerful fleet was retained, but it was not necessary to probe too deeply to uncover weaknesses and shortcomings in essential categories.

By a vigorous programme spread over ten years (1935–44) the German Navy hoped to cut back their disparity in strength to acceptable limits, happily aware that they were not the only navy the British fleet sought to contain. But they suffered two severe setbacks at an early stage: the first was the 1937 British re-armament, and subsequent, programmes; the second was the folly of their leaders in prematurely precipitating a war two years later. The re-armament programme was on a scale not witnessed since pre-1914 which, within the industrial and economic capacity of Great Britain, set out rapidly and drastically to make good the deficiencies in its fleet. It came so late, almost too late, that its impact was never fully appreciated in Germany: they had, in fact, already lost the naval race. German shipbuilding could not keep pace with, much less outstrip, the British capacity, and even had war not intervened there was every indication that German naval construction was under close scrutiny, and that any significant action on their part would result in an immediate, and larger, British counteraction.

From the outbreak of war, therefore, construction of German surface ships generally languished, while construction mainly was concentrated on submarines. They could dispute but never attain for themselves the command of the seas as they lacked the means to exercise command had they been successful. There is no doubt that sea communications were gravely threatened, but the threat was not basically from the German surface fleet which is listed in this book. It was the nucleus of a fleet that never reached maturity and, as such, was confined to the sidelines. This small fleet conducted itself well in covering the German invasion of Norway but when the ultimate issue presented itself, the invasion of Great Britain, its task was hopeless. There was no way round the stern bulwark presented by the Royal Navy, cast once more in its historic role of defending its native shores. The projected invasion was abandoned. The German Navy achieved some singular and spirited success with their surface ships but these did not affect the main issues. Meanwhile, its submarine arm relentlessly pursued a *guerre du course* against trade, following a classic but nevertheless false doctrine which has yet to achieve success. The German Navy fought hard, fought long, fought gallantly, but lost. At the outbreak of war their C-in-C was under no illusion of the task ahead and had remarked that "the surface forces . . . are so inferior in number and strength to those of the British fleet that . . . they can do no more than show that they know how to die gallantly. . . ." These proved to be prophetic words.

# REBUILDING A FLEET: 1919–1939

The Treaty of Versailles dealt a heavy blow to the *Kaiserliche Marine* in 1919. Its best ships—already in custody in British waters—were to be surrendered for division among the victorious Allied powers, while only a token force of obsolescent pre-1914 vessels was to be retained to preserve a precarious *status quo* in the Baltic.

This force was sufficient to ensure that in the chaotic conditions following the 1917 Russian revolution, and subsequent counter-revolution, that Germany was not left entirely defenceless and had some means of resistance at her disposal. The threat was clearly recognised as coming from the east, and such military forces that Germany was allowed to retain were to act as an initial bulwark against any proposed, or probable, Bolshevik onslaught. Regardless of whether or not the negotiations conducted at Versailles were successful, there can be little doubt that the permitted strength of the German Navy allowed by this treaty was slender, and comprised:

(*a*) the battleships *Braunschweig, Elsass, Hannover, Hessen, Lothringen, Preussen, Schlesien,* and *Schleswig-Holstein*
(*b*) the light cruisers *Amazone, Arcona, Berlin, Hamburg, Medusa, Niobe, Nymphe,* and *Thetis*
(*c*) the destroyers *T.175, T.185, T.190, T.196, V.1, V.2, V.3, V.5, V6, G.7, G.8, G.10, G.11, S.18, S.19,* and *S.23*
(*d*) the torpedo boats *T.135, T.139, T.141, T.143, T.144, T.146, T.148, T.149, T.151, T.152, T.153, T.154, T.156, T.157, T.158,* and *T.168*
(*e*) ancillary vessels such as minesweepers, surveying vessels, etc.

The active strength was limited to six battleships, six light cruisers, twelve destroyers, and twelve torpedo boats, and vessels in excess of this number were to be held in reserve. No submarines or aircraft were allowed to be kept or built. With personnel restricted to 15,000, the German Navy experienced considerable difficulty in keeping even this small force fully manned, and the active fleet did not, in practice, ever attain its full allotted strength. Replacement tonnage was allowed in all categories, once vessels became over-age, subject to the following limitations: battleships 10,000 tons, light cruisers 6,000 tons, destroyers 600 tons, and torpedo boats 200 tons. If the treaty makers at Versailles showed good judgement on the material side, they failed lamentably on the psychological side if they imagined, by these tonnage limitations, that the German Navy would simply replace old vessels of limited fighting value by only slightly superior new construction. If a single trait was outstandingly obvious with the German race it was their ability and capacity for detailed planning—especially in the field of military science. Viewed in this light the Versailles Treaty was a challenge in which every artifice was used by the German armed forces to circumvent the restrictive clauses of the treaty: first by guile and falsehood, and later by open defiance.

In 1922 a new light cruiser, the *Emden*, was proposed whose design was little advanced on that of the *Dresden* class, the final First World War design to be built. The original provision was to have eight guns twin-mounted on the centre line, but as these mountings failed to materialise she received eight single mountings instead, arranged four on the centre line and four on the broadside. Two years later the first six replacement destroyers, allocated the hull numbers W.102–106, were projected. Ostensibly of 600 tons (they later proved to be over 900 tons[1]) they were not outstanding craft, and followed the traditional German line of flotilla craft with the torpedo armament predominating.

The programmes for 1925 and 1926 embraced three light cruisers, six further destroyers and a torpedo boat. The light cruisers were of 6,000 tons (6,650 tons), and with a main armament of nine 5.9inch guns introduced triple mountings to the German Navy. The turrets were disposed one forward and two aft, and the after turrets were arranged *en echelon* to widen their bow arcs and supplement ahead fire. The original provision for four single A.A. guns was increased to six, all twin-mounted, while building, and the torpedo armament of twelve deck tubes was the heaviest fitted to contemporary, or subsequent, non-British cruisers. Not in keeping with the usual German practice was the meagre scale of protection comprising a narrow waterline belt with thin plating to decks and turrets, and was most probably the result of tonnage restrictions which, with these vessels, was not greatly exceeded. The machinery installation consisted of geared turbines and 10-cylinder diesel engines coupled to twin shafts and this arrangement was one of the earliest

---

[1] Hereafter, the actual displacement in parentheses will follow the officially stated figures given prior to the outbreak of the Second World War.

examples of separate prime movers for full speed and cruising purposes.

The torpedo boat, hull number W.108, was not finally proceeded with as the 200-ton restriction proved too severe to enable a useful type of craft to be developed, but the destroyers, hull numbers W.109–114, were generally similar to the earlier type with the addition of some 15 feet in length, while two units carried guns of heavier calibre.

In 1928 work started on a further light cruiser, the *Leipzig,* which adopted a three-shaft machinery arrangement but was otherwise similar to the "K" class above. The geared turbines were coupled to the wing shafts, and four 7-cylinder diesel engines to the centre shaft for cruising purposes. The variable pitch propeller on the centre shaft feathered when the turbines only were used while conversely, when cruising solely on the diesel engines, the wing shafts were spun by B.H.P. 500 motors. The following year's programme included the first battleship replacement, a combined gunnery training and minelaying vessel, two fishery protection vessels, and the first series of motor minesweepers.

It is here relevant to recall broadly the term of the Washington Naval Treaty which limited capital ships to 35,000 tons and 16inch guns, and cruisers to 10,000 tons and 8inch guns. Between them there existed a virtually forbidden zone into which only aircraft carriers encroached, with their upper limit initially placed at 27,000 tons and their ordnance restricted to 8inch guns. When the treaty was framed particular concern had been expressed that an intermediate class—approximating to the old armoured cruiser—might result between capital ships and cruisers which would completely outclass the latter; two safeguards were therefore incorporated: a total tonnage limitation on capital ships, and the 8inch gun restriction on aircraft carriers which were precisely defined as "decked vessels primarily designed to operate aircraft"[2]. This effectively prevented vessels exceeding the cruiser limits being built, as they would then rank as capital ships and be included in the total tonnage for that class, and none of the signatories to the treaty had any margin to spare in that category[3]. Similarly, the Treaty of Versailles had restricted German replacement battleship tonnage to 10,000 tons and 11inch guns, and while apparently keeping within these limits, the German Navy announced details of the first ship they proposed to build to these limitations.

[2] This resulted in the large British cruisers *Courageous* and *Glorious*, armed with 15inch guns, either being included in the total tonnage for capital ships or being scrapped. Their retention was secured, however, by converting them to aircraft carriers.

[3] France, Italy, Japan, United Kingdom, and United States of America.

She was to be of 10,000 tons (11,700 tons), 26 knots speed, and primarily armed with six 11inch guns. With the exception of eight battlecruisers then extant (four British and four Japanese) she justified the claim that she could outfight any vessel she could not outrun. In fact, the German Navy had utilised replacement battleship tonnage to build a vessel which made no pretensions to capital rank, and fell into the forbidden zone the Washington Treaty had so laboured to avoid. For the German naval architects it was a *tour de force* as, compared with her, all foreign cruisers built to the upper limit of the Washington Treaty cut a sorry figure. The pride of nation and navy were fully expressed when she was named *Deutschland*. In the popular press she was hailed as a "pocket battleship", most probably because she was neither one nor the other, but in the German Navy she was simply rated as a *panzerschiff* (armoured ship), which could be liberally translated as armoured cruiser.

Novel features introduced in her construction, for a vessel of her size, were electric welding and main propulsion by diesel engines: both weight saving items, particularly the latter, which gave her a large radius of action on a modest bunkerage, and clearly marked her as a corsair intended to operate against trade. Nor was the impact of the *Deutschland* on the naval world lessened by the fact that the German Navy could legally build six such vessels, and fully intended to implement her rights under the Treaty.

The *Deutschland* completely overshadowed the remaining vessels included in the programme for the year, but they were not without interest. The dual purpose *Bremse* was a fast minelayer thinly disguised as a gunnery training ship, and was also largely experimental. She was the test bed for the diesel machinery installed in the *Deutschland*, and also mounted the 5inch guns later to be fitted to destroyers. The two sloops on the other hand, built for fishery protection duties, were without merit, but the motor minesweepers, *R.1–16*, were the prototypes of a subsequent large series which performed ubiquitous service comparable to the British Fairmile "B" motor launches. They provided early experience in the construction of small, fast, round bilge form craft, and were equally adaptable for patrol, anti-submarine, or escort work besides their designed role.

The small craft programme was continued in the following year with the first motor torpedo boats, and as a result a significant step was taken a few years later when the German Navy placed a development contract with M.A.N. and Daimler-Benz to produce a suitable lightweight diesel engine for coastal craft. In the interim, hull form was further developed, after extensive tank tests had resulted in the adoption of the round bilge form for seaworthiness, and a high L:B ratio for speed. Alone among the navies of the world the German Navy introduced, and retained, this hull for their MTBs; again alone they had the prime advantage of being able to power them with diesel engines; and technically their development and subsequent production was of the highest order.

The programmes for the years 1931 and 1932 each included further armoured ships, the *Admiral Scheer* and *Admiral Graf Spee*, and the following year included a battlecruiser, light cruiser, eight fast sloops, eight submarines, two submarine depot ships, a yacht, and additional MTBs.

The armoured ships basically followed the *Deutschland* but with modified bridge and superstructure and heavier calibre A.A. guns, increased from 3.5inch to 4.1inch. However, the introduction of the *Deutschland* had not passed un-challenged and resulted in the French Navy laying down two 26,000-ton battlecruisers, which not unnaturally completely outclassed her, and there were indications that the French action would be followed by other navies.

In Germany a new leader had emerged: an outspoken militarist determined to regain for Germany her former greatness, and by force where other means failed. He shrewdly recognised that the victors of the First World War now only possessed the illusion of great powers, were unwilling in the military sense to pay the price this role demanded, and that their voices carried lessening conviction in proportion to their annually declining armed strength. Faced with former allies that no longer acted in concert, and all possessing strong pacifist elements, he used this disunity to full advantage and rallied all Germany behind him. The name of Adolf Hitler has since passed into history, and with his rise to power a cloak of deception fell over German naval activities. There was no point in proceeding with the fourth "Deutschland" as planned—the type had been surpassed—and the vessel was consequently turned into a 26,000-ton (31,800-ton) battlecruiser, the *Scharnhorst*, a fast and robust vessel which sacrificed gunpower, and not protection, for speed. Although submarine construction had been banned design work had been undertaken as outlined in the later section on submarines, and eight coastal submarines, *U.1–8*, and two depot ships were ordered. But these orders were cloaked in secrecy, although the enlarged *Scharnhorst* was suspected. Thus, in little over a decade, the Versail'es Treaty was abrogated, but a further two years were to pass before this was officially recognised.

No secret was made about the remaining vessels of the programme. The light cruiser *Nürnberg*, 6,000 tons (6,980 tons), closely followed the *Leipzig* but with the A.A. armament increased to eight 3.5inch guns, all twin mounted. Of 600 tons (712 tons) the sloops were fast and well armed, but their exact function was obscure as they were too superior for some roles, and inferior for others. For escort, or antisubmarine work they possessed a large excess of speed, while they were too slow for employment with the torpedo flotillas, and had too restricted a radius to work with the fleet. The German Navy tended to assign dual purpose roles to their minor war vessels in order that they could be fully employed as combatant units in time of war, but the results were sometimes surprising. The yacht *Grille*, officially rated as a sloop, was an expensive luxury but a suitable status symbol for the Head of State. Although possessing a good turn of speed and all adequate radius of action she lacked any military value.

Undisclosed in the 1934 programme was another battlecruiser, the *Gneisenau*, two heavy cruisers, sixteen destroyers, and twenty-eight submarines; while two further sloops, another gunnery training ship, and additional MTBs and MMSs were publicised. The *Gneisenau* was a sister ship to the previous year's *Scharnhorst*, and together they matched the French pair built to counter the "Deutschlands". The heavy cruisers *Admiral Hipper* and *Blücher*, 10,000 tons (13,900 tons) and armed with eight 8inch guns, and the destroyers *Z.1–Z.16*, 1,625 tons (2,170/2,270 tons) and armed with five 5inch guns and eight torpedo tubes, were also in plain defiance of the Versailles Treaty, and taken together with the battlecruisers were the nucleus of a fleet whose horizon was no longer limited by the Baltic and coastal waters.

Filling the dual roles of training ship and minelayer was the *Brummer*. Unlike the *Bremse* she adopted turbine machinery and was considerably slower, but like her she was used experimentally and was fitted with very high pressure boilers that were later installed in cruisers, destroyers and torpedo boats. In spite of the success they enjoyed in the *Brummer* they were, on the whole, rather a disastrous innovation, which resulted in many boiler failures under the rigours of war steaming, with its frequent demands for high and sustained steam production. The large mine deck could stow four hundred and fifty mines, and when stripped could accommodate the same number of men for training purposes.

The MTBs, *S.10–13*, were similar to the previous year's boats, *S.7–9*, except that they had Daimler-Benz instead of M.A.N. diesel engines, but the MMSs, *R.17–24*, were considerably increased in size over the prototypes, with displacement raised from 60 tons to 115 tons, and the installed engine power practically trebled with a corresponding rise in speed. Even though the development project placed with diesel engine manufacturers had not yet borne fruit, there was still no difficulty in obtaining suitable units for installation *pro tem*, and no other navy in the world was so advantageously placed in this respect.

By 1935 there was no longer any doubt that Germany was re-arming on a large scale, although precise details were lacking. Any doubts were soon dispelled when, in an historic statement in the early part of the year, Hitler publicly repudiated the Versailles Treaty, and proclaimed Germany's right to determine her own future. In the total absence of any concerted action by the convening powers at Versailles to check this growth, the British and German governments entered into an agreement whereby the German Navy limited itself to 35 per cent of the Royal Navy in total tonnage. Included in this total figure were submarines, but in this category Germany reserved the right to equality with the Royal Navy, but stated her intention not to exceed 45 per cent without giving further notice. It is interesting to note that limitations were in terms of total tonnage, and not qualitative or quantitative, and any increase in submarines over 35 per cent would, therefore, be balanced by an equal reduction in other categories. This bi-lateral agreement did not meet with universal accord, but the British government was on firm ground whereby they limited German naval re-armament in the absence of any restriction that could be placed on it.

Based on the existing strength of the Royal Navy at that time, and while it was still subject to the Washington and (first) London naval treaties, this agreement allowed the German Navy the following tonnages against the principal categories shown:

| Type | Total tonnage | Built or building | Balance for new construction |
|---|---|---|---|
| Battleships | 183,750 tons | 82,000 tons | 101,750 tons |
| Heavy cruisers | 51,380 tons | 20,000 tons | 31,380 tons |
| Light cruisers | 67,270 tons | 35,600 tons | 31,670 tons |
| Aircraft carriers | 47,250 tons | | 47,250 tons |
| Destroyers and torpedo boats | 52,500 tons | 35,600 tons | 16,900 tons |
| Submarines[4] | 18,445 tons | 12,425 tons | 6,020 tons |
| Totals | 420,595 tons | 185,625 tons | 234,970 tons |

[4] The tonnage for submarines using the 45 per cent ratio was 23,715 tons, leaving a balance of 11,290 tons for new construction.

From the foregoing it will be seen that the tonnage available for new construction enabled the German Navy, providing they kept within the general qualitative restrictions to which they were not subject, to add the following vessels: three battleships of 35,000 tons each; three heavy cruisers of 10,000 tons each; four light cruisers of 8,000 tons each; two aircraft carriers of 23,000 tons each; six destroyers of 1,625 tons each; twelve torpedo boats of 600 tons each; and eight submarines of 740 tons each.

The overt construction planned before the 1935 agreement could now be revealed, and if added to the balance available for new construction outlined above, entailed a large programme of construction which would have to be spread over several years. Not surprisingly the programme for 1935 was a large one, and comprised one battleship, the *Bismarck*, of 35,000 tons (41,700 tons); one heavy cruiser, the *Prinz Eugen*, of 10,000 tons (14,800 tons); one aircraft carrier, the *Graf Zeppelin*, of 19,250 tons (23,200 tons); six destroyers, *Z.17–22*, each of 1,811 tons (2,411 tons); twelve torpedo boats, *T.1–12*, each of 600 tons (840 tons); eight submarines, *U.37–44*, each of 740 tons (1,032 tons); and twelve minesweepers, *M.1–12*, each of 600 tons (717 tons). There was thus no category in which the standard displacement was not exceeded, and in some cases grossly so. It is, however, fair to add that as none of the first three vessels was completed until after the outbreak of the Second World War, their actual displacements were the result of further increases from this date when, naturally, all restrictions ceased to apply. In this respect the actual breakdown of weights for the *Bismarck* are of considerable interest, and are listed below.

The most interesting feature of the *Bismarck* was the extent of her protection, which absorbed more than 40 per cent of her standard displacement, associated with her great beam. Her main belt was 16 feet deep and enclosed the end barbettes, and over this was placed an upper belt which gave her armoured freeboard over the greater part of her length. The upper deck was $3\frac{1}{4}$ inches thick at its outer edge and thinned to 2 inches amidships, while the lower deck was similarly $4\frac{1}{2}$ inches (sloped) and $3\frac{1}{4}$ inches (flat) except over the magazines were it was thickened to $4\frac{3}{4}$ inches and 4 inches respectively. Inboard of the main belt was an armoured longitudinal bulkhead $1\frac{1}{2}$ inches thick above, and $1\frac{3}{4}$ inches thick below, the lower deck. The turret crowns were angled to increase the obliquity of impact and could consequently be made thinner than the vertical walls. The *Bismarck's* main armament of eight 15inch guns was not outstanding, but the equal of any afloat, and she adhered to secondary and tertiary batteries, for use against light surface craft and aircraft, whereas American and British contemporaries were more economically minded with their dual purpose secondary armament.

| | | | | | |
|---|---|---|---|---|---|
| Hull | 11,691 | tons | Stores | $155\frac{1}{2}$ | tons |
| Armour | 17,540 | tons | Fresh water | | |
| Main | | | (domestic) | 167 | tons |
| machinery | 2,800 | tons | | | |
| Auxiliary | | | *Standard* | $42,343\frac{1}{2}$ | tons |
| machinery | 1,428 | tons | | | |
| Armament | 5,973 | tons | Oil fuel | 6,452 | tons |
| Aircraft fittings | 83 | tons | Gas oil | 193 | tons |
| Light arms | 8 | tons | Lub. oil | 160 | tons |
| Equipment | 408 | tons | Petrol | 34 | tons |
| | | | Feed water | 375 | tons |
| *Light ship* | 39,931 | tons | Reserve feed | | |
| | | | water | $389\frac{1}{4}$ | tons |
| Ammunition | $1,510\frac{1}{2}$ | tons | | | |
| Small arms | | | *Full load* | $49,946\frac{3}{4}$ | tons |
| ammunition | $2\frac{1}{2}$ | tons | Emergency | | |
| Complement | $243\frac{1}{2}$ | tons | oil fuel | 1,009 | tons |
| Provisions | $194\frac{1}{4}$ | tons | | | |
| Fresh water | | | *Emergency* | | |
| (drinking) | $139\frac{1}{4}$ | tons | *full load* | $50,955\frac{3}{4}$ | tons |

The *Graf Zeppelin* was the German Navy's first experience with an aircraft carrier, and in this respect they were at a severe disadvantage. Coupled to this was the complete lack of co-operation between the German naval and air forces, and at no stage in the *Graf Zeppelin's* chequered career was her air group ready and available to be embarked. Her A.A. armament was good but not ideally placed, before and abaft the island superstructure, where it could only engage targets to port by firing across the flight deck and impede, if not to wholly arrest, simultaneous flying operations. Eight twin 5.9inch guns, carried on the broadside in armoured casemates at main deck level, were needless additional weight, and such protection as there was confined to the hull leaving the hangars and flight deck quite unprotected. Her construction was halted in August, 1940, when 80 per cent complete, resumed in 1942 to a modified design, but was finally suspended again in April, 1943.

The *Prinz Eugen* generally followed the lines of the earlier heavy cruisers with a slight all-round increase in dimensions and displacement unaccompanied by any other improvements, and the same applied to the second group of destroyers. The torpedo boats, on the other hand, clearly showed the German propensity for the torpedo and were armed with six deck tubes but only a single gun, mounted right aft. The minesweepers were modern counterparts to those built during the First World War, but this was not a class of vessel in which outstanding advances were to be expected. They could do their job, were seaworthy, and although they reverted to reciprocating machinery this was no retrograde step but a clear recognition of available facilities, both in peace and war.

The programmes for the two following years were extensions to that for 1935, and underlined the difficulties experienced by the German Navy in attaining the total tonnage permitted by the Anglo-German Naval agreement. The shipyards were incapable of the required rate of production, and added to this was the difficulty in providing adequate numbers of trained personnel. Ships proposed in 1936 were the battleships *Tirpitz*, a sister ship to the *Bismarck*; a second aircraft carrier; two 10,000-ton (14,800-ton) cruisers, the *Seydlitz* and *Lützow*, to be armed with twelve 5.9inch guns; eleven submarines, *U.45–55*, each of 517 tons (753 tons); and the depot ship *Tanga*; to be followed in 1937 by a third battleship, six torpedo boats, twenty-six submarines, six more minesweepers, and two depot ships.

Also in 1937 the German government signed a further naval agreement with the United Kingdom which, in effect, secured their adherence to the qualitative restrictions of the (second) London Naval Treaty. An additional clause was not to build cruisers exceeding 8,000 tons armed with guns larger than 6inch calibre, which inferred the abandonment of construction of the *Seydlitz* and *Lützow*. However, these two vessels were only shortly in abeyance as the next year Germany legally exercised her rights, under both agreements, to expand her submarine arm up to parity with the Royal Navy, and not only to complete the two cruisers but to arm them with 8inch guns. Her reasons were based on reports of Russian cruiser and submarine construction to which she felt compelled to reply, although the more reasonable counter to submarines appeared at the time to be anti-submarine vessels and not craft of the same type.

In retrospect, the years 1937/8 were of more than passing interest. They saw the beginning of the British naval rearmament programme whose implications were not fully realised at the time: especially in Germany where the inevitability of war with the United Kingdom was recognised, but not until about 1944/5. The German Navy accordingly drew up plans for the fleet required for this purpose in order to wage war principally against trade on, below, and above the seas, and the estimates were for:

Six battleships to be completed by 1944,

Four heavy cruisers by 1943, and four more by 1945,
Four light cruisers by 1944, and thirteen more by 1948,
Two aircraft carriers by 1941, and two more by 1947, and
One hundred and twenty-eight submarines by 1943, and
Ninety-five more by 1947.

To this could be added the existing fleet of two battleships (both building), two battlecruisers, three armoured cruisers, three heavy and five light cruisers (*Emden* was excepted), and forty-four submarines. The plan was modified, from time to time, to suit tactical re-assessment and building capacity, and at least two of the heavy cruisers were dropped and three battlecruisers added. As was stated earlier, there was no denying the German ability for detailed military planning: but where they failed was to distinguish between actual and proposed. Of the proposed additions only one battleship, two aircraft carriers, and two heavy cruisers had been ordered by the German Navy, and the remainder were still paper projects in 1937 and a long way from fulfilment. At the same time the Royal Navy possessed a present overwhelming superiority in all categories, and the fact to be considered, once the extent of the German programme was known, was to what extent would the United Kingdom retaliate. The answer was to be found in the British estimates for 1937 which were on a higher ratio than ship-for-ship. The German plan could have succeeded only if the subsequent British estimates up to 1941 —as ships laid down during these years would have been available by 1944/5—had been nil: an improbability which hardly merited consideration. The British estimates had already shown their awareness of the increased tempo in warship building, and in a building race Germany could not match, far less surpass, the United Kingdom capacity. The German threat was very real in that the Royal Navy could not concentrate the entire fleet in Home waters, in view of heavy commitments in both the Far East and the Mediterranean, but nor did the Royal Navy contemplate having to wage war simultaneously in all three theatres completely unaided.

With the build-up of tension the 1938 programme was not unnaturally a heavy one, and comprised two battleships, two light cruisers, six destroyers, three torpedo boats, thirty-five submarines, six minesweepers, two depot ships, and two icebreakers, plus a variety of smaller craft.

The two battleships, together with the one ordered in the preceding year, were armed as the *Bismarck* and *Tirpitz* except that the main guns were increased to 16inch calibre, but size rose sharply to 56,200 tons for a dimensionally larger hull. Protection was on the same generous scale as the smaller battleships but sub-division was enhanced by a further increase of beam to $123\frac{1}{4}$ feet. To secure a large radius of action main propulsion was by twelve 9-cylinder diesel engines coupled to three shafts and totalled B.H.P. 165,000—the most powerful diesel installation ever envisaged.

The light cruisers kept within the limits of the Anglo-German agreements, and were vessels of 7,800 tons, with a main armament of eight 5.9inch guns, disposed in four turrets, and stowage for 160 mines. They were only lightly armoured, as the *Nürnberg*, with the main deck made a little thicker, and adopted a similar machinery layout, geared turbines coupled to wing shafts and four 12-cylinder diesel engines to the centre shaft, but with power much increased for a top speed of 35½ knots. The destroyers, *Z.23–28*, were a further increase in size to accommodate the heavier gun armament which had increased to 5.9inch in calibre: the two forward guns being housed in a twin turret. There was no change in the design of the torpedo boats, *T.19–21*, or in the six minesweepers, *M.19–24*, which were continuations of earlier series. The two depot ships and two icebreakers indicated the need for other than pure fighting ships in the balanced build-up of a fleet, and the former were supplemented by four mercantile conversions.

In the field of smaller craft the diesel engine development project placed in 1934 had borne fruit and resulted in the final adoption of a 20-cylinder Daimler-Benz V-form unit— which was to give sterling service in the ensuing years—in preference to the M.A.N. in-line engine. The new engine was first fitted to the MTBs *S.18–25* and proved superior to the alternative unit fitted in the MTBs *S.14–17*. Production was standardised around these boats, which were otherwise identical and had given every satisfaction in service. However, if the Daimler-Benz engine was more suited to the MTBs, the M.A.N. engine was preferred for the lower powered and slower MMSs which shipped them to the exclusion of all else. The smaller series of MMSs, *FR.1–12*, were for river work and were only briefly perpetuated. In spite of being lengthened they were unsuitable for work in open waters, and there was little need to specialise with a purely river craft whose functions, when the need arose, could be undertaken by requisitioning suitable commercial craft, of which there was no shortage.

Also planned in 1938 was a destroyer designed to be mass produced and act as a screen for the raiding squadrons of capital ships, cruisers, and aircraft carriers under construction. They were of more modest dimensions than the heavy units built, or building, and would probably have served the German Navy better than the programme of larger and more complicated vessels on which they were embarked. The flush decked design embraced four 5inch guns in twin turrets fore and aft, eight torpedo tubes in two deck mountings, a wholly adequate speed of 36½ knots, and the exceptional radius of 9,500 miles: on which figures they ranked with comparable vessels anywhere in the world.

In spite of the proposed build-up of the German Navy, the programme for 1939 had to be tailored to suit the available building capacity, and was limited to one battleship, two light cruisers, nine destroyers, three torpedo boats, eleven submarines, three minelayers, six minesweepers, one depot ship (plus two mercantile conversions), a surveying vessel, and further MMSs.

The battleship was the fourth 56,200-ton unit, and the light cruisers, destroyers (*Z.29–37*), submarines, and minesweepers (*M.25–30*) further additions to earlier classes. The three torpedo boats, *T.22–24*, were of an enlarged type with the gun armament increased to four 4.1inch pieces and a reduction in speed of some two knots. The minelayers approached cruiser dimensions and were propelled by geared turbines at 28 knots. They were armed with eight 4.1inch A.A. guns, twin mounted, except for one unit which shipped four single 5inch guns and doubled as a gunnery training ship, and could stow up to four hundred mines. Provision was also made for a single aircraft, stowed in a hangar aft, and handled by a crane or otherwise recovered by the Hein mat method, which could be streamed aft through a cut made in the stern. Once again these ships illustrated the lack of precise function which characterised intermediate types of German warships. They were too slow to carry out lays in enemy waters, expensively fast—to the detriment of other qualities—for lays in waters free from enemy interference, and although possessing a good A.A. armament had too restricted a radius to work with the fleet, and were too large and vulnerable to expose as convoy escorts, if employed in an anti-aircraft role in both instances.

The diesel-engined surveying vessel had a quite exceptional radius sufficient to circumnavigate the world, but was also designed with a military view in mind, and was both fast and well armed to fill a detached marauding role against trade. The MMSs, *R.41* up, were a little larger than, but otherwise similar to, the preceding series, while the smaller type, *MR.1–10*, similarly increased in size, were the final effort in this direction after which further development with these craft was abandoned.

Thus, in spite of intensive building up to the outbreak of the Second World War, which descended precipitately on the German Navy, the fleet was no match for the Anglo-French combination with which it was now confronted. For the German Navy it was a time of painful reappraisal to meet a new and unexpected turn of events. There was now no question of challenging the command of the seas, only a war against trade to conduct, but without the backing of a main fleet—the sole means by which command, once gained, was exercised. Force of circumstances had committed the German Navy to a *guerre du course*: a popular but false doctrine yet to be justified.

# WAR CONSTRUCTION: 1939–1945

Although it was originally intended to proceed with the construction of the major units outlined in the 1936/9 programmes, the German Navy, in committing itself to a mainly trade war, soon found that submarine construction was awarded the highest priority, and that all plans for a balanced fleet had to be abandoned.

Limited numbers of destroyers, torpedo boats, etc., were built during the war years, but the major constructive effort among surface vessels was in motor torpedo boats, and fleet and motor minesweepers. For the mining, minesweeping, and the safe passage of convoys along a coastline stretching from the North Cape to the French Biscay ports, a considerable force of auxiliary vessels was put into service, which were essentially dependent on land-based air power for support. Therefore, with the exception of some sporadic forays by small groups of, or individual ships, surface operations were largely restricted to that within the radius of shore-based aircraft, and vitally dependent on their availability. These conditions did not apply in the Baltic and, to a lesser extent, the Black seas where, in the face of weak opposition, the German Navy was able to secure local command.

War alterations followed a similar pattern experienced by other combatant navies. Firstly, the A.A. armament was augmented by the simple addition of several light pieces—usually single 20mm—and sea and air warning RDF was added. Next, the light A.A. armament was further augmented by the addition of multiple 20mm and single and twin 37mm mountings, which entailed the removal of some original items of equipment to compensate for the increased topweight, and more sophisticated warning and gunnery control RDF was added. This latter enabled aircraft, where carried, to be landed as although RDF did not possess the range of reconnaissance aircraft it gave ample warning, which could be extended depending on the number of vessels operating together, and resulted in a welcome reduction in topweight.

In summarising war construction it is more convenient to

work right through each category of ship, as to arrange the sequence of events chronologically would break continuity, and entail considerable repetition in the absence of precise details of the annual war programmes which were recast several times in the course of a single year.

**Battleships:** Two further units of 56,200 tons were projected bringing the total of this class to six. Of these, only the first two were ever laid down, no work took place on the remainder, and all were cancelled in 1940. The following design studies were undertaken during the war, but they were never more than interesting paper projects which illustrate the dimensions to which the German Navy was prepared to expand to secure invulnerability for ships of capital rank. The *H.41* design was for a battleship of 64,000 tons, but this was soon abandoned for the undermentioned successive, and more ambitious, projects:

*H.42 design:* 83,265 tons (90,000 tons full): $1001\frac{1}{4} \times 140\frac{1}{2} \times 38\frac{3}{4}$ ($62\frac{3}{4}$d.) feet: belt 15 inches, deck 13 inches; geared turbines (outer shafts) and diesel motors (inner shafts) S.H.P. 160,000 + B.H.P. 120,000 = $32\frac{1}{4}$ knots.

*H.43 design:* 103,342 tons (111,000 tons full): $1083\frac{1}{4} \times 140\frac{1}{2} \times 39\frac{1}{4}$ (66d.) feet: geared turbines (inner shafts) and diesel motors (outer shafts) S.H.P. 160,000 + B.H.P. 120,000 = 31 knots: eight 19.7inch (4 × 2) guns.

*H.44 design:* 122,000 tons (141,500 tons full): $1132\frac{1}{4} \times 169 \times 41\frac{1}{2}$ (69d.) feet: geared turbines (inner shafts) and diesel motors (outer shafts) S.H.P. 160,000 + B.H.P. 120,000 = 30 knots: eight 20inch (4 × 2) guns.

**Battlecruisers:** Three units were projected but no constructional work was undertaken on them, and they, too, were cancelled in 1940. The overriding requirement was for speed and radius, and armament and protection was sacrificed to this end. Main propulsion was by four 24-cylinder V-form diesel engines coupled to each wing shaft, for sustained high speed cruising, boosted by geared turbines coupled to the centre shaft to attain the designed full speed of $33\frac{1}{2}$ knots. On a larger scale they were a reversion to the principle adopted by the *Deutschland* of outrunning whatever they could not outfight, and there is no doubt that their destruction could only have been accomplished by (*a*) the heavy gunfire of capital ships providing they could be brought to action, or by (*b*) torpedoes from fast surface vessels and/or aircraft. Their armament was limited to six 15inch guns in twin turrets, two forward and one aft, and to six 5.9inch and eight 4.1inch A.A. guns, all twin-mounted. These were numerically light batteries but underlined their role, which was more to run than fight, and lure enemy capital ships engaging them towards the heavy support groups formed by the battleships referred to above. Although vertical protection, and that to the main turrets and barbettes, was scaled down, horizontal protection remained on practically the same scale as that given to the *Bismarck* and *Tirpitz*.

It was also intended to rearm the *Scharnhorst* and *Gneisenau* by replacing their triple 11inch with twin 15inch turrets, but this was not proceeded with following the complete abandonment of the capital ship programme. The light A.A. armament of these ships was, however, considerably augmented by the addition of a large number of 20mm guns, in quadruple, twin, and single mountings, disposed overall. All combatant navies engaged in the Second World War experienced the same necessity for this modification in all types of vessels.

**Aircraft Carriers:** Principally because of the lack of co-operation between the naval and air forces the progress of these units were not greatly advanced. In conjunction with the battleships and battlecruisers they were to be used against trade, besides providing air cover and long range reconnaissance for the heavy units. In 1940 the *Graf Zeppelin* was suspended as her heavy A.A. armament had been purloined for use ashore, and it would take another year to manufacture and install a new outfit, in addition to the added difficulties in providing fire control equipment for which there were higher priorities in other categories. The second carrier, only a little advanced on the slips, was cancelled owing to shortages of material and labour, but even at this early stage the conversion of a heavy cruiser, the *Seydlitz*, to a carrier was put in hand. By 1942 the need for carriers to support heavy units operating against convoys bound to and from Russia by the northern route was stressed, and work on the *Graf Zeppelin* was resumed with the following mercantile conversions also being proposed:

*Europa* (1930) 49,746 tons gross: 890 × 102 × 48d. feet: 4-shaft geared turbines S.H.P. 95,000 = 27½ knots: twelve 4.1inch A.A. (6 × 2), twenty 37mm A.A., thirty-six 20mm A.A. guns, forty-two aircraft, two catapults.

*Gneisenau* (1935) 18,160 tons gross: 610 × 74 × 45d. feet: 2-shaft geared turbines S.H.P. 26,000 = 21 knots: eight 4.1inch A.A. (4 × 2), ten 37mm A.A., twenty-four 20mm A.A. guns, twenty-four aircraft, two catapults.

*Potsdam* (1935) 17,528 tons gross: 597 × 74 × 45d. feet: 2-shaft turbo-electric S.H.P. 26,000 = 21 knots: eight 4.1inch A.A. (4 × 2), ten 37mm A.A., twenty-four 20mm A.A. guns, twenty-four aircraft, two catapults.

In addition, work was proceeding with decking over the *Seydlitz*, and her armament had been altered to ten 4.1inch A.A. (5 × 2), eight 37mm A.A., and twenty-four 20mm A.A. guns, twenty-four aircraft, and two catapults.

In spite of determined efforts none of the carriers was finally completed and the mercantile conversions not even started, and although better relations existed between the naval and air forces from 1943 it was too late by then to offset the critical shortages in material and labour which finally hampered progress.

**Cruisers:** The final pair of heavy cruisers, the *Seydlitz* and the *Lützow*, were never completed. The former was selected for conversion to an aircraft carrier (see above), and the latter was sold to the Russian Navy while still under construction, and her name given to the armoured ship *Deutschland*. The ex-*Lützow* was delivered in an incomplete state to the Russians, lacking all fire control equipment, and under cover of a multitude of excuses its delivery was deliberately withheld. Although the machinery was installed, it had never been operated, and after she had been sunk in shallow water by German aircraft she was used as a battery by the Russians. After the end of hostilities, the Russian Navy—having meanwhile acquired the *Seydlitz*—intended refitting both ships, which included replacing the twin 8inch by triple 7.1inch turrets, but the work involved was so extensive that the project was finally abandoned.

Two more 7,800-ton light cruisers were ordered, but they—together with the four earlier units— were not proceeded with and cancelled between 1941/3. But to provide some screening force for heavy units already completed, the orders for three type 1936A (Mob) destroyers, *Z.40–42*, placed in 1940 were cancelled, and replaced in the following year by an equal number of scout cruisers. This was basically a blown-up destroyer design, with the foc's'le deck extended well aft and the main armament of 5.9inch guns paired in three turrets, one forward and two aft, and the addition of a twin 3.5inch A.A. mounting, also placed aft. A three-shaft machinery arrangement was adopted, with geared turbines on the wing shafts and four diesel engines coupled to the centre shaft, and by this means the radius was increased to the wholly adequate figure of 12,000 miles. Quintuple banks for torpedo tubes were first projected with this design, and two mountings were placed amidships on the foc's'le deck between the funnels, while upper deck stowage was provided for one hundred and forty mines, almost double that usually carried by a destroyer. Except for thin plating to the turrets and barbettes, no armour was worked into the design, whose most noticeable feature was the concentration aft of the gun armament, superimposed at three levels on the centre line.

The regular cruisers were supplemented by eleven auxiliary units, converted from suitable fast cargo ships, for use against trade. Between them they sank one hundred and thirty-five ships totalling 830,588 tons gross and one cruiser, the *Sydney*, a most creditable performance, and one which outshone the record of the six regular warships used against trade who accounted for sixty-two ships of 352,027 tons gross and two auxiliary cruisers, the *Rawalpindi* and *Jervis Bay*[5].

**Destroyers:** Five more destroyers, *Z.38–42*, were added to the type 1936A (Mob) making twelve in all: but of these the contracts for the final three were cancelled and replaced by orders for three scout cruisers (see above). The destroyers of this, and the preceding series (type 1936A), carried their two forward 5.9inch guns in a twin turret, with the exception of *Z.28, Z.35,* and *Z.36.* However, as the production of these turrets was subject to delay, a single mounting was placed temporarily forward, and the reduction in weight enabled the light A.A. armament to be augmented forward of the bridge. When the turret was finally made available and shipped, these additional light A.A. guns were resited, much farther aft, in place of "C" gun (at the fore end of the after shelter deck) which was removed. The *Z.28* was designed as a flotilla leader and differed in that her four guns were all carried singly, two forward and two aft, and extra accommodation was provided at the fore end of the after shelter for the flotilla staff instead of the fifth gun mounted there in the other vessels of these series. The increase in calibre to 5.9inch for the gun was not a great success, as it was not accompanied by any sensible increase in beam, and the addition of uncompensated top-weight made them poorer seaboats in consequence.

With the *Z.35* and *Z.36,* and three subsequent units, *Z.43–45,* forming the type 1936B, the 5.9inch guns were replaced by the lighter 5inch, all mounted singly, and the entire group benefited by the reduced topweight. Five later units, *Z.46–50,* while retaining a similar hull and general arrangements as the type 1936B, adopted a new calibre 5.1inch gun, housed in three twin turrets placed one forward and two aft, and were classed as type 1936C. Although of limited elevation, this new gun could be used as a dual-purpose weapon, and a high-angle director was placed aft so that the vessels of this group could engage aerial targets with controlled fire.

The last destroyers ordered during the war met requirements

[5] These were the battlecruisers *Scharnhorst* and *Gneisenau*; the armoured ships *Deutschland, Admiral Scheer,* and *Admiral Graf Spee*; and the heavy cruiser *Admiral Hipper*.

for operations in Northern waters in conjunction with a much greater radius of action. As the very high pressure boilers used in preceding destroyers had far from provided the expected economy, coupled with lack of reliability, the problem was startlingly resolved by adopting diesel engines for main propulsion—the first time they had been applied to destroyers[6]. Not unnaturally work first proceeded with a prototype, the *Z.51*, which had a diesel engine coupled to each wing shaft, and four units geared to the centre shaft, while the entire installation totalled over B.H.P. 57,000 for a speed of 36 knots. The radius of 13,500 miles was unmatched by any other war-built destroyer at the time. The dual-purpose 5.1inch gun, introduced with the type 1936C, was retained, and four were equally disposed fore and aft in single mountings, and the usual eight torpedo tubes provided. This vessel was succeeded by the series *Z.52–58*, which were larger than the prototype and were, in fact, the largest German destroyers contemplated. Although they retained a three-shaft arrangement, the layout was uniform with four diesel engines coupled to each shaft, and the total output was B.H.P. 76,000 for a speed of 37½ knots. The radius was set even higher, at 16,000 miles. They still adhered to the 5.1inch gun, twin-mounted in three turrets sited two forward and one aft, but introduced new light calibre A.A. guns comprising three 55mm, grouped around the after funnel, and seven twin 30mm mountings positioned on the bridge, abreast the fore funnel, and well aft. Two high-angle directors forward and aft for the main guns, and the absence of funnel caps gave them a distinctive profile among German destroyers. The final outcome was that none was completed: the *Z.51* was the furthest advanced and was bombed while completing, material shortages compelled the early cancellation of *Z.52–56*, and *Z.57* and *Z.58* were never more than projected.

**Torpedo Boats:** With the authorisation of the type 1934 destroyers, the earlier destroyers of the *Möwe* and *Wolf* classes were re-classed as torpedo boats, and as has already been noted, the type continued in production. A further twelve type 1939 were ordered, bringing the total to fifteen, and were followed by fifteen similar fleet units with slightly greater power and improved bunkerage and radius.

The next group of nine vessels, *T.52–60*, dropped the un-

---

[6] In this respect some claim has been made for the US Navy's diesel-electric destroyer escorts, which anticipated the German destroyers in service. But the German vessels were destroyers in the fullest sense, which the American vessels were not, added to which the latter secured their drive by electric motors. In fact, there is no conflict of claim, and both types of vessels introduced novel main propulsion within their categories.

dulating flush-decked hull for a gently sheered long foc's'le with the break occurring well aft. The 4.1inch guns were grouped in twin A.A. mountings forward and aft with their high-angle director placed on the bridge, and were supplemented by a uniform light A.A. armament of twin 30mm guns. The final group, *T.61–72*, were all ordered from Netherlands shipyards and their design ante-dated that of their predecessors. Their construction was retarded on every pretext and no more than three reached German ports for final arming and fitting-out. Close on 2,000 tons, their inclusion among torpedo boats is open to question, and they too adopted the raised foc's'le but with the break now placed amidships, abreast the funnel. Unlike other flotilla craft, with the exception of the types 1935 and 1937 torpedo boats, their boiler rooms were adjacent and resulted in a single trunked funnel and distinctive appearance. The gun armament was heavier and comprised four single 5inch on low angle mountings: an installation not in keeping with then current practice which required main guns to be at least dual-purpose, if not solely anti-aircraft pieces, in view of the heavy air attacks to which they would be exposed at this stage of the war.

**Torpedo Recovery Vessels:** The provision of these craft is not easily appreciated in that they possessed the refinements of a small torpedo boat and must, therefore, have absorbed essential building capacity which could have been more profitably utilised. Had they been built pre-war, as non-combatant vessels not subject to restrictions or limitations, with the ulterior view to being employed, for example, as coastal anti-submarine vessels, their inception would have been understood even if not wholly approved. They had the silhouette of a small torpedo boat, were defensively armed with only two 20mm A.A. guns, were propelled at $23\frac{1}{2}$ knots by geared turbines, and seemed an expensive way with which to recover practice torpedoes. Eight were built in Germany, *TF.1–8*, a further sixteen, *TF.9–24*, were ordered in the Netherlands, and they were all generally similar. They perhaps best reflect the intensity of the German Navy for torpedo warfare, in which they excelled, with the natural corollary that they devoted more than ordinary effort to training that required such specialised vessels.

**Sloops:** One further class, *G.1–24*, were ordered which were enlarged developments of the earlier class. Their power output dropped by 50 per cent by the necessity to adopt reciprocating machinery and low pressure boilers, so that an additional boiler was required, and a proportion of their greater size was so absorbed by less efficient and bulkier machinery, but did enable them to enhance the armament by pairing the 4.1inch A.A. guns mounted fore and aft. Only *G.1* was laid down but was lost incomplete while building in an air raid, and the construction of the remainder, in German and Netherlands shipyards, was abandoned. Later, a smaller series of multi-purpose vessels, *MZ.1–12*, were put in hand, and were remarkable for the heavy armament of guns and torpedoes accommodated on a small displacement. They were powered by a single diesel engine of B.H.P. 1,000 for a speed of 14 knots but had a restricted radius, at this speed, of only a 1,000 miles. After the initial unit was completed it was planned to lengthen them by $16\frac{1}{2}$ feet but all subsequent construction was cancelled.

**Minesweepers:** It was in this category that the largest additions were made to the surface fleet. Another two hundred and thirty were ordered of the type commenced pre-war before construction was switched to a smaller, coal burning design for which two hundred and forty-one contracts were placed. Fifteen of the latter were provided with two torpedo tubes on the fo'c'sle for training purposes. The final series were increased in size but remained coal-burning, and over four hundred were projected. They were also designed to be used as anti-submarine or torpedo recovery vessels as the need arose. Of the more than nine hundred additions planned about one hundred each of the first and second series, and about four hundred of the final series, were cancelled.

**Minelayers:** Another five large minelayers were projected but, together with the three units planned pre-war, were all cancelled. It should be noted that all destroyers, torpedo boats, and motor torpedo boats were equipped for mine-laying and were often used in this role, so that there was no shortage of fast craft to undertake lays in enemy waters. In addition, increasing use was made of submarines and aircraft for this purpose.

**Motor Torpedo Boats:** The construction of these boats had been standardised shortly before the outbreak of war, and construction naturally adhered to an established and proven design to speed production. Modifications subsequently incorporated principally related to increased power output and gun armament. The first order for standard boats finally totalled one hundred and five (*S.26–29, 38–53, 62–138,* and *159–166*), of which three (*S.100, 136,* and *138*) had super-charged engines of greater power which were adopted for the second series of four hundred and forty-six boats (*S.139–150, 167–500,* and *701–800*). Power was further increased in two of the latter series (*S.170* and *228*) but it was too late by then to incorporate this advance in a further series, although it was selected for two experimental projects, for hard chine and armoured boats, neither of which finally materialised.

The first standard boats were armed with two 20mm A.A. guns, placed singly fore and aft, in addition to the two torpedo tubes and two reloads. The torpedo tubes, placed well forward, were enclosed by a half-height foc's'le deck so that the forward gun, mounted between the tubes, was in a well. This innovation was retained throughout the war and considerably added to the seakeeping qualities of these craft. The gun armament was increased, in *S.62* up, by replacing the after 20mm with a 37mm A.A. gun; by adding a further 20mm A.A. gun amidships in *S.211* up; while *S.701* up shipped a uniform armament of twin 20mm A.A. in all three positions. Earlier boats were later brought up to a comparable standard by substituting a 37mm for the after 20mm A.A. gun and the addition of a twin 20mm mounting.

The only departure from the standard boats was for sixteen slightly smaller units (*S.30–37* and *54–61*) which were lower powered and slower, and whatever unaccountable idea inspired their construction was thereafter dropped.

All these boats could secure an increase in speed of about 2 knots, when running at speed, by the use of side rudders. This adjusted their trim by the stern to a nearly horizontal running plane and resulted in a smaller slope drag.

Two much smaller classes of MTBs, *LS.1–20* and *KS.201–220*, of a size that could be hoisted by larger surface vessels, were put in hand. But the restricted employment of such craft, essentially dependent on good weather, outweighed their merits and they were not further developed. One each was carried in the auxiliary cruisers *Komet* (*LS.2*), *Kormoran* (*LS.3*), and *Michel* (*LS.4*), with the boats in the first two altered to stow mines instead of torpedoes.

**Motor Minesweepers:** Unlike the motor torpedo boats, the dimensions of these craft varied with each succeeding group, but the type was otherwise basically unaltered. The group *R.130* up advanced to 140 tons from the 125 tons of the group *R.41* up; dropped to 125 tons for the group *R.151* up; then again rose to 140 tons (*R.218* up) and 175 tons (*R.301* up) for the next two groups, which also had more powerful engines; and finally dropped to 140 tons for the last group, *R.401* up. Two 21inch torpedo tubes were added to the largest group and they were renumbered *GR.301–320* and used for patrol work, while the gun armament in all boats was strengthened by the addition of three/six 20mm A.A. guns.

**Motor Launches:** Only a small number of these craft were built, and none of them in German yards, as patrol and escort work was largely undertaken by the motor minesweepers in addition to their specialised role. Twelve 70/80-ton craft were built in Denmark, four much smaller boats in Norway, and forty-nine large units in Italy.

**Motor Minelayers:** These were small, hard chine form craft, able to carry four mines. Their limited radius of action was on the low side, even for the short distances involved in the southern North Sea, and they were later fitted with two 18inch torpedo tubes and reclassed as MTBs.

**Experimental Boats:** These embraced some interesting designs of hydrofoil craft for patrol, minelaying, transport, and torpedo duties. The principal advantage of hydrofoils lay not in securing a higher speed for a given power, an advantage they none the less possessed, but in their ability to better maintain speed in adverse conditions. The technical difficulties to be overcome, however, were complex, and were not fully resolved even under the stimulus of war conditions.

**Trawlers and MFVs:** Like those of the Royal Navy these vessels were principally drawn from the fishing fleets for patrol, anti-submarine, and minesweeping duties. But a small trawler and large MFV programme was also put in hand, and design embraced the best mercantile practice and was largely left in the hands of experienced commercial yards.

**Ferries, Lighters and Transports:** The first ferries were built for the projected invasion of the United Kingdom in 1940 and were double-ended pontoon supported motor rafts for the carriage of troops and equipment. The later transport ferries were mainly used in the Mediterranean and Black Seas for running supplies and were flat-bottomed but more seaworthy craft, well armed, and partly armoured with 1-inch plate over the engine room and vitals. Some one hundred and twenty were converted to carry a much heavier armament and act as escorts, as these craft were constantly harassed by attacks from aircraft and light naval forces. The supply lighters, and their gun versions, were similarly employed but in less exposed waters.

All these craft were built in various shipyards at Ancona, Budapest, Castellammare, Genoa, Leghorn, Linz, Monfalcone, Nicolaev, and Vienna under licence from Deutsche Werft, Hamburg.

**Miscellaneous Vessels:** Although further depot ships of the same type as the *Otto Wunsche* were proposed, none were actually built, and the only additions in this category were two more mercantile conversions. Two icebreakers were built in Sweden and a third in the Netherlands, the latter to replace one of the two vessels projected in 1938 but subsequently cancelled.

**Ex-enemy Vessels:** Quite considerable additions were made from this source following the successive campaigns in Poland in 1939; Norway, Denmark, Belgium, the Netherlands, and France in 1940, and finally Italy in 1943. From Italy were seized vessels which they had themselves secured from France, Greece, and Yugoslavia during 1940/1. In addition, a small number of British warships were captured. These additions less submarines are summarised below, but it should be noted that not all were put into service with the German Navy:

*Polish Navy:* four minesweepers and one old sloop.
*Royal Norwegian Navy:* two coast defence ships, six destroyers (two incomplete), thirteen old torpedo boats, one large and two small minelayers, and two minesweepers.
*Royal Danish Navy:* two coast defence ships, eight torpedo boats, three sloops, six minesweepers, two minelayers, and one depot ship.
*Royal Belgian Navy:* two sloops (one incomplete) and two old torpedo boats.
*Royal Netherlands Navy:* two coast defence ships, one old cruiser, one destroyer (incomplete), two old torpedo boats, three sloops (all incomplete), three minesweepers, ten MTBs (all incomplete), and six MMSs (all incomplete).
*French Navy:* two destroyers (one incomplete), eleven torpedo boats (six incomplete and three ex-Italian), ten sloops (two incomplete), four corvettes (all incomplete), four large (all incomplete) and three small aircraft tenders, one minesweeper, and eight submarine chasers.
*Royal Hellenic Navy:* one destroyer (ex-Italian).
*Royal Yugoslav Navy:* two destroyers (both ex-Italian), one old torpedo boat (ex-Italian), one seaplane carrier, five MTBs (ex-Italian).
*Royal Italian Navy:* five destroyers, twenty-nine torpedo boats (fifteen incomplete), twenty-four corvettes (fourteen incomplete), forty-three MTBs, and eighteen MA/SBs.
*Royal Navy:* one MTB and one M/L.

Many of the captured warships were elderly vessels of doubtful value, and the task of maintaining them—with non-standard armament and equipment—resulted in them proving more "paper" assets than of material value. The conversion of old coast defence ships and old cruisers to heavy A.A.

batteries showed, however, the versatility to which structurally sound hulls were adaptable, and they gave good service. Where local geographical features favoured the employment of numerous patrol vessels, and in this respect almost any type of vessel sufficed, many captured units rendered useful service and so reduced the demand on war production which could further concentrate on more essential categories. As almost any type of vessel—naval or mercantile—could be adapted for minelaying in areas not contested by the enemy, many conversions to this role were made from all manner of sources including captured and obsolete tonnage.

As several of these vessels had been scuttled or sabotaged to prevent them from falling into German hands, they did not rapidly re-inforce the German Navy as perhaps a mere examination of figures indicated.

**Auxiliary Vessels:** Like most major combatant navies, the German Navy during the war acquired a considerable amount of mercantile tonnage to supplement its regular warships. Space does not permit more than passing reference to them, and vessels taken over were placed in service as armed merchant cruisers, escort vessels, anti-submarine and anti-aircraft vessels, patrol vessels, minelayers, minesweepers; mine destroyers, netlayers, cable vessels, weather ships, experimental vessels, training ships of all kinds, target ships, depot ships, repair ships, accommodation vessels, hospital ships, tankers and supply ships, tugs, tenders, etc.

# Battleships
# and Battlecruisers

### *Battleships:* **Schlesien** and **Schleswig-Holstein**

These were the last pre-dreadnought battleships to be built for the German Navy, and originally comprised six units of which one, the *Pommern*, was sunk at the Battle of Jutland. Their appearance was not greatly altered but "between the wars" the two foremost funnels were trunked into a single casing, the four upper deck 5.9inch guns removed, and four single 3.5inch A.A. guns added on the after superstructure. By the outbreak of war they had been relegated to training, but were used for bombardment purposes in the Polish campaign. They were later reduced to harbour service, had their main deck 5.9inch guns removed, and the A.A. armament considerably augmented.

*The old battleship* Schlesien *had her two forward funnels trunked together when reconstructed in 1936.* (Drüppel)

*Displacement:* 12,100 tons (14,900 tons full)

*Dimensions:* 413½(pp) 419(oa) × 72¾ × 25¼ feet

*Machinery:* Eight Marine (oil-fired) + four Marine (coal-fired for training) boilers (pressure 235 lb.); three shafts; reciprocating (VTE), I.H.P. 17,000 = 18 knots

*Bunkers & Radius:* O.F. 1,130 tons, coal 436 tons; 5,900 miles at 10 knots

*Protection:* Main w.l. belt 4 inches (ends)–9½ inches (amid.), upper belt 8 inches, battery 6¾ inches. Deck 1½–2¾ inches. Turrets 6¾–11¼ inches, barbettes 11¼ inches. C.T. 5½–12 inches (fwd) and 5½ inches (aft)

*Armament:* Four 11inch (2 × 2), ten 5.9inch (10 × 1), four 3.5inch A.A. (4 × 1), four 20mm A.A. (4 × 1) guns

*Complement:* 725

*Notes:* In 1944 the 5.9inch and 3.5inch guns were removed, and the A.A. armament increased to six 4.1inch (6 × 1), ten 40mm (10 × 1), twenty-two 20mm (4 × 4 and 3 × 2) guns

**Name** *Schlesien* **Built by** Schichau (Danzig) **Launched** 28.5.06 **Fate** Scuttled off Swinemünde 4.5.45 after being mined 3.5.45, salved and towed to Königsberg 1947; scrapped 1949

**Name** *Schleswig-Holstein* **Built by** Germania Werft (Kiel) **Launched** 17.12.06 **Fate** Scuttled Gdynia 21.3.45 after being bombed RAF aircraft 18.12.44

## *Armoured ship:* **Deutschland**

The Treaty of Versailles, by restricting replacement battleship tonnage to 10,000 tons and 11inch guns, had thought to ensure that new construction would broadly adhere to the pre-dreadnought design, typefied by the *Schlesien* and *Schleswig-Holstein*. But by adopting diesel propulsion and abandoning thick belt and turret armour sufficient weight was saved for a powerful armament and a good turn of speed. Although exceeding the specified limit the illusion was given that the *Deutschland* did not, and every weight saving expedient was exercised in her construction, such as welding, triple turrets for the main armament, etc. The heavy A.A. armament originally comprised four single 3.5inch guns, all mounted abaft the funnel, but this was later increased to three twin 4.1inch mountings wider dispersed. The torpedo tubes were carried in armoured shields on the quarterdeck.

*Displacement:* 11,700 tons (15,900 tons full)

*Dimensions:* 593(pp) 616¾(oa) × 68 × 19/23¾ feet

*Machinery:* Two shafts; 9-cylinder M.A.N. diesel motors (four/shaft), B.H.P. 56,800 = 26 knots

*Bunkers & Radius:* O.F. 2,784 tons; 10,000 miles at 19 knots

*The armoured ship*
Deutschland *was completed*
*with single 88mm AA guns,*
*as seen in this photograph.*
*Later she was given a catapult*
*between the tower mast and*
*the funnel, and during the war*
*she had a cap fitted to the*
*funnel.* (Drüppel)

*Protection:* Main w.l. belt $3\frac{1}{4}$ inches, longitudinal bulkheads $1\frac{3}{4}$ inches. Foc's'le deck $\frac{3}{4}$ inch, main deck $1\frac{1}{4}$–$1\frac{1}{2}$–3 (over magazines) inches. Turrets $5\frac{1}{2}$ (face) 2/3 (sides)–$\frac{1}{2}$ (rear) inches, barbettes 4 inches. C.T. $5\frac{1}{2}$ (sides)–2 (crown) inches. Externally bulged

*Armament:* Six 11inch (2 × 3), eight 5.9inch (8 × 1), six 4.1inch A.A. (3 × 2), eight 37mm A.A. (4 × 2), ten 20mm A.A. (10 × 1) guns; eight 21inch (2 × 4) T.T.; two aircraft and one catapult

*Complement:* 1,150

*Notes:* A.A. armament augmented by the addition of twelve 20mm (1 × 4 and 8 × 1) guns and funnel cap added

**Name** *Deutschland* **Built by** Deutsche Werke (Kiel)
**Launched** 19.5.31 **Fate** *Lützow* (1940); scuttled Swinemünde 4.5.45 after being bombed Allied aircraft 16.4.45, salved and towed Königsberg 1947; Russian, and scrapped Leningrad 1948/9

## *Armoured Ships:* **Admiral Graf Spee** and **Admiral Scheer**

Modifications of the *Deutschland* with the bridge work made more compact and extended higher, and the aircraft catapult resited abaft the funnel. Dimensions were little altered except for a 3-foot increase in beam, but the main belt was shorter and thicker, and the bunkerage—and consequently radius—slightly reduced. In the *Admiral Graf Spee* the belt armour was reduced to $2\frac{1}{4}$/$3\frac{1}{4}$ inches in thickness but the belt was made deeper.

*Displacement:* 12,100 tons (16,200 tons full)
*Dimensions:* 597 (wl) $616\frac{3}{4}$(oa) × $71\frac{1}{4}$ × 19/24 feet
*Machinery:* Two shafts; 9-cylinder M.A.N. diesel motors (four/shaft), B.H.P. 56,800 = 26 knots
*Bunkers & Radius:* O.F. 2,436 tons *Ad. Scheer*, 2,523 tons *Ad. Graf Spee*; 9,000 miles at 19 knots

*Protection:* Main w.l. belt 4 inches, longitudinal bulkheads $1\frac{3}{4}$
inches. Foc's'le deck $\frac{3}{4}$ inch, main deck $\frac{3}{4}$–$1\frac{1}{4}$–$1\frac{1}{2}$–$2\frac{1}{4}$–3
(over magazines) inches. Turrets $5\frac{1}{2}$ (face)–2/3 (sides)–$\frac{1}{2}$
(rear) inches, barbettes 4 inches. C.T. $5\frac{1}{2}$ (sides)–2 (crown)
inches. Externally bulged
*Armament:* Six 11inch (2 × 3), eight 5.9inch (8 × 1), six 4.1inch
A.A. (3 × 2), eight 37mm A.A. (4 × 2), ten 20mm A.A. (10 ×
1) guns; eight 21inch (2 × 4) T.T.; two aircraft and one
catapult
*Complement:* 1,124
*Notes:* Clinker screen added to funnel and light A.A. augmented
by addition of twenty-six 20mm guns—later replaced by twelve
37mm (6 × 2) guns—in *Admiral Scheer* only

*The* Admiral Graf Spee *and*
Admiral Scheer *differed from
the* Deutschland *in having a
heavy tower bridge. This view
is of the* Graf Spee*'s bridge as
completed (pre-1938).*
(Samuel L. Morison)

*Two USN intelligence photographs of the* Graf Spee *showing the damage inflicted during the Battle of the River Plate. Note the camouflage scheme on the upperworks and turrets and the false bow wave.* (Samuel L. Morison)

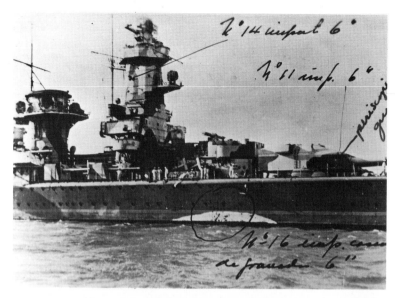

**Name** *Admiral Graf Spee* **Built by** Naval Dockyard (Wilhelms-haven) **Launched** 30.6.34 **Fate** Scuttled off Montevideo 17.12.39 after being damaged by gunfire of RN cruisers *Achilles, Ajax* and *Exeter* 13.12.39

**Name** *Admiral Scheer* **Built by** Naval Dockyard (Wilhelmshaven) **Launched** 1.4.33 **Fate** Bombed Allied aircraft and capsized Kiel 9.4.45 while in dry dock, and buried when dock was filled in

*In 1940 the armoured ship
Admiral Scheer had several
alterations, including a funnel
cap and increased AA
armament. In these two ships
the catapult was sited abaft the
funnel.*(Drüppel)

## *Battlecruisers:* **Gneisenau** and **Scharnhorst**

These two vessels gave a new slant to the battlecruiser
definition mainly by sacrificing weight of armament instead
of protection to secure high speed. The heavy A.A. armament
of fourteen guns, coupled with four high-angle directors, was
unmatched for its time. The aircraft catapults were carried
high, and mounted over the hangars placed abaft the funnel.
The *Scharnhorst* originally had a vertical stem, but this was
later altered to the clipper shape adopted by the *Gneisenau*,
and she had her mainmast moved further aft from where it
was previously stepped, close abaft the funnel, while *Gneisenau*
retained this arrangement.

In 1942, while undergoing repairs, the *Gneisenau* was to
be lengthened forward and be re-armed, with twin 15inch
replacing the triple 11inch turrets and probably by twin
5.2inch D.P. replacing the 5.9inch and 4.1inch turrets, but
all work on her was abandoned after she sustained further
severe damage from air attack.

*Displacement:* 31,800 tons (38,900 tons full)
*Dimensions:* $741\frac{1}{2}$(wl) $770\frac{3}{4}$(oa) $\times$ $98\frac{1}{2}$ $\times$ $27/32\frac{1}{2}$ feet
*Machinery:* Twelve Wagner boilers (pressure eight at 661 lb. and
    four at 735 lb.); three shafts; Brown-Boveri geared turbines,
    S.H.P. 160,000 = 32 knots
*Bunkers & Radius:* O.F. 6,200 tons; 10,000 miles at 17 knots

*A pre-war view of* Gneisenau *showing her after alteration with a clipper bow and funnel cap. From this time she differed from* Scharnhorst *in having her mainmast stepped against the funnel.* (Drüppel)

*Protection:* Main w.l. belt $1\frac{1}{4}$ (fwd)–$9\frac{3}{4}$ (amid.)–$1\frac{1}{4}$ (aft) inches, closed by bulkheads 6/8 inches. Upper deck 2 inches, main deck $\frac{3}{4}$ (slope)–2 (flat) inches. Main turrets 4 (rear)–$9\frac{3}{4}$ (side)–$13\frac{1}{4}$ (face) inches, barbettes $8/12\frac{3}{4}$ inches, secondary turrets $2/5\frac{1}{2}$ inches, barbettes 6 inches, shields $\frac{3}{4}$ inch

*Armament:* Nine 11inch (3 × 3), twelve 5.9inch (4 × 2 and 4 × 1), fourteen 4.1inch A.A. (7 × 2), sixteen 37mm A.A. (8 × 2), eight 20mm A.A. (8 × 1) guns; six 21inch (2 × 3) T.T.; two aircraft and two catapults

*Complement:* 1,840

*Notes:* The catapult was removed from 'Y' turret early in the war, and the light A.A. armament was augmented first by the addition of two 20mm (2 × 1), and then eight 20mm (2 × 4), guns. For the Channel breakthrough operation in 1942 sixteen 20mm A.A. (4 × 4) were temporarily shipped; and while one quadruple mounting was subsequently retained by the *Scharnhorst*, the *Gneisenau* was later stripped of all light A.A. guns after sustaining heavy bomb damage

**Name** *Gneisenau* **Built by** Deutsche Werke (Kiel) **Launched** 8.12.36 **Fate** Bombed RAF aircraft Kiel 26.7.42, repairs suspended and scuttled Gdynia 28.3.45; salved 13.9.51 and scrapped

**Name** *Scharnhorst* **Built by** Naval Dockyard (Wilhelmshaven) **Launched** 3.10.36 **Fate** Gunfire of RN battleship *Duke of York* and torpedoed cruiser *Jamaica* and destroyers *Musketeer*, *Opportune*, *Scorpion* and *Virago* off North Cape 26.11.43

*The battlecruiser* Scharnhorst *was completed without a funnel cap or clipper bow, and had two aircraft catapults.*

*In 1940 the* Scharnhorst *emerged from a refit completely altered, with an "Atlantic" clipper bow, funnel cap and augmented AA. She is seen here in 1943 with a two-tone camouflage scheme.* (Credit: Drüppel)

## *Battleships:* **Bismarck** and **Tirpitz**

The retention of secondary and tertiary batteries was an unusual feature of these vessels when most foreign contemporaries had adopted dual-purpose batteries for use against light surface craft and aircraft. This was probably accounted for by the fact that the standard 4.1inch A.A. gun was considered too light for driving off light craft, whereas the United States Navy had adopted a 5inch gun, and the Royal Navy a 5.25inch or 4.5inch gun for their dual-purpose batteries. The secondary battery was well disposed, in twin turrets, and the tertiary of sixteen A.A. guns, controlled by six high-angle directors (owing to shortages only four were installed on the *Bismarck*), was unmatched anywhere. A fixed athwartship catapult was placed abaft the funnel, but a second to be placed abaft "B" turret, together with its hangar, was not finally put in. Only the *Tirpitz* carried two sets of torpedo tubes, mounted on the upper deck abaft the catapult, while the light A.A. armament was considerably increased from the original provision of twelve 20mm (12 × 1) guns.

*The* Bismarck *on trials in the Baltic early in 1941.* (Drüppel)

Bismarck *at Bergen just before the breakout in May 1941. The diagonal recognition bands are believed to have been painted out, with the false bow wave and two-tone bow and stern, just before the ship sailed, but the turret-tops were painted yellow.* (PPL)

*Displacement:* Bismarck 41,676 tons (50,153 tons full), *Tirpitz* 42,900 tons (52,600 tons full)

*Dimensions:* 794(wl) $822\frac{3}{4}$(oa) × $118\frac{1}{4}$ × $28\frac{1}{2}/33\frac{1}{2}$ except *Tirpitz* $29\frac{1}{2}/34\frac{3}{4}$ feet

*Machinery:* Twelve Wagner boilers (pressure 808 lb.); three shafts; Brown-Boveri geared turbines, S.H.P. 138,000 = 29 knots

*Bunkers & Radius:* Bismarck O.F. 7,450 tons; 8,100 miles at 19 knots. *Tirpitz* O.F. 8,780 tons; 9,000 miles at 19 knots

*Protection:* Main w.l. belt $12\frac{3}{4}$ inches, upper belt $2\frac{1}{2}$ (fwd)–$5\frac{3}{4}$ (amid.)–$3\frac{1}{4}$ (aft) inches, closed by bulkheads $5\frac{3}{4}$–$8\frac{3}{4}$–7 (fwd) and $5\frac{3}{4}$–$4\frac{1}{4}$–7 (aft) inches, internal longitudinal bulkhead $1\frac{1}{2}$–$1\frac{3}{4}$ inches. Upper deck 2 (amid.)–$3\frac{1}{4}$ (outer edge) inches, lower deck $3\frac{1}{4}$ (flat)–$4/4\frac{3}{4}$ (slope) inches, over steering gear $4\frac{1}{4}$ inches. Main turrets $14\frac{1}{4}$ (face)–$6/8\frac{3}{4}$ (side)–$12\frac{1}{4}$ (rear) inches and crown $5/7\frac{1}{4}$ inches, barbettes $8\frac{3}{4}$ (below UD)–$13\frac{1}{2}$ (above UD) inches. Secondary turrets 4 (face)–$1\frac{1}{2}$ (sides and rear)–$\frac{3}{4}/1\frac{1}{2}$ (crown) inches, barbettes 4 inches. Fwd C.T. $13\frac{3}{4}$ (face)–$8\frac{3}{4}$ (crown) inches, R/F hood 4/8 inches, tube $8\frac{3}{4}$ inches; aft C.T. $1\frac{1}{4}$–6 inches, R/F hood 2/4 inches, tube 2 inches

*Armament:* Eight 15inch (4 × 2), twelve 5.9inch (6 × 2), sixteen 4.1inch A.A. (8 × 2), sixteen 37mm A.A. (8 × 2), *Bismarck* thirty-six/*Tirpitz* seventy 20mm A.A. (4 × 4, 6 × 2 and 8 × 1/ 11 × 4, 16 × 2 and 10 × 1) guns; eight 21inch (2 × 4) T.T. in *Tirpitz* only; six aircraft and one catapult

*Complement:* Bismarck 1,989 (2,192 as flag), *Tirpitz* 2,530

Above: *The* Bismarck's *sister* Tirpitz *differed in minor respects, having quadruple torpedo-tubes and the upper deck abaft the catapult, and additional AA guns. The aircraft was mounted a deck higher than in* Bismarck *to improve handling of the floatplanes.* (Drüppel)

Left and above left: *Two views of the* Tirpitz.(Drüppel)

Above: *A stern view of the Tirpitz*. (Drüppel)

Above right: *A salvo of 15-inch shells from the after turrets of the* Tirpitz *during gunnery practice*. (Drüppel)

**Name** *Bismarck* **Built by** Blohm & Voss (Hamburg)
**Launched** 14.2.39 **Fate** Gunfire RN battleships *King George V* and *Rodney*, and torpedoed cruiser *Dorsetshire*, aircraft (810, 818 & 820 Sqns.) of fleet carrier *Ark Royal,* and destroyers North Atlantic 27.5.41

**Name** *Tirpitz* **Built by** Naval Dockyard (Wilhelmshaven)
**Launched** 1.4.39 **Fate** Bombed RAF aircraft (617 Sqn.) and capsized Tromso 12.11.44; scrapped *in situ* 1948

## *Battleships:* **Six projected**

The first two battleships of this class were laid down before even their final plans were completed, and when these were eventually drawn-up their size was increased by over 10,000 tons from that first envisaged. Nearly all this additional weight was put into hull strength and protection, which in turn required heavier double bottom plating than that already worked, while the armament was similar to that of the *Bismarck* and *Tirpitz* except that the calibre of the main guns was increased to 16inch. To extend their radius diesel propulsion was adopted, and they were to be organised as support groups, able to keep the seas indefinitely, on which the raiding squadron could fall back when opposed by a heavier concentration. Both the units laid down were broken up on the slips, by which time 1,200 tons had been worked into "H" and

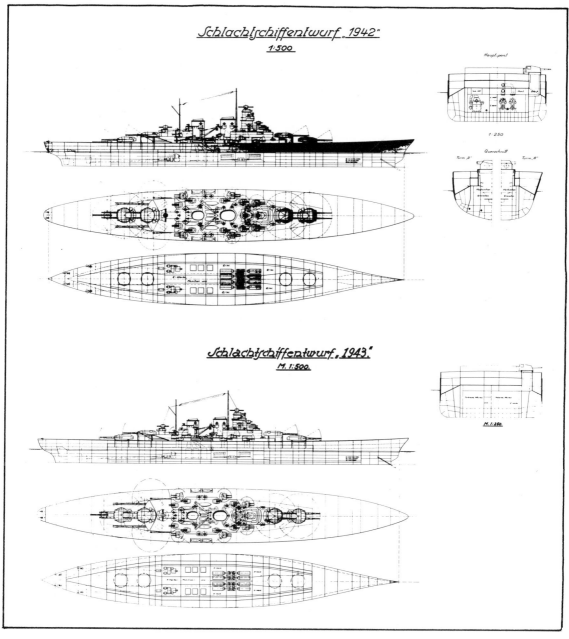

several hundred tons into "J", and the remainder were never started. The fixed athwartship catapult was placed across the quarterdeck, abaft "D" turret, and the aircraft stowed in an upper deck hangar placed between the after funnel and "C" turret: a neat arrangement that dispensed with high superstructure. They represented the culmination of German capital ship design, and had they been proceeded with would have inspired a new cycle of large and costly ships.

Top: *The "1942" battleship design, a project which was put forward as a successor to the* Bismarck *and* Tirpitz.

Bottom: *The "1943" battleship project was even larger but followed the general layout of the previous project.*

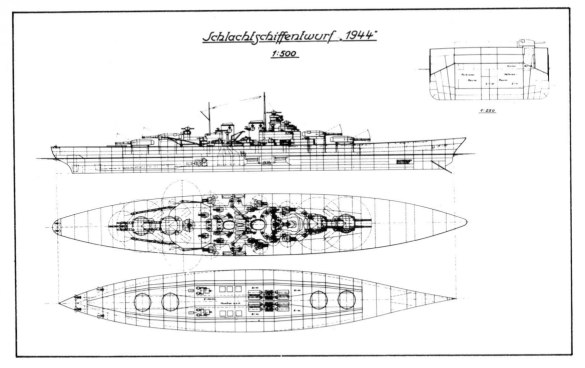

*Schlachtschiffentwurf „1944"*
*1:500*

*1:250*

*The "1944" battleship design was the last design prepared by the German design-team, by which time there was no conceivable likelihood of the ships being built. All three should be seen as extensions and improvements on the original "H" to "N" class of 56,000-tonners stopped in 1940. [PPL (all 3)]*

*Displacement:* 56,200 tons (68,000 tons full)

*Dimensions:* $872\frac{3}{4}$(pp) 912(oa) $\times$ $123\frac{1}{4}$ $\times$ $31\frac{1}{2}/36\frac{3}{4}$ feet

*Machinery:* Three shafts; M.A.N. diesel motors (four per shaft), B.H.P. 165,000 = 29 knots

*Bunkers & Radius:* O.F. 10,000 tons; 16,000 miles at 19 knots

*Protection:* Main w.l. belt $12\frac{3}{4}$ inches, upper belt $2\frac{1}{2}$ (fwd)–6 (amid.)–$1\frac{1}{4}/3\frac{1}{2}$ (aft) inches. Upper deck 2 inches, main deck 4 inches. Main turrets $9\frac{1}{2}$ (rear)–$14\frac{1}{2}$ (side)–$15\frac{1}{2}$ (face) inches, barbettes $14\frac{1}{2}$ inches, secondary turrets 4 inches. C.T. $15\frac{1}{2}$ inches

*Armament:* Eight 16inch (4 $\times$ 2), twelve 5.9inch (6 $\times$ 2), sixteen 4.1inch A.A. (8 $\times$ 2), sixteen 37mm A.A. (8 $\times$ 2), twenty-four 20mm A.A. (6 $\times$ 4) guns; six 21inch (6 $\times$ 1—fixed and fwd) T.T.; six aircraft and two catapults

*Complement:* 2,600

**Name** *"H"* **Built by** Blohm & Voss (Hamburg) **Fate** Scrapped on slip 1940

**Name** *"J"* **Built by** AG Weser (Bremen) **Fate** Scrapped on slip 1940

**Name** *"K"* **Built by** AG Weser (Bremen) **Fate** Projected

**Name** *"L"* **Built by** Naval Dockyard (Wilhelmshaven) **Fate** Projected

**Name** *"M"* **Built by** Blohm & Voss (Hamburg) **Fate** Projected

**Name** *"N"* **Built by** Deutsche Werke (Kiel) **Fate** Projected

## *Battlecruisers:* **Three projected**

In the traditional manner these battlecruisers sacrificed armament and protection for speed and were real corsairs which, in spite of mounting only six main guns, could only have been successfully engaged by ships of capital rank. Their deck protection was nearly as strong as that of the battleships so that aircraft from a carrier group would have experienced great difficulty in inflicting bomb damage, but their A.A. armament of six guns and two high-angle directors was too light to withstand sustained attacks. A large radius of action was provided by diesel propulsion to the wing shafts, with which they could make 25 knots, while a turbine plant on the centre shaft only was brought in for full speed. No units of this class were laid down and they were the final capital ship project to be seriously advanced.

*Displacement:* 32,300 tons (38,200 tons full)
*Dimensions:* 807(pp) $843\frac{1}{4}$(oa) $\times$ $98\frac{1}{2}$ $\times$ 25/$29\frac{1}{2}$ feet
*Machinery:* Four Wagner boilers; three shafts; M.A.N. diesel motors (four per wing shafts) and Brown-Boveri geared turbines (centre shaft), B.H.P. 110,000 + S.H.P. 60,000 = $33\frac{1}{2}$ knots
*Bunkers & Radius:* O.F. 5,100 tons; 14,000 miles at 19 knots
*Protection:* Main w.l. belt $7\frac{1}{4}$ inches, upper belt $3\frac{1}{4}$ inches. Upper deck $1\frac{1}{4}$ inches, main deck $3\frac{1}{4}$ inches, lower deck $4\frac{1}{2}$ inches. Main turrets $8\frac{1}{2}$ inches, barbettes $7\frac{1}{4}$ inches, secondary turrets $\frac{1}{2}$ inch
*Armament:* Six 15inch (3 $\times$ 2), six 5.9inch (3 $\times$ 2), eight 4.1inch A.A. (4 $\times$ 2), eight 37mm A.A. (4 $\times$ 2), twenty 20mm A.A. (5 $\times$ 4) guns; four aircraft and one catapult
*Complement:* 1,900

**Name** "*O*" **Built by** Deutsche Werke (Kiel) **Fate** Projected

**Name** "*P*" **Built by** Naval Dockyard (Wilhelmshaven) **Fate** Projected

**Name** "*Q*" **Built by** Germania Werft (Kiel) **Fate** Projected

# Aircraft Carriers

## Aircraft Carriers: **Graf Zeppelin** and **One** more

Aircraft carriers filled a vital role either operating with, or in support of, the raiding squadrons in providing fighter air cover, and strike and reconnaissance aircraft. But ship rather than aircraft features predominated in the design and cut back aircraft capacity. The heavy A.A. armament of twelve guns, controlled by four high-angle directors, amply met defensive requirements but their disposition, all along the starboard side, was open to criticism. It restricted flight deck operations when engaging air targets to port, and was an undue concentration more easily liable to disruption by only localised damage. In view of the extra high speed steaming undertaken by carriers when operating their aircraft, the radius of action was on the short side, while, to aid manoeuvrability, two Voith-Schneider cycloidal propellers, powered by electric motors, were fitted forward. As neither of these vessels was finally completed two further 12,000-ton carriers, which had only been contemplated pre-war, were not further advanced.

*The hull of the carrier* Graf Zeppelin *after launching in 1938.* (Drüppel)

*Displacement:* 23.200 tons (32,600 tons full)

*Dimensions:* $820\frac{1}{4}$(wl) $862\frac{3}{4}$(oa) $\times$ $103\frac{1}{4}$ $\times$ $21/26\frac{1}{2}$ feet (flight deck 790 $\times$ $118\frac{3}{4}$ feet)

*Machinery:* Sixteen Lamont boilers (pressure 1,249 lb.); four shafts; Brown-Boveri geared turbines, S.H.P. 200,000 = $33\frac{3}{4}$ knots

*Bunkers & Radius:* O.F. 6,400 tons; 8,000 miles at 19 knots

*Protection:* Main w.l. belt 4 inches. Flight deck $\frac{3}{4}$ inch, main deck $1\frac{1}{2}$ (flat)–$2\frac{1}{2}$ (slope) inches. Casemates and barbettes $1\frac{1}{4}$ inches, turrets $\frac{1}{2}$ inch

*Armament:* Sixteen 5.9inch (8 $\times$ 2), twelve 4.1inch A.A. (6 $\times$ 2), twenty-two 37mm A.A. (11 $\times$ 2), twenty-eight 20mm. A.A. (28 $\times$ 1) guns; forty aircraft and two catapults

*Complement:* 1,760

*Notes:* Full load displacement increased to 34,000 tons after 1942 modification

**Name** *Graf Zeppelin* **Built by** Deutsche Werke (Kiel)
**Launched** 8.12.38 **Fate** Construction suspended 1940, resumed to modified design 1942, again suspended 1943; scuttled Stettin 25.4.45, salved and Russian; mined 15m north of Rügen 15.8.47

**Name** Unnamed **Built by** Germania Werft (Kiel) **Fate** Scrapped incomplete on slip 1940

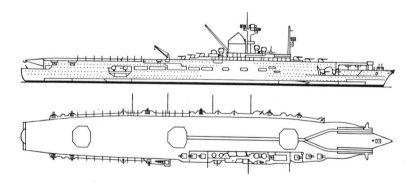

*The* Graf Zeppelin's *design was revised in 1942 to include a heavier AA armament.*

# Cruisers

### *Light Cruiser:* **Emden**

In the absence of any design studies undertaken in the years immediately following the First World War, this vessel was developed from the latest proven design with which war experience was available. The draft provision to have the main guns twin-mounted on the centre line was not implemented, and single mountings were shipped in these positions supplemented by four single mountings on the broadside. For active employment during the Second World War the *Emden* lacked sufficient A.A. guns and deck protection and was principally employed on minelaying and training duties.

*Displacement:* 5,600 tons (6,990 tons full)
*Dimensions:* $492\frac{1}{2}$(pp) $508\frac{1}{2}$(oa) $\times$ 47 $\times$ 19/$21\frac{3}{4}$ feet
*Machinery:* Ten Marine boilers (pressure 235 lb.); two shafts; Blohm & Voss geared turbines, S.H.P. 46,500 = 29 knots
*Bunkers & Radius:* O.F. 1,266 tons; 5,300 miles at 18 knots
*Protection:* Main belt 2 inches, decks $\frac{3}{4}$ inch (upper and main), gunshields $\frac{1}{2}-\frac{3}{4}$ inch, C.T. 3 inches
*Armament:* Eight 5.9inch (8 $\times$ 1), three 3.5inch A.A. (3 $\times$ 1), four 37mm A.A. (4 $\times$ 1) guns; four 21inch (2 $\times$ 2) T.T.; one hundred and twenty mines
*Complement:* 630
*Notes:* At least four 20mm A.A. (1 $\times$ 4) guns, if not more, were added

*The light cruiser* Emden *was based on the last light cruiser built during World War I and was used mainly on training and minelaying during the War.* (Drüppel)

**Name** *Emden* **Built by** Naval Dockyard (Wilhelmshaven)
**Launched** 7.1.25 **Fate** Scuttled Heikendorfer Bight 3.5.45 after
being bombed RAF aircraft Kiel 14.4.45; scrapped 1947

## *Light Cruisers:* **Karlsruhe, Köln,** and **Königsberg**

Although these cruisers were intended to operate with the
raiding squadrons and introduced mixed turbine and diesel
propulsion to extend their radius, the weight of armament
carried heavily loaded the hull and the position of the forward turret and bridge represented a concentration of weight
forward which prejudiced seakeeping qualities. The heavy
A.A. guns were first mounted singly aft, then paired on the
centre line and finally—with the addition of a further twin
mounting—the two forward mountings were winged out. The
*Karlsruhe* was the only unit refitted pre-war when the fore
funnel was heightened, caps added to both funnels, a heavier
tripod mainmast added abaft the after funnel, and was
externally bulged, which added much needed beam.

*The* Karlsruhe *as completed, with light rig and aerials carried to spreaders on the after funnel.* (Drüppel)

Karlsruhe *after her 1939 refit, with capped funnels, extra platforms on the foremast, and tripod mast stepped against the funnel.* (Drüppel)

*The* Köln *lying damaged on the bottom of Wilhelmshaven Dockyard in 1945. Note that the after 5·9-inch gun turrets were staggered to widen their forward arcs of fire on each side.*

*Displacement:* 6,650 tons (8,130 tons except *Karlsruhe* 8,350 tons full)

*Dimensions:* 554½(wl) 570¾(oa) × 50¼ except *Karlsruhe* 54½ (over bulges) × 17¾/21¼ feet

*Machinery:* Six Marine boilers (pressure 235 lb.); two shafts; Germania (*Karlsruhe*) Blohm & Voss (*Köln*) or Schichau (*Königsberg*) geared turbines and M.A.N. diesel motors, S.H.P. 68,000 + B.H.P. 1,800 = 32 except *Karlsruhe* 30 knots

*Bunkers & Radius:* O.F. 1,145 + 261 tons; 18,000/5,200 miles at 10/19 knots

*Protection:* Main w.l. belt 2 inches. Main deck ¾ inch. Main turrets and barbettes 1¼ inches, secondary turrets ½ inch. C.T. 3 inches

*Armament:* Nine 5.9inch (3 × 3), six 3.5inch A.A. (3 × 2), eight 37mm A.A. (4 × 2), four 20mm A.A. (4 × 1) guns; twelve 21inch (4 × 3) T.T.; two aircraft and one catapult

*Complement:* 820

*Notes:* At least four 20mm A.A. (1 × 4) guns, if not more, were added in *Köln*, the aircraft and catapult were removed, and the after bank of torpedo tubes on each side were taken out and the hull plated over

*The* Königsberg *and her two sisters were largely experimental in design and suffered accordingly. She is seen here pre-war.*

**Name** *Karlsruhe* **Built by** Deutsche Werke (Kiel) **Launched** 20.8.27 **Fate** Torpedoed RN submarine *Truant* south of Christiansand 10.4.40

**Name** *Köln* **Built by** Naval Dockyard (Wilhelmshaven) **Launched** 23.5.28 **Fate** Bombed 8th USAAF aircraft Wilhelmshaven 30.3.45; scrapped 1946

**Name** *Königsberg* **Built by** Naval Dockyard (Wilhelmshaven) **Launched** 26.3.27 **Fate** Bombed RN aircraft (800 & 803 Sqns.) Bergen 10.1.40; salved 1943, capsized 22.9.44 and abandoned

## *Light Cruiser:* **Leipzig**

A modification of the *Königsberg* class with 3-feet more beam, both after turrets placed on the centre line, the funnels trunked into a single uptake positioned nearly amidships with the aircraft catapult placed forward of it, a third shaft added for a more powerful cruising diesel installation, and the main belt extended forward and aft.

*Displacement:* 6,710 tons (8,290 tons full)
*Dimensions:* $544\frac{1}{2}$(pp) $580\frac{3}{4}$(oa) × $53\frac{1}{4}$ × 17/$21\frac{3}{4}$ feet
*Machinery:* Eight Marine boilers (pressure 235 lb.); three shafts; Parsons geared turbines (wing shafts) and 7-cylinder M.A.N. diesel motors (four on centre shaft), S.H.P. 66,000 + B.H.P. 12,400 = 32 knots
*Bunkers & Radius:* O.F. 1,183 + 348 tons; 5,700 miles at 19 knots
*Protection:* Main w.l. belt 2 inches. Main deck $\frac{3}{4}$ (flat)–1 (slope) inch. Main turrets and barbettes $1\frac{1}{4}$ inches, secondary turrets $\frac{1}{2}$ inch. C.T. 2 inches
*Armament:* Nine 5.9inch (3 × 3), six 3.5inch A.A. (3 × 2), eight 37mm A.A. (4 × 2), ten 20mm A.A. (2 × 4 and 2 × 1) guns; twelve 21inch (4 × 3) T.T.; two aircraft and one catapult

*The light cruiser* Leipzig *was an improved version of the* Karlsruhe *Class with funnels trunked together and other improvements; a pre-war view.* (Drüppel)

*Complement:* 850
*Notes:* Six T.T. removed in 1941, and the remainder in 1944, together with the forward boiler room, when converted for training duties, and *ca.* ten 20mm A.A. (2 × 4 and 2 × 1) guns added

**Name** *Leipzig* **Built by** Naval Dockyard (Wilhelmshaven)
**Launched** 18.10.29 **Fate** Scuttled south-west of Lister 20.7.46

## *Light Cruiser:* **Nürnberg**

A further modification of the *Königsberg* class and *Leipzig* with the hull lengthened and main belt extended to the stem, the heavy A.A. armament further augmented and moved more amidships instead of being concentrated aft, the single trunked funnel moved further forward and the aircraft catapult resited abaft it, and a light mizzen mast added.

*Displacement:* 6,980 tons (8,380 tons full)
*Dimensions:* $557\frac{3}{4}$(pp) $593\frac{3}{4}$(oa) × $53\frac{3}{4}$ × $16\frac{1}{2}$/21 feet
*Machinery:* Eight Marine boilers (pressure 235 lb.); three shafts; Parsons geared turbines (wing shafts) and M.A.N. diesel motors (four on centre shaft), S.H.P. 60,000 + B.H.P. 12,400 = 32 knots
*Bunkers & Radius:* O.F. 1,100 + 348 tons; 5700 miles at 19 knots
*Protection:* Main w.l. belt 2 inches. Main deck $\frac{3}{4}$ (slope)–1 (flat) inch. Main turrets and barbettes $1\frac{1}{4}$ inches, secondary turrets $\frac{1}{2}$ inch. C.T. 3 inches
*Armament:* Nine 5.9inch (3 × 3), eight 3.5inch A.A. (4 × 2), eight 37mm A.A. (4 × 2), four 20mm A.A. (4 × 1) guns; twelve 21inch (3 × 4) T.T.; two aircraft and one catapult

The Nürnberg *was an improved* Leipzig *with heavier AA armament; a pre-war view.* (Drüppel)

The Nürnberg *in Arctic waters, showing the disruptive effect of her camouflage; her aircraft, catapult and after torpedo-tubes have been removed.* (Drüppel)

*Complement:* 896
*Notes:* Catapult and two after banks of T.T. removed, and A.A. armament augmented by addition of two 37mm and twenty-nine 20mm (2 × 4, 10 × 2 and 1 × 1) guns

**Name** *Nürnberg* **Built by** Deutsche Werke (Kiel) **Launched** 8.12.34 **Fate** Russian *Admiral Makarov* (1946)

## *Heavy Cruisers:* **Admiral Hipper** and **Blücher**

The German Navy was late in the field of heavy cruiser construction, but benefited by the much publicised shortcomings of earlier foreign cruisers of this type. In spite of being intended for raiding operations only turbine machinery was fitted and their radius reduced in consequence, which proved an embarrassment during war operations. They were well

*The heavy cruiser* Admiral Hipper *on completion in 1939, with uncapped funnel and vertical stem. During the War she was given an "Atlantic" bow and a funnel cap, and additional AA.* (Drüppel)

protected, for their type, with the belt continued to the bows. The heavy A.A. was good and was enhanced by the ultimate provision of four high-angle directors, but only the superimposed turrets were fitted with rangefinders for the 8inch guns. The *Admiral Hipper* was completed with a vertical stem and only two high-angle directors forward but later embodied the clipper stem, had two more high-angle directors put in aft, and a funnel cap added—all as in *Blücher*. The catapult was placed aft, over the after end of the hangar.

*Displacement:* 12,500 tons (16,000 tons full/17,250 tons max)
*Dimensions:* 639$\frac{3}{4}$(wl) 675$\frac{3}{4}$(oa) × 70 × 19/25$\frac{1}{4}$ feet
*Machinery:* Twelve Lamont (pressure 1,175 lb.—*Admiral Hipper*), or Wagner (pressure 1,028 lb.—*Blücher*) boilers; three shafts; Blohm & Voss (*Admiral Hipper*) or AG Weser (*Blücher*) geared turbines, S.H.P. 132,000 = 32$\frac{1}{2}$ knots
*Bunkers & Radius:* O.F. 4,250 tons; 6,800 miles at 19 knots
*Protection:* Main w.l. belt 2$\frac{3}{4}$–3$\frac{1}{4}$ inches, longitudinal bulkheads $\frac{3}{4}$ inch. Upper deck $\frac{1}{2}$ (fwd)–1$\frac{1}{4}$ (abreast fwd turrets)–$\frac{1}{2}$ (amid.)–1$\frac{1}{4}$ (abreast aft turrets)–$\frac{1}{2}$ (aft) inches, main deck $\frac{3}{4}$ (fwd)–1$\frac{1}{4}$/1$\frac{1}{2}$ (flat)–2 (slopes) amid.–$\frac{3}{4}$ (aft) inches. Main turrets 4$\frac{1}{4}$ (face)–2$\frac{3}{4}$ (sides)–2$\frac{3}{4}$ (crown) inches, barbettes 3$\frac{3}{4}$ inches, secondary turrets $\frac{1}{2}$ inch. Fwd C.T. 6 (sides)–2 (crown) inches, aft C.T. 1$\frac{1}{4}$ (sides)–$\frac{3}{4}$ (crown) inches, R/F hoods $\frac{3}{4}$ inch. Externally bulged
*Armament:* Eight 8inch (4 × 2), twelve 4.1inch A.A. (6 × 2), twelve 37mm A.A. (6 × 2), four 20mm A.A. (4 × 1) guns; twelve 21inch (3 × 4) T.T.; three aircraft and one catapult
*Complement:* 1,600
*Notes:* About four 20mm A.A. (4 × 1) guns were added in *Blücher*, while thirty-five 20mm A.A. (8 × 2 and 3 × 1) guns were added in *Admiral Hipper*

**Name** *Admiral Hipper* **Built by** Blohm & Voss (Hamburg) **Launched** 6.2.37 **Fate** Scuttled Heikendorfer Bight 3.5.45; scrapped 1946

**Name** *Blücher* **Built by** Deutsche Werke (Kiel) **Launched** 8.6.37 **Fate** Torpedoed and gunfire shore batteries Drobak 9.4.40

*The* Blücher *was a sister of the* Hipper *but she was completed with the modifications added to* Hipper *subsequently.* (Drüppel)

## *Heavy Cruisers:* **Lützow, Prinz Eugen,** and **Seydlitz**

Generally similar to the *Admiral Hipper* class but with more pronounced clipper stem and funnel cap. The former was added while building and increased length by 16 ft. The aircraft crane was moved further forward where it was less liable to mask the fire of the amidships heavy A.A. guns mounted on the upper deck, and in consequence the catapult was resited over the fore end of the hangar where the crane could plumb it. A speed of 22 knots could be attained using only the centre shaft, or 27 knots using only the wing shafts, while all three shafts were required for full speed. Provision was also made to carry 900 troops, all of which could be berthed in portable 3-tier bunks.

Of this group only the *Prinz Eugen* was completed; the *Lützow* was sold incomplete to the Russian Navy, who were never able to complete her; and the *Seydlitz* was converted to an aircraft carrier. How far this conversion progressed is not precisely known, but she is believed to have advanced to the stage of having her hull decked over.

*The* Prinz Eugen *was the last German heavy cruiser to be completed and so incorporated more modifications than her sisters. She is seen here in the Spring of 1941 at the time of the* Bismarck's *breakout, with recognition bands, two-tone camouflage and false bow- and stern-waves.* (Drüppel)

*Two views of* Prinz Eugen *at the end of the War, with heavily augmented close-range AA armament.* (Drüppel, L. J. Baée)

*Displacement:* 12,750 tons (16,200 tons full/18,400 tons max)

*Dimensions:* 654½(wl) 697½(oa) × 71¾ × 21/26 feet

*Machinery:* Nine Wagner boilers (pressure 881 lb.) except *Prinz Eugen* twelve boilers (pressure 1,012 lb.); three shafts; AG Weser except *Prinz Eugen* Brown-Boveri geared turbines, S.H.P. 132,000 = 32 knots

*Bunkers & Radius:* O.F. 4,250 tons; 7,600/6,750/5,500/2,050 miles at 12/15/18/32 knots

*Protection:* Main w.l. belt 2¾–3¼ inches, longitudinal bulkheads ¾ inch. Upper deck ½ (fwd)–1¼ (abreast fwd turrets)–½ (amid.)–1¼ (abreast aft turrets)–½ (aft) inches, main deck ¾ (fwd)–1¼/1½ (flat)–2 (slope) amid.–¾ (aft) inches. Main turrets 4¼ (face–2¾ (sides)–2¾ (crown) inches, barbettes 3¼ inches, secondary turrets ½ inch. Fwd C.T. 6 (sides)–2 (crown) inches, aft C.T. 1¼ (sides)–¾ (crown) inches, R/F hoods ¾ inch. Externally bulged

*Armament:* Eight 8inch (4 × 2), twelve 4.1inch A.A. (6 × 2), twelve 37mm A.A. (6 × 2), eight 20mm A.A. (8 × 1) guns; twelve 21inch (3 × 4) T.T.; three aircraft and one catapult

*Complement:* 1,600

*Notes:* During 1942 the light A.A. armament of the *Prinz Eugen* was increased to twenty-eight 20mm (5 × 4 and 8 × 1), and for the Channel breakthrough operation to fifty-six 20mm (6 × 4 and 16 × 2) guns. In 1944 the twin 37mm A.A. mountings were taken out, and the light A.A. altered to eighteen 40mm (18 × 1) and twenty-eight 20mm (6 × 4 and 4 × 1) guns. Maximum bunkerage was increased from 3,250 tons to 4,250 tons. Boilers not pressed higher than 750 lb.

*Facing page: Danish troops guard the* Prinz Eugen *in Copenhagen in 1945. Note the radar "mattress" on her control-top and the 37-mm AA guns which had replaced the 20-mm quads, twins and singles by the end of the War.* (Associated Press)

**Name** *Prinz Eugen* **Built by** Germania Werft (Kiel)
**Launched** 22.8.38 **Fate** USN (1946); expended as target
Kwajalein 15.11.47

**Name** *Seydlitz* **Built by** AG Weser (Bremen) **Launched** 19.1.39
**Fate** Construction halted 1942 and converted to aircraft carrier,
scuttled incomplete Königsberg 10.4.45, salved and Russian
*Poltava*; construction abandoned 1950

**Name** *Lützow* **Built by** AG Weser (Bremen) **Launched** 1.7.39
**Fate** Russian (1940), completion abandoned 5.41, bombed
German aircraft Leningrad 4.42, floating battery *Tallin* (1942),
*Petropavlovsk* (1944) construction abandoned 1950

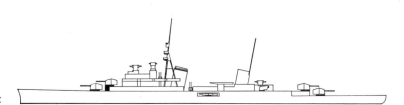

*Light cruiser.*

## *Light Cruisers:* **Six projected**

To secure speed and seaworthiness the armament in these
vessels was reduced, compared to that carried in the earlier
light cruisers, while the mixed turbine and diesel installation
was retained for the necessary radius of action. But with only
a single high-angle director and two twin heavy A.A. mountings they had little to offer in the way of air defence. The belt
extended between the end barbettes, and was taken up to the
level of the upper deck for the greater part of its length
abreast the machinery spaces. Their large mine capacity
indicated a further role well suited to their high speed for
which they possessed ample gun power to ward off any interference from surface craft able to catch them. Only the first
three ships of the class were laid down but were not greatly
advanced before they were scrapped on the slips.

*Displacement:* 7,800 tons (10,400 tons full)
*Dimensions:* 584(wl) $600\frac{1}{2}$(oa) $\times$ $55\frac{3}{4}$ $\times$ $19\frac{3}{4}/23\frac{3}{4}$ feet
*Machinery:* Four Wagner boilers (pressure 1,028 lb.); three shafts;
    Wagner geared turbines (wing shafts) + M.A.N. diesel motors
    (four on centre shaft), S.H.P. 100,000 + B.H.P. 16,500 = $35\frac{1}{2}$
    knots
*Bunkers & Radius:* O.F. 1,080 + 520 tons; 8,000 miles at 19 knots
*Protection:* Main w.l. belt 2 inches. Main deck 1 (flat)–$1\frac{1}{2}$ (slope)
    inches. Main turrets $\frac{3}{4}$–$3\frac{1}{4}$ (faces) inches, barbettes $1\frac{1}{4}$–$2\frac{1}{2}$ inches,
    secondary turrets $\frac{1}{2}$ inch. C.T. 2 (crown)–4 (sides) inches

*Armament:* Eight 5.9inch (4 × 2), four 4.1inch A.A. (2 × 2), eight
   37mm A.A. (4 × 2), four 20mm A.A. (4 × 1) guns; eight
   21inch (2 × 4) T.T.; one hundred and sixty mines; two aircraft
   and one catapult
*Complement:* 920

**Name** "*M*" **Built by** Deutsche Werke (Kiel) **Fate** Scrapped on slip
1941–3

**Name** "*N*" **Built by** Naval Dockyard (Wilhelmshaven)
**Fate** Scrapped on slip 1941–3

**Name** "*O*" **Built by** Germania Werft (Kiel) **Fate** Scrapped on slip
1941–3

**Name** "*P*" **Built by** Germania Werft (Kiel) **Fate** Cancelled

**Name** "*Q*" **Built by** Schichau (Danzig) **Fate** Cancelled

**Name** "*R*" **Built by** Deutsche Werke (Kiel) **Fate** Cancelled

*Scout cruiser.*

## *Scout Cruisers:* **Sp.1–3.**

The cancellation of the 7,800-ton light cruisers left those
capital ships already completed devoid of any screen as none
of the existing light cruisers could match them for prolonged
high speed steaming, and the heavy cruisers were short on
endurance. As a temporary expedient an enlarged destroyer
design was proposed with the addition of a third centre shaft
to which a powerful diesel installation was coupled. By this
means their radius was increased to 25–33 per cent above that
possessed by the battleships *Bismarck* and *Tirpitz*: an ample
margin for their purpose. The concentration of the gun
armament aft left no doubt of their course of action on sighting the enemy, and they could not hope to press home a
reconnaissance. The old axiom that armour, not speed, was
vision could, perhaps, be disregarded to some extent now that
RDF was available, but unfortunately its development in
the German Navy was not so marked as in the American and
British navies. Under these circumstances the employment of
fast, but unarmoured, small scouts was problematical, but
the dilemma was resolved by the premature loss of the
*Bismarck*, the crippling effect this had on the employment of
the *Tirpitz*, and the scout cruiser project was abandoned after
the initial unit only had been laid down.

*Displacement:* 4,542 tons (5,900 tons full)

*Dimensions:* 475$\frac{3}{4}$(wl) 498$\frac{3}{4}$(oa) × 48 × 15/18$\frac{1}{4}$ feet

*Machinery:* Four Wagner boilers (pressure 1,028 lb.); three shafts; Wagner geared turbines (wing shafts) + M.A.N. diesel motors (four on centre shaft), S.H.P. 77,500 + B.H.P. 14,500 = 36 knots

*Bunkers & Radius:* O.F. 1,102 + 250 tons; 12,000 miles at 19 knots

*Protection:* Longitudinal bulkheads (amid.) $\frac{3}{4}$ inch. Upper deck (amid.) $\frac{3}{4}$ inch, main turrets 1 inch, barbettes $\frac{1}{2}$ inch, secondary turret $\frac{1}{2}$ inch

*Armament:* Six 5.9inch (3 × 2), two 3.5inch A.A. (1 × 2), eight 37mm A.A. (4 × 2), twelve 20mm A.A. (3 × 4) guns; ten 21inch (2 × 5) T.T.; one hundred and forty mines

*Complement:* 583

**Name** *Sp.1* (ex-*Z.40*) **Built by** Germania Werft (Kiel)
**Fate** Scrapped on slip 7.43

**Name** *Sp.2* (ex-*Z.41*) **Built by** Germania Werft (Kiel)
**Fate** Cancelled 3.42

**Name** *Sp.3* (ex-*Z.42*) **Built by** Germania Werft (Kiel)
**Fate** Cancelled 3.42

# Destroyers

*Destroyer type 1934 :* **Z.1–16**

In building up the destroyer flotillas the underlying principle was to offset quantity by quality, and consequently the first series of destroyers were among the largest in the world. The design was one of robust simplicity—with an adequate but not outstanding armament for their tonnage—except for the main machinery where the adoption of very high boiler pressures did not prove a great success. The need to augment the A.A. armament led to the eventual removal of "C" gun and the addition of several light pieces, mounted overall, but to no uniform pattern in individual ships. By the end of the war Z.5, in addition to the two twin 37mm mountings originally carried abreast the after funnel, mounted a twin 20mm on the foc's'le, a twin 20mm before and two twin 37mm abaft "B" gun, two twin 20mm in the bridge wings, two twin 37mm in lieu of "C" gun, one twin 37mm and two twin 20mm on the shelter between "C" and "D" guns, and a single 20mm abaft "D" gun—a total of fourteen 37mm and thirteen 20mm. As completed they had vertical stems but Z.4 and Z.5 were lengthened in 1944 when they were given clipper stems.

*Displacement:* Z1–4: 2,232 tons (3,156 tons full); Z.5–8: 2,171 tons (3,100 tons full); Z.9–13: 2,270 tons (3,190 tons full); Z.14–16: 2,239 tons (3,165 tons full)
*Dimensions:* 374(pp) 390½(oa) except Z.9–16 380½(pp) 397(oa) × 37 × 12½/14 feet
*Machinery:* Six Wagner (pressure 1,028 lb.) except Z.9–16 Benson (pressure 1,616 lb.) boilers; two shafts; Wagner geared turbines, S.H.P. 70,000 = 38 knots except Z.1–4 38¼ knots
*Bunkers & Radius:* O.F. 752 tons; 4,400 miles at 19 knots
*Armament:* Five 5inch (5 × 1), four 37mm A.A. (2 × 2) guns; eight 21inch (2 × 4—sixteen torpedoes) T.T.; sixty mines
*Complement:* 325

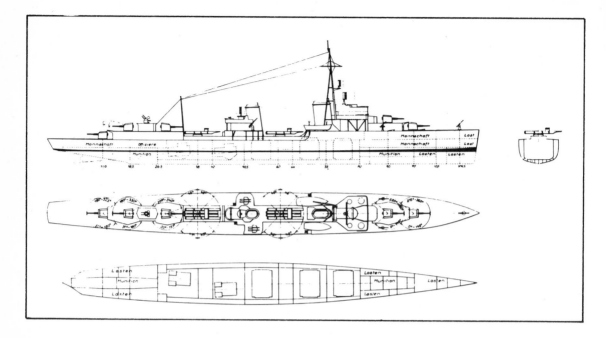

Z.1 to Z.16 *General Arrangement showing basic layout.*

**Name** *Z.1* (*Leberecht Maass*) **Built by** Deutsche Werke (Kiel) **Launched** 18.8.35 **Fate** Bombed in error German aircraft north-west of Borkum 22.2.40

**Name** *Z.2* (*Georg Thiele*) **Built by** Deutsche Werke (Kiel) **Launched** 18.8.35 Scuttled Rombaksfjord 13.3.40

**Name** *Z.3* (*Max Schultz*) **Built by** Deutsche Werke (Kiel) **Launched** 30.11.35 **Fate** Bombed in error German aircraft north-west of Borkum 22.2.40

**Name** *Z.4* (*Richard Beitzen*) **Built by** Deutsche Werke (Kiel) **Launched** 30.11.35 **Fate** RN *H.97* (1945); sold C. W. Dorkin, arrived Gateshead 10.1.49 and scrapped

**Name** *Z.5* (*Paul Jacobi*) **Built by** AG Weser (Bremen) **Launched** 24.3.36 **Fate** RN (1945), French *Desaix* (1946); scrapped 1954

**Name** *Z.6* (*Theodor Riedel*) **Built by** AG Weser (Bremen) **Launched** 22.4.36 **Fate** RN (1945), French *Klèber* (1946); scrapped 1958

**Name** *Z.7* (*Hermann Schoemann*) **Built by** AG Weser (Bremen) **Launched** 16.7.36 **Fate** Gunfire RN cruiser *Edinburgh* Arctic 2.5.42

**Name** *Z.8* (*Bruno Heinemann*) **Built by** AG Weser (Bremen) **Launched** 15.9.36 **Fate** Mined English Channel 25.1.42

**Name** *Z.9* (*Wolfgang Zenker*) **Built by** Germania Werft (Kiel) **Launched** 27.3.36 **Fate** Scuttled Rombaksfjord 13.4.40

**Name** *Z.10* (*Hans Lody*) **Built by** Germania Werft (Kiel) **Launched** 14.5.36 **Fate** RN *R.38* (1945); scrapped Sunderland 1949

Georg Thiele (Z.2) *was an early casualty and so had virtually no additions to her armament.* (Drüppel)

*The destroyer* Max Schultz *(Z.3) as completed. The hull number indicated her position in the flotilla.* (Drüppel)

Paul Jacobi (Z.5) *as completed. During the War her light armament was increased to seven twin 37-mm AA, six twin 20-mm and a single 20-mm gun, while "C" gun at the forward end of the after deckhouse was removed.* (Drüppel)

Theodor Riedel (Z.6) *seen at the time of the Spanish Civil War, with national markings on the shield of "B" gun to assist recognition. During the War "C" gun was removed and the light AA augmented.* (Drüppel)

Below: Friedrich Ihn (Z.14) *belonged to a slightly enlarged second group of destroyers built 1936–7, but were otherwise very similar to the earlier boats.* (Drüppel)

**Name** *Z.11* (*Bernd von Arnim*) **Built by** Germania Werft (Kiel) **Launched** 8.7.36 **Fate** Scuttled Rombaksfjord 13.4.40

**Name** *Z.12* (*Erich Giese*) **Built by** Germania Werft (Kiel) **Launched** 12.3.37 **Fate** Scuttled Ofotfjord 13.4.40

**Name** *Z.13* (*Erich Koellner*) **Built by** Germania Werft (Kiel) **Launched** 18.3.37 **Fate** Scuttled Ofotfjord 13.4.40

**Name** *Z.14* (*Friedrich Ihn*) **Built by** Blohm & Voss (Hamburg) **Launched** 5.11.35 **Fate** Russian *Zorki* (1946); scrapped 1961

Bottom: Erich Steinbrinck (Z.15) *in wartime camouflage but still retaining "C" gun.* (Drüppel)

**Name** *Z.15* (*Erich Steinbrinck*) **Built by** Blohm & Voss (Hamburg) **Launched** 24.9.36 **Fate** Russian *Pylki* (1946); scrapped 1961

**Name** *Z.16* (*Friedrich Eckoldt*) **Built by** Blohm & Voss (Hamburg) **Launched** 21.3.37 **Fate** Gunfire RN cruiser *Sheffield* off Bear Island 31.12.42

## *Destroyer type 1936:* **Z.17–22**

These vessels were generally similar to the preceding class except that the last three units, *Z.20–22*, were completed with clipper stems. The extra buoyancy so provided forward improved seaworthiness and was adopted for all subsequent construction. The overloading and frequent breakdowns of the high pressure boilers under arduous war steaming conditions led to the forming of a special committee, before the end of 1939, to enquire into the problem. The sole surviving unit of this class after 1940, the *Z.20*, was altered similarly to the earlier vessels and had two 37mm A.A. (1 × 2) and twelve 20mm A.A. (1 × 4, 3 × 2 and 2 × 1) guns added.

*Displacement:* 2,411 tons (3,415 tons full)
*Dimensions:* $393\frac{3}{4}$(wl) $403\frac{1}{2}$(oa) except *Z.20–22* 410(oa) × $38\frac{3}{4}$ × $12\frac{1}{2}/14\frac{3}{4}$ feet
*Machinery:* Six Wagner boilers (pressure 1,028 lb.); two shafts; Wagner geared turbines, S.H.P. 70,000 = 38 knots
*Bunkers & Radius:* O.F. 760 tons; 4,850 miles at 19 knots
*Armament:* Five 5inch (5 × 1), four 37mm A.A. (2 × 2) guns; eight 21inch (2 × 4—sixteen torpedoes) T.T.; sixty mines
*Complement:* 323

Karl Galster (Z.20) *belonged to a large third group (Z.17–22), of which Z.20–22 had clipper stems to improve seaworthiness. The funnel caps were less prominent than before. Note that "C" gun has been removed.* (Drüppel)

**Name** *Z.17* (*Diether von Roeder*) **Built by** AG Weser (Bremen)
**Launched** 19.8.37 **Fate** Scuttled Rombaksfjord 13.4.40

**Name** *Z.18* (*Hans Lüdemann*) **Built by** AG Weser (Bremen)
**Launched** 1.12.37 **Fate** Scuttled Rombaksfjord 13.4.40

**Name** *Z.19* (*Hermann Künne*) **Built by** AG Weser (Bremen)
**Launched** 22.12.37 **Fate** Scuttled Rombaksfjord 13.4.40 after torpedoed RN destroyer *Eskimo*

**Name** *Z.20* (*Karl Galster*) **Built by** AG Weser (Bremen)
**Launched** 15.6.38 **Fate** Russian *Protschny* (1946)

**Name** *Z.21* (*Wilhelm Heidkamp*) **Built by** AG Weser (Bremen)
**Launched** 20.8.38 **Fate** Torpedoed RN destroyers Narvik 10.4.40

**Name** *Z.22* (*Anton Schmitt*) **Built by** AG Weser (Bremen)
**Launched** 20.9.39 **Fate** Torpedoed RN destroyers Narvik 10.4.40

## *Destroyer type 1936A:* **Z.23–30**

With this class the calibre of the main guns was increased to 5.9inch and the two forward guns housed in a turret except in *Z.28*, fitted as a flotilla leader, which had single mountings throughout and had "C" gun suppressed for additional accommodation. To compensate for this additional weight of armament the hull dimensions were slight enlarged, but on nowhere near an adequate scale, and the twin turret cramped internal arrangements and weakened the hull structure forward. Owing to the shortage of twin 5.9inch turrets only a single gun was mounted forward on completion together with additional light A.A. guns before the bridge. The twin turret was available from the end of 1942 and was fitted to all except *Z.26*, but shortly afterwards "C" gun was removed so that further light A.A. guns could be added. Typical of this class were *Z.25* and *Z.29* which had one 20mm on the fo'c'sle, two twin 20mm A.A. mountings abaft the turret, two twin 37mm before the bridge, two twin 20mm in the bridge wings, two twin and two single 37mm around the after funnel, two single 37mm in lieu of "C" gun, and two quadruple 20mm on the deckhouse forward of "D" gun which, with "C" gun out, had been extended to the fore end of the after shelter deck, and one 20mm at the after end.

*Z.25–27 General Arrangement showing layout.*

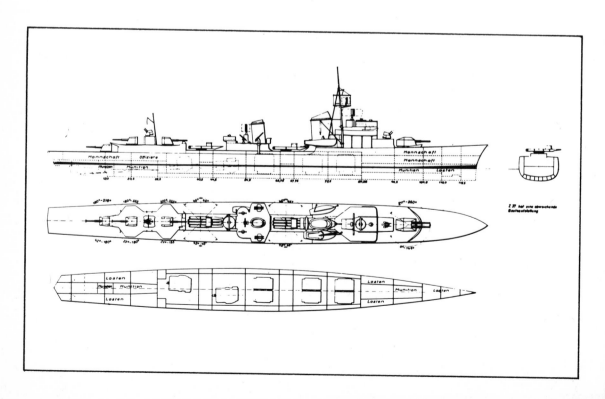

*Displacement:* 2,603 tons (3,605 tons full except *Z.29* and *30* 3,597 tons full) except *Z.25–27* 2,543 tons (3,543 tons full) and *Z.28* 2,596 tons (3,519 tons full)

*Dimensions:* $393\frac{1}{2}$(pp) $400\frac{1}{4}$(wl) $416\frac{3}{4}$(oa) × $39\frac{1}{4}$ × $12\frac{3}{4}$/15 feet

*Machinery:* Six Wagner boilers (pressure 1,028 lb.); two shafts; Wagner geared turbines, S.H.P. 70,000 = $38\frac{1}{2}$ knots

*Bunkers & Radius:* O.F. 752 tons except *Z.28* 804 tons and *Z.29* and *30* 825 tons; 5,000 miles except *Z.28* 5,800 miles and *Z.29–30* 5,900 miles at 19 knots

*Armament:* Five except *Z.28* four 5.9inch (1 × 2 and 3 × 1 except *Z.28* 4 × 1), six 37mm A.A. (2 × 2 and 2 × 1) guns; eight except *Z.28* seven 20mm A.A. (2 × 4 except *Z.28* 1 × 2 and 5 × 1), eight 21inch (2 × 4—twelve torpedoes) T.T.; sixty mines

*Complement:* 321 except *Z.28* 327

**Name** *Z.23* **Built by** AG Weser (Bremen) **Launched** 15.12.39
**Fate** Scuttled La Pallice 21.8.44 after being bombed RAF aircraft

**Name** *Z.24* **Built by** AG Weser (Bremen) **Launched** 7.3.40
**Fate** Driven ashore rocket fire RAF aircraft Le Verdon 25.8.44

**Name** *Z.25* **Built by** AG Weser (Bremen) **Launched** 16.3.40
**Fate** RN (1945), French *Hoche* (1946)

**Name** *Z.26* **Built by** AG Weser (Bremen) **Launched** 2.4.40
**Fate** Gunfire RN cruiser *Trinidad* and destroyer *Eclipse* North Sea 29.3.42

Z.24 *as completed with a single 5.9-inch gun on the forecastle. From 1942 as the twin turret became available it was shipped in Z.24 and others, and "C" gun then had to be sacrificed to make way for extra AA guns.* (Drüppel)

Because of her loss in 1942 Z.26 was the only boat to retain the single 5.9-inch gun forward. (Drüppel)

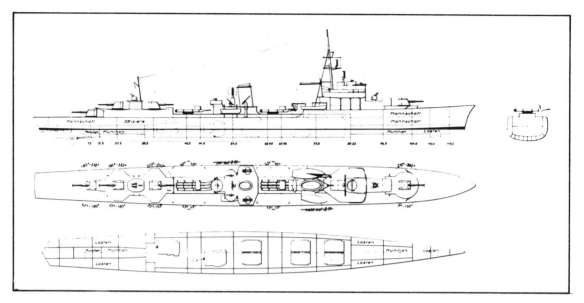

*Z.28 General Arrangement showing differences as a flotilla leader, with extra accommodation aft.*

**Name** *Z.27* **Built by** AG Weser (Bremen) **Launched** 1.8.40
**Fate** Gunfire RN cruisers *Enterprise* and *Glasgow* Bay of Biscay 28.12.43

**Name** *Z.28* **Built by** AG Weser (Bremen) **Launched** 20.8.40
**Fate** Bombed Allied aircraft Sassnitz 6.3.45

**Name** *Z.29* **Built by** AG Weser (Bremen) **Launched** 15.10.40
**Fate** USN (1945); scuttled Skagerak 1946

**Name** *Z.30* **Built by** AG Weser (Bremen) **Launched** 8.12.40
**Fate** RN (1945); expended as experimental vessel 1948

*Z.28 was unique among the Z.23–30 group in having two single 5.9-inch guns forward throughout her career.* (Drüppel)

*Z.29 in Arctic waters before the replacement of the single 5.9-inch gun forward.* (Drüppel)

## *Destroyer type 1936A (Mob)*: **Z.31–34** and **Z.37–39**

Generally similar to the preceding class and only *Z.31* was completed without the twin turret forward. This was, however, installed in 1944, only to be removed the following year, when undergoing damage repairs, and replaced by a single 4.1inch A.A. and additional light A.A. guns. The final armament carried by *Z.31* was three 5.9inch (3 × 1) all aft, one 4.1inch A.A. forward, two single and two twin 37mm A.A. before the bridge, two 20mm A.A. in the bridge wings, four single 37mm A.A. around the after funnel, and two single 37mm A.A. and one quadruple 20mm A.A. between "C" and "D" guns on the after shelter deck. As completed *Z.33* and *Z.34* had a light A.A. armament of four 37mm (2 × 2) and twenty-one 20mm (2 × 4, 2 × 2, and 7 × 1) guns.

*Displacement:* 2,603 tons (3,597 tons full)
*Dimensions:* 400¼(wl) 416¾(oa) × 39¼ × 12¾/15 feet
*Machinery:* Six Wagner boilers (pressure 1,028 lb.); two shafts;
  Wagner geared turbines, S.H.P. 70,000 = 38½ knots
*Bunkers & Radius:* O.F. 825 tons; 5,900 miles at 19 knots
*Armament:* Five 5.9inch (1 × 2 and 3 × 1), six 37mm A.A. (2 ×
  2 and 2 × 1), eight 20mm A.A. (2 × 4) guns; eight 21inch
  (2 × 4—twelve torpedoes) T.T.; sixty mines
*Complement:* 321 except *Z.32–34* 320

*Z.31–34 and Z.37–39 General Arrangement.*

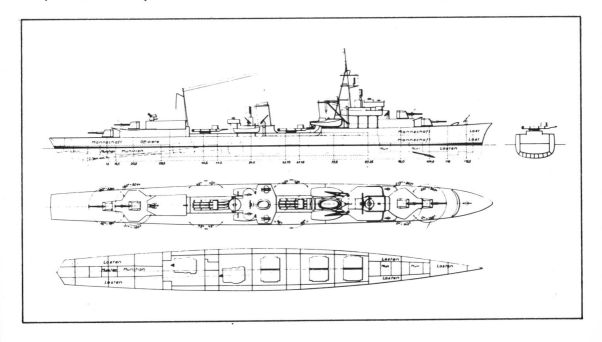

**Name** *Z.31* **Built by** AG Weser (Bremen) **Launched** 15.5.41
**Fate** RN (1945), French *Marceau* (1946); scrapped 1956

**Name** *Z.32* **Built by** AG Weser (Bremen) **Launched** 15.8.41
**Fate** Driven ashore gunfire RCN destroyers *Haida* and *Huron*, Ushant 9.6.44

**Name** *Z.33* **Built by** AG Weser (Bremen) **Launched** 15.9.42
**Fate** Russian *Provorny* (1946)

**Name** *Z.34* **Built by** AG Weser (Bremen) **Launched** 5.5.42
**Fate** USN (1945); scuttled Skagerrak 26.3.46

**Name** *Z.37* **Built by** Germania Werft (Kiel) **Launched** 24.2.41
**Fate** Scuttled Bordeaux 24.8.44

**Name** *Z.38* **Built by** Germania Werft (Kiel) **Launched** 5.8.41
RN *Nonsuch* (1945); scrapped 1949

**Name** *Z.39* **Built by** Germania Werft (Kiel) **Launched** 2.12.41
**Fate** USN *DD.939* (1945); French (1948) and cannibalised for spares and used as floating pier

Z.31 *became the French* Marceau *in 1946 and is seen here virtually unchanged apart from the substitution of 40-mm Bofors guns for her 37-mm weapons.* (ECPA)

Z.33 *in Norway showing her twin 5.9-inch turret, radar etc.* (Drüppel)

Z.34 *mounted the full armament of a twin 5.9-inch turret forward and three singles aft. Note the external degaussing coil just below the edge of the weather deck.* (Drüppel)

Z.38 *served in the Royal Navy as* HMS Nonsuch *from 1945 to 1949 and is seen here under the White Ensign.* (Drüppel)

## *Destroyer·type 1936B:* **Z.35 & 36** and **Z.43–45**

The adoption of 5.9inch guns had not, on the whole, been a complete success, as the additional weight carried, especially with the twin turret concentration forward, had been to the detriment of seakeeping qualities despite slightly increased but inadequate hull dimensions. Not only that, the need to supplement the light A.A. armament had resulted in a critical weight problem entailing the removal of at least one 5.9inch gun so that the weight of the broadside remained virtually unaffected in spite of shipping a heavier calibre gun. Therefore, this class reverted to the lighter 5inch gun, all in single mountings, and the designed light A.A. armament was improved to include six 37mm (2 × 2 and 2 × 1) around the after funnel, and thirteen 20mm (3 × 4 and 1 × 1) mounted in the wings of the upper bridge and aft together with a solitary mounting on the fo'c'sle.

*Displacement:* 2,527 tons (3,507 tons full)
*Dimensions:* 400¼(wl) 416¾(oa) × 39¼ × 11½/14 feet
*Machinery:* Six Wagner boilers (pressure 1,028 lb.); two shafts; Wagner geared turbines, S.H.P. 70,000 = 38 knots
*Bunkers & Radius:* O.F. 825 tons; 5,900 miles at 19 knots
*Armament:* Five 5inch (5 × 1), six 37mm A.A. (2 × 2 and 2 × 1), thirteen 20mm A.A. (3 × 4 and 1 × 1) guns; eight 21inch (2 × 4—sixteen torpedoes) T.T.; seventy-six mines
*Complement:* 321

**Name** *Z.35* **Built by** AG Weser (Bremen) **Launched** 2.10.42
**Fate** Mined Gulf of Finland 12.12.44

**Name** *Z.36* **Built by** AG Weser (Bremen) **Launched** 15.5.43
**Fate** Mined Gulf of Finland 12.12.44

**Name** *Z.40–42* **Built by** Germania Werft (Kiel) **Fate** See under scout cruisers *Sp.1–3*

**Name** *Z.43* **Built by** AG Weser (Bremen) **Launched** 9.43
**Fate** Scuttled Geltinger Bight 3.5.45 after being mined and bombed Allied aircraft; salved and scrapped 1953

**Name** *Z.44* **Built by** AG Weser (Bremen) **Launched** 20.1.44
**Fate** Bombed Allied aircraft Bremen 29.7.44; scuttled incomplete 20.7.46

**Name** *Z.45* **Built by** AG Weser (Bremen) **Launched** 1944
**Fate** Suspended 1944; scuttled incomplete 20.7.46

## *Destroyer type 1938Ac:* **Z.40–42**
See under scout cruisers *Sp.1–3*.

## *Destroyer type 1936C :* **Z.46–50**

This class was generally similar to the earlier types but with the gun armament completely rearranged following the introduction of a new 5.1inch D.P. gun twin-mounted in turrets. The turrets were disposed one forward and two aft, the three 37mm A.A. twin mountings were placed one before the bridge and two abreast the after funnel, and the four twin 20mm A.A. mountings in wing positions on the bridge and abaft the after funnel. The addition of an RDF-fitted high-angle director at the fore end of the shelter deck considerably enhanced the A.A. capabilities of the main guns.

*Displacement:* 2,574 tons (3,594 tons full)
*Dimensions:* 397(wl) 413½(oa) × 40 × 11¾/14½ feet
*Machinery:* Six Wagner boilers (pressure 1,028 lb.); two shafts;
    Wagner geared turbines, S.H.P. 70,000 = 37½ knots
*Bunkers & Radius:* O.F. 860 tons; 6,000 miles at 19 knots
*Armament:* Six 5.1inch D.P. (3 × 2), six 37mm A.A. (3 × 2),
    eight 20mm A.A. (4 × 2) guns; eight 21inch (2 × 4—sixteen
    torpedoes) T.T.; sixty mines
*Complement:* 320

**Name** *Z.46* **Built by** AG Weser (Bremen) **Fate** Bombed Allied aircraft Bremen while building and scrapped on slip 1945

**Name** *Z.47* **Built by** AG Weser (Bremen) **Fate** Bombed Allied aircraft Bremen while building and scrapped on slip 1945

**Name** *Z.48–50* **Built by** AG Weser (Bremen) **Fate** Cancelled

Z.46–50 *General Arrangement.*

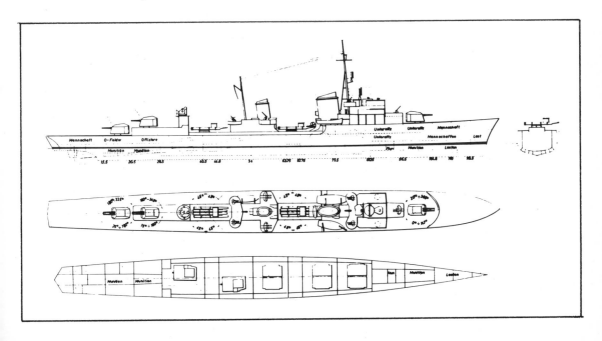

## Destroyer type 1938B

This was a pre-war mass production project that was not followed-up to provide long range destroyers able to accompany the raiding squadrons. The design was kept simple to ease production, and embodied a flush-decked hull of moderate dimensions with the main guns arranged in twin turrets fore and aft. The turrets afforded shelter for guns' crews as under ocean conditions they would have been subject to the penalties of exposure with a corresponding loss of efficiency at the guns.

*Displacement:* 1,971 tons (2,747 tons full)
*Dimensions:* $354\frac{1}{4}$(wl) $367\frac{1}{2}$(oa) × 37 × $10\frac{1}{2}$/13 feet
*Machinery:* Four Wagner boilers (pressure 1,028 lb.); two shafts;
    Wagner geared turbines, S.H.P. 50,000 = $36\frac{1}{2}$ knots
*Bunkers & Radius:* O.F. 563 tons; 9,500 miles at 19 knots
*Armament:* Four 5inch (2 × 2), one 37mm A.A., two 20mm A.A.
    (2 × 1) guns; eight 21inch (2 × 4) T.T.
*Complement:* 239

## Destroyer type 1942: **Z.51**

This vessel was an uncompleted prototype which introduced diesel main propulsion to destroyers to secure the extended radius dictated in staff requirements for operations in Northern waters. The hull form closely resembled that of the type 1938B project, which was never put into production, except that a raised fo'c'sle was added in view of the more severe weather conditions experienced in Northern waters. Primarily a floating test bed to examine the feasibility of the installed machinery, the armament was of almost secondary consideration and included the new 5.1inch D.P. gun, in four single mountings, equally disposed fore and aft, four twin 37mm A.A. mountings placed abreast the two funnels, and three quadruple 20mm mountings, two before the bridge and one aft: an improved arrangement, nevertheless, than before. But the lack of a high-angle director would not have enabled the 5.1inch guns to be fought very effectively as A.A. weapons. This heavy gun armament, for her size, was partly compensated for by reductions in the torpedo armament and mine load.

*Displacement:* 2,053 tons (2,632 tons full)
*Dimensions:* $354\frac{1}{4}$(pp) 374(oa) × 36 × $12\frac{1}{4}$/$14\frac{1}{2}$ feet
*Machinery:* Three shafts; 24-cylinder M.A.N. diesels (one per
    wing shafts and four on centre shaft), B.H.P. 57,120 = 36 knots

*Bunkers & Radius:* O.F. 551 tons; 13,500 miles at 19 knots
*Armament:* Four 5.1inch (4 × 1), eight 37mm A.A. (4 × 2),
    twelve 20mm A.A. (3 × 4) guns; six 21inch (2 × 3) T.T.; fifty
    mines
*Complement:* 235

**Name** *Z.51* **Built by** AG Weser (Bremen) **Launched** 1944
**Fate** Bombed Allied aircraft Bremen while building and
construction suspended; scrapped

## *Destroyer type 1942C:* **Z.52–56**

This was the final, and largest, destroyer design put into
production. None were ever completed and their performance,
therefore, cannot be assessed, but if it matched their symmetry
they would have proved most successful vessels. They were
outstanding in both main propulsion and armament, and
also adopted diesel main propulsion for unmatched radius
with no appreciable loss of speed as compared with the
turbine-engined destroyers. The main guns were the new
5.1inch D.P., again twin-mounted in three turrets, but this
time placed two forward and one aft, and controlled by
RDF-fitted high-angle directors mounted on the bridge and
aft. New and heavier calibre light A.A. guns were also
incorporated: three single 55mm around the after funnel, and
seven twin 30mm, with three mountings on the bridge, two
abreast the fore funnel, and two aft. In spite of the heavy gun
armament there was no reduction in the torpedo armament
or the mine load which equalled that of earlier types.

*Z.52–56 General Arrangement.*

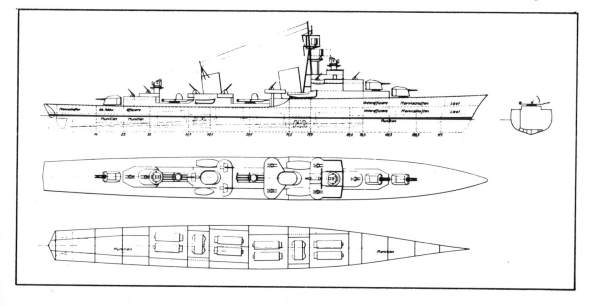

*Displacement:* 2,818 tons (3,703 tons full)
*Dimensions:* 413½(wl) 433(oa) × 41¼ × 13½/16 feet
*Machinery:* Two shafts; M.A.N. diesel motors (four per shaft),
    B.H.P. 76,000 = 37½ knots
*Bunkers & Radius:* O.F. 630 tons; 16,000 miles at 19 knots
*Armament:* Six 5.1inch D.P. (3 × 2), three 55mm A.A. (3 × 1),
    fourteen 30mm A.A. (7 × 2) guns; eight 21inch (2 × 4) T.T.;
    sixty mines
*Complement:* 320

**Name** *Z.52–56* **Built by** AG Weser (Bremen) **Fate** Cancelled
1944/5

**Name** *Z.57* and *58* **Built by** Germania Werft (Kiel) **Fate** Cancelled
1945

## *Destroyer type 1945*

Project for high performance type which reverted to geared
turbines and sacrificed radius for speed. They were to be
solely gun-armed and were provided fore and aft with RDF-
fitted high-angle directors.

*Displacement:* 2,657 tons (3,700 tons full)
*Dimensions:* 397(wl) 413½(oa) × 39¼ × 12¾/15 feet
*Machinery:* Six Wagner boilers (pressure 1,028 lb.); two shafts;
    Wagner geared turbines, S.H.P. 80,000 = 40 knots
*Bunkers & Radius:* O.F. 800 tons; 3,600 miles at 19 knots
*Armament:* Eight 5.1inch D.P. (4 × 2), four 55mm A.A. (4 × 1),
    twelve 30mm A.A. (6 × 2) guns; eight 21inch (2 × 4—16
    torpedoes) T.T.; one-hundred mines
*Complement:* 365

## *Ex-RNeth.N destroyer:* **ZH.1**

*Displacement:* 1,204 tons (2,228 tons full)
*Dimensions:* 344½(pp) 347¾(oa) × 34¾ × 9¼/11½ feet
*Machinery:* Three Yarrow boilers (pressure 412 lb.), two shafts,
    Werkspoor geared turbines S.H.P. 49,500 = 37½ knots
*Bunkers & Radius:* O.F. 560 tons; 5,400 miles at 19 knots
*Armament:* Five 4.7inch (2 × 2 and 1 × 1), four 37mm A.A.
    (2 × 2), four 20mm A.A. (1 × 4) guns, eight 21inch (2 × 4)
    T.T.
*Complement:* 236

**Name** *ZH.1* (ex-*Gerard Callenburgh*) **Built by** Rotterdam D.D.
**Launched** 12.10.39   **Fate** Scuttled Rotterdam 14.5.40, salved and
German (1942); gunfire RN destroyers *Ashanti* and *Tartar*
20 m north-west Ile de Batz 9.6.44

## Ex-French destroyer: **ZF.2**

*Displacement:* 2,070 tons (2,910 tons full)
*Dimensions:* 333¼(pp) 371(oa) × 36½ × 8½/11¼ feet
*Machinery:* Four Indret boilers (pressure 412 lb.); two
   shafts; Rateau geared turbines S.H.P. 58,000 = 37 knots
*Bunkers & Radius:* O.F. 820 tons; 4,700 miles at 19 knots
*Armament:* Five 5inch (1 × 2 and 3 × 1), four 37mm A.A.
   (2 × 2), ten 20mm A.A. (1 × 4 and 6 × 1) guns, eight 21inch
   (2 × 4) T.T.
*Complement:* 245
*Notes:* Was originally armed with six 5.1inch (3 × 2), four 37mm
   A.A. (2 × 2), four 13mm A.A. (2 × 2) guns, seven 21.7inch
   (1 × 3 and 2 × 2) T.T.

**Name** *ZF.2* (ex-*Opiniatre*) **Built by** Fges. & Ch. de la Gironde
(Bordeaux) **Fate** Retroceded incomplete 1945 and scrapped

## Ex-RHN destroyer: **ZG.3**

*Displacement:* 1,414 tons (2,008 tons full)
*Dimensions:* 312(pp) 331¼(oa) × 33½ × 8½/10½ feet
*Machinery:* Three Yarrow boilers (pressure 235 lb.); two shafts;
   Parsons geared turbines S.H.P. 34,000 = 36 knots
*Bunkers & Radius:* O.F. 455 tons; 4,800 miles at 19 knots
*Armament:* Four 5inch (4 × 1), four 37mm A.A. (4 × 1), four
   20mm A.A. (4 × 1) guns, eight 21inch (2 × 4) T.T.
*Complement:* 220

**Name** *ZG.3* (ex-*Vasilevs Georgios I*) **Built by** Yarrow (Scotstoun)
**Launched** 3.3.38   **Fate** Scuttled Piraeus 20.4.41, salved and
German *Hermes,* (1943); scuttled west of La Goulette 7.5.43 after
being bombed by Allied aircraft

## Ex-RNN destroyers: **ZN.4** and **5**

*Displacement:* 1,278 tons (1,694 tons full)
*Dimensions:* 300(pp) 328(oa) × 34¾ × 8¾/10½ feet
*Machinery:* Three Yarrow boilers (pressure 470 lb.); two shafts;
   De Laval geared turbines S.H.P. 30,000 = 34 knots
*Bunkers & Radius;* O.F. 300 tons; 3,100 miles at 19 knots
*Armament:* Four 4.7inch (1 × 2 and 2 × 1), two 37mm A.A.
   (1 × 2), six 20mm A.A. (6 × 1) guns, four 21inch (1 × 4) T.T.
*Complement:* 162

**Name** *ZN.4* **Built by** Naval Dockyard (Horten) **Launched** 1941
**Fate** *TA.7* (1941), sabotaged while building 1945, retroceded
incomplete R.N.N. *Aalesund* (1945); construction abandoned 1950

**Name** *ZN.5* **Built by** Naval Dockyard (Horten) **Launched** 1941
**Fate** *TA.8* (1941), sabotaged while building 1945, retroceded
incomplete 1945 and scrapped

# Torpedo Boats

*Torpedo boat type 1923:* **Albatros, Falke, Greif, Kondor, Möwe** and **Seeadler**

The design of these boats generally followed that of the latest craft built during the First World War (types *V.125–130, S.131–139,* and *H.140–147*) and although dimensions were enlarged to make them more weatherly they were still inclined to be wet owing to the absence of sheer and lack of freeboard. Novel constructional features were longitudinal framing and a double bottom to the hull outside of the machinery spaces. The low bridge accentuated the height of the tall fore funnel, which ensured that smoke was carried well clear, but it was later necessary to raise the bridge level. The lead ship of the class, the *Möwe,* was slightly shorter and beamier than the remainder. Whereas the fo'c'sle and quarter-deck guns were

*General Arrangement of the* Möwe *Class torpedo boats.*

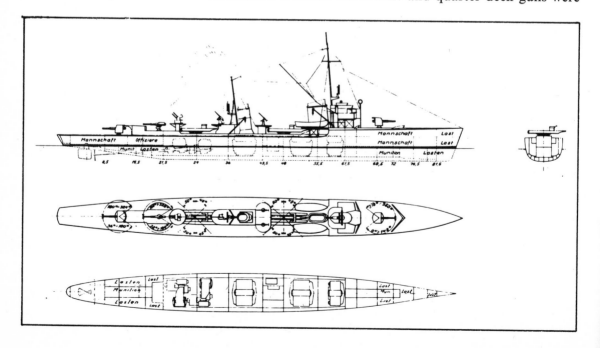

placed behind shields, the superfiring gun aft was on an open high-angle mounting, and the light A.A. armament was augmented during the war by the addition of one 37mm and four 20mm (1 × 4) guns.

*Displacement:* 924 tons (1,290 tons full)
*Dimensions:* 278¾(pp) 288¾(oa) except *Möwe* 285½(oa) × 27¼ except *Möwe* 27¾ × 9¼/11½ feet
*Machinery:* Three Marine boilers (pressure 264 lb.); two shafts; *Albatros & Kondor* Schichau, *Falke & Greif* Vulcan, *Möwe* Blohm & Voss, and *Seeadler* Germania geared turbines, S.H.P. 23,000 = 33 knots except *Möwe* 32 knots
*Bunkers & Radius:* O.F. 340 tons; 3,100 miles at 17 knots
*Armament:* Three 4.1inch (3 × 1), two 20mm A.A. (2 × 1) guns; six 21inch (2 × 3) T.T.
*Complement:* 122

**Name** *Albatros* **Built by** Naval Dockyard (Wilhelmshaven) **Launched** 15.7.26 **Fate** Gunfire RNN minelayer *Olav Tryggvason* Oslofjord 10.4.40

**Name** *Falke* **Built by** Naval Dockyard (Wilhelmshaven) **Launched** 22.9.26 **Fate** Bombed RAF aircraft Le Havre 14.6.44

**Name** *Greif* **Built by** Naval Dockyard (Wilhelmshaven) **Launched** 15.7.26 **Fate** Bombed Allied aircraft Seine estuary 25.5.44

Albatros *was typical of the early torpedo boats or light destroyers built under the terms of the Versailles Treaty.* (Drüppel)

Greif *and her sisters had their light AA increased during the War.* (Drüppel)

**Name** *Kondor* **Built by** Naval Dockyard (Wilhelmshaven)
**Launched** 22.9.26 **Fate** Scuttled Le Havre 28.6.44 after being
bombed RAF aircraft

**Name** *Möwe* **Built by** Naval Dockyard (Wilhelmshaven)
**Launched** 24.3.26 **Fate** Bombed RAF aircraft Le Havre 14.6.44

**Name** *Seeadler* **Built by** Naval Dockyard (Wilhelmshaven)
**Launched** 15.7.26 **Fate** Torpedoed RN MTB north of Boulogne
13.5.42

## *Torpedo boat type 1924:* **Iltis, Jaguar, Leopard, Luchs, Tiger (i),** and **Wolf**

Similar to the preceding class except that the hull was
lengthened by about 15 feet and the beam slightly increased.
Two units, the *Leopard* and *Luchs*, mounted heavier calibre
5inch guns, which were later adopted for destroyers. The light
A.A. armament was increased during the war by the addition
of one 37mm and two 20mm (2 × 1) guns.

Intervening between this and the previous class, which
were originally rated as destroyers, was a 200-ton torpedo
boat project which was not advanced as no useful craft could
be produced within such a limited parameter.

*Two views of the* Iltis *in rough weather showing the problems of seakeeping with a heavy armament forward and lack of freeboard.* (Drüppel)

*The* Leopard *was the only one
of her class to mount the new
5-inch (127-mm) gun.*

*Displacement:* 933 tons (1,320 tons full)
*Dimensions:* 292(pp) 305(oa) × 28½ × 9¼/11½ feet
*Machinery:* Three Marine boilers (pressure 264 lb.); two shafts;
   *Iltis & Tiger* Vulcan, *Jaguar & Luchs* Schichau, and *Leopard &
   Wolf* Brown Boveri geared turbines, S.H.P. 23,000 = 33 knots
*Bunkers & Radius:* O.F. 380 tons; 3,100 miles at 17 knots
*Armament:* Three 4.1inch except *Leopard* and *Luchs* 5inch (3 × 1),
   two 20mm A.A. (2 × 1) guns; six 21inch (2 × 3) T.T.
*Complement:* 123

**Name** *Iltis* **Built by** Naval Dockyard (Wilhelmshaven)
**Launched** 12.10.27 **Fate** Torpedoed RN MTB north of Boulogne
13.5.42

**Name** *Jaguar* **Built by** Naval Dockyard (Wilhelmshaven)
**Launched** 15.3.28 **Fate** Bombed RAF aircraft Le Havre 14.6.44

**Name** *Leopard* **Built by** Naval Dockyard (Wilhelmshaven)
**Launched** 15.3.28 **Fate** Lost collision with *Preussen* Skagerrak
30.4.40

**Name** *Luchs* **Built by** Naval Dockyard (Wilhelmshaven)
**Launched** 15.3.28 **Fate** Torpedoed RN submarine *Swordfish* North
Sea 26.7.40

**Name** *Tiger* (*i*) **Built by** Naval Dockyard (Wilhelmshaven)
**Launched** 15.3.28 **Fate** Lost collision with *Z.3* (*Max Schultz*)
east of Bornholm 25.8.39

**Name** *Wolf* **Built by** Naval Dockyard ((Wilhelmshaven)
**Launched** 12.10.27 **Fate** Mined north of Dunkerque 8.1.41

## Torpedo boat type 1935: **T.1–12**

These boats were diminutives of the earlier classes, sacrificed
gunpower to retain both banks of torpedo tubes, and were over
2 knots faster but with a more limited radius. They were
lengthened during the war to 285½(oa) feet by the addition
of a clipper stem, one 40mm A.A. gun replaced the after set
of torpedo tubes, and six 20mm A.A. (6 × 1) guns were
added.

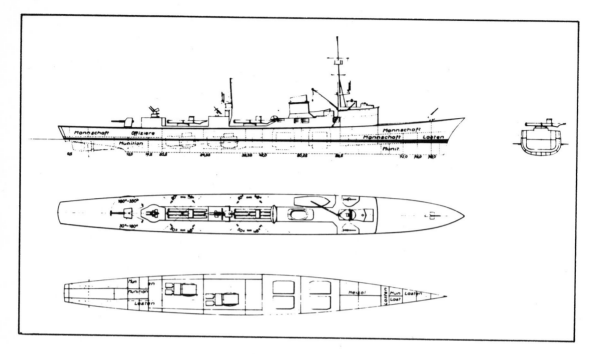

*General Arrangement of the*
*T.1–12 group.*

*Displacement:* 844 tons (1,088 tons full) except *T.9–12* 839 tons
    (1,082 tons full)
*Dimensions:* 269(wl) 275½(oa) × 28¼ × 7½/9½ feet
*Machinery:* Four Wagner boilers (pressure 1,028 lb.); two shafts;
    Wagner geared turbines, S.H.P. 31,000 = 35½ knots
*Bunkers & Radius:* O.F. 205 tons; 2,400 miles at 19 knots
*Armament:* One 4.1inch, three 20mm A.A. (3 × 1) guns; six
    21inch (2 × 3) T.T.; thirty mines
*Complement:* 119

*The* T.1 *was the prototype of a*
*new single-funnelled type.*
*(Drüppel)*

**Name** *T.1* **Built by** Schichau (Elbing) **Launched** 1938
**Fate** Bombed Allied aircraft Kiel 10.4.45

**Name** *T.2* **Built by** Schichau (Elbing) **Launched** 1938
**Fate** Bombed USAAF aircraft Bremen 29.7.44; salved 1944 and
scrapped Cuxhaven 1945

**Name** *T.3* **Built by** Schichau (Elbing) **Launched** 1938
**Fate** Bombed RAF aircraft Le Havre 19.9.40; salved 1941; mined
north of Hela 14.3.45

**Name** *T.4* **Built by** Schichau (Elbing) **Launched** 1938
**Fate** USN (1945); RDN (1947); for disposal 1951

**Name** *T.5* **Built by** AG Weser (Bremen) **Launched** 22.11.37
**Fate** Mined north of Hela 14.3.45

**Name** *T.6* **Built by** AG Weser (Bremen) **Launched** 16.12.37
**Fate** Mined west of Shetlands 7.11.40

**Name** *T.7* **Built by** AG Weser (Elbing) **Launched** 18.6.38
**Fate** Bombed USAAF aircraft Bremen 29.7.44; salved and
scrapped 1945

**Name** *T.8* **Built by** AG Weser (Bremen) **Launched** 10.8.38
**Fate** Scuttled Strander Bight (Kiel) 3.5.45

**Name** *T.9* **Built by** Schichau (Elbing) **Launched** 1939
**Fate** Scuttled Strander Bight (Kiel) 3.5.45

**Name** *T.10* **Built by** Schichau (Elbing) **Launched** 1939
**Fate** Bombed RAF aircraft Gdynia 18.12.44

**Name** *T.11* **Built by** AG Weser (Bremen) **Launched** 1.3.39
**Fate** RN (1945), French *Bir Hakeim* (1946); for disposal 1949

**Name** *T.12* **Built by** AG Weser (Bremen) **Launched** 12.4.39
**Fate** Russian *Podvischny* (1946)

T.11 *seen under the AA guns of
a larger warship.* (Drüppel)

## Torpedo boat type 1937: **T.13–21**

Practically repeats of the preceding class but with a slightly increased radius of action and 37mm in lieu of 20mm A.A. guns. The light A.A. armament was augmented during the war by replacing the after set of torpedo tubes by one 40mm gun, and the addition of one 37mm and ten 20mm (2 × 4 and 2 × 1) guns.

*Displacement:* 853 tons (1,098 tons full)
*Dimensions:* 269(wl) 278$\frac{3}{4}$(oa) × 29$\frac{1}{4}$ × 8$\frac{1}{4}$/10$\frac{1}{4}$ feet
*Machinery:* Four Wagner boilers (pressure 1,028 lb.); two shafts;
    Wagner geared turbines, S.H.P. 31,000 = 35$\frac{1}{2}$ knots
*Bunkers & Radius:* O.F. 216 tons; 3,000 miles at 19 knots
*Armament:* One 4.1inch, two 37mm A.A. (2 × 1) guns; six 21inch
    (2 × 3) T.T.; thirty-eight mines
*Complement:* 119

**Name** *T.13* **Built by** Schichau (Elbing) **Launched** 15.6.39
**Fate** Bombed Allied aircraft Kattegat 10.4.45

**Name** *T.14* **Built by** Schichau (Elbing) **Launched** 1939
**Fate** USN (1945); French *Dompaire* (1947); discarded 1949

**Name** *T.15* **Built by** Schichau (Elbing) **Launched** 1939
**Fate** Bombed USAAF aircraft Kiel 13.12.43

**Name** *T.16* **Built by** Schichau (Elbing) **Launched** 1940/1
**Fate** Paid-off Frederikshavn 13.4.45 after being bombed Allied aircraft; scrapped

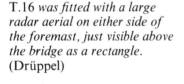

*T.16 was fitted with a large radar aerial on either side of the foremast, just visible above the bridge as a rectangle.* (Drüppel)

**Name** *T.17* **Built by** Schichau (Elbing) **Launched** 1940/1
**Fate** Russian *Porivisty* (1946)

**Name** *T.18* **Built by** Schichau (Elbing) **Launched** 1940/1
**Fate** Bombed Russian aircraft Gulf of Finland 17.9.44

**Name** *T.19* **Built by** Schichau (Elbing) **Launched** 1941
**Fate** USN (1945); RDN (1947); discarded 1951

**Name** *T.20* **Built by** Schichau (Elbing) **Launched** 10.41
**Fate** RN (1945); French *Baccarat* (1946); discarded 1949

**Name** *T.21* **Built by** Schichau (Elbing) **Launched** 11.41
**Fate** USN (1945); scuttled Skagerrak 1946

T.17 *was fitted for minelaying and carried a barrage balloon.* (Drüppel)

*A clearer view of the rectangular radar aerials carried in* T.17. (Drüppel)

## *Torpedo boat type 1939:* **T.22–36**

The shortcomings of the two previous classes in possessing mainly a torpedo armament and little else was that, except for minelaying, their operational scope was limited to use against ship targets. Consequently, an adequate gun armament was incorporated in this class which enabled them to be more flexibly employed. As they were completed after hostilities had broken out they benefited from war experience and carried a more numerous light A.A. armament from the onset.

*Displacement:* 1,294 tons (1,754 tons full)
*Dimensions:* $318\frac{1}{4}$(wl) $334\frac{3}{4}$(oa) × $32\frac{3}{4}$ × $8\frac{1}{2}/10\frac{1}{2}$ feet
*Machinery:* Four Wagner boilers (pressure 1,028 lb.); two shafts; Wagner geared turbines, S.H.P. 32,000 = $33\frac{1}{2}$ knots
*Bunkers & Radius:* O.F. 401 tons; 5,000 miles at 19 knots
*Armament:* Four 4.1inch (4 × 1), four 37mm A.A. (2 × 2), nine except *T.23* and *24* seven 20mm A.A. (1 × 4 and 3/5 × 1), two 15mm A.A. (2 × 1) guns; six 21inch (2 × 3) T.T.; fifty mines
*Complement:* 198

**Name** *T.22* **Built by** Schichau (Elbing) **Launched** 1941
**Fate** Mined Narva Bay 18.8.44

**Name** *T.23* **Built by** Schichau (Elbing) **Launched** 11.41
**Fate** RN (1945); French *Alsacien* (1946)

**Name** *T.24* **Built by** Schichau (Elbing) **Launched** 11.41
**Fate** Driven ashore rocket fire of RAF aircraft Le Verdon 24.8.44

**Name** *T.25* **Built by** Schichau (Elbing) **Launched** 1942
**Fate** Gunfire RN cruisers *Enterprise* and *Glasgow* Bay of Biscay 28.12.43

*General Arrangement of the T.22 group.*

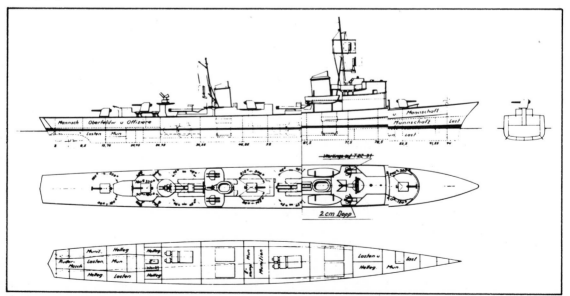

**Name** *T.26* **Built by** Schichau (Ebling) **Launched** 1942
**Fate** Gunfire RN cruisers *Enterprise* and *Glasgow* Bay of Biscay
28.12.43

**Name** *T.27* **Built by** Schichau (Elbing) **Launched** 1942
**Fate** Driven ashore gunfire RCN destroyer *Haida* off Ushant
29.4.44, and torpedoed RN MTB and RAF aircraft 7.5.44

**Name** *T.28* **Built by** Schichau (Elbing) **Launched** 11.41
**Fate** RN (1945); French *Lorrain* (1946)

**Name** *T.29* **Built by** Schichau (Elbing) **Launched** 11.41
**Fate** Gunfire RN destroyers *Ashanti*, RCN *Athabaskan*, *Haida*
and *Huron* off Ushant 26.4.44

**Name** *T.30* **Built by** Schichau (Elbing) **Launched** 1943
**Fate** Mined Narva Bay 18.8.44

**Name** *T.31* **Built by** Schichau (Elbing) **Launched** 1943
**Fate** Mined and torpedoed Russian MTB Gulf of Finland 20.6.44

**Name** *T.32* **Built by** Schichau (Elbing) **Launched** 1944
**Fate** Mined Narva Bay 18.8.44

**Name** *T.33* **Built by** Schichau (Elbing) **Launched** 1943
**Fate** Russian *Primierny* (1946)

**Name** *T.34* **Built by** Schichau (Elbing) **Launched** 1944
**Fate** Mined west of Arkona 20.11.44

**Name** *T.35* **Built by** Schichau (Elbing) **Launched** 1944
**Fate** USN DD.935 (1945); French (1947) and cannibalised for
spares

**Name** *T.36* **Built by** Schichau (Elbing) **Launched** 1944
**Fate** Mined and bombed Allied aircraft off Swinemünde 4.5.45

*T.26 was one of the T.22 group, known to the British as the "Elbing" Class. They were better armed and were virtually destroyers by comparison with the earlier torpedo boats.* (Drüppel)

## Fleet torpedo boat type 1941: **T.37–51**

Closely similar to the preceding class but with the bridge structure modified to include a low-angle director for the main guns, the light A.A. armament more advantageously regrouped, and the radius of action increased. Only the first three units, *T.37–39*, nearly approached completion.

*Displacement:* 1,493 tons (2,155 tons full)
*Dimensions:* 334¾(wl) 347¾(oa) × 33¼ × 9½/12¼ feet
*Machinery:* Four Wagner boilers (pressure 1,028 lb.); two shafts; Wagner geared turbines, S.H.P. 40,000 = 34 knots
*Bunkers & Radius:* O.F. 582 tons; 6,500 miles at 19 knots
*Armament:* Four 4.1inch (4 × 1); six 37mm A.A. (3 × 2), eight 20mm A.A. (1 × 4 and 2 × 2) guns; six 21inch (2 × 3) T.T.
*Complement:* 210

**Name** *T.37* **Built by** Schichau (Elbing) **Launched** 1945
**Fate** Scuttled Bremerhaven 1945

**Name** *T.38* **Built by** Schichau (Elbing) **Launched** 1945
**Fate** Scuttled Kiel 1945

**Name** *T.39* **Built by** Schichau (Elbing) **Launched** 1945
**Fate** Scuttled Kiel 1945

**Name** *T.40* **Built by** Schichau (Elbing) **Launched** 1945
**Fate** Scuttled incomplete Elbing 3.45

**Name** *T.41* **Built by** Schichau (Elbing) **Launched** 1945
**Fate** Scuttled incomplete Elbing 3.45

**Name** *T.42* **Built by** Schichau (Elbing) **Launched** 1945
**Fate** Scuttled incomplete Elbing 3.45

**Name** *T.43* **Built by** Schichau (Elbing) **Launched** 1945
**Fate** Scuttled incomplete Elbing 3.45

**Name** *T.44–51* **Built by** Schichau (Elbing) **Launched** 1945
**Fate** Destroyed on slip Elbing 3.45

## Fleet torpedo boat type 1944: **T.52–60**

Although essentially similar to the two preceding classes the design was recast to embrace a long fo'c'sle deck with the break positioned abaft the after funnel, the 4.1inch guns were placed in twin A.A. mountings controlled by a high-angle director on the bridge, the light A.A. armament was a homogeneous battery of ten 30mm (5 × 2) guns, and speed was increased at the expense of the radius. This class never advanced further than the planning stage and none were ever laid down.

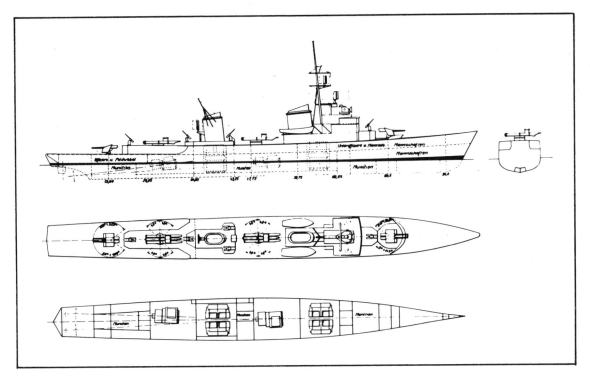

*Displacement:* 1,418 tons (1,794 tons full)
*Dimensions:* 321½(wl) 338(oa) × 33¼ × 9½/12¼ feet
*Machinery:* Four Wagner boilers (pressure 1,028 lb.); two shafts;
   Wagner geared turbines, S.H.P. 52,000 = 37¼ knots
*Bunkers & Radius:* O.F. 300 tons; 4,500 miles at 19 knots
*Armament:* Four 4.1inch A.A. (2 × 2), ten 30mm, A.A. (5 × 2)
   guns; six 21inch (2 × 3) T.T.
*Complement:* 214

*General Arrangement of the
1944 Type,* T.52–60.

**Name** *T.52–60* **Built by** Schichau (Elbing) **Fate** Cancelled

## *Fleet torpedo boat type 1940:* **T.61–72**

Chronologically the design of these boats preceded that of the
previous class, and was equally influenced by the material
available, and that could be manufactured, in the Netherlands,
where their construction was undertaken. Their advancement
was hampered and retarded at every turn and although
ordered late in 1940, only eight of the twelve were laid down
by 1942 and of these only three reached launching stage.
They broke away from the flush decked design and had a
fo'c'sle deck, with the break just aft of the bridge, and the
boiler rooms were all adjacent and their uptakes trunked into
a single funnel. The 4.1inch guns were equally disposed fore

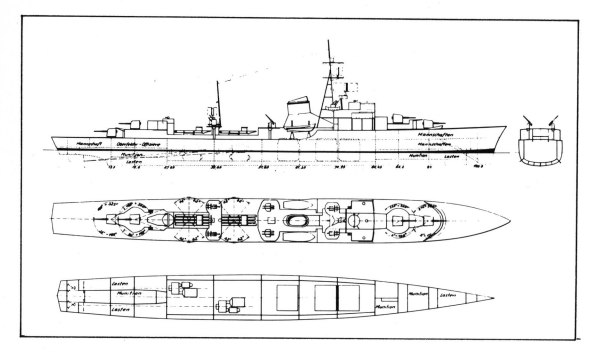

*General Arrangement of the T.61 group of torpedo boats, ordered from Dutch shipyards late in 1940 but never completed.*

and aft with the inner mountings superimposed over the outer ones, two twin 37mm A.A. mountings were placed abaft the funnel, four quadruple 20mm A.A. mountings were winged out on the upper bridge and farther aft between the torpedo tubes, and control positions were provided fore and aft. They were the largest of the torpedo boats—and would have ranked as destroyers in any other navy—but had no opportunity to show their merits.

*Displacement:* 1,931 tons (2,566 tons full)
*Dimensions:* 361(wl) 374(oa) × 37 × $10\frac{1}{2}$/$12\frac{1}{2}$ feet
*Machinery:* Three Yarrow boilers (pressure 411 lb.); two shafts; Werkspoor geared turbines, S.H.P. 49,500 = 35 knots
*Bunkers & Radius:* O.F. 570 tons; 5,000 miles at 19 knots
*Armament:* Four 5inch (4 × 1), four 37mm A.A. (2 × 2), sixteen 20mm A.A. (4 × 4) guns; eight 21inch (2 × 4) T.T.
*Complement:* 223

**Name** *T.61* **Built by** Wilton-Fijenoord (Schiedam) **Launched** 6.44 **Fate** Capsized on launching and salved; torpedoed incomplete while in tow by Allied aircraft off West Frisian Islands 13.9.44

**Name** *T.62* **Built by** Wilton-Fejenoord (Schiedam) **Fate** Destroyed on slip, Rotterdam 1944

**Name** *T.63* **Built by** Rotterdam D.D. **Launched** 28.10.44 **Fate** Scuttled incomplete Kiel 2.5.45

**Name** *T.64* **Built by** Rotterdam D.D. **Fate** Destroyed on slip Rotterdam 1944

**Name** *T.65* **Built by** De Schelde (Flushing) **Launched** 8.7.44
**Fate** Scuttled incomplete Kiel 1946

**Name** *T.66* **Built by** De Schelde (Flushing) **Fate** Bombed Allied
aircraft while building 1944, and construction abandoned

**Name** *T.67* **Built by** Wilton-Fijenoord (Schiedam) **Fate** Cancelled

**Name** *T.68* **Built by** Wilton-Fejenoord (Schiedam) **Fate** Cancelled

**Name** *T.69* **Built by** Rotterdam D.D. **Fate** Destroyed on slip
Rotterdam

**Name** *T.70* **Built by** Rotterdam D.D. **Fate** Destroyed on slip
Rotterdam

**Name** *T.71* **Built by** De Schelde (Flushing) **Fate** Cancelled

**Name** *T.72* **Built by** De Schelde (Flushing) **Fate** Cancelled


## *Torpedo Boat:* **Pfeil**

*Displacement:* 660 tons except *Komet* 675 tons (800 tons full)
*Dimensions:* 237¾(pp) 242¼(oa) × 25½ × 10¼/10½ feet
*Machinery:* four Schultz boilers (pressure 280 lb.), two shafts,
   reciprocating (VTE) I.H.P. 10,900 = 30 knots
*Bunkers & Radius:* O.F. 181 tons (3,500 miles at 17 knots)
*Armament:* one 3.5-inch, one 20mm. A.A. except *Komet* and
   *E. Jungmann* disarmed: complement 87


## *Torpedo Boats:* **Komet, Eduard Jungmann** and **T.155–158**

*Displacement:* 530 tons (685 tons full)
*Dimensions:* 230¼(pp) 232(oa) × 25½ × 10/10½ feet
*Machinery:* Schultz Thornycroft boilers (pressure 280 lb.), two
   shafts, reciprocating (VTE) I.H.P. 11,000 = 30 knots
*Bunkers & Radius:* O.F. 200 tons (3,000 miles at 17 knots)
*Armament:* disarmed: *complement* 87


## *Torpedo Boat:* **Blitz**

*Displacement:* 761 tons (858 tons full)
*Dimensions:* 241½(pp) 242½(oa) × 25¾ × 10½/10¾ feet
*Machinery:* three Schultz-Thornycroft boilers (pressure 265 lb.),
   two shafts, A.E.G. turbines S.H.P. 17,750 = 30 knots
*Bunkers & Radius:* O.F. 198 tons (1,400 miles at 17 knots)
*Armament:* disarmed: complement 87.

**Name** *Pfeil* (ex-*T.139*, ex-*S.139*) **Built by** Schichau (Elbing) **Launched** 12.11.06 **Fate** Target service

**Name** *Komet* (ex-*T.151*, ex-*V.151*) **Built by** Vulcan (Stettin) **Launched** 14.9.07 **Fate** Target service, T.R.V.; U.S.N. (1945); scrapped Netherlands 1949

**Name** *Eduard Jungmann* (ex-*T.153*, ex-*V.153*) **Built by** Vulcan (Stettin) **Launched** 13.11.07 **Fate** Gunnery school tender, T.R.V.; U.S.N. (1945); scrapped Netherlands 1949

**Name** *T.155* (ex-*V.155*) **Built by** Vulcan (Stettin) **Launched** 28.1.08 **Fate** Submarine tender, T.R.V.; scuttled Swinemüude 22/4/45.

**Name** *T.156* (ex-*V.156*) **Built by** Vulcan (Stettin) **Launched** 29.2.08 **Fate** Submarine tender, T.R.V.; scuttled Kiel 3.5.45.

**Name** *T.157* (ex-*V.157*) **Built by** Vulcan (Stettin) **Launched** 29.5.08 **Fate** Submarine tender, T.R.V.; mined New Waterway 22.10.43

**Name** *T. 158* (ex-*V.158*) **Built by** Vulcan (Stettin) **Launched** 23.6.08 **Fate** New Waterway 22.10.43. Submarine tender, T.R.V.; Russian *Prozorlivi* (1945)

**Name** *Blitz* (ex-*T.185*, ex-*V.185*) **Built by** Vulcan (Stettin) **Launched** 9.4.10 **Fate** Target service; Russian *Vystrel* (1945).

Eduard Jungmann (*ex*-T.156) *was an old torpedo boat used as a gunnery tender.*

## *Torpedo Boat:* **Claus von Bevern**

*Displacement:* 755 tons (860 tons full)
*Dimensions:* 241½(pp) 242½(oa) × 26 × 10/10½ feet
*Machinery:* three Schultz Thornycroft boilers (pressure 265 lb.), two shafts, AEG-Vulcan turbines S.H.P. 18,000 = 30½ knots
*Bunkers & Radius:* O.F. 198 tons (1,400 miles at 17 knots)
*Armament:* one 4.1-inch, two 20mm. A.A. (2 × 1) guns: complement 99.

Claus van Bevern (ex-T.190)
*was another old torpedo boat
used for experimental purposes.*
(Drüppel)

## *Torpedo Boat:* **T.196**

*Displacement:* 755 tons (875 tons full)
*Dimensions:* 241½(pp) 242¾(oa) × 26¼ × 10½/10¾ feet
*Machinery:* three Schultz-Thornycroft boilers (pressure 265 lb.),
  two shafts, Germania turbines S.H.P. 18,200 = 32½ knots
*Bunkers & Radius:* O.F. 204 tons (1,850 miles at 19 knots)
*Armament:* two 4.1-inch (2 × 1), two 20mm. A.A. (2 × 1) guns:
  complement 99

**Name** *Claus von Bevern* (ex-*T.190*, ex-*V.190*) **Built by** Vulcan
(Stettin) **Launched** 12.4.11 **Fate** Experimental vessel; scuttled
Skagerrak 1946.

**Name** *T.196* (ex-*G196*) **Built by** Vulcan (Stettin) **Launched** 24.5.11
**Fate** Fleet tender; Russian *Pronzitelny* (1945)

## *Torpedo Boats:* **T.107, 108, 110** and **111**

*Displacement:* 760 tons (885 tons full)
*Dimensions:* 247¾(pp) 249¾(oa) × 25 × 10¼/10½ feet
*Machinery:* three Schultz-Thornycroft boilers (pressure 265 lb.),
  two shafts, Germania turbines S.H.P. 16,000 = 31 knots
*Bunkers & Radius:* O.F. 173 tons (1,900 miles at 17 knots)
*Armament:* one 4.1-inch, two 22mm. A.A. (2 × 1) guns, three
  19.7-inch (1 × 3—*T.108* and *110*) or three 21-inch (1 × 3)
  and one 19.7-inch (*T.107* and *T.111*) T.T.: complement 85
*Notes:* Were lengthened by 14¾ feet 1928/31

**Name** *T.107* (ex-*G.7*) **Built by** Germania Werft (Kiel) **Launched**
7.11.11 **Fate** Torpedo school tender, T.R.V.; Russian
*Poraschayuschy* (1945)

**Name** *T.108* (ex-*G.8*) **Built by** Germania Werft (Kiel) **Launched**
21.12.11 **Fate** Torpedo school tender; R.N. (1945) and scrapped

**Name** *T.110* (ex-*G.10*) **Built by** Germania Werft (Kiel) **Launched**
15.3.12 **Fate** Torpedo school tender; scuttled Travemünde 5.5.45
**Name** *T.111* (ex-*G.11*) **Built by** Germania Werft (Kiel) **Launched**
23.4.12 **Fate** Torpedo school tender; scuttled after bomb damage
Kiel 3.5.45

## *Ex-RNN torpedo boats:* **Leopard, Löwe, Panther,** and **Tiger**

*Displacement:* 597 tons (708 tons full)
*Dimensions:* 236¼(pp) 243¾(oa) × 25½ × 6½/9¼ feet
*Machinery:* Three Yarrow boilers (pressure 450 lb.); two shafts;
   De Laval geared turbines, S.H.P. 12,500 = 32 knots
*Bunkers & Radius:* O.F. 100 tons; 3,500 miles at 15 knots
*Armament:* One 3.9inch, two/four 20mm A.A. (2/4 × 1), two
   8mm A.A. (2 × 1) guns, two 21inch (1 × 2) T.T.
*Complement:* 72
*Notes:* Were originally armed with three 3.9inch (3 × 1) and one
   40mm A.A. guns. T.T. were later removed

**Name** *Leopard* (ex-*Balder*) **Built by** Naval Dockyard (Horton)
**Launched** 11.10.39 **Fate** Retroceded 1945

**Name** *Löwe* (ex-*Gyller*) **Built by** Naval Dockyard (Horton)
**Launched** 2.7.38 **Fate** Retroceded 1945

**Name** *Panther* (ex-*Odin*) **Built by** Naval Dockyard (Horton)
**Launched** 17.1.39 **Fate** Retroceded 1945

**Name** *Tiger* (*ii*) (ex-*Tor*) **Built by** Frederiksstad Mek. Verksted
**Launched** 9.9.39 **Fate** Scuttled Frederiksstad 9.4.40, salved and
German; retroceded 1945

*General Arrangement of the
Tiger Class, formerly
Norwegian torpedo boats
Balder, Gyller, Odin and Tor.*

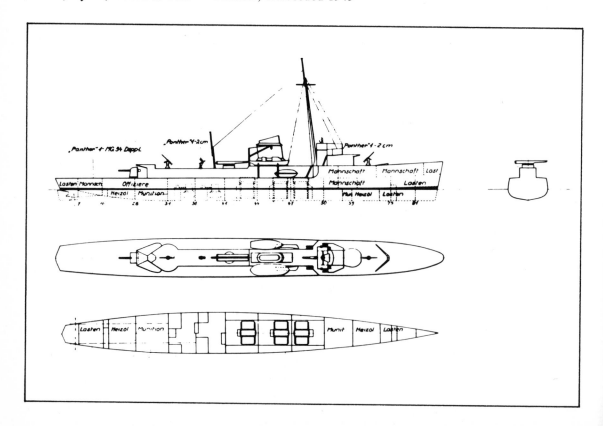

*The* Panther *was the ex-Norwegian* Odin, *armed with one 3.9-inch gun aft, two single 20-mm AA guns and twin torpedo-tubes abaft the funnel.* (Drüppel)

## Ex-French torpedo boats: **TA.1–6**

*Displacement:* 1,087 tons (1,443 tons full)
*Dimensions:* 295¼(pp) 305(oa) × 30½ × 10¼/12¾ feet
*Machinery:* Two boilers (pressure 270 lb.); two shafts; Rateau except *TA.4–6* Parsons geared turbines, S.H.P. 28,000 = 34 knots

*General Arrangement of TA.1–6, formerly French torpedo boats of the* Agile *Class.*

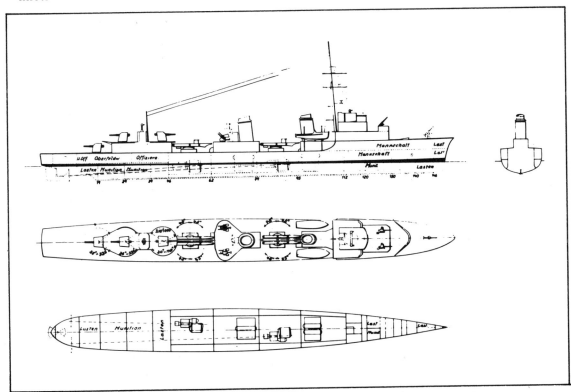

*Bunkers & Radius:* O.F. 290 tons; 2,170 miles at 19 knots
*Armament:* Three 4.1inch A.A. (3 × 1), two 37mm A.A. (1 × 2), nine 20mm A.A. (2 × 4 and 1 × 1) guns, six 21inch (2 × 3) T.T.
*Complement:* 147
*Notes:* Were originally armed with four 3.9inch (4 × 1), four 40mm A.A. (2 × 2) guns, four 21.7inch (2 × 2) T.T.

# *Ex-RNN torpedo boats:* **TA.7** and **8**

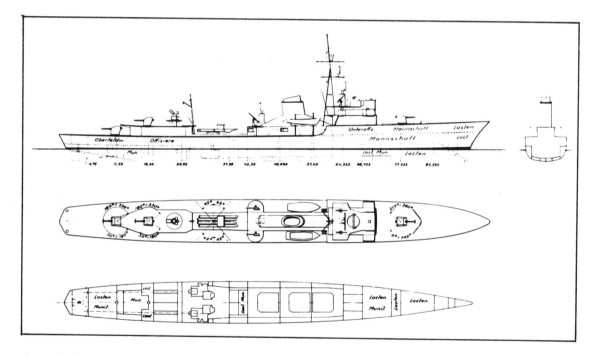

*General Arrangement of TA.7–8, formerly Dutch ZN.4 and ZN.5.*

# *Ex-French torpedo boats:* **TA.9–13**

*Displacement:* 610 tons (970 tons full)
*Dimensions:* 245$\frac{1}{4}$(pp) 264$\frac{3}{4}$(oa) × 25$\frac{1}{4}$ × 9$\frac{1}{4}$/11 feet
*Machinery:* Two boilers (pressure 270 lb.); two shafts; Parsons geared turbines, S.H.P. 22,000 = 34$\frac{1}{2}$ knots
*Bunkers & Radius:* O.F. 90 tons; 1,880 miles at 18 knots
*Armament:* Two 3.9inch (2 × 1), two 37mm A.A. (1 × 2), fourteen 20mm A.A. (2 × 4 and 6 × 1) guns
*Complement:* 95
*Notes:* Three boats had first been acquired by the RIt.N before being taken over by the German Navy. Original armament included two 21.7inch T.T. (1 × 2) but excluded the 20mm A.A. guns

## *Ex-RIt.N destroyer:* **TA.14**

*Displacement:* 1,092 tons (1,355 tons full)
*Dimensions:* 299½(pp) 308½(oa) × 30½ × 9½/11¼ feet
*Machinery:* Three Express boilers; two shafts; Parsons geared
   turbines S.H.P. 40,000 = 36 knots
*Bunkers & Radius:* O.F. 270 tons; 2,800 miles at 15 knots
*Armament:* Four 4.7inch (2 × 2), two 40mm A.A. (1 × 2) guns,
   six 21inch (2 × 3) T.T.
*Complement:* 120

## *Ex-RIt.N torpedo boat:* **TA.15**

*Displacement:* 965 tons (1,260 tons full)
*Dimensions:* 275½(pp) (oa) × 27 × 9¾ feet
*Machinery:* Three Thornycroft boilers; two shafts; Belluzzo
   geared turbines, S.H.P. 36,000 = 35 knots
*Bunkers & Radius:* O.F. 255 tons; 2,750 miles at 15 knots
*Armament:* Four 4.7inch (2 × 2), two 40mm A.A. (1 × 2) guns,
   four 21inch (2 × 2) T.T.
*Complement:* 120

## *Ex-RIt.N torpedo boats:* **TA.16** and **19**

*Displacement:* 876 tons (1,090 tons full)
*Dimensions:* 262½(pp) 278¾(oa) × 26¼ × 9½ feet
*Machinery:* Four Thornycroft boilers (pressure 265 lb.); two
   shafts; Zoelly geared turbines, S.H.P. 22,000 = 32 knots
*Bunkers & Radius:* O.F. 200 tons; 2,000 miles at 15 knots
*Armament:* Two 4inch (1 × 2), six 20mm A.A. (6 × 1) guns, four
   21inch (2 × 2) T.T.; ten mines
*Complement:* 105

## *Ex-RIt.N torpedo boats:* **TA.17** and **18**

*Displacement:* 824 tons (1,040 tons full)
*Dimensions:* 256½(pp) 262½(oa) × 26¼ × 9¼ feet
*Machinery:* Four Thornycroft boilers (pressure 265 lb.); two
   shafts; Zoelly geared turbines, S.H.P. 22,000 = 32 knots
*Bunkers & Radius:* O.F. 170 tons; 2,000 miles at 15 knots
*Armament:* Two 4inch (2 × 1), six 20mm A.A. (6 × 1) guns, four
   21inch (2 × 2) T.T.; ten mines
*Complement:* 105

## *Ex-RIt.N torpedo boat:* **TA.20**

*Displacement:* 629 tons (1,010 tons full)
*Dimensions:* 275(pp) 287½(oa) × 27¾ × 8 feet
*Machinery:* Three Yarrow boilers; two shafts; Brown Curtis
    turbines, S.H.P. 22,000 = 31 knots
*Bunkers & Radius:* O.F. 252 tons; 2,180 miles at 15 knots
*Armament:* Orig. seven 4in/35, later two 4inch (2 × 1), six 20mm
    A.A. (6 × 1) guns, orig. four 18inch, later four 21inch (2 × 2)
    T.T.; ten mines
*Complement:* 113

## *Ex-RIt.N torpedo boats:* **TA.22** and **35**

*Displacement:* 697 tons (865 tons full)
*Dimensions:* 236¼(pp) 239½(oa) × 24 × 8¾/10¾ feet except *TA.22*
    7½ feet
*Machinery:* Four Thornycroft boilers (pressure 265 lb.); two
    shafts; Tosi turbines, S.H.P. 15,500 = 30 knots
*Bunkers & Radius:* O.F. 150 tons; 1,190 miles at 14 knots
*Armament:* Two 4inch (2 × 1), six 20mm A.A. (6 × 1) guns, two
    18inch (1 × 2) T.T.; ten mines
*Complement:* 105
*Notes:* Were originally armed with five 5inch/40 (5 × 1), two
    40mm A.A. (2 × 1), four machine guns, four 18inch (4 × 1)
    T.T.

## *Ex-RIt.N torpedo boat:* **TA.21**

*Displacement:* 686 tons (860 tons full)
*Dimensions:* 238(pp) (oa) × 24 × 8¾/10¾ feet
*Machinery:* Four Thornycroft boilers (pressure 265 lb.); two
    shafts; Tosi turbines, S.H.P. 15,000 = 29 knots
*Bunkers & Radius:* O.F. 128 tons; 1,200 miles at 14 knots
*Armament:* two 4inch (2 × 1), six 20mm A.A. (6 × 1) guns, two
    18inch (1 × 2) T.T.; ten mines
*Complement:* 105
*Notes:* Was originally armed with five 4inch (5 × 1), one 40mm
    A.A., four machine guns, four 18inch (1 × 2 and 2 × 1) T.T.

## *Ex-RIt.N torpedo boats:* **TA.23, 25** and **26**

*Displacement:* 1,204 tons (1,709 tons full)
*Dimensions:* 282¼(pp) 292(oa) × 32½ × 9½/11½ feet
*Machinery:* Two Yarrow boilers; two shafts; Tosi geared turbines,
    S.H.P. 16,000 = 25 knots

*Bunkers & Radius:* O.F. 430 tons; 2,140 miles at 20 knots
*Armament:* Three except *TA.26* two 3.9inch A.A. (2/3 × 1), six
    except *TA.26* ten 20mm A.A. (1/2 × 4 and 2 × 1) guns, four
    18inch (2 × 2) T.T.; thirty mines
*Complement:* 175

## *Ex-RIt.N torpedo boats:* **TA.24, 27–30, 36–42, 45–47**

*Displacement:* 797 except *TA.24* 791 tons (1,033 tons full)
*Dimensions:* 259¼(pp) 269(oa) × 27¼ × 8/9¾ feet
*Machinery:* Two boilers; two shafts; Tosi geared turbines, S.H.P.
    22,000 = 25 knots
*Bunkers & Radius:* O.F. 200 tons; 1,020 miles at 20 knots
*Armament:* Two 3.9inch A.A. (2 × 1), four 37mm A.A. (4 × 1),
    twelve 20mm A.A. (2 × 4 and 4 × 1) guns, six 18inch T.T.
    (2 × 3), twenty-eight mines
*Complement:* 94

## *Ex-RIt.N destroyer:* **TA.31**

*Displacement:* 1,206 tons (1,450 tons full)
*Dimensions:* 302½(pp) 315(oa) × 32¼ × 10½ feet
*Machinery:* Three Thornycroft boilers; two shafts; Parsons geared
    turbines, S.H.P. 44,000 = 38 knots
*Bunkers & Radius:* O.F. 310 tons; 1,500 miles at 20 knots
*Armament:* Four 4.7inch (2 × 2), four 37mm A.A. (4 × 1), seven
    20mm A.A. (1 × 4 and 3 × 1) guns, three 21inch (1 × 3) T.T.
*Complement:* 156
*Notes:* After bank of T.T. removed to augment light A.A.
    armament

## *Ex-RYN destroyer:* **TA.32**

*Displacement:* 1,880 tons (2,400 tons full)
*Dimensions:* 345(pp) 371½(oa) × 35 × 11¾/000 feet
*Machinery:* Three Yarrow boilers; two shafts; Parsons geared
    turbines, S.H.P. 48,000 = 37 knots
*Bunkers & Radius:* O.F. 590 tons; 1,700 miles at 20 knots
*Armament:* Four 5.1inch (4 × 1), two 3.4inch A.A. (1 × 2), seven
    40mm A.A. (7 × 1), two 20mm A.A. (2 × 1) guns; three
    21inch (1 × 3) T.T.; six mines
*Complement:* 200
*Notes:* After bank of T.T. removed to augment light A.A.
    armament. Was formerly RIt.N *Premuda* before being
    acquired by the German Navy

## *Ex-RIt.N destroyers:* **TA.33** and **34**

*Displacement:* 1,830 tons (2,460 tons full)
*Dimensions:* 341¼(pp) 351(oa) × 33½ × 11¾/14 feet
*Machinery:* Three boilers; two shafts; Tosi geared turbines, S.H.P.
     48,000 = 38½ knots
*Bunkers & Radius:* O.F. 544 tons; 1,890 miles at 20 knots
*Armament:* Five 4.7inch (2 × 2 and 1 × 1), twenty 20mm A.A.
     (3 × 4, 2 × 2 and 4 × 1) guns, three 21inch (1 × 3) T.T.;
     fifty mines
*Complement:* 207
*Notes:* After bank of T.T. removed to augment light A.A.
     armament

## *Ex-RYN destroyer:* **TA.43**

*Displacement:* 1,210 tons (1,350 tons full)
*Dimensions:* 313(pp) 321½(oa) × 30¾ × 10¾ feet
*Machinery:* Three Yarrow boilers (pressure 400 lb.); two shafts;
     Parsons geared turbines, S.H.P. 44,000 = 37 knots
*Bunkers & Radius:* O.F. 120 tons; 1,000 miles
*Armament:* Four 4.7inch (4 × 1), seven 37mm A.A. (1 × 2 and
     5 × 1), two 20mm A.A. (2 × 1) guns, three 21inch (1 × 3)
     T.T.; thirty mines
*Complement:* 145
*Notes:* After bank of T.T. removed to augment light A.A.
     armament. Was formerly RIt.N *Sebenico* before being
     acquired by the German Navy

## *Ex-RIt.N destroyer:* **TA.44**

*Displacement:* 1,944 tons (2,580 tons full)
*Dimensions:* 354¼(oa) × 33½ × 10¾/12¾ feet
*Machinery:* Four Thornycroft boilers; two shafts; Belluzzo geared
     turbines, S.H.P. 50,000 = 39 knots
*Bunkers & Radius:* O.F. 553 tons; 1,450 miles at 26 knots
*Armament:* Six 4.7inch (3 × 2), nine 20mm A.A. (9 × 1) guns;
     four 21inch (2 × 2) T.T.; fifty-two mines
*Complement:* 185

## *Ex-RYN torpedo boat:* **TA.48**

*Displacement:* 240 tons (262 tons full)
*Dimensions:* 188¼(pp) 190¼(oa) × 18¾ × 5/6 feet
*Machinery:* Two Yarrow boilers (pressure 255 lb.); two shafts;
     Parsons turbines, S.H.P. 5,000 = 28 knots
*Bunkers & Radius:* Coal 18 tons + O.F. 24 tons; 220 miles at 20
     knots

*Armament:* Two 3inch A.A. (2 × 1), two 20mm A.A. (2 × 1)
  guns; two 18inch (1 × 2) T.T.
*Complement:* 52


## *Ex-RIt.N torpedo boat:* **TA.49**

*Displacement:* 689 tons (799 tons full)
*Dimensions:* 254¾(wl) 265¾(oa) × 26 × 7¾/9¼ feet
*Machinery:* Two Yarrow boilers; two shafts; Tosi geared turbines,
  S.H.P. 19,000 = 34 knots
*Bunkers & Radius:* O.F. 215 tons; 1,260 miles at 20 knots
*Armament:* Three 3.9inch A.A. (3 × 1), fourteen 20mm A.A.
  (2 × 4 and 6 × 1) guns; two 18inch (2 × 1) T.T.; thirty mines
*Complement:* 94

**Name** *TA.1* (ex-*Le Fier*) **Built by** At. & Ch. de la Bretagne (Nantes)
**Launched** 12.3.40 **Fate** Scuttled incomplete Nantes 11.8.44

**Name** *TA.2* (ex-*L'Agile*) **Built by** At. & Ch. de la Bretagne (Nantes)
**Launched** 23.5.40 **Fate** Bombed USA aircraft Nantes 16.9.43
while building; scuttled incomplete 11.8.44

**Name** *TA.3* (ex-*L'Alsacien*) **Built by** At. & Ch. de la Bretagne
(Nantes) **Launched** 5.40 **Fate** Retroceded incomplete 1945 and
scrapped

**Name** *TA.4* (ex-*L'Entreprennant*) **Built by** At. & Ch. de la Loire
(Nantes) **Launched** 25.4.41 **Fate** Bombed USA aircraft Nantes
16.9.43 while building; retroceded incomplete 1945 and scrapped

**Name** *TA.5* (ex-*Le Farouche*) **Built by** At. & Ch. de la Loire
(Nantes) **Launched** 19.10.40 **Fate** Scuttled incomplete Nantes
11.8.44

**Name** *TA.6* (ex-*Le Corse*) **Built by** At. & Ch. de la Loire (Nantes)
**Launched** 4.4.42 **Fate** Scuttled incomplete Nantes 11.8.44

**Name** *TA.9* (ex-*FR.41,* ex-*Bombarde*) **Built by** At. & Ch. de la
Loire (St. Nazaire) **Launched** 23.3.36 **Fate** Scuttled Bizerta
30.11.42; salved RIt.N *FR.41*, German (1943); bombed USA
aircraft Toulon 23.8.44

**Name** *TA.10* (ex-*FR.42,* ex-*La Pomone*) **Built by** At. & Ch. de la
Loire (St. Nazaire) **Launched** 25.1.35 **Fate** Scuttled Bizerta
30.11.42; salved and RIt.N *FR.42* German (1943); scuttled
Rhodes 23.1.44 after gunfire RN destroyer *Eclipse* 17.1.44

**Name** *TA.11* (ex-*FR.43,* ex-*L'Iphigenie*) **Built by** At. & Ch. de la
Loire (St. Nazaire) **Launched** 18.4.35 **Fate** Scuttled Bizerta
30.11.42; salved and RIt.N *FR.43*, German (1943); beached
Piombino 17.9.43 after gunfire of Italian tanks 10.9.43

**Name** *T.12* (ex-*Baliste*) **Built by** At. & Ch. de France
(Dunkerque) **Launched** 17.3.37 **Fate** Scuttled Toulon 27.11.42;
salved and German; bombed Allied aircraft Rhodes 22.8.43

**Name** *TA.13* (ex-*La Bayonnaise*) **Built by** Ch. Sud-Ouest (Bordeaux) **Launched** 28.1.36 **Fate** Scuttled Toulon 27.11.42; salved and German; scuttled Toulon 25.8.44

**Name** *TA.14* (ex-*Turbine*) **Built by** Odero-Terni-Orlando (Leghorn) **Launched** 21.4.27 **Fate** Bombed USA aircraft Salamis 15.9.44

**Name** *TA.15* (ex-*Francesco Crispi*) **Built by** Pattison (Naples) **Launched** 12.9.25 **Fate** Bombed RAF aircraft Candia 8.3.44; salved and scuttled Piraeus 13.10.44

**Name** *TA.16* (ex-*Castelfidardo*) **Built by** Orlando (Leghorn) **Launched** 4.6.22 **Fate** Scuttled Piraeus 8.9.43, salved and German; bombed Allied aircraft Heraklion 2.6.44

**Name** *TA.17* (ex-*San Martino*) **Built by** Orlando (Leghorn) **Launched** 8.9.20 **Fate** Scuttled Piraeus 8.9.43, salved and German; bombed RAF aircraft off Piraeus 12.10.44

**Name** *TA.18* (ex-*Solferino*) **Built by** Orlando (Leghorn) **Launched** 28.4.20 **Fate** Gunfire RN destroyers *Termagant* and *Tuscan* south of Volos 19.10.44

**Name** *TA.19* (ex-*Calatafirmi*) **Built by** Orlando (Leghorn) **Launched** 17.3.23 **Fate** *Achilles* (1944); torpedoed RHN submarine *Pipinos* off Karlovassi 9.8.44

**Name** *TA.20* (ex-*Audace*) **Built by** Yarrow (Scotstoun) **Launched** 27.9.16 **Fate** Gunfire RN escort destroyers *Avon Vale* and *Wheatland* off Pag Island 3.11.44

**Name** *TA.21* (ex-*Insidioso*) **Built by** Pattison (Naples) **Launched** 30.9.13 **Fate** Scuttled Pola 10.9.43, salved and German; torpedoed RN destroyers north of Adria 9.8.44, salved; bombed RAF aircraft Fiume 5.11.44

**Name** *TA.22* (ex-*Giuseppe Missori*) **Built by** Odero-Terni-Orlando (Genoa) **Launched** 20.12.15 **Fate** Scuttled Durazzo 10.9.43, salved and German; bombed Allied aircraft Trieste 25.6.44, salved; scuttled 2.5.45

**Name** *TA.23* (ex-*Impavido*) **Built by** Tirreno (Riva Trigoso) **Launched** 24.2.43 **Fate** Scuttled off Elba 8.9.43, salved and German; mined west of Capri 25.4.44

**Name** *TA.24* (ex-**Arturo**) **Built by** Ansaldo (Genoa) **Launched** 27.3.43 **Fate** Gunfire RN destroyers *Lookout* and *Meteor* south of Genoa 18.3.45

**Name** *TA.25* (ex-*Intrepido*) **Built by** Tirreno (Riva Trigoso) **Launched** 8.9.43 **Fate** Scuttled incomplete Genoa 9.9.43, salved and German; torpedoed RN MTB west of Spezia 15.7.44

**Name** *TA.26* (ex-*Ardito*) **Built by** Ansaldo (Genoa) **Launched** 16.3.42 **Fate** Sabotaged Rapallo 6.7.44

**Name** *TA.27* (ex-*Auriga*) **Built by** Ansaldo (Genoa) **Launched** 15.4.43 **Fate** Bombed USAAF aircraft off Elba 9.6.44

**Name** *TA.28* (ex-*Rigel*) **Built by** Ansaldo (Genoa)
**Launched** 22.5.43 **Fate** Bombed RAF aircraft Genoa 4.9.44,
salved; scuttled 5.45

**Name** *TA.29* (ex-*Eridano*) **Built by** Ansaldo (Genoa)
**Launched** 12.7.43 **Fate** Gunfire RN destroyers *Lookout* and
*Meteor* south of Genoa 18.3.45, and scuttled 19.3.45

**Name** *TA.30* (ex-*Dragone*) **Built by** Ansaldo (Genoa)
**Launched** 14.8.43 **Fate** Torpedoed RN MTB west of Spezia
15.6.44

**Name** *TA.31* (ex-*Dardo*) **Built by** Ansaldo (Genoa)
**Launched** 6.9.30 **Fate** Bombed Allied aircraft Genoa 25.10.44;
scuttled 25.4.45, salved and scrapped

**Name** *TA.32* (ex-*Premuda*, ex-*Dubrovnik*) **Built by** Yarrow
(Scotstoun) **Launched** 11.10.31 **Fate** Scuttled Genoa 25.4.45 after
gunfire of RN destroyers

**Name** *TA.33* (ex-*Corsaro*, ex-*Squadrista*) **Built by** Odero-Terni-
Orlando (Leghorn) **Launched** 12.9.42 **Fate** Bombed USA aircraft
Genoa 4.9.44 while building and construction abandoned;
scrapped 1946

**Name** *TA.34* (ex-*Carrista*) **Built by** Odero-Terni-Orlando
(Leghorn) **Fate** Bombed Allied aircraft Leghorn 7.43 while
building and construction abandoned; scrapped on slip 5.45

**Name** *TA.35* (ex-*Giuseppe Dezza*) **Built by** Odero-Terni-Orlando
(Genoa) **Launched** 26.10.15 **Fate** Scuttled Fiume 16.9.43, salved
and German; torpedoed off Pola 20.8.44, salved; scuttled Trieste
3.5.45 and scrapped

**Name** *TA.36* (ex-*Stella Polare*) **Built by** Quarnaro (Fiume)
**Launched** 1.4.44 **Fate** Mined off Quarnaro 15.9.44

**Name** *TA.37* (ex-*Giadio*) **Built by** Cant. Riuniti dell'Adriatico
(Trieste) **Launched** 15.6.43 **Fate** Gunfire RN destroyer
*Termagant* Gulf of Salonika 7.10.44

**Name** *TA.38* (ex-*Spada*) **Built by** Cant. Riuniti dell'Adriatico
(Trieste) **Launched** 1.7.43 **Fate** Scuttled Volos 13.10.44 after being
bombed Allied aircraft

**Name** *TA.39* (ex-*Daga*) **Built by** Cant. Riuniti dell'Adriatico
(Trieste) **Launched** 15.7.43 **Fate** Scuttled Salonika 16.10.44 after
gunfire RN destroyer

**Name** *TA.40* (ex-*Pugnale*) **Built by** Cant. Riuniti dell'Adriatico
(Trieste) **Launched** 1.8.43 **Fate** Scuttled Trieste 4.5.45 after
being bombed Allied aircraft 20.2.45

**Name** *TA.41* (ex-*Lancia*) **Built by** Cant. Riuniti dell'Adriatico
(Trieste) **Launched** 7.5.44 **Fate** Scuttled San Rocco 1.5.45 after
being bombed Allied aircraft 17.2.45

**Name** *TA.42* (ex-*Alabarda*) **Built by** Cant. Riuniti dell'Adriatico (Trieste) **Launched** 7.5.44 **Fate** Scuttled Venice 21.3.45 after being bombed RAF aircraft

**Name** *TA.43* (ex-*Sebenico*, ex-*Beograd*) **Built by** At. & Ch. de la Loire/Yarrow (Scotstoun) **Launched** 23.12.37 **Fate** Scuttled Trieste 1.5.45; salved and scuttled 19.7.46

**Name** *TA.44* (ex-*Da Verrazzano*) **Built by** Quarnaro (Fiume) **Launched** 10.11.29 **Fate** Scuttled Fiume 10.9.43, salved and German; bombed Allied aircraft Trieste 17.2.45

**Name** *TA.45* (ex-*Spica*) **Built by** Quarnaro (Fiume) **Launched** 30.1.44 **Fate** Torpedoed RN MTBs *670* and *697* Aegean 13.4.45

**Name** *TA.46* (ex-*Fionda*) **Built by** Quarnaro (Fiume) **Launched** 31.1.43 **Fate** Bombed Allied aircraft Fiume 20.2.45; salved and Yugoslavian *Velebit* (1948)

**Name** *TA.47* (ex-*Balestra*) **Built by** Quarnaro (Fiume) **Launched** 4.10.47 **Fate** Bombed Allied aircraft Fiume 20.2.45; salved and Yugoslavian *Ucka* (1948)

**Name** *TA.48* (ex-*T.3*) **Built by** Stab. Tecnico (Trieste) **Launched** 1913 **Fate** Bombed Allied aircraft Trieste 20.2.45

**Name** *TA.49* (ex-*Lira*) **Built by** Quarnaro (Fiume) **Launched** 12.9.37 **Fate** Scuttled Spezia 9.9.43, salved and German; bombed RAF aircraft Spezia 4.11.44

# Ex-Enemy Torpedo Boats

## Ex-RNN torpedo boats: **DRAGONER, KURASSIER** and **MESKETIER**

*Displacement:* 45 tons
*Dimensions:* $114\frac{3}{4}$(pp) × $12\frac{1}{2}$ × $5\frac{1}{2}$ feet
*Machinery:* Two boilers, 1-shaft reciprocating (VTE) I.H.P.
   650 = 19 knots
*Bunkers & Radius:* Coal 13 tons; 900 miles at 12 knots
*Armament:* Two 37mm (2 × 1) guns, two 18inch (1 fixed bow
   and 1 × 1) T.T.
*Complement:* 14
*Notes:* Former torpedo boats which had their T.T. removed and
   used for patrol work

## Ex-RNN torpedo boat: **GRENADIER**

*Displacement:* 94 tons
*Dimensions:* $134\frac{1}{2}$(pp) × $14\frac{3}{4}$ × 7 feet
*Machinery:* Two boilers, 1-shaft reciprocating (VTE) I.H.P.
   1,700 = 25 knots
*Bunkers & Radius:* Coal 16 tons; 1,250 miles at 12 knots
*Armament:* One 3inch gun, three 18inch (3 × 1—1 fixed bow and
   2 × 1) T.T.
*Complement:* 21

**Name** *KT.4* (ex-*Blink*) **Built by** Christiana **Launched** 1896
**Fate** *Kürassier* (1941)

**Name** *KT.3* (ex-*Lyn*) **Built by** Christiana **Launched** 1897
**Fate** *Musketier* (1941)

**Name** *KT.2* (ex-*Kvik*) **Built by** Christiana **Launched** 1896
**Fate** *Dragoner* (1941)

**Name** *KT.1* (ex-*Kjell*) **Built by** Karl Johans Verksted (Horten)
**Launched** 1912 **Fate** *Grenadier* (1941).

### Ex-RNN torpedo boat: **TARANTEL**

*Displacement:* 90 tons
*Dimensions:* $131\frac{1}{4}$(pp) × 16 × 7 feet
*Machinery:* Two boilers, 1-shaft reciprocating (VTE) I.H.P.
  1,000 = 19 knots
*Bunkers & Radius:* Coal 17 tons; 1,250 miles at 12 knots
*Armament:* Two 37mm (2 × 1) guns
*Complement:* 19
*Notes:* Former torpedo boat which had her T.T. removed and
  used for patrol work

### Ex-RNN torpedo boats: **KROKODIL, QUALLE, SCHILDKRÖTE** and **SEESTERN**

*Displacement:* 65 tons
*Dimensions:* $114\frac{3}{4}$(pp) × $14\frac{3}{4}$ × 6 feet
*Machinery:* Two boilers, 1-shaft reciprocating (VTE) I.H.P.
  700 = 19 knots
*Bunkers & Radius:* 13 tons; 900 miles at 12 knots
*Armament:* Two 37mm (2 × 1) guns
*Complement:* 14
*Notes:* Former torpedo boats which had their T.T. removed and
  used for patrol work

### Ex-RNN torpedo boats: **EIDECHSE** and **SCHLANGE**

*Displacement:* 70 tons
*Dimensions:* 118(pp) = $14\frac{3}{4}$ = $6\frac{1}{4}$ feet
*Machinery:* Two boilers, 1-shaft reciprocating (VTE) I.H.P.
  1,000 = 23 knots
*Bunkers & Radius:* Coal 13 tons; 900 miles at 12 knots
*Armament:* Two 37mm (2 × 1) guns
*Complement:* 16
*Notes:* Former torpedo boats which had their T.T. removed and
  used for patrol work

**Name** *Tarantel* (ex-*Hval*) **Built by** Schichau (Elbing)
**Launched** 1896 **Fate** Not known

**Name** *Krokodil* (ex-*Hauk*) **Built by** Christiana **Launched** 1903
**Fate** Not known

**Name** *Qualle* (ex-*Falk*) **Built by** Christiana **Launched** 1903

**Name** *Schildkröte* (ex-*Kjaek*) **Built by** Christiana **Launched** 1900

**Name** *Seestern* (ex-*Hvas*) **Built by** Christiana **Launched** 1900

**Name** *Eidechse* (ex-*Lom*) **Built by** Christiana **Launched** 1906

**Name** *Schlange* (ex-*Orn*) **Built by** Christiana **Launched** 1904
**Fate** Not known

# Torpedo Recovery Vessels

## *Torpedo recovery vessels type 1942:* **TF.1–8**

The provision of these vessels is in no way extraordinary, but what is unusual is the building of vessels of such high quality for this task, especially during war time when building and turbine blade cutting capacity were fully extended. In appearance they resembled small torpedo boats, and the first two groups closely resembled each other, except that the German-built boats had the bridge structure faired into the funnel casing and had derricks at either end of the after deck, while the boats built in the Netherlands had their bridge sited slightly more forward and a less conspicuous funnel casing and only a single derrick amidships on the after deck. No boats of the third group were ever laid down.

*General Arrangement of the torpedo-recovery vessels TF.1–8.*

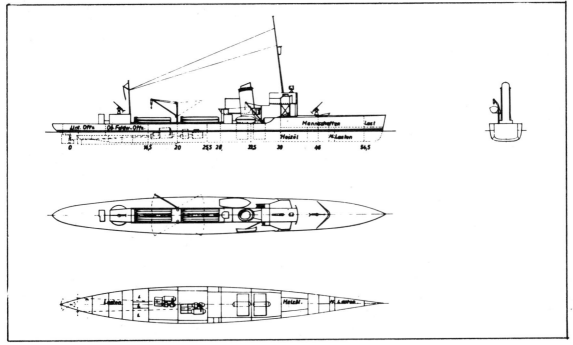

*Displacement:* 381 tons (483 tons full) × ×
*Dimensions:* 190¼(pp) 203½(oa) × 22 × 6¼/8 feet
*Machinery:* Two boilers; two shafts; Schichau geared turbines,
　　S.H.P. 6,000 = 23½ knots
*Bunkers & Radius:* O.F. 71 tons; 2,000 miles at 19 knots
*Armament:* Two 20mm A.A. (2 × 1) guns
*Complement:* 61
*Notes:* Deck stowage for fourteen torpedoes

**Name** *TF.1* **Built by** Schichau (Elbing) **Launched** 1941
**Fate** Not known

**Name** *TF.2* **Built by** Schichau (Elbing) **Launched** 1941
**Fate** Russian (1945)

**Name** *TF.3* **Built by** Schichau (Elbing) **Launched** 1941
**Fate** Not known

**Name** *TF.4* **Built by** Schichau (Elbing) **Launched** 1941/2
**Fate** Russian (1945)

**Name** *TF.5* **Built by** Schichau (Elbing) **Launched** 1941/2
**Fate** Scuttled 5.45

**Name** *TF.6* **Built by** Schichau (Elbing) **Launched** 1941/2
**Fate** Scuttled 14.6.45

**Name** *TF.7* **Built by** Schichau (Elbing) **Launched** 1941/2
**Fate** Not Known

**Name** *TF.8* **Built by** Schichau (Elbing) **Launched** 1941/2
**Fate** Not known

## *Torpedo recovery vessels type 1943:* **TF.9–24**

*Displacement:* 380 tons (491 tons full)
*Dimensions:* 190¼(pp) 203½(oa) × 22¼ × 6½/8 feet
*Machinery:* Two boilers; two shafts; Werkspoor geared turbines,
　　S.H.P. 6,240 = 24 knots
*Bunkers & Radius:* O.F. 72 tons; 2,000 miles at 19 knots
*Armament:* Two 20mm A.A. (2 × 1) guns
*Complement:* 61
*Notes:* Deck stowage for fourteen torpedoes

## *Torpedo recovery vessels type 1942:* **TF.25–36**

*Displacement:* 473 tons (625 tons full)
*Dimensions:* 203½(pp) 216½(oa) × 26 × 6½/8¾ feet
*Machinery:* Two boilers; two shafts; Schichau geared turbines,
　　S.H.P. 8,000 = 23½ knots
*Bunkers & Radius:* O.F. 120 tons; 3,200 miles at 19 knots
*Armament:* One 37mm A.A., four 20mm A.A. (1 × 4) guns
*Complement:* 76
*Notes:* Deck stowage for fourteen torpedoes

**Name** *T.F.9* **Built by** Netherlands Dock & Sbdg. (Amsterdam)
**Launched** 6.6.43 **Fate** Russian (1945)

**Name** *T.F.10* **Built by** Netherlands Dock & Sbdg. (Amsterdam)
**Launched** 10.7.43 **Fate** Scuttled 5.45

**Name** *T.F.11* **Built by** Netherlands Dock & Sbdg. (Amsterdam)
**Launched** 28.8.43 **Fate** Scuttled 5.45

**Name** *T.F.12* **Built by** Netherlands Dock & Sbdg. (Amsterdam)
**Launched** 2.10.43 **Fate** Scuttled 5.45

**Name** *T.F.13* **Built by** Rotterdam D.D. **Launched** 18.9.43
**Fate** Scuttled 5.45

**Name** *T.F.14* **Built by** Rotterdam D.D. **Launched** 10.11.43
**Fate** Scuttled 5.45

**Name** *T.F.15* **Built by** Wilton-Fijenoord **Launched** 1943
**Fate** Russian (1945)

**Name** *T.F.16* **Built by** Wilton-Fijenoord **Launched** 1943
**Fate** Scuttled 5.45

**Name** *T.F.17* **Built by** Wilton-Fijenoord **Launched** 1943
**Fate** Russian (1945)

**Name** *T.F.18* **Built by** Wilton-Fijenoord **Launched** 1943
**Fate** Scuttled 5.45

**Name** *T.F.19* **Built by** Rotterdam D.D. **Launched** 27.5.43
**Fate** Scuttled 5.45

**Name** *T.F.20* **Built by** Rotterdam D.D. **Launched** 29.7.43
**Fate** Not known

**Name** *T.F.21* **Built by** Van der Giessen (Krimpen) **Launched** 14.5.43
**Fate** Not known

**Name** *T.F.22* **Built by** Van der Giessen (Krimpen) **Launched** 8.7.43
**Fate** Not known

**Name** *T.F.23* **Built by** Netherlands Dock & Sbdg. (Amsterdam)
**Launched** 3.7.43 **Fate** Not known

**Name** *T.F.24* **Built by** Netherlands Dock & Sbdg. (Amsterdam)
**Launched** 14.8.43 **Fate** Not known

**Name** *T.F.24–36* **Built by** Schichau (Elbing) **Fate** Cancelled

## *Ex-RDN torpedo recovery vessels:* **TFA.1–3**

*Displacement:* 290 tons (335 tons full)
*Dimensions:* $198\frac{3}{4} \times 19\frac{1}{2} \times 7\frac{3}{4}/8\frac{1}{2}$ feet
*Machinery:* Two Thornycroft boilers; two-shaft Atlas geared
    turbines, S.H.P. 6,000 = $27\frac{1}{2}$ knots
*Bunkers & Radius:* O.F. 40 tons
*Armament:* Two 3.5inch (2 × 1), two 20mm A.A. (2 × 1),
    two 8mm A.A. (2 × 1) guns, six 18inch (2 FB and 2 × 2) T.T.
*Complement:* 55

### *Ex-RDN torpedo recovery vessels:* **TFA.4–6**

*Displacement:* 290 tons (335 tons full)
*Dimensions:* $198\frac{3}{4}$(oa) × $19\frac{1}{2}$ × $7\frac{3}{4}/8\frac{1}{2}$ feet
*Machinery:* Two Thornycroft boilers; two-shaft Brown Boveri
   except *TFA.6* Atlas geared turbines, S.H.P. 6,000 = $27\frac{1}{2}$ knots
*Bunkers:* O.F. 40 tons
*Armament:* Two 3inch (2 × 1), two 20mm A.A. (2 × 1),
   two 8mm A.A. (2 × 1) guns, eight 18inch (2 FB and 2 × 3)
   T.T.
   *Complement:* 51
*Notes:* Former torpedo boats

### *Ex-Polish torpedo recovery vessels:* **TFA.7, 8, 11** *and* **OXHOFT**

*Displacement:* 183 tons
*Dimensions:* $139\frac{1}{2}$(pp × $21\frac{1}{4}$ × $5\frac{1}{2}$ feet
*Machinery:* Two-shaft diesel motors, B.H.P. 1,040 = 15 knots
*Bunkers:* O.F.
*Armament:* One 3inch gun
*Complement:* 30
*Notes:* Former minesweepers

### *Ex-RNeth.N torpedo recovery vessels:* **TFA.9**

*Displacement:* 180 tons (230 tons full)
*Dimensions:* $162\frac{1}{2}$(pp) × 17 × $4\frac{1}{2}/5\frac{3}{4}$ feet
*Machinery:* Two-shaft reciprocating (VTE) I.H.P. 2,600 = 25
   knots
*Bunkers:* Coal 44 tons
*Armament:* Two 3inch (2 × 1) guns, three 17.7inch (3 × 1) T.T.
*Complement:* 27

*The torpedo recovery vessel
TFA.9 was an ex-Netherlands
Navy torpedo boat.* (Drüppel)

## *Ex-RNeth.N torpedo recovery vessels:* **TFA.10**

*Displacement:* 144 tons (185 tons full)
*Dimensions:* 154¼(pp) × 16½ × 6/8 feet
*Machinery:* One-shaft reciprocating (VC) I.H.P. 2,000 = 25 knots
*Bunkers & Radius:* Coal 40 tons; 1,230 miles at 8 knots
*Armament:* Two 4 pdr. (2 × 1) guns, three 17.7inch (3 × 1) T.T.
*Complement:* 24
*Notes:* Former torpedo boats. Foc's'le was extended to abaft
   bridge and funnels trunked into a single casing. *TFA.10* had
   been removed from the effective list in 1930

**Name** *TFA.1* (ex-*Hogen*) **Built by** Naval Dockyard (Copenhagen)
**Launched** 1933 **Fate** Heavily damaged when depot ship *Donau*
blew-up Flensburg 14.6.45

**Name** *TFA.2* (ex-*Ornen*) **Built by** Naval Dockyard (Copenhagen)
**Launched** 19.10.34 **Fate** Heavily damaged when depot ship *Donau*
blew-up Flensburg 14.6.45

**Name** *TFA.3* (ex-*Glenten*) **Built by** Naval Dockyard (Copenhagen)
**Launched** 1933 **Fate** Heavily damaged when depot ship *Donau*
blew-up Flensburg 14.6.45

**Name** *TFA.4* (ex-*Dragen*) **Built by** Naval Dockyard (Copenhagen)
**Launched** 12.29 **Fate** Mined Geltinger Bight 14.5.45

**Name** *TFA.5* (ex-*Hvalen*) **Built by** Naval Dockyard (Copenhagen)
**Launched** 1930 **Fate** Heavily damaged when depot ship *Donau*
blew-up Flensburg 14.6.45

**Name** *TFA.6* (ex-*Laxen*) **Built by** Naval Dockyard (Copenhagen)
**Launched** 1930 **Fate** Heavily damaged when depot ship *Donau*
blew-up Flensburg 14.6.45

**Name** *TFA.7* (ex-*Mewa*) **Built by** Gdynia **Launched** 1935
**Fate** Not known

**Name** *TFA.8* (ex-*Rybitwa*) **Built by** Modlin **Launched** 26.4.35
**Fate** Not known

**Name** *TFA.11* (ex-*Czajka*) **Built by** Modlin **Launched** 10.4.35
**Fate** *Westerplatte* (1942)

**Name** *Oxhoft* (ex-*Zuraw*) **Built by** Gdynia **Launched** 22.8.38
**Fate** Experimental vessel

**Name** *TFA.9* (ex-*G.16*) **Built by** Wilton-Fijennord (Schiedam)
**Launched** 1914 **Fate** Scuttled Kiel 3.5.45 and scrapped

**Name** *TFA.10* (ex-*G.22*) **Built by** De Schelde (Flushing)
**Launched** 1904 **Fate** Scuttled Kiel 5.45

# Submarines

## INTRODUCTION

This section is devoted to the submarines of the German Navy, a potent arm which for the second time within twenty-five years nearly severed the Allied lines of communication. Had this occurred the outcome of the Second World War would have been in doubt. It only failed because the intensive anti-submarine measures adopted coupled with outstanding technical advances—especially with sonar—finally defeated the submarine. Towards the end of the war Germany had new classes of very effective submarines entering service. They were produced too late to avert defeat, but their earlier introduction would have undoubtedly prolonged the issue. With their sea communications eventually secured the Allies were subsequently able to deploy their overwhelming military strength to their advantage culminating in the invasion and occupation of enemy countries. But there can be no doubt that the submarines were the greatest single obstacle to Allied success: a fact which Germany fully appreciated and evidenced by the size of the underwater fleet they created. It was indeed fortunate for the Allied powers that the submarine programme was not completed in its entirety.

German submarine classes were each given a type number with the addition of a simple, or compound, suffix if the basic type was further developed or modified. These type numbers are chronologically arranged in the text, and against them are shown the range of numbers of submarines forming the class. This arrangement of type numbers only loosely follows the date order, as it will be appreciated that the later mark of a low type number was often not contemplated until after the initial mark of a higher type number had been put in hand, but this was considered the more logical arrangement.

The following standard format for the legend, with the oblique stroke used in the conventional manner to indicate surfaced/submerged details respectively, has been used throughout:

*Displacement:* Surfaced (standard)/submerged (full load) in tons.

*Dimensions:* Waterline length × maximum breadth, over saddle tanks where fitted × mean draught at surfaced standard displacement

*Machinery:* Number of shafts, horse power and type of surfaced/ submerged machinery, speed surfaced/submerged, and details of auxiliary propulsion where fitted

*Bunkers & Radius:* O.F. (diesel-engined boats) or perhydrol (turbine-engined boats) in tons; radius and speed surfaced/ submerged; and cargo O.F. where carried

*Armament:* Number and calibre of guns (single or multiple mountings); number and calibre of torpedo tubes (position of tubes—number of torpedoes and/or mines, and number of cargo torpedoes where carried)

*Complement:* Full war

*Notes:* Details of variation, or alteration, in the above legend

The tabulated lists give details of the type number; individual submarine number; builder; launch date; and fate. The submarines are arranged chronologically in the lists to facilitate entry, while submarine losses are summarised at the end for each month of the war. Following the German surrender, a large number of submarines in home ports were scuttled, principally as a final defiant gesture, but these are separated from, and form no part of, the war losses as their inclusion would only confuse any analytical study of the losses incurred. Generally, all ships and aircraft known to have participated in the sinking of a German submarine have been equally credited with the success, and not just the particular ship, or aircraft, which delivered the *coup-de-grace*. The loss details are largely, but by no means solely, based on the official Admiralty accounts, but a small number of these differ, by a few days in some instances, from German records. The latter contend, not without justification, that in the case of prolonged hunts which ultimately resulted in a sinking, the Admiralty policy was to date a "kill" from the day on which initial contact was made, while the German Navy recorded the date of actual loss. This posed the question of adequately defining the date of a war loss when attack and sinking did not occur on the same day, which further posed defining a war loss itself: as a ship did not necessarily have to sink to be so reckoned.

Accepting as a loss a ship which is no longer capable of further combatant service for the duration of hostilities, whether actually sunk or not, the relevant date would then be the actual date on which she was sunk, qualified, where necessary, by an earlier date on which she received damage which either directly resulted in her loss, or in her being written-off as a constructive total loss. For the latter, the date on which damage occurred is more relevant than when officially written- or paid-off. The loss dates given herein are, therefore, based on these contentions where possible, but cannot in all cases be so simply resolved owing to the lack of precise details.

A further point of interest is that with submarines sunk by aircraft the cause is frequently and incorrectly attributed to bombing. The naval depth charge was available to maritime aircraft of the Royal Air Force from the outbreak of war but, because of its size and shape, could only be carried by a few of the larger aircraft; the smaller aircraft were provided with a special anti-submarine bomb. In July, 1940, however, bombs were abandoned for depth charges of naval design which were subsequently developed to ensure proper trajectories in both air and water. The depth charge was similarly the principal anti-submarine weapon of naval vessels, and even when the cause of a submarine loss is stated as from gunfire, or ramming, this was, in nearly all cases, brought about by submarines being first forced to the surface by depth charges before succumbing to a secondary cause. Submarines sunk by missiles from the Hedgehog or Squid ahead throwing mortar are also listed as being depth charged.

# SUBMARINE DEVELOPMENT: 1934–1939

Under the terms of the Treaty of Versailles Germany was not permitted to retain any submarines but later, when this treaty was abrogated, one of the first steps taken was to recreate the submarine arm of the German Navy. In 1934 the second, and greatest, submarine fleet the world had ever seen was re-established. Although over fifteen years had passed since submarines had been built in German shipyards, they were still rich with experience from the First World War, a factor no treaty could obliterate, nor had the German Navy been exactly idle in submarine design during the years the treaty had been in force. Two sea-going submarines[1] were built in the Netherlands in 1927 for Turkey; three sea-going and one coastal unit[2] were locally built in 1930/1 for the Finnish Navy; a further sea-going craft[3] was built in Spain in 1932 for Turkey; and the following year a coastal submarine[4] was

---

[1] *Birinci Inonu* and *Ikinci Inonu* (Wilton-Fijenoord) 505/620 tons.
[2] *Vetehinen, Vesihiisi* and *Iko-Turso* (Crichton-Vulkan) 490/715 tons, and *Saukko* (Hietalahden Laivatelakka) 100/136 tons.
[3] *Gur* (Echavarrieta y Larrinaga) 750/960 tons.
[4] *Vesikko* (Crichton-Vulkan) 250/300 tons.

again locally built for the Finnish Navy. All these submarines were of German design, albeit prepared outside their country of origin.

The experience gained with those eight boats, allied to that gained during the First World War, led the German naval staff to consider five basic types for the new submarine arm, viz.:

(*a*) sea-going craft of *ca.* 500–750 tons
(*b*) ocean-going craft of *ca.* 1,000 tons fitted for minelaying
(*c*) submarine-cruisers of *ca.* 1,500 tons
(*d*) coastal craft of *ca.* 250 tons
(*e*) coastal minelayers of *ca.* 500 tons

Successful prototypes had been tested for all five types. For the sea-going and coastal boats, for which there was the highest priority, there was the recent experience with the Turkish *Gur* and the Finnish *Vesikko*, while the ocean-going boats, the submarine-cruisers, and the coastal mine-layers could all draw on that obtained with the *U.81*, *U.151*, and *UC.80* types during the First World War.

The immediate need for sea-going and coastal craft was implemented by the construction of the types I and II. The type IA were 862-ton boats capable of speeds of $17\frac{3}{4}/8\frac{1}{4}$ knots with twin-shaft diesel/electric propulsion. They were armed with a 4.1inch and a 20mm A.A. guns and six torpedo tubes—four forward and two aft. The smaller type IIA were of 254 tons with speeds of 13/7 knots, and were armed with three bow torpedo tubes plus a single 20mm A.A. gun. The subsequent types IIB and IIC were closely similar but were progressively larger to accommodate additional bunkers. This was attended with a slight loss of speed as their twin-shaft diesel/electric machinery remained virtually unchanged. The rapidity with which these types were built, following Germany's declaration that they no longer considered themselves bound by the Treaty of Versailles, was a marked indication of their ability in this field: and if this fact was conveniently ignored by the British Government of the day, it certainly was not by the Royal Navy.

Factors to be taken into account were the improved methods of detecting submarines by both ships and aircraft. It is opportune to mention here that the salient fact relating to submarines built during this period, and for the greater part of the Second World War, was their limited radius of action when proceeding submerged[5]. They spent the greater part of their time on the surface and generally only submerged during daylight hours to escape detection, or in the closing stages of an attack. When their batteries were exhausted they were

[5] Usually limited to about one hour at full speed and between 12/24 hours, depending on type, at reduced speeds.

compelled to surface to recharge them and so, if they could be kept continually submerged, their effectiveness was greatly reduced owing to their extremely limited radius of action when dived. The use of maritime aircraft in this role is obvious as with their large field of vision they could continually harry submarines proceeding on the surface which would have little option except to dive once sighted, and then have no means of knowing when the watching aircraft had departed. It was not even necessary for aircraft to attack to be effective, although naturally they would do so if the opportunity occurred, but they could do little once the submarine had dived and subsequent detection and counter measures were the province of the anti-submarine vessels[6]. The pre-war radius of maritime aircraft was also limited but it did permit an effective coastal patrol to be maintained so that there would be little opportunity for coastal submarines, fitted with either mines or torpedoes, to emulate their counterparts of the First World War, in addition to which the mining of enemy coastal waters could be more efficiently undertaken by aircraft themselves. Thus the type II submarines were, from an early stage, mainly used for training purposes, while the requirement for a coastal minelayer was not pursued. This does not mean that submarine mining was completely dropped but only that the specific requirement for a coastal minelayer became superfluous. Practically every type of German submarine could carry mines in lieu of its outfit of torpedoes, and they were discharged via the torpedo tubes.

A novel requirement considered for the type III submarine, based on the type I design, was the carriage of two small MTBs in hangars abaft the conning tower. The MTBs were launched by the parent vessel flooding down until they were awash and could be floated out. However, as such an operation was completely dependent on suitable weather conditions their use was considered too restricted and the project was abandoned, but a similar idea was later taken up by the British, Italian and Japanese navies for the carriage of chariots[7]. Following three further projected designs, types IV, V and VI, which never progressed further than the drawing board, the next class put into production was the type VIIA sea-going boat: a general diminutive of type I which nevertheless met all staff requirements. This type turned out

[6] Although specific vessels were built for anti-submarine warfare practically any vessel could be pressed into this service whose speed exceeded 10 knots, a speed only a very few submarines could exceed when running submerged.
[7] These were manned torpedoes for penetrating defended enemy harbours and were fitted with detachable warheads for securing to ships found therein. They were transported by submarines close to their area of operations, and were stowed on the upper casing, either uncovered or in metal cylinders.

to be the principal operational unit of the German Navy and gave an excellent return within moderate dimensions. They also had the unhappy distinction of suffering one of the first and the last submarine losses to be sustained by the German Navy, proof in itself of their enduring high quality, while the first boat to surrender after the German capitulation also belonged to this class[8].

Another design project, type VIII, was interspersed between the next production type, the ocean-going type IXA. With the latter most of the additional size was taken up with more powerful diesel engines, considerably increased bunkerage, and double the number of torpedoes than carried by the type VIIA: all sound basic requirements for boats designed to to undertake prolonged patrols.

The next two designs, types XA and XI, completely eclipsed the type IX in size. The former was a large minelayer of 2,500 tons with mines carried in side shafts amidships, external to the pressure hull, and within the pressure hull aft. The type XI met the submarine-cruiser requirement and tonnage rose sharply to 3,140 tons with the pressure hull formed of two parallel cylinders set abreast. Designed to fight on the surface with guns they were armed with four 5inch guns in two twin turrets, one forward and one aft, while two 37mm and two 20mm A.A. pieces were grouped around the conning tower. Eight torpedo tubes (six forward and two aft) plus four reloads, and a scouting seaplane, rounded off the armament. Neither type was put into production. The internal arrangements of the type XA were considered uneconomical and a fresh design drawn up, while the limited use of the type XI was correctly gauged. Designed for 23 knots the latter would have proved the fastest and most powerful diesel-engined submarines in the world.

As noted above the type XA was abandoned for a fresh design, type XB, that was drawn up for a large ocean-going minelayer. Whereas the external mineshafts were retained on each side amidships, the internal ones were moved from aft to forward where two bow torpedo tubes were also incorporated. The six internal shafts forward could stow three mines apiece while the twenty-four amidship shafts (twelve a side) stowed two each. In spite of the considerable provision made for mining these craft were not often used in this role but principally in supplying submarines at sea with bunkers and provisions. This system of keeping raiders supplied at sea was not new to German tactics, but to widen the scope to include submarine raiders and then serve them with supply submarines was an unexpected turn of events which the

[8] *U.27* lost 30/9/39: *U.320* lost 7/5/45: *U.249* surfaced and surrendered off The Lizard 8/5/45 and then proceeded to Weymouth.

German Navy ably exploited, and used more extensively as the war progressed.

This was as far as the design stage had advanced up to the outbreak of hostilities in 1939, and the submarines building and completing by then are summarised below:

| | | |
|---|---|---|
| *Type IA:* | *U.25* and *26* | 2 |
| *Type IIA:* | *U.1–6* | 6 |
| *Type IIB:* | *U7.–24* | 18 |
| *Type IIC:* | *U.56–63* | 8 |
| *Type VIIA:* | *U27 -36* | 10 |
| *Type VIIB:* | *U.45–55* | 11 |
| *Type IXA:* | *U.37–44* | 8 |
| *Type IXB:* | *U.64* and *65* | 2 |
| | Total | 65 |

Following the outbreak of war construction was considerably stepped-up and, for the early stages, was mainly confined to types VIIB and C and IXB and C, the former predominating, although the initial programme was for a further series of type IID coastal craft fitted with saddle tanks and their radius of action further extended. At first, even the coastal boats were pressed into undertaking war patrols, but were soon diverted to training—an equally essential role considering the large submarine programme contemplated by Germany.

To meet the need for a mercantile submarine able to transport limited amounts of essential commodities to and from the Far East, modifications were effected with the type $IXC$ resulting in the type $IXD_1$. Lengthened by some 25 feet, they had a cargo deadweight of 252 tons, and could be used either as transport or supply submarines. Military requirements were sacrificed for cargo capacity, and although provision was originally made to ship torpedo tubes these, together with their weighty control arrangements, were finally omitted; part of the battery was removed as submerged endurance was not so vitally important; and only a defensive gun armament carried on deck. Intended at first for operational service they had been fitted with three MTB type fast running diesel engines per shaft, totalling B.H.P. 9,000 for a speed of $20\frac{3}{4}$ knots, but these had proved unsatisfactory and had been removed and replaced by a lower powered slower running installation more suited to their transport role.

The military version of the above was the type $IXD_2$, similarly intended for Far Eastern operations. By fitting two diesel engines per shaft the power was practically doubled, and the bunkerage more than doubled to give them the widest radius of action possessed by any German submarine. This radius was further extended by the addition of two diesel-generators, of combined B.H.P. 1,000, which increased their range to 31,500 miles at 10 knots using diesel-electric drive. With engines and bunkers absorbing a great deal of the available space the armament was not relatively heavy and comprised six torpedo tubes (four forward and two aft) and eighteen reloads while the surface gun, for which there was a much greater scope in more distant waters, was curiously discarded for a more numerous light A.A. armament. They may be regarded as the culmination of German submarine design and were the final conventional boats to be put into production, and were the largest and fastest of this type.

Following the initial war programme, which was basically aimed at numerically expanding the submarine arm with as little deviation from standard types as possible, came the second phase of expansion which incorporated war experience and led to more diversification of type. Existing type designs were modified to suit new and changing requirements in the manner calculated to least impede the flow of production. Thus, the types VII and IX, to instance two large production examples, passed through many modifications until the stage was reached that the basic design needed entire recasting so that equipment, space, and weight could be reallocated to better advantage; but always with the proviso that an uninterrupted flow of production was the prime consideration.

Designs which resulted in production difficulties could not be entertained, and the German Navy was not alone in following this line as an examination of the Allied naval war construction clearly showed. Having once adopted a new design, however, the German Navy ruthlessly cut back on the construction of the type supplanted, which accounts for the large blocks of cancelled orders which occur in the tabulated lists. Further, the individual numbers allocated to submarines of a particular type were spread over a wide range, and did not follow a strict chronological sequence, as part of a deliberate policy to confuse the Allied naval command. This resulted in submarines receiving high numbering being completed well in advance of lower numbered boats of differing type.

The German submarines soon found that counter measures were far more effective than in the First World War, and that the Royal Navy was as skilled in anti-submarine warfare as they were in waging submarine war. Maritime aircraft, operating both on their own and in conjunction with naval forces, confirmed the high hopes held pre-war as to their effectiveness. They rapidly denied to German submarines the use of U.K. coastal waters, but this was more than offset following the tragic events of 1940 when, after overruning continental Europe, the German Navy was able to deploy its submarines from a long stretch of coastline extending from the North Cape to the French Biscay ports. Nor was the overall position eased by the entry of Italy into the war on the German side or the loss of the British ally, France. In addition, the threat of invasion now hung over the British Isles resulting in a concentration of naval forces in Home waters which temporarily greatly reduced the number of vessels available for convoy escort and anti-submarine duties.

The introduction of escort carriers in 1941 greatly extended the range of maritime aircraft but they were woefully short in numbers in the first instance. Their introduction did mean, that convoys, when they were available, could proceed under continuous air cover to their dispersal points, and it was not until after the entry of the United States into the war that they were made available in anything approaching sufficient numbers.

When radar was sufficiently developed so that an ASV set[9] could be fitted to aircraft they enjoyed an unparalleled success against German submarines which lacked any form of radar. No longer dependent on visual sighting alone, aircraft were able to detect and attack submarines proceeding on the surface under conditions which the latter normally accepted as safe: such as at night, or in overcast conditions. Consequently, submarines proceeding to and from their patrol areas suffered losses comparable to those in the open sea, outside the range of aircraft, where naval escort vessels, worked-up to matchless war-acquired efficiency, were dealing them similar heavy blows. It is not intended to digress here on submarine or anti-submarine tactics, which were continually varied on both sides to meet ever changing conditions, but only to indicate the effect they had on German submarine development.

To withstand concentrated air attacks the initial answer lay in augmenting the anti-aircraft armament of submarines. This led to the removal of the low-angle gun shipped for surface use and the addition of several light A.A. pieces on the conning tower, which was extended to accommodate them, and was also armoured as a measure of protection against shell-firing aircraft. Below is tabulated the progressively increasing A.A. armament fitted to the type VIIC boats to meet the threat from the air. Originally mounting a 3.5inch gun before the conning tower, and a single 20mm A.A. abaft it, supplemented by two 30-calibre machine guns, the surface gun was taken out and the A.A. armament increased to:

[9] Initial development with radar had utilised the decimetre wavelengths. Whereas Germany had not pursued their experiments in the shorter wavebands Great Britain had done so and went, step by step, to shorter and shorter wavelengths which enabled radar sets compact enough to be fitted into aircraft to be produced.

(*a*) two 20mm (2 × 1) guns
(*b*) four 20mm (2 × 2) guns
(*c*) one 37mm and four 20mm (2 × 2) guns
(*d*) eight 20mm (1 × 4 and 2 × 2) guns
(*e*) two 37mm (2 × 1) and four 20mm (2 × 2) guns
(*f*) four 37mm (4 × 1) guns

The same modifications were extended to operational units of all types put into production up to type X, with the exception of the small units of type II which were limited to four 20mm A.A. (2 × 2) guns and only when operationally employed, and a quantity of armour plating was worked into the conning tower to protect the bridge personnel and guns' crews. These measures were partly but not wholly effective, led to some diminution of loss from air attack, and resulted in maritime aircraft shipping guns of heavier calibre (40mm in place of 20mm) with which to engage submarines outside the effective range of their guns. The ultimate step was to provide Mosquito aircraft with 6-pounder guns. Later, rockets supplemented the guns in aircraft and had the added advantage that they could be fitted to smaller aircraft that could not otherwise accommodate the 40mm gun.

A more passive and less effective measure was the fitting of a radar detecting receiver which indicated whether radar was being operated in the vicinity. This was switched on when surfaced or surfacing and if it gave a positive indication, the submarine dived until it could surface in an area free of radar emissions. In spite of the technical capability of Germany—especially in the electronics field—they were unable to produce a suitable radar set for their submarines which blunted their most potent weapon at sea[10].

The third measure—and by far the most successful—to halt the slaughter from the air was the *schnorchel*, or air-mast, enabling submarines to remain submerged for longer periods, as it was only in the ocean depths that they could seek immunity. A somewhat similar installation had been tried in 1938 in the Royal Netherlands Navy submarine *O.19*, but principally as a means of ventilating the boat, while the German adoption was far more embracing and entailed using the *schnorchel* as an air supply so that the main diesel engines could be run while submerged. By this means the prime need to surface to recharge batteries was eliminated and, if forced to go deep by surface vessels, submarines could descend to

[10] This situation was primarily brought about by a High Command order in 1940 that restricted all research on technical projects that could not be completed in one year. At that time the German Navy was investigating centimetre wavebands for radar, and could only subsequently pursue their investigations with limited facilities.

the depths and run on their electric motors with the comforting thought that they had a full charge in their batteries. The use of the *schnorchel* had, however, one inherent drawback in that speed was restricted to about 6 knots while it was being used. If the submarine was to remain submerged for the whole of her patrol she lost the tactical advantage of speed and her sphere of operations was severely curtailed. If the *schnorchel* aided the survival of submarines it was only at the severe cost that a craft of wide tactical deployment was now reduced to a still unseen, but crawling, hunter with restricted day vision, limited to the periscope, and quite blind at night as the noise of the diesel engines rendered the hydrophones useless. They could only regain their mobility by coming to the surface, but that was to court disaster, and the only answer lay in the "true" submarine capable of high and prolonged speed submerged with machinery independent of the atmosphere.

Equally important was the effect on morale with the use of the *schnorchel*. Its use was accompanied by some discomfort to the crew at a time when they had to be specially alert to maintain a good trim, owing to the sharply varying air pressure. Moreover there was the cramping effect it had on initiative as, at the slow speed to which the submarine was reduced, there could be no selection of target and no manoeuvre to obtain an attacking advantage. But in this respect the resilience of the German crews was equal to the occasion, and their sagging morale was boosted as their technique improved. By 1943 most existing German operational submarines had been equipped with *schnorchel* which was, of course, a built-in requirement with new construction.

The ubiquitous type VII, which had already progressed through three marks before the outbreak of war, was taken a stage further with the type VIID. With this type an additional 25-foot section was added abaft the conning tower and fitted with five vertical mine shafts able to stow three mines apiece. These shafts, like those fitted forward in the type XB, projected above and below the pressure hull and were free-flooding. Less successful was the type VIIE project which was based around a new type of engine that, it was anticipated, would result in considerable saving in machinery weight. However, as the engine failed to materialise the project proceeded no farther. As mentioned earlier the German Navy, to extend the radius of their operational submarines, had developed supply submarines to bunker and provision these units at sea. These tactics were further advanced by the type VIIF. They were generally similar to the type VIID except that the additional section was fitted with a hatch and carried twenty-five torpedoes in lieu of mines. The transfer of torpedoes at sea, however, proved a risky operation as it necessitated both submarines being on the surface with hatches open and a large number of the crew employed on the upper deck. In this state they were wide open to sudden attack by aircraft with little opportunity to rapidly dive, and consequently the idea found little favour afloat. Therefore the type VIIF were mainly used as torpedo transports from base-to-base rather that replenishing the boats at sea.

# SUBMARINE DEVELOPMENT: 1939–1945

The desire to possess fleet submarines had, at one time or another, obsessed most of the major navies, and the German Navy was no exception. The existence of the fleet submarine had hardly ever been justified by any firm requirement and it was somewhat surprising to note that, with the type XII, this project was again considered by the German Navy while fully engaged in a war of attrition on Allied sea-borne trade. Based on the type IX hull, power was raised to B.H.P./S.P.H. 7,000/1,680 for higher speeds of 22/10 knots, together with a large radius of action on the surface. Not surprisingly the project was not advanced, and paradoxically the following project, type XIII, swung the other way and was a design developed from the type II coastal boat enlarged to *ca.* 400 tons with greater surface speed. The type XIII could hardly supplant the type VII, a sea-going boat of the minimum size which could most certainly not afford to make any sacrifice in tonnage, and was unreasonably larger than the type II, which quite satisfactorily met training requirements, and as a result this study too was dropped.

The next three types were all supply submarines, and indicated the increasing importance attached to this role by the German Navy. The type XIV—known as the "broad beam" supply boats—were considerably shorter, but much beamier and deeper, than the type IXD$_1$, and had a much improved cargo oil deadweight of 432 tons, plus four externally stowed torpedoes, and showed the advantage of a specially designed supply type over an adapted war boat. Types XV and XVI were much more ambitious projects intended to supply bunkers, stores, and torpedoes, as well as possessing workshop facilities for undertaking limited repairs. The former adopted a triple cylinder (all set abreast) hull form and had a displacement of *ca.* 2,500 tons, while the latter doubled this displacement while retaining the same hull form. But by the time these designs were prepared the ever increasing number of maritime aircraft fitted with radar had, within their sphere of action, practically driven the submarine from the surface and, for practical purposes, supplying submarines at sea had become a hazardous undertaking.

Long before maritime aircraft had made the surface so unsafe for submarines, the German Navy had been experimenting with closed-cycle engines with the object of producing a "true" submarine: one that could operate continuously submerged with a speed and radius comparable to that of the diesel-engined boats. War had naturally given impetus to these experiments, and the critical year of 1943 now made imperative the successful conclusion of this prolonged research work if German submarines were to continue to operate in the radically changed conditions that now existed. In fact, the very survival of submarines was at stake, and the introduction of the *schnorchel* could only be regarded as a stop gap measure at the best. The most promising development lay in the Walter turbine, which had been fitted in the experimental submarine *V.80* as long back as 1940, but this installation had encountered many difficulties which were never completely overcome although sufficient success had been obtained to merit its adoption.

The essence of the Walter system was a closed-circuit turbine activated by the thermal energy produced by the decomposition of a high concentration of hydrogen peroxide (perhydrol). This resulted in the formation of hot gas under considerable natural pressure quite sufficient in itself to drive a turbine. The system was a complex one by which the perhydrol was forced up by water pressure from its containers stowed at the bottom of the hull to a porcelain-lined chamber where it encountered the catalyst necessary to bring about its decomposition. This resulted in steam and oxygen at a high temperature ($1,765°F$) which passed to a combustion chamber where they met to ignite the oil fuel, while water was sprayed on the gas to increase its volume and descrease its temperature (to $986°F$). This combination of gas and steam was then led to the turbine, and from there to the condenser, where the water was extracted and the residual carbon dioxide generated in the combustion chamber drawn off.

The greatest difficulties, however, arose with the manufacture and storage of the perhydrol which reacted powerfully with any impurity present. This latter could serve as a catalytic agent, causing decomposition and a rise of temperature until spontaneous combustion resulted. Absolute clinical cleanliness was essential in preparing and storing the concentrate (which was expensive to produce, costing approximately eight times as much as fuel oil), and after a variety of tests flexible synthetic rubber was found to be the most suitable storage container. For submarine propulsion a further advantage of the Walter system, beside it being quite independent of external air, was its power/weight ratio of about $11\frac{1}{4}$ lb./S.H.P. which resulted in a compact unit, but this was rather offset by its high rate of consumption at full speed.

The first naval boat to receive the Walter turbine, the *U.791*, had a two-shaft installation developing S.H.P. 4,360 for a speed of 19 knots. The boat was not, in the final instance, commissioned, but proved a suitable test bed from which to plan a production series. Conventional diesel/electric drive was also provided to expand the radius which, at full speed, was limited to a little over 200 miles with the Walter turbine.

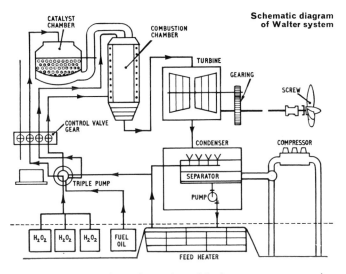

Schematic diagram of Walter system

The type XVII, therefore, heralded a new generation of German submarines, and were coastal boats with only a single shaft to which was coupled two Walter geared turbines and the normal diesel/electric motors. The designed speed of 26 knots with the turbines was not evidently quite attained, but this in no way detracted from what was otherwise a major advance in submarine propulsion. The two succeeding types, types XVIIB and XVIIG, were slightly larger but the former only had one geared turbine coupled to the single shaft, although two had been originally intended, but even then the submerged speed was in excess of 20 knots. The type XVIIK used a closed-cycle diesel engine drawing on stored oxygen but was far less successful than the turbine boats, and none was finally completed. Limited success with the Walter system then inspired the ocean-going type XVIII with turbines coupled to two shafts together with diesel/electric motors as well. This too rapid advance, however, outstripped progress and the project had to be abandoned.

With the type XVII submarines surface sea-keeping characteristics were now subjugated to secure the form of hull least resistful for submerged propulsion. This took a "figure-of-eight" shape, the lower cylinder having a much smaller radius than the upper one, and the deck casing—so long a conspicuous feature of the conventional boats—was much reduced in size. The hull form adopted, with a L:B ratio of 10:1 was too long and thin for optimum performance submerged, but it dispensed with all restriction on draught that had applied to the conventional boats, which would otherwise have imposed a needless restriction on boats intended to operate continuously submerged.

Types XIX and XX again reverted to transport submarines: principally brought about by the economic crisis in certain essential raw materials. The former was a submarine tanker of *ca.* 2,000 tons with a double cylinder (set abreast) hull form, but whose development was arrested by diesel engines of new design which failed to materialise. The type XX was an even larger craft of *ca.* 2,700 tons which had a cargo deadweight of 800 tons, and was primarily intended to carry rubber from the Far East. Normal diesel/electric propulsion to two shafts was adopted, but their construction was later halted owing to deficiencies that subsequently arose in more essential categories.

Although the Walter turbine held great promise for the not too distant future, this nevertheless left a void between the *schnorchel*-fitted submarines and the Walter boats which had to be bridged until the latter could be further developed, as their complex machinery installation was not completely satisfactory, and to this was added the difficulties experienced in the manufacture of perhydrol. This resulted in the type XXI, a conventional but nevertheless outstanding submarine whose design embraced accumulated war experience and which proved to be a most formidable adversary for Allied anti-submarine forces.

The basic design was for a boat that could operate silently and continuously submerged with conventional propulsion, in which submerged performance took priority over that on the surface, and to this end the hull was fully streamlined and had a figure-of-eight form. The power of the electric motors was greatly increased, the battery capacity trebled to extend the radius submerged and, known as the "all electric boat", the two-shaft diesel/electric machinery developed B.H.P./ S.H.P. 4,000/5,000 for speeds of $15\frac{1}{2}/16$ knots. They were, naturally, equipped with *schnorchel*—principally to run their diesel engines submerged for battery charging—and, in addition, had silent electric motors coupled to each shaft with which they could proceed at a creep speed of about

5 knots. To speed production the hull was prefabricated in eight welded sections in 15 shipyards which were then transported to three main yards for welded assembly and completion. A marked feature of all German submarines to this date had been the paucity of comfort provided for the crew, but it was recognised that the type XXI would operate under arduous conditions and they were, in consequence, air-conditioned—the first German submarines to be so equipped. A special power-operated twin 30mm anti-aircraft mounting was prepared for these boats but few, if any, were so fitted owing to production difficulties, and they had to make do with the lighter twin 20mm mounting. There was, however, no deficiency with the torpedo armament, which comprised six bow tubes together with seventeen internally-stowed reloads. To speed production on the type XXI all work on boats of types VII, IX, XVI and XX then under construction or on order was halted, and building capacity diverted to the new boats.

Studies were also made of modifications to the basic type XXI design but they were not actively pursued as they would have disrupted the flow of production. The types XXIB and XXIC were slightly altered to increase the torpedo armament, while the types XXID, XXIE, XXIT and XXIV were supply submarines incorporating as much of the basic type XXI material as possible. Experiments with underwater refuelling had been conducted with the *UD.5* (the former Royal Netherlands Navy submarine *O.27*), but the stage had not yet been reached which envisaged the employment of supply submarines also able to operate continuously submerged.

Another return was made to the turbine boat with the type XXII, a single-shaft coastal boat of 155 tons. But a coastal boat adopting type XXI features, proportionately scaled down, was a more attractive proposition, so that the type XXII project was shelved for the type XXIII, which were very austere diminutives of the type XXI. Their construction was arranged on the same lines as their larger prototypes, and their figure-of-eight hull form was similarly fabricated in four sections at various yards and taken to two main shipyards for welded assembly. They proved to be very difficult to detect, and were armed with only two bow tubes into which the torpedoes were loaded externally by raising the bows sufficiently clear of the water with a crane.

The type XXIV was yet another return to the turbine boat, and this time of ocean-going size, with the displacement running up to 1,800 tons and a twin-shaft arrangement of machinery. The prepared design could hardly be more successful than the smaller coastal boats which, if in no way a failure, were no better than an unqualified success at this stage, and consequently the type XXIV was never put into production. The original provision was for eighteen torpedo tubes, disposed six in the bow and six on each side, but this was decreased to twelve tubes by halving the number carried on the broadside. Few details are available on the succeeding type XXV all-electric coastal boat, while the type XXVI was a reduced edition of the type XXIV with only one turbine coupled to a single shaft. Far less dependence was placed on the secondary diesel/electric propulsion with this type but a separate diesel-generator was provided. They were armed with ten torpedo tubes, four in the bow and six on the broadside: the latter being angled 10 deg. from the centre line; increased to twelve tubes (six bow and six sided) in the types XXVIA and XXVIB. Generally similar were the types XXVIE/F/G in which conventional propulsion supplanted the turbine, no conning tower was fitted, and the torpedo tubes, reduced to eight, were equally disposed in the bow and sides. Neither types, however, advanced further than the planning stage.

The types XXVIIA and XXVIIB were the largest of the midget craft built by the German Navy, and had the distinction of being awarded type numbers. The type XXVIIA, originally intended as a minelayer, was never operationally employed and was relegated to training at an early stage in its development, while the torpedo-armed type XXVIIB was primarily built for anti-invasion duties and to be used against ship targets. Although production of these midget craft was planned on a large scale there was little use for them after the Allied invasion of the European continent had been mounted. They showed the limited capabilities of midget craft which, outside of a specific role, have no general purpose function. They were, however, the highest type number put into production, and all subsequent types were no more than projects that could not be fulfilled, but were nevertheless interesting in indicating the future trend had not hostilities been brought to a close.

Not without reason the German Navy had pinned great faith on their types XXI and XXIII, but they were developed too late to swing the tide of events. There is no denying that they were formidable craft, and that their earlier introduction might have resulted in unforeseen possibilities, but the inescapable fact was that they came too late. As far as is known only two of type XXI and seven of type XXIII made operational patrols, although large numbers had been completed but were still working-up.

In briefly covering the remaining types of projected German submarine designs, it must be recalled that production difficulties steadily increased as the Second World War moved to a close in Europe. Round-the-clock bombing relentlessly wore down manufacturing capacity, and interrupted transport facilities on which the mass-produced types were vitally dependent. Under such conditions, with the addition of hostile armies advancing on two frontiers, the German Navy could not embark on any long-term project, and design was governed more by what was available rather than what was needed. None the less, some of the following projects showed a detachment from reality which was remarkable for the times.

Another attempt at a closed-cycle coastal turbine boat of *ca.* 200 tons was made with the type XXVIII on which relatively few details are available, and whose design was not greatly advanced. The type XXIX, however, reverted to conventional diesel/electric propulsion for a sea-going boat, and the principal object of the design was to enlarge the submerged radius of action. Types XXIXA, XXIXB and XXIXC had the output of the electric motors progressively increased, but were uniformly armed with eight bow torpedo tubes. This armament was increased to twelve tubes in the type XXIXD and XXIXG, the additional tubes being added on the broadside, but was reduced to six tubes in the type XXIXH. All these types had a diesel generator provided which could supply current to the electric motors so that both main diesel and electric motors could be run simultaneously, when the need arose, without drawing on the batteries for the latter. The types $XXIXK_{1/4}$ adopted closed-cycle diesel engines for main propulsion.

The ocean-going craft of types XXX and XXXI were expanded type XXI designs: the former having no conning tower, and the latter a low conning tower with a very short figure-of-eight hull form. Machinery and armament was the same in both types and comprised diesel/electric motors coupled to a single-shaft and twelve torpedo tubes, eight forward and four on the broadside. The succeeding type XXXII was an ocean-going boat whose design was not completed in detail. A closed-cycle engine was chosen for the type XXXIII, a coastal boat fitted with four bow torpedo tubes and two re-loads, while displacement dropped to under 100 tons with the type XXXIV which were powered by a closed cycle MTB type fast-running diesel engine for a submerged speed of 22 knots, and was armed with two torpedoes carried externally in clamps. The type XXXV was the final attempt with the Walter turbine, and was a single shaft sea-going boat of *ca.* 850 tons armed with eight torpedo tubes, six forward and two aft, and the type XXXVI also embraced a closed-cycle machinery installation comprising four MTB type fast running diesel engines coupled to two shafts.

No further serious design studies appear to have been undertaken after this, but it was apparent that the German Navy strived hard to perfect a closed-cycle engine which would provide them with a "true" submarine they so urgently needed. They sought the solution in the final stages with submarines ranging from 90 tons to 1,200 tons, whereby they would have continued to contest the issue, from below the surface, in coastal waters, in the narrow seas, and on the wider oceans.

In spite of enduring calamitous losses the German submarine arm, to quote from the British official account *The Battle of the Atlantic*, fought "to the very end . . . with discipline and efficiency. There was no relaxation of effort or hesitation to incur risks." Over 39,000 officers and men served in German submarines, and of these some 32,000 were killed in action: a high proportion of loss that was unequalled in any other branch of the armed forces of any of the belligerents involved in the Second World War. In 1940. Admiral Dönitz had said ". . . the U-boat alone can win this war . . . nothing is impossible . . ." He was nearly right.

## SPECIAL MODIFICATIONS

Examination of the U-Boats surrendered at Lisahally showed that a number of interesting features had been tried out in different boats.

*Schnorchel* masts varied from the normal hinging type forward of the conning tower, in the Type VIIC, IXC and $IXD_2$. *U.255* was selected to try a fixed mast, and was subsequently used for training. Some vessels had the induction pipe taken down to the heel of the mast. It is interesting to note that this type of mast had been tried in HMS *Truant* by June 1945. The Type XXI and XXIII boats had the "periscope" type mast, with induction and exhaust pipes going through separate glands but the whole being raised by rack and pinion on one tube.

There were three types of valve, the ball float valve as already tried in the *Truant*, the ring float valve, and the electro-pneumatic valve. The ball float valves were often covered with corrugated rubber and coated with aluminium paint. Ring float valves were covered similarly, or with unpainted wood fitted in 2 in. $\times$ $\frac{1}{2}$ in. strips, or a painted plastic material. The electro-pneumatic type normally had the corrugated rubber covering. All these expedients were adopted to reduce the echo on a centimetric radar set, but were of limited effectiveness.

The Type XXI Boats adopted a novel torpedo-reloading system to reduce the time taken to fire a second salvo. Two pairs of inclined arms on either side of the torpedo room carried three torpedoes each. Beneath these were a further pair of arms on either side, supported from below and carrying two torpedoes. There was stowage on the centreline on the bottom of the pressure hull, making a total of 23 torpedoes carried, including the six in the tubes.

To conserve battery power as much as possible the Type XXI boats ran the capstan, torpedo-loading warping barrel and main vents off the High Pressure Air System, but this idea was hindered by the unreliable Junker compressors carried. The telemotor system ran the periscopes, tilted and housed the hydroplanes, steered the boat and worked the bow caps to the torpedo tubes, whereas the older U-Boats used electric motors for this purpose.

After preliminary trials with the Type XXI it was proposed to blank off some of the free-flooding holes for increased speed (and also silence, if post-war experience is anything to go by). The supercharger was to be removed as it had been found impossible to draw in enough air when using the *schnorchel*. The underwater exhaust was to be moved above the waterline as the M.A.N. 6-cylinder diesel ran better without back pressure. Direct telemotor power was to be provided from the control room to the forward and after hydroplanes, in place of a local valve operated by the control room telemotor. These changes had all been incorporated in the prototype *U.2502* and would have been made in the other boats.

The other innovation in the later U-boats was automatic depth-keeping and trimming, which acted like an automatic pilot in an aircraft to reduce fatigue during normal running. The IXC and IXD$_2$ U-boats often had the foredeck cut away to reduce the diving time. The original U-boat designs emphasised a broad flat casing to facilitate a good turn of speed on the surface, but when the aircraft menace became acute in 1942/3 this was found to be a severe disadvantage. The broad casing acted like a plane, and made the boat "stick"; by reducing the area of the casing the diving time could be cut from 45 seconds to 33 seconds, a vital factor in reducing losses. By comparison British submarines had always had narrow deck-casings, and the "S" Class could dive in about 25 seconds in good conditions.

Some periscopes were fitted with a device to reduce "feathering", the tell-tale plume of spray. Two circular clamps about 32 inches apart were bolted to the conical upper part of the periscope, and five 1-cm wires were wound in a spiral around the periscope between them.

One Type VIIC boat, *U.1105* (known as the Black Panther) had her hull coated entirely with rubber, excepting the wooden deck, in an attempt to absorb Asdic pulses. The thickness was about $\frac{3}{16}$ in., but in two layers, of which the bottom one was perforated.

## *Type IA:* **U.25** and **U.26**

Sea-going boats, based on the Turkish *Gur*, which were used for training prior to the outbreak of the Second World War, but were then employed operationally.

*Displacement:* 862/983 tons
*Dimensions:* 237½ × 20¼ × 14 feet
*Machinery:* 2-shaft diesel/electric motors, B.H.P./S.H.P. 2,800/ 1,000 = 17¾/8¼ knots
*Bunkers & Radius:* O.F. 96 tons; 6,700/78 miles at 12/4 knots
*Armament:* One 4.1inch, one 20mm A.A. guns; six 21inch torpedo tubes (four fwd and two aft—fourteen torpedoes)
*Complement:* 43
*Notes:* A.A. armament not augmented although provision made for shipping it

*U.25 (Type IA) was the prototype for future seagoing types, and was based on the Turkish* Gur. **(IWM)**

Above: U.2, *a Type IIA coastal submarine seen in rough weather pre-war.* (Associated Press)

Right: *The 1st U-Boat Flotilla (known as the Weddigen Flotilla) with their depot ship* Saar. (Drüppel)

## Type IIA: **U.1–U.6**

Coastal boats, based on the UB II series of the First World War and the Finnish *Vesikko*, and mainly used for training owing to limited radius.

*Displacement:* 254/303 tons
*Dimensions:* $134\frac{1}{4} \times 13\frac{1}{2} \times 12\frac{1}{2}$ feet
*Machinery:* 2-shaft diesel/electric motors, B.H.P./S.H.P. 700/
　　360 = 13/7 knots

*Bunkers & Radius:* O.F. 12 tons; 1,050/35 at 12/4 knots
*Armament:* One 20mm A.A. gun; three 21inch torpedo tubes
  (all fwd—six torpedoes or eight mines)
*Complement:* 25
*Notes:* A.A. armament increased to four 20mm (2 × 2) guns
  when operationally employed

*U.9 (Type IIB) shows distinctive features of pre-war U-Boats: net cutter forward and D/F loop forward of the conning tower. (IWM)*

## *Type IIB:* **U.7–U.24, U.120 and U.121**

Improved type IIA, with bunkers and radius increased, and mainly used for training.

*Displacement:* 279/329 tons
*Dimensions:* 140 × $13\frac{1}{2}$ × $12\frac{3}{4}$ feet
*Machinery:* 2-shaft diesel/electric motors, B.H.P./S.H.P.
  700/360 = 13/7 knots
*Bunkers & Radius:* O.F. 21 tons; 1,300/43 miles at 12/4 knots
*Armament:* One 20mm A.A. gun; three 21inch torpedo tubes
  (all fwd—six torpedoes or eight mines)
*Complement:* 25
*Notes:* A.A. armament increased to four 20mm (2 × 2) guns
  when operationally employed. *U.120* and *U.121* were building
  for the Royal Yugoslav Navy when acquired on the outbreak
  of the Second World War. Their conning towers differed from
  those fitted in type IIB, and were generally similar to those in
  type IID

*L. to r.* U.9, U.8 *and* U.11
*(Type IIB) pre-war.*
(Drüppel)

## Type IIC: **U.56–U.63**

Improved type IIB, with bunkers and radius increased, and slightly more powerful electric motors. Mainly used for training.

*Displacement:* 291/341 tons
*Dimensions:* 144 × 13¾ × 12½ feet
*Machinery:* 2-shaft diesel/electric motors, B.H.P./S.H.P. 700/410
    = 12/7 knots
*Bunkers & Radius:* O.F. 23 tons; 1,900/43 miles at 12/4 knots
*Armament:* One 20mm A.A. gun; three 21inch torpedo tubes
    (all fwd—six torpedoes or eight mines)
*Complement:* 25
*Notes:* A.A. armament increased to four 20mm (2 × 2) guns
    when operationally employed

## Type IID: **U.137–U.152**

Improved type IIC, with addition of saddle tanks, part of which were used to increase bunkers and radius. Initially used for coastal patrols, but were later relegated to training.

*Displacement:* 314/364 tons
*Dimensions:* 144¼ × 16 × 12¾ feet
*Machinery:* 2-shaft diesel/electric motors, B.H.P./S.H.P. 700/410
    = 12¾/7¼ knots
*Bunkers & Radius:* O.F. 38 tons; 3,500/56 miles at 12/4 knots
*Armament:* One 20mm A.A. gun; three 21inch torpedo tubes
    (all fwd—six torpedoes or eight mines)
*Complement:* 25

*L. to r.* U.23, U.15, U.16, U.12 *and* U.14, *with* U.20 *etc. behind.* (Drüppel)

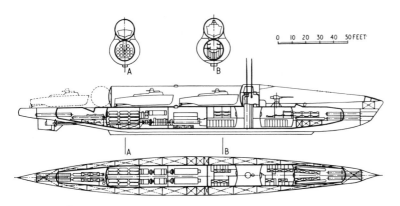

*Type III*

## Type III.

A design prepared in 1933, basically similar to type IA, with arrangements for carrying two small 10-ton MTBs in circular hangars abaft the conning tower. These boats were launched by flooding down the submarine until they were waterborne in their hangar, and they were then floated out. As this was essentially a smooth water operation the scope of this type was considered too limited, and the design was not proceeded with further.

*Displacement:* Not known
*Dimensions:* $254\frac{1}{4} \times 26\frac{1}{4} \times 17$ feet
*Machinery:* 2-shaft diesel/electric motors, B.H.P./S.H.P. 2,800/1,000 = 17/8 knots
*Bunkers & Radius:* Not known
*Armament:* One 4.1inch gun; six 21inch torpedo tubes (four fwd and two aft—eight torpedoes); two MTBs
*Complement:* 65 (inc. MTB crews)

## Types IV, V and VI.

Various projected designs not proceeded with and for which no details are available.

### TYPE IIA

**Name** *U.1* **Built by** Deutsche Werke (Kiel) **Launched** 15.6.35
**Fate** Torpedoed RN submarine *Porpoise* south-west of Stavanger 16.4.40

**Name** *U.2* **Built by** Deutsche Werke (Kiel) **Launched** 1.7.35
**Fate** Lost by collision west of Pillau 8.4.44

**Name** *U.3* **Built by** Deutsche Werke (Kiel) **Launched** 19.7.35
**Fate** Surrendered 5.45 and scrapped

**Name** *U.4* **Built by** Deutsche Werke (Kiel) **Launched** 31.7.35
**Fate** Surrendered 5.45 and scrapped

**Name** *U.5* **Built by** Deutsche Werke (Kiel) **Launched** 14.8.35
**Fate** Lost by collision west of Pillau 19.3.43

**Name** *U.6* **Built by** Deutsche Werke (Kiel) **Launched** 21.8.35
**Fate** Surrendered 5.45 and scrapped

### TYPE IIB

**Name** *U.7* **Built by** Germania Werft (Kiel) **Launched** 29.6.35
**Fate** Lost by collision west of Pillau 18.2.44

**Name** *U.8* **Built by** Germania Werft (Kiel) **Launched** 16.7.35
**Fate** Scuttled Kiel 5.45

**Name** *U.9* **Built by** Germania Werft (Kiel) **Launched** 30.7.35
**Fate** Bombed Russian aircraft Constanta 20.8.44

*The Type VIIA was the prototype for the standard model of wartime U-Boat. l. to r. U.34, U.28, U.29, U.30 and U.36. (Drüppel)*

**Name** *U.10* **Built by** Germania Werft (Kiel) **Launched** 13.8.35
**Fate** Surrendered 5.45 and scrapped

**Name** *U.11* **Built by** Germania Werft (Kiel) **Launched** 27.8.35
**Fate** Surrendered 5.45 and scrapped

**Name** *U.12* **Built by** Germania Werft (Kiel) **Launched** 11.9.35
**Fate** Mined Dover Straits 8.10.39

**Name** *U.13* **Built by** Deutsche Werke (Kiel) **Launched** 9.11.35
**Fate** Depth charged RN sloop *Weston* 31.5.40

**Name** *U.14* **Built by** Deutsche Werke (Kiel) **Launched** 18.12.35
**Fate** Scuttled Wilhelmshaven 2.5.45

**Name** *U.15* **Built by** Deutsche Werke (Kiel) **Launched** 15.2.36
**Fate** Lost collision with German torpedo boat *Iltis* Baltic 1.2.40

**Name** *U.16* **Built by** Deutsche Werft (Kiel) **Launched** 28.4.36
**Fate** Mined Goodwins 24.10.39 after being depth charged by RN
sloop *Puffin* and trawler *Cayton Wyke* on 23.10.39

**Name** *U.17* **Built by** Deutsche Werke (Kiel) **Launched** 14.11.35
**Fate** Scuttled Wilkelmshaven 5.45

**Name** *U.18* **Built by** Deutsche Werke (Kiel) **Launched** 7.12.35
**Fate** Scuttled Constanza 10.9.44; salved and used by Russians for
training; scrapped (1960)

**Name** *U.19* **Built by** Deutsche Werke (Kiel) **Launched** 21.12.35
**Fate** Scuttled Black Sea (off Turkish coast) 10.9.44

**Name** *U.20* **Built by** Deutsche Werke (Kiel) **Launched** 14.1.36
**Fate** Scuttled Black Sea (off Turkish coast) 10.9.44

**Name** *U.21* **Built by** Deutsche Werke (Kiel) **Launched** 13.7.36
**Fate** Paid-off Neustadt 5.8.44; scrapped 2.45

**Name** *U.22* **Built by** Deutsche Werke (Kiel) **Launched** 29.7.36
**Fate** Mined Skagerrak 25.4.40

**Name** *U.23* **Built by** Deutsche Werke (Kiel) **Launched** 28.8.36
**Fate** Scuttled Black Sea (off Turkish coast) 10.9.44

**Name** *U.24* **Built by** Deutsche Werke (Kiel) **Launched** 24.9.36
**Fate** Scuttled Constanza 10.9.44; salved by Russians for training

**TYPE IA**
**Name** *U.25* **Built by** AG Weser (Bremen) **Launched** 14.2.36
**Fate** Mined north of Terschelling 3.8.40

**Name** *U.26* **Built by** AG Weser (Bremen) **Launched** 14.3.36
**Fate** Depth charged RN corvette *Gladiolus* and RAAF aircraft
(10 Sqn.) south-west of Bishops Rock 3.7.40

## TYPE VIIA

**Name** *U.27* **Built by** AG Weser (Bremen) **Launched** 24.6.36
**Fate** Depth charged RN destroyers *Forester* and *Fortune* 60 m
west of Hebrides 20.9.39

**Name** *U.28* **Built by** AG Weser (Bremen) **Launched** 14.7.36
**Fate** Lost by accident off Neustadt 3.44

**Name** *U.29* **Built by** AG Weser (Bremen) **Launched** 22.8.36
**Fate** Scuttled Flensburg 5.5.45

**Name** *U.30* **Built by** AG Weser (Bremen) **Launched** 4.8.36
**Fate** Scuttled Flensburg 5.5.45

**Name** *U.31* **Built by** AG Weser (Bremen) **Launched** 25.9.36
**Fate** Bombed RAF aircraft Schillig Roads 11.3.40, later salved;
depth charged RN destroyer *Antelope* north-west of Ireland
2.11.40

**Name** *U.32* **Built by** AG Weser (Bremen) **Launched** 25.2.37
**Fate** Depth charged RN destroyers *Harvester* and *Highlander*
north-west of Ireland 30.10.40

**Name** *U.33* **Built by** Germania Werft (Kiel) **Launched** 11.6.36
**Fate** Depth charged RN minesweeper *Gleaner* Firth of Clyde
12.2.40

**Name** *U.34* **Built by** Germania Werft (Kiel) **Launched** 17.7.36
**Fate** Collision German depot ship *Lech* off Memel 5.8.43, later
salved; scrapped

*The conning tower of* U.38
*pre-war.* (IWM)

**Name** *U.35* **Built by** Germania Werft (Kiel) **Launched** 29.9.36
**Fate** Depth charged RN destroyers *Icarus, Kashmir* and *Kingston* east of Shetlands 29.11.39

**Name** *U.36* **Built by** Germania Werft (Kiel) **Launched** 4.11.36
**Fate** Torpedoed RN submarine *Salmon* south-west of Stavanger 4.12.39

## TYPE IXA

**Name** *U.37* **Built by** AG Weser (Bremen) **Launched** 14.5.38
**Fate** Scuttled Eckernforde 3.5.45

**Name** *U.38* **Built by** AG Weser (Bremen) **Launched** 3.8.38
**Fate** Scuttled Weser estuary 5.45

**Name** *U.39* **Built by** AG Weser (Bremen) **Launched** 22.9.38
**Fate** Depth charged RN destroyers *Faulknor, Foxhound* and *Firedrake* north-west of Ireland 14.9.39

**Name** *U.40* **Built by** AG Weser (Bremen) **Launched** 9.11.38
**Fate** Mined Dover Strait 13.10.39

**Name** *U.41* **Built by** AG Weser (Bremen) **Launched** 20.1.39
**Fate** Depth charged RN destroyer *Antelope* south of Ireland 5.2.40

**Name** *U.42* **Built by** AG Weser (Bremen) **Launched** 16.2.39
**Fate** Depth charged RN destroyers *Ilex* and *Imogen* south-west of Ireland 13.10.39

*The victorous* U.47 *under Gunther Prien returns to a hero's welcome after sinking the battleship* Royal Oak. (Drüppel)

**Name** *U.43* **Built by** AG Weser (Bremen) **Launched** 23.5.39
**Fate** Depth charged USN aircraft of escort carrier *Santee* (VC.29) south-west of Azores 30.7.43

**Name** *U.44* **Built by** AG Weser (Bremen) **Launched** 5.8.39
**Fate** Depth charged RN destroyer *Fortune* south-west of Narvik 20.3.40

**TYPE VIIB**

**Name** *U.45* **Built by** Germania Werft (Kiel) **Launched** 27.4.38
**Fate** Depth charged French destroyer *Cyclone* Bay of Biscay 16.10.39

**Name** *U.46* **Built by** Germania Werft (Kiel) **Launched** 10.9.38
**Fate** Scuttled Flensburg 5.45

**Name** *U.47* **Built by** Germania Werft (Kiel) **Launched** 29.10.38
**Fate** Depth charged RN corvettes *Arbutus* and *Camellia* off Rockall 7.3.41

**Name** *U.48* **Built by** Germania Werft (Kiel) **Launched** 8.3.39
**Fate** Scuttled Neustadt 3.5.45

**Name** *U.49* **Built by** Germania Werft (Kiel) **Launched** 24.6.39
**Fate** Depth charged RN destroyer *Fearless* Vaagsofjord 15.4.40

*An early Type VIIC in dock showing the saddle tanks.* (Ullstein)

**Name** *U.50* **Built by** Germania Werft (Kiel) **Launched** 1.11.39
**Fate** Depth charged RN destroyers *Amazon* and *Witherington*
north of Shetlands 29.4.40

**Name** *U.51* **Built by** Germania Werft (Kiel) **Launched** 11.6.38
**Fate** Torpedoed RN submarine *Cachalot* Bay of Biscay 20.8.40

**Name** *U.52* **Built by** Germania Werft (Kiel) **Launched** 21.12.38
**Fate** Scuttled Kiel 5.45

**Name** *U.53* **Built by** Germania Werft (Kiel) **Launched** 6.5.39
**Fate** Depth charged French destroyer *Fantasque* North Atlantic
21.2.40

**Name** *U.54* **Built by** Germania Werft (Kiel) **Launched** 15.8.39
**Fate** Torpedoed RN submarine *Salmon* North Sea 12.4.40

**Name** *U.55* **Built by** Germania Werft (Kiel) **Launched** 11.10.39
**Fate** Depth charged RN destroyer *Whitshed*, sloop *Fowey*, and
RAF aircraft (228 Sqn.) 100 m west of Ushant 30.1.40

## TYPE IIC

**Name** *U.56* **Built by** Deutsche Werke (Kiel) **Launched** 3.9.38
**Fate** Bombed RAF and USAAF aircraft Kiel 28.4.45

*Another view of a Type VIIC
in dry dock, showing the
fairings over the bow
torpedo tubes.* (Südd Verlag)

**Name** *U.57* **Built by** Deutsche Werke (Kiel) **Launched** 3.9.38
**Fate** Collision S.S. *Rona* Brunsbuttel 3.9.40, later salved; scuttled
Kiel 5.45

**Name** *U.58* **Built by** Deutsche Werke (Kiel) **Launched** 14.10.38
**Fate** Scuttled Kiel 5.45

**Name** *U.59* **Built by** Deutsche Werke (Kiel) **Launched** 12.10.38
**Fate** Surrendered Kiel 5.45 and scrapped

**Name** *U.60* **Built by** Deutsche Werke (Kiel) **Launched** 1.6.39
**Fate** Scuttled Wilhelmshaven 5.45

**Name** *U.61* **Built by** Deutsche Werke (Kiel) **Launched** 15.6.39
**Fate** Scuttled Wilhelmshaven 5.45

**Name** *U.62* **Built by** Deutsche Werke (Kiel) **Launched** 16.11.39
**Fate** Scuttled Wilhelmshaven 5.45

**Name** *U.63* **Built by** Deutsche Werke (Kiel) **Launched** 6.12.39
**Fate** Depth charged RN destroyers *Escort, Imogen* and *Inglefield*
south-east of Shetlands 25.2.40

### TYPE IXB

**Name** *U.64* **Built by** AG Weser (Bremen) **Launched** 20.9.39
**Fate** Bombed RN aircraft of battleship *Warspite* (700 Sqn.)
Rombaksfjord 13.4.40; salved 8.57 and scrapped

**Name** *U.65* **Built by** AG Weser (Bremen) **Launched** 6.11.39
**Fate** Depth charged RN corvette *Gladiolus* south of Iceland
28.4.41

### TYPE IXC

**Name** *U.66* (ex-*U.122*) **Built by** AG Weser (Bremen)
**Launched** 10.10.40 **Fate** Depth charged USN aircraft of escort
carrier *Block Island* (VC.55), and destroyer escort *Buckley* west
of Cape Verde Islands 6.5.44

*U.93 and* U.94 *(Type VIIC) show the distinctive spray deflectors fitted halfway up the conning tower as a result of war experience.* (Drüppel)

**Name** *U.67* (ex-*U.123*) **Built by** AG Weser (Bremen)
**Launched** 30.10.40 **Fate** Depth charged USN aircraft of escort
carrier *Core* (VC.13) Saragossa Sea 16.7.43

**Name** *U.68* (ex-*U.124*) **Built by** AG Weser (Bremen)
**Launched** 12.11.40 **Fate** Depth charged USN aircraft of escort
carrier *Guadacanal* (VC.58) north of Madeira 10.4.44

**TYPE VIIC**

**Name** *U.69* (ex-*U.99*) **Built by** Germania Werft (Kiel)
**Launched** 19.9.40 **Fate** Depth charged RN destroyer *Viscount*
North Atlantic 17.2.43

**Name** *U.70* (ex-*U.100*) **Built by** Germania Werft (Kiel)
**Launched** 12.10.40 **Fate** Depth charged RN destroyer *Wolverine*
south of Iceland 8.3.41

**Name** *U.71* (ex-*U.101*) **Built by** Germania Werft (Kiel)
**Launched** 31.10.40 **Fate** Scuttled Wilhelmshaven 5.45

**Name** *U.72* (ex-*U.102*) **Built by** Germania Werft (Kiel)
**Launched** 22.11.40 **Fate** Bombed USAAF aircraft Bremen
30.3.45

**TYPE V.IIB**

**Name** *U.73* **Built by** Bremer Vulkan (Vegesack) **Launched** 27.7.40
**Fate** Depth charged USN destroyers *Trippe* and *Woolsey* off Oran
16.12.43

**Name** *U.74* **Built by** Bremer Vulkan (Vegesack) **Launched** 31.5.40
**Fate** Depth charged RN destroyers *Wishart* and *Wrestler*, and
RAF aircraft (202 Sqn.) south-east of Valencia 2.5.42

*A Type IXB boat, probably U.106, under air attack. Note the wide casing characteristic of these larger U-Boats. (IWM)*

**Name** *U.75* **Built by** Bremer Vulkan (Vegesack) **Launched** 18.10.40
**Fate** Depth charged RN destroyer *Kipling* off Mersa Matruh
28.12.41

**Name** *U.76* **Built by** Bremer Vulkan (Vegesack) **Launched** 3.10.40
**Fate** Depth charged RN destroyer *Wolverine*, and sloop
*Scarborough* south of Iceland 5.4.41

## TYPE VIIC

**Name** *U.77* **Built by** Bremer Vulkan (Vegesack) **Launched** 23.11.40
**Fate** Depth charged RAF aircraft (48 & 233 Sqns.) east of
Cartagena 28.3.43

**Name** *U.78* **Built by** Bremer Vulkan (Vegesack) **Launched** 7.12.40
**Fate** Harbour service (1945); gunfire Russian shore batteries off
Pilau 16.4.45

**Name** *U.79* **Built by** Bremer Vulkan (Vegesack) **Launched** 25.1.41
**Fate** Depth charged RN destroyers *Hasty* and *Hotspur* off Bardia
23.12.41

**Name** *U.80* **Built by** Bremer Vulkan (Vegesack) **Launched** 11.2.41
**Fate** Lost by accident west of Pilau 28.11.44

**Name** *U.81* **Built by** Bremer Vulkan (Vegesack) **Launched** 22.2.41
**Fate** Bombed USAAF aircraft Pola 9.1.44

**Name** *U.82* **Built by** Bremer Vulkan (Vegesack) **Launched** 15.3.41
**Fate** Depth charged RN sloop *Rochester*, and corvette *Tamarisk*
Azores area 6.2.42

## TYPE VIIB

**Name** *U.83* **Built by** Flenderwerft (Lübeck) **Launched** 9.12.40
**Fate** Depth charged RAF aircraft (500 Sqn.) east of Cartagena
4.3.43

**Name** *U.84* **Built by** Flenderwerft (Lübeck) **Launched** 26.2.41
**Fate** Depth charged USN aircraft of escort carrier *Core* (VC.13)
Azores area 24.8.43

**Name** *U.85* **Built by** Flenderwerft (Lübeck) **Launched** 10.4.41
**Fate** Depth charged USN destroyer *Roper* off Cape Hatteras
14.4.42

**Name** *U.86* **Built by** Flenderwerft (Lübeck) **Launched** 10.5.41
**Fate** Depth charged USN aircraft of escort carrier *Bogue* (VC.19)
Azores area 29.11.43

**Name** *U.87* **Built by** Flenderwerft (Lübeck) **Launched** 21.6.41
**Fate** Depth charged RCN destroyer *St. Croix*, and frigate
*Shediac* west of Oporto 4.3.43

**Name** *U.88* **Built by** Flenderwerft (Lübeck) **Launched** 16.8.41
**Fate** Depth charged RN destroyer *Onslow* Bear Island area
14.9.42

**Name** *U.89* **Built by** Flenderwerft (Lübeck) **Launched** 20.9.41
**Fate** Depth charged RN destroyer *Broadway*, frigate *Lagan,* and
aircraft of escort carrier *Biter* (811 Sqn.) North Atlantic 14.5.43

**Name** *U.90* **Built by** Flenderwerft (Lübeck) **Launched** 25.10.41 **Fate** Depth charged RCN destroyer *St. Croix* North Atlantic 24.7.42

**Name** *U.91* **Built by** Flenderwerft (Lübeck) **Launched** 30.10.41 **Fate** Depth charged RN frigates *Affleck, Gore* and *Gould* North Atlantic 25.2.44

**Name** *U.92* **Built by** Flenderwerft (Lübeck) **Launched** 10.1.42 **Fate** Bombed RAF aircraft Bergen 4.10.44, salved and paid-off 12.10.44; scrapped 1944–5

**Name** *U.93* **Built by** Germania Werft (Kiel) **Launched** 8.6.40 **Fate** Depth charged RN destroyer *Hesperus* west of Cape St. Vincent 15.1.42

**Name** *U.94* **Built by** Germania Werft (Kiel) **Launched** 12.6.40 **Fate** Depth charged RCN corvette *Oakville* and USN aircraft (VP.92) south of Haiti 28.8.42

**Name** *U.95* **Built by** Germania Werft (Kiel) **Launched** 18.7.40 **Fate** Torpedoed RNeth.N submarine 0.21 east of Gibraltar 28.11.41

**Name** *U.96* **Built by** Germania Werft (Kiel) **Launched** 4.8.40 **Fate** Bombed USAAF aircraft Wilhelmshaven 30.3.45

**Name** *U.97* **Built by** Germania Werft (Kiel) **Launched** 15.8.40 **Fate** Depth charged RAAF aircraft (459 Sqn.) south of Cyprus 16.6.43

**Name** *U.98* **Built by** Germania Werft (Kiel) **Launched** 31.8.40 **Fate** Depth charged RAF aircraft (608 Sqn.) west of Gibraltar 19.11.42

## TYPE VIIB

**Name** *U.99* (ex-*U.69*) **Built by** Germania Werft (Kiel) **Launched** 12.3.40 **Fate** Torpedoed RN destroyer *Walker* north-west of Hebrides 17.3.41

**Name** *U.100* (ex-*U.70*) **Built by** Germania Werft (Kiel) **Launched** 13.1.40 **Fate** Depth charged RN destroyers *Vanoc* and *Walker*, finally rammed by former, north-west of Hebrides 17.3.41

**Name** *U.101* (ex-*U.71*) **Built by** Germania Werft (Kiel) **Launched** 10.2.40 **Fate** Paid-off 11.43; surrendered Neustadt 1945 and scrapped

**Name** *U.102* (ex-*U.72*) **Built by** Germania Werft (Kiel) **Launched** 21.3.40 **Fate** Lost by unknown cause North Sea 21.8.40

## TYPE IXB

**Name** *U.103* **Built by** AG Weser (Bremen) **Launched** 12.4.40 **Fate** Bombed Allied aircraft Gdynia 15.4.45

**Name** *U.104* **Built by** AG Weser (Bremen) **Launched** 15.5.40
**Fate** Depth charged RN corvette *Rhododendron* south of Rockall
21.11.40

**Name** *U.105* **Built by** AG Weser (Bremen) **Launched** 15.6.40
**Fate** Depth charged French aircraft (141 Sqn.) off Dakar 2.6.43

**Name** *U.106* **Built by** AG Weser (Bremen) **Launched** 17.6.40
**Fate** Depth charged RAF and RAAF aircraft (228 & 461 Sqns.)
north-west of Cape Ortegal 2.8.43

**Name** *U.107* **Built by** AG Weser (Bremen) **Launched** 2.7.40
**Fate** Depth charged RAF aircraft (201 Sqn.) west of La Rochelle
18.8.44

**Name** *U.108* **Built by** AG Weser (Bremen) **Launched** 15.7.40
**Fate** Bombed Allied aircraft Hamburg 11.4.44, and paid-off
17.7.44; scuttled 1945

**Name** *U.109* **Built by** AG Weser (Bremen) **Launched** 14.8.40
**Fate** Depth charged RAF (86 Sqn.) aircraft south of Ireland
4.5.43

**Name** *U.110* **Built by** AG Weser (Bremen) **Launched** 25.8.40
**Fate** Depth charged RN destroyers *Broadway* and *Bulldog*, and
corvette *Aubrieta*, and finally rammed by the first; captured and
foundered in tow south-west of Ireland 9.5.41

**Name** *U.111* **Built by** AG Weser (Bremen) **Launched** 6.9.40
**Fate** Depth charged trawler *Lady Shirley* west-south-west of
Tenerife 4.10.41

## TYPE XI
**Name** *U.112–115* **Built by** AG Weser (Bremen) **Fate** Projected
1938 but not built

## TYPE XB
**Name** *U.116* **Built by** Germania Werft (Kiel) **Launched** 3.5.41
**Fate** Depth charged USN aircraft (VP.74) Atlantic 20.10.44

**Name** *U.117* **Built by** Germania Werft (Kiel) **Launched** 26.7.41
**Fate** Depth charged USN aircraft of escort carrier *Card* (VC.1)
west of Flores 7.8.43

**Name** *U.118* **Built by** Germania Werft (Kiel) **Launched** 28.9.41
**Fate** Depth charged USN aircraft of escort carrier *Bogue* (VC.9)
west of Canary Islands 12.6.43

**Name** *U.119* **Built by** Germania Werft (Kiel) **Launched** 6.1.42
**Fate** Depth charged RN sloop *Starling* north-west of Cape
Ortegal 24.6.43

## TYPE IIB
**Name** *U.120* (ex-RYN) **Built by** Flenderwerft (Lübeck)
**Launched** 16.3.40 **Fate** Scuttled Bremerhaven 5.45

**Name** *U.121* (ex-RYN) **Built by** Flenderwerft (Lübeck)
**Launched** 20.4.40 **Fate** Scuttled Weser estuary 5.45

## TYPE IXB

**Name** *U.122* (ex-*U.66*) **Built by** AG Weser (Bremen)
**Launched** 12.12.39 **Fate** Lost by unknown cause North Sea
21.6.40

**Name** *U.123* (ex-*U.67*) **Built by** AG Weser (Bremen)
**Launched** 2.3.40 **Fate** Paid-off Lorient 19.8.44 and surrendered
1945; French *Blaison* (1947); discarded (1957)

**Name** *U.124* (ex-*U.68*) **Built by** AG Weser (Bremen)
**Launched** 9.3.40 **Fate** Depth charged RN sloop *Black Swan*, and
corvette *Stonecrop* west of Oporto 2.4.43

## TYPE IXC

**Name** *U.125* **Built by** AG Weser (Bremen) **Launched** 10.12.40
**Fate** Depth charged RN destroyer *Vidette* east-south-east of
Newfoundland 6.5.43

**Name** *U.126* **Built by** AG Weser (Bremen) **Launched** 31.12.40
**Fate** Depth charged RAF aircraft (172 Sqn.) north-west of Cape
Ortegal 3.7.43

**Name** *U.127* **Built by** AG Weser (Bremen) **Launched** 1.2.41
**Fate** Depth charged RAN destroyer *Nestor* south-west of Cape St.
Vincent 15.12.41

**Name** *U.128* **Built by** AG Weser (Bremen) **Launched** 20.2.41
**Fate** Depth charged USN destroyers *Jouett* and *Moffett*, and
aircraft (VP.74) 200 m east-north-east of Bahia 17.5.43

**Name** *U.129* **Built by** AG Weser (Bremen) **Launched** 28.2.41
**Fate** Paid-off Lorient 7.44; scuttled 8.44

**Name** *U.130* **Built by** AG Weser (Bremen) **Launched** 19.3.41
**Fate** Depth charged USN destroyer *Champlin* west of Azores
12.3.43

**Name** *U.131* **Built by** AG Weser (Bremen) **Launched** 1.4.41
**Fate** Depth charged RN destroyer *Stanley*, escort destroyers
*Blakeney* and *Exmoor*, sloop *Stork*, corvette *Pentstemon*, and
aircraft of escort carrier *Audacity* (802 Sqn.) off Cape St. Vincent
17.12.41

## TYPE VIIC

**Name** *U.132* **Built by** Bremer Vulkan (Vegesack) **Launched** 10.4.41
**Fate** Depth charged RAF aircraft (120 Sqn.) south of Cape
Farewell 5.11.42

**Name** *U.133* **Built by** Bremer Vulkan (Vegesack) **Launched** 28.4.41
**Fate** Mined off Salamis 14.3.42

**Name** *U.134* **Built by** Bremer Vulkan (Vegesack) **Launched** 7.5.41
**Fate** Depth charged RAF aircraft (179 Sqn.) off Vigo 24.8.43

**Name** *U.135* **Built by** Bremer Vulkan (Vegesack) **Launched** 13.6.41 **Fate** Depth charged RN sloop *Rochester*, and corvettes *Balsam* and *Mignonette* off Canary Islands 15.7.43

**Name** *U.136* **Built by** Bremer Vulkan (Vegesack) **Launched** 5.7.41 **Fate** Depth charged RN sloop *Pelican*, frigate *Spey*, and French destroyer *Léopard* north-west of Canary Islands 11.7.42

## TYPE IID

**Name** *U.137* **Built by** Deutsche Werke (Kiel) **Launched** 18.5.40 **Fate** Scuttled Wilhelmshaven 5.45

**Name** *U.138* **Built by** Deutsche Werke (Kiel) **Launched** 18.5.40 **Fate** Depth charged RN destroyers *Faulknor*, *Fearless*, *Forester*, *Foresight* and *Foxhound* 100 m west Cape Trafalgar 18.6.41

**Name** *U.139* **Built by** Deutsche Werke (Kiel) **Launched** 26.6.40 **Fate** Scuttled Wilhelmshaven 5.45

**Name** *U.140* **Built by** Deutsche Werke (Kiel) **Launched** 28.6.40 **Fate** Scuttled Wilhelmshaven 5.45

**Name** *U.141* **Built by** Deutsche Werke (Kiel) **Launched** 27.7.40 **Fate** Scuttled Wilhelmshaven 5.45

**Name** *U.142* **Built by** Deutsche Werke (Kiel) **Launched** 27.7.40 **Fate** Scuttled Wilhelmshaven 5.45

**Name** *U.143* **Built by** Deutsche Werke (Kiel) **Launched** 10.8.40 **Fate** Surrendered Wilhelmshaven 5.45 and scuttled North Atlantic 1945/6

**Name** *U.144* **Built by** Deutsche Werke (Kiel) **Launched** 24.8.40 **Fate** Torpedoed Russian submarine *Shch. 307* Gulf of Finland 9.8.41

**Name** *U.145* **Built by** Deutsche Werke (Kiel) **Launched** 21.9.40 **Fate** Surrendered Wilhelmshaven 5.45 and scuttled North Atlantic 1945/6

**Name** *U.146* **Built by** Deutsche Werke (Kiel) **Launched** 21.9.40 **Fate** Scuttled Wilhelmshaven 5.45

**Name** *U.147* **Built by** Deutsche Werke (Kiel) **Launched** 16.11.40 **Fate** Depth charged RN destroyer *Wanderer*, and corvette *Periwinkle* north-west of Ireland 2.6.41

**Name** *U.148* **Built by** Deutsche Werke (Kiel) **Launched** 16.11.40 **Fate** Scuttled Wilhelmshaven 5.45

**Name** *U.149* **Built by** Deutsche Werke (Kiel) **Launched** 19.10.40 **Fate** Surrendered Wilhelmshaven 5.45 and scuttled North Atlantic 1945/6

**Name** *U.150* **Built by** Deutsche Werke (Kiel) **Launched** 19.10.40 **Fate** Surrendered Wilhelmshaven 5.45; expended as RCN experimental vessel 22.10.47

**Name** *U.151* **Built by** Deutsche Werke (Kiel) **Launched** 14.12.40
**Fate** Scuttled Wilhelmshaven 5.45

**Name** *U.152* **Built by** Deutsche Werke (Kiel) **Launched** 14.12.40
**Fate** Scuttled Wilhelmshaven 5.45

## TYPE IXC

**Name** *U.153* **Built by** AG Weser (Bremen) **Launched** 5.4.41
**Fate** Depth charged by USN destroyer *Landsdowne* off Colon
13.7.42

**Name** *U.154* **Built by** AG Weser (Bremen) **Launched** 21.4.41
**Fate** Depth charged USN destroyer escorts *Frost* and *Inch* west of
Madeira 3.7.44

**Name** *U.155* **Built by** AG Weser (Bremen) **Launched** 12.5.41
**Fate** Surrendered Wilhelmshaven 5.45 and scuttled North
Atlantic 1945/6

**Name** *U.156* **Built by** AG Weser (Bremen) **Launched** 21.5.41
**Fate** Depth charged USN aircraft (VP.53) east of Barbados
8.3.43

**Name** *U.157* **Built by** AG Weser (Bremen) **Launched** 5.6.41
**Fate** Depth charged USCG cutter *Thetis* north of Havana 13.6.42

**Name** *U.158* **Built by** AG Weser (Bremen) **Launched** 21.6.41
**Fate** Depth charged USN aircraft (VP.74) west of Bermuda
30.6.42

**Name** *U.159* **Built by** AG Weser (Bremen) **Launched** 1.7.41
**Fate** Depth charged USN aircraft (VP.32) south of Haiti 15.7.43

**Name** *U.160* **Built by** AG Weser (Bremen) **Launched** 12.7.41
**Fate** Depth charged USN aircraft of escort carrier *Santee* (VC.29)
west of Azores 14.7.43

**Name** *U.161* **Built by** Seebeckwerft (Bremerhaven)
**Launched** 15.2.41 **Fate** Depth charged USN aircraft (VP.74)
north-east of Bahia 27.9.43

**Name** *U.162* **Built by** Seebeckwerft (Bremerhaven)
**Launched** 15.2.41 **Fate** Depth charged RN destroyers *Pathfinder*,
*Quentin* and *Vimy* north-east of Trinidad 3.9.42

**Name** *U.163* **Built by** Seebeckwerft (Bremerhaven)
**Launched** 30.4.41 **Fate** Torpedoed USN submarine *Herring* Bay of
Biscay 21.3.43

**Name** *U.164* **Built by** Seebeckwerft (Bremerhaven)
**Launched** 30.4.41 **Fate** Depth charged USN aircraft (VP.83) off
Natal (Brazil) 6.1.43

**Name** *U.165* **Built by** Seebeckwerft (Bremerhaven)
**Launched** 15.8.41 **Fate** Depth charged RAF aircraft (825 Sqn.)
Bay of Biscay 27.9.42

**Name** *U.166* **Built by** Seebeckwerft (Bremerhaven)
**Launched** 3.11.41 **Fate** Depth charged USCG aircraft (V.212) off
New Orleans 1.8.42

### TYPE IXC$_{40}$

**Name** *U.167* **Built by** Seebeckwerft (Bremerhaven)
**Launched** 5.3.42 **Fate** Depth charged RAF aircraft (233 Sqn.) off
Canary Islands 5.4.43, and scuttled next day; salved 1951 by
Spanish Navy and scrapped

**Name** *U.168* **Built by** Seebeckwerft (Bremerhaven)
**Launched** 5.3.42 **Fate** Torpedoed RNeth.N submarine
*Zwaardvisch* off Java 5.10.44

**Name** *U.169* **Built by** Seebeckwerft (Bremerhaven)
**Launched** 6.6.42 **Fate** Depth charged RAF aircraft (206 Sqn.)
north of Rockall 27.4.43

**Name** *U.170* **Built by** Seebeckwerft (Bremerhaven)
**Launched** 6.6.42 **Fate** Surrendered Horten 5.45 and scuttled
North Atlantic 1945/6

### TYPE IXC

**Name** *U.171* **Built by** AG Weser (Bremen) **Launched** 22.7.41
**Fate** Mined off Lorient 9.10.42

**Name** *U.172* **Built by** AG Weser (Bremen) **Launched** 5.8.41
**Fate** Depth charged USN aircraft of escort carrier *Bogue* (VC.19)
and destroyers *Clemson, Dupont* and *George E. Badger*, and
destroyer escort *George W. Ingram* 600 m north-north-west of
Cape Verde Islands 13.12.43

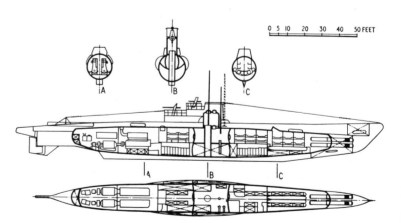

*Type VIIA*

## *Type VIIA:* **U.27–U.36**

Sea-going boats, based on the Finnish *Vetehinen*, to meet
requirements for minimum operational size, so that the
greatest number possible could be built under the total

tonnage limitations of the London Naval Treaty. They proved most successful, were developed as the main operational type, and were later relegated to training. Part of bunkers and torpedo reloads stowed externally.

*Displacement:* 626/745 tons
*Dimensions:* 211¾ × 19¼ × 14½ feet
*Machinery:* 2-shaft diesel/electric motors, B.H.P./S.H.P. 2,100/750 = 16/8 knots
*Bunkers & Radius:* O.F. 67 tons; 4,300/90 miles at 12/4 knots
*Armament:* One 3.5inch, one 20mm A.A. guns; five 21inch torpedo tubes (four fwd and one aft—eleven torpedoes)
*Complement:* 44
*Notes:* Surface speed increased to 17 knots when not carrying O.F. in external bunker tanks

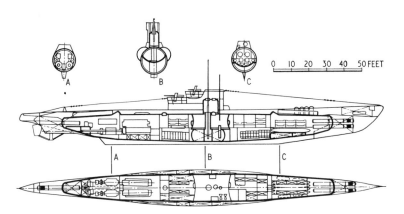

*Type VIIB*

## *Type VIIB:* U.45–U.55, U.73–U.76, U.83–U.87, U.99–U.102

Slightly enlarged type VIIA, with saddle tanks modified to improve seaworthiness and increase bunkers and radius, and more powerful diesel engines installed to raise surfaced speed.

*Displacement:* 753/857 tons
*Dimensions:* 218¼ × 20¼ × 15½ feet
*Machinery:* 2-shaft diesel/electric motors, B.H.P./S.H.P. 2,800/750 = 17¼/8 knots
*Bunkers & Radius:* O.F. 108 tons; 6,500/80 miles at 12/4 knots
*Armament:* One 3.5inch, one 20mm A.A. guns; five 21inch torpedo tubes (four fwd and one aft—twelve torpedoes or fourteen mines)
*Complement:* 44
*Notes:* *Schnorchel* added. A.A. armament increased to one 37mm and two 20mm (2 × 1) guns, and 3.5inch gun removed

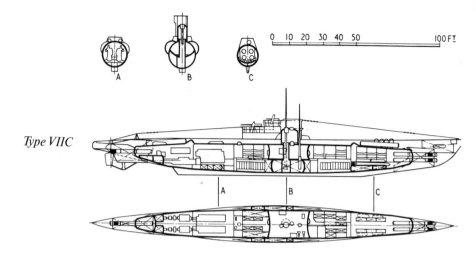

*Type VIIC*

## *Type VIIC:* **U.69–U.72, U.77–U.82, U.88–U.98, U.132–U.136, U.201–U.212, U.221–U.232, U.235–U.458, U.465–U.486, U.551–U.790, U.821–U.840, U.901–U.1058, U.1063–U.1080**

Improved type VIIB, with addition of two externally stowed torpedo re-loads, and heavier light anti-aircraft armament.

*Displacement:* 769/871 tons

*Dimensions:* $165\frac{3}{4}$(pp)/$218\frac{1}{4}$(oa) × $20\frac{1}{4}$ × $15\frac{1}{2}$ feet

*Machinery:* 2-shaft 6-cyl. diesel/electric motors, B.H.P./S.H.P. 2,800/750 = $17/7\frac{1}{2}$ knots

*Bunkers & Radius:* O.F. $105\frac{1}{4}$–$113\frac{1}{2}$ tons; 8,500/6,500/3,250 miles at 10/12/17 knots surfaced, 80/30 miles at 4/2 knots submerged

*Armament:* One 3.5inch, one 37mm A.A., two 20mm A A. (2 × 1) guns; five 21inch torpedo tubes (four fwd and one aft—fourteen torpedoes or thirty-nine mines)

*Complement:* 44

*Notes: Schnorchel* added. A.A. armament increased by substituting twin 20mm for single 20mm guns, and 3.5inch gun removed. *U.441* (and possibly others) had one 37mm and eight 20mm (2 × 4) before and abaft conning tower, the latter being extended forward. *U.428–430* and *U.746–750* were completed as Royal Italian Navy *S.1, 4, 6, 2, 3, 5, 7* and *9* respectively, but were retroceded in 1943 and retook original numbers *U.573* was sold to the Spanish Navy in 1943 while interned and re-numbered *G.7.* Most units had the G.W.-6-1400 diesel, but *U.255* and possibly others had the M.A.N. type. *U.485* is reported to have had a rubber-coated hull as a protection against Asdic. *U.826* had automatic hydroplane depth-keeping gear. *U.255* was the first to have a fixed *schnorchel* mast

## *Type VIIC$_{41/2}$:* **U.1101–U.1220, U.1271– U.1330**

Generally similar to type VIIC, but pressure hull strengthened for deeper diving.

*Displacement:* 769/871 tons
*Dimensions:* 220¼ × 20¼ × 15¾ feet
*Machinery.* 2-shaft 6-cyl. diesel/electric motors, B.H.P./S.H.P.
  2,800/750 = 17/7½ knots
*Bunkers & Radius:* O.F. 114 tons; 6,500/80 miles at 12/4 knots
*Armament:* One 3.5inch, one 37mm A.A., two 20mm A.A.
  (2 × 1) guns; five 21inch torpedo tubes (four fwd and one aft—
  fourteen torpedoes or fourteen mines)
*Complement:* 44
*Notes: Schnorchel* added: A.A. armament increased by substituting
  four 20mm (1 × 4) for single 37mm (in some), and twin for
  single 20mm guns, and 3.5inch gun removed. *U.1161* was
  completed as Royal Italian Navy *S.8*, but was retroceded in
  1943 and retook original number. *U.1105* had automatic
  hydroplane depth-keeping gear and a rubber-coated hull.

## *Type VIIC$_{42}$:* **U.1093–U.1100, U.1331–U.1404, U.1417–U.1500, U.1801–U.2110, U.2301– U.2320**

Improved type VIIC$_{41/2}$, with bunkers and radius increased, pressure hull further strengthened, conning tower armoured, and A.A. armament augmented.

*Displacement:* 999/1,050 tons
*Dimensions:* 225½ × 22¼ × 16¼ feet
*Machinery:* 2-shaft diesel/electric motors, B.H.P./S.H.P.
  2,700/750 = 16¾/7½ knots
*Bunkers & Radius:* O.F. 180 tons; 10,000/80 miles at 12/4 knots
*Armament:* One 3.5inch, one 37mm A.A., four 20mm A.A.
  (2 × 2) guns; five 21inch torpedo tubes (four fwd and one
  aft—fourteen torpedoes or fourteen mines)
*Complement:* 45
*Notes: Schnorchel* added. A.A. armament increased to two 37mm
  (2 × 1) and two 20mm (1 × 2), or four 37mm (4 × 1) guns,
  and 3.5inch gun removed

### TYPE IXC

**Name** *U.173* **Built by** AG Weser (Bremen) **Launched** 11.8.41
**Fate** Depth charged USN destroyers *Quick, Swanson* and *Woolsey*
off Casablanca 16.11.42

**Name** *U.174* **Built by** AG Weser (Bremen) **Launched** 21.8.41
**Fate** Depth charged USN aircraft (VB.125) south-east of
Newfoundland 27.4.43

**Name** *U.175* **Built by** AG Weser (Bremen) **Launched** 2.9.41
**Fate** Gunfire of USCG cutter *Spencer* south-west of Cape Clear
17.4.43

**Name** *U.176* **Built by** AG Weser (Bremen) **Launched** 12.9.41
**Fate** Depth charged Cuban chaser *CS.13* and USN aircraft
(VS.62) north of Havana 15.5.43

**TYPE IXD$_2$**
**Name** *U.177* **Built by** AG Weser (Bremen) **Launched** 1.10.41
**Fate** Depth charged USN aircraft (VB.107) north-west of
Ascension 6.2.44

**Name** *U.178* **Built by** AG Weser (Bremen) **Launched** 25.10.41
**Fate** Scuttled Bordeaux 20.8.44

**Name** *U. 179* **Built by** AG Weser (Bremen) **Launched** 18.11.41
**Fate** Depth charged RN destroyer *Active* off Capetown 8.10.42

**TYPE IXD$_1$**
**Name** *U.180* **Built by** AG Weser (Bremen) **Launched** 10.12.41
**Fate** Mined off Gironde estuary 22.8.44

**TYPE IXD$_2$**
**Name** *U.181* **Built by** AG Weser (Bremen) **Launched** 30.12.41
**Fate** IJN *I.501* (1945); surrendered Singapore 16.8.45 and
scuttled off Singapore 12.2.46

**Name** *U.182* **Built by** AG Weser (Bremen) **Launched** 3.3.42
**Fate** Depth charged USN destroyer *Mackenzie* north-east of
Madeira 16.5.43

**TYPE IXC$_{40}$**
**Name** *U.183* **Built by** AG Weser (Bremen) **Launched** 9.1.42
**Fate** Torpedoed USN submarine *Besugo* Java Sea 23.4.45

**Name** *U.184* **Built by** AG Weser (Bremen) **Launched** 21.2.42
**Fate** Depth charged RNN corvette *Potentilla* north-east of
Newfoundland 20.11.42

**Name** *U.185* **Built by** AG Weser (Bremen) **Launched** 2.3.42
**Fate** Depth charged USN aircraft of escort carrier *Core* (VC.13)
North Atlantic 24.8.43

**Name** *U.186* **Built by** AG Weser (Bremen) **Launched** 11.3.42
**Fate** Depth charged RN destroyer *Hesperus* north of Azores
12.5.43

**Name** *U.187* **Built by** AG Weser (Bremen) **Launched** 16.3.42
**Fate** Depth charged RN destroyers *Beverley* and *Vimy* 600 m
south-east of Cape Farewell 4.2.43

**Name** *U.188* **Built by** AG Weser (Bremen) **Launched** 31.3.42
**Fate** Scuttled Bordeaux 20.8.44

**Name** *U.189* **Built by** AG Weser (Bremen) **Launched** 1.5.42
**Fate** Depth charged RAF aircraft (120 Sqn.) south-west of
Iceland 23.4.43

**Name** *U.190* **Built by** AG Weser (Bremen) **Launched** 3.6.42
**Fate** Surrendered Halifax 5.45; RCN experimental vessel,
expended off Halifax 22.10.47

**Name** *U.191* **Built by** AG Weser (Bremen) **Launched** 3.7.42
**Fate** Depth charged RN destroyer *Hesperus* south-west of
Iceland 23.4.43

**Name** *U.192* **Built by** AG Weser (Bremen) **Launched** 31.7.42
**Fate** Depth charged RN corvette *Pink* south of Greenland
5.5.43

**Name** *U.193* **Built by** AG Weser (Bremen) **Launched** 24.8.42
**Fate** Depth charged RAF aircraft (612 Sqn.) west of Nantes
28.4.44

**Name** *U.194* **Built by** AG Weser (Bremen) **Launched** 22.9.42
**Fate** Depth charged RAF aircraft (120 Sqn.) south-west of
Iceland 24.6.43

## TYPE IXD$_1$

**Name** *U.195* **Built by** AG Weser (Bremen) **Launched** 8.4.42
**Fate** IJN *I.506* (1945); surrendered Surabaya 8.45 and scrapped
1947

## TYPE IXD$_2$

**Name** *U.196* **Built by** AG Weser (Bremen) **Launched** 24.4.42
**Fate** Lost by unknown cause Sunda Strait 30.11.44

**Name** *U.197* **Built by** AG Weser (Bremen) **Launched** 21.5.42
**Fate** Depth charged RAF aircraft (259 & 265 Sqns.) south of
Madagascar 20.8.43

**Name** *U.198* **Built by** AG Weser (Bremen) **Launched** 15.6.42
**Fate** Depth charged RIN sloop *Godarvari*, RCN frigate *Findhorn*,
and RN aircraft of *Begum* (832 Sqn.) and *Shah* (851 Sqn.) north-
west of Seychelles 12.8.44

**Name** *U.199* **Built by** AG Weser (Bremen) **Launched** 11.7.42
**Fate** Depth charged USN (VP.74) and Brazilian aircraft off
Rio de Janeiro 31.7.43

**Name** *U.200* **Built by** AG Weser (Bremen) **Launched** 10.8.42
**Fate** Depth charged USN aircraft (VP. 84) south-west of Iceland
24.6.43

**TYPE VIIC**

**Name** *U.201* **Built by** Germania Werft (Kiel) **Launched** 7.12.40
**Fate** Depth charged RN destroyer *Fame* south-east of Greenland
17.2.43

**Name** *U.202* **Built by** Germania Werft (Kiel) **Launched** 10.2.41
**Fate** Depth charged RN sloop *Starling* 315 m south of Cape
Farewell 1.6.43

**Name** *U.203* **Built by** Germania Werft (Kiel) **Launched** 4.1.41
**Fate** Depth charged RN aircraft of escort carrier *Biter* (811 Sqn.)
and destroyer *Pathfinder* 290 m south-east of Cape Farewell
25.4.43

**Name** *U.204* **Built by** Germania Werft (Kiel) **Launched** 23.1.41
**Fate** Depth charged RN sloop *Rochester* and corvette *Mallow*
Straits of Gibraltar 19.10.41

**Name** *U.205* **Built by** Germania Werft (Kiel) **Launched** 20.3.41
**Fate** Depth charged RN destroyer *Paladin* and SAAF aircraft
(15 Sqn.) off Benghazi 17.2.43

**Name** *U.206* **Built by** Germania Werft (Kiel) **Launched** 4.4.41
**Fate** Depth charged RAF aircraft (502 Sqn.) west of Nantes
30.11.41

**Name** *U.207* **Built by** Germania Werft (Kiel) **Launched** 24.4.41
**Fate** Depth charged RN destroyers *Leamington* and *Veteran*
Denmark Strait 11.9.41

**Name** *U.208* **Built by** Germania Werft (Kiel) **Launched** 21.5.41
**Fate** Depth charged RN corvette *Bluebell* west of Gibraltar
11.12.41

**Name** *U.209* **Built by** Germania Werft (Kiel) **Launched** 28.8.41
**Fate** Depth charged RN frigates *Jed* and *Sennen* North Atlantic
19.5.43

**Name** *U.210* **Built by** Germania Werft (Kiel) **Launched** 23.12.41
**Fate** Depth charged RCN destroyer *Assinboine* North Atlantic
6.8.42

**Name** *U.211* **Built by** Germania Werft (Kiel) **Launched** 15.1.42
**Fate** Depth charged RAF aircraft (179 Sqn.) off Azores 19.11.43

**Name** *U.212* **Built by** Germania Werft (Kiel) **Launched** 11.3.42
**Fate** Depth charged RN frigates *Curzon* and *Ekins* 47 m
south-east of Brighton 21.7.44

**TYPE VIID**

**Name** *U.213* **Built by** Germania Werft (Kiel) **Launched** 24.7.41
**Fate** Depth charged RN sloops *Erne, Rochester* and *Sandwich*
west of Punta Delgada 31.7.42

**Name** *U.214* **Built by** Germania Werft (Kiel) **Launched** 18.9.41
**Fate** Depth charged RN frigate *Cooke* 16 m south-south-east
of Start Point 26.7.44

**Name** *U.215* **Built by** Germania Werft (Kiel) **Launched** 9.10.41
**Fate** Depth charged RN armed yacht *Le Tigre* off Nantucket
Island 3.7.42

**Name** *U.216* **Built by** Germania Werft (Kiel) **Launched** 23.10.41
**Fate** Depth charged RAF aircraft (224 Sqn.) west-south-west of
Ireland 20.10.42

**Name** *U.217* **Built by** Germania Werft (Kiel) **Launched** 15.11.41
**Fate** Depth charged USN aircraft of escort carrier *Bogue* (VC.9)
North Atlantic 5.6.43

**Name** *U.218* **Built by** Germania Werft (Kiel) **Launched** 5.12.41
**Fate** Surrendered Bergen 5.45, and scuttled North Atlantic
1945/6

## TYPE XB

**Name** *U.219* **Built by** Germania Werft (Kiel) **Launched** 6.10.42
**Fate** IJN *I.505* (1945); surrendered Batavia 8.45 and scrapped
1947

**Name** *U.220* **Built by** Germania Werft (Kiel) **Launched** 16.1.43
**Fate** Depth charged USN aircraft of escort carrier *Block Island*
(VC.1) off Newfoundland 28.10.43

## TYPE VIIC

**Name** *U.221* **Built by** Germania Werft (Kiel) **Launched** 14.3.42
**Fate** Depth charged RAF aircraft (58 Sqn.) south-west of Ireland
27.9.43

**Name** *U.222* **Built by** Germania Werft (Kiel) **Launched** 28.3.42
**Fate** Lost by collision off Danzig 2.9.42

**Name** *U.223* **Built by** Germania Werft (Kiel) **Launched** 16.4.42
**Fate** Depth charged RN destroyers *Laforey* and *Tumult*, and
escort destroyers *Blencathra* and *Hambledon* north-east of
Palermo 30.3.44

**Name** *U.224* **Built by** Germania Werft (Kiel) **Launched** 7.5.42
**Fate** Depth charged RCN corvette *Ville de Quebec* west of Algiers
13.1.43

**Name** *U.225* **Built by** Germania Werft (Kiel) **Launched** 28.5.42
**Fate** Depth charged USCG cutter *Spencer* North Atlantic 21.2.43

**Name** *U.226* **Built by** Germania Werft (Kiel) **Launched** 18.6.42
**Fate** Depth charged RN sloops *Kite*, *Starling* and *Woodcock* off
Newfoundland 6.11.43

**Name** *U.227* **Built by** Germania Werft (Kiel) **Launched** 9.7.42
**Fate** Depth charged RAF aircraft (455 Sqn.) north of Faroes
30.4.43

**Name** *U.228* **Built by** Germania Werft (Kiel) **Launched** 30.7.42
**Fate** Bombed RAF aircraft Bergen 4.10.44, salved and paid-off
5.10.44; surrendered 1945 and scrapped

**Name** *U.229* **Built by** Germania Werft (Kiel) **Launched** 20.8.42
**Fate** Depth charged RN destroyer *Keppel* North Atlantic 22.9.43

**Name** *U.230* **Built by** Germania Werft (Kiel) **Launched** 10.9.42
**Fate** Scuttled Toulon 21.8.44

**Name** *U.231* **Built by** Germania Werft (Kiel) **Launched** 1.10.42
**Fate** Depth charged RAF aircraft (172 Sqn.) west of Cape
Finisterre 13.1.44

**Name** *U.232* **Built by** Germania Werft (Kiel) **Launched** 15.10.42
**Fate** Depth charged USAAF aircraft (2nd A/S Sqn.) west of
Oporto 8.7.43

## TYPE XB

**Name** *U.233* **Built by** Germania Werft (Kiel) **Launched** 8.5.43
**Fate** Depth charged USN destroyer escorts *Baker* and *Thomas*
south-east of Halifax 5.7.44

**Name** *U.234* **Built by** Germania Werft (Kiel) **Launched** 23.12.43
**Fate** Surrendered Portsmouth (N.H.) 16.5.45, USN experimental
vessel (1945); expended off Cape Cod 11.46 (torpedoed)

## TYPE VIIC

**Name** *U.235* **Built by** Germania Werft (Kiel) **Launched** 4.11.42
**Fate** Depth charged in error German torpedo boat *T.17* Kattegat
14.4.45

**Name** *U.236* **Built by** Germania Werft (Kiel) **Launched** 24.11.42
**Fate** Bombed and damaged RAF aircraft (236 & 254 Sqns.)
Kattegat 4.5.45, and scuttled Schleimündung later same day

**Name** *U.237* **Built by** Germania Werft (Kiel) **Launched** 17.12.42
**Fate** Bombed USAAF aircraft Kiel 4.4.45

**Name** *U.238* **Built by** Germania Werft (Kiel) **Launched** 7.1.43
**Fate** Depth charged RN sloops *Kite, Magpie* and *Starling* south-
west of Ireland 9.2.44

**Name** *U.239* **Built by** Germania Werft (Kiel) **Launched** 28.1.43
**Fate** Bombed RAF aircraft Kiel 23.7.44, later salved and scrapped

**Name** *U.240* **Built by** Germania Werft (Kiel) **Launched** 18.2.43
**Fate** Depth charged RAF aircraft (330 Norge Sqn.) 200 m west
of Trondheim 16.5.44

**Name** *U.241* **Built by** Germania Werft (Kiel) **Launched** 25.6.43
**Fate** Depth charged RAF aircraft (210 Sqn.) north-east of Faroes
18.5.44

**Name** *U.242* **Built by** Germania Werft (Kiel) **Launched** 20.2.43
**Fate** Depth charged RN destroyers *Havelock* and *Hesperus* off
UK coast 30.4.45

**Name** *U.243* **Built by** Germania Werft (Kiel) **Launched** 2.9.43
**Fate** Depth charged RAAF aircraft (10 Sqn.) west of Nantes
8.7.44

U.249 *surrenders in the English Channel on May 9, 1945.* (British Official)

**Name** *U.244* **Built by** Germania Werft (Kiel) **Launched** 2.9.43
**Fate** Surrendered Bergen 5.45, and scuttled North Atlantic 1945/6

**Name** *U.245* **Built by** Germania Werft (Kiel) **Launched** 25.11.43
**Fate** Surrendered Bergen 5.45, and scuttled North Atlantic 1945/6

**Name** *U.246* **Built by** Germania Werft (Kiel) **Launched** 7.12.43
**Fate** Depth charged RN frigate *Duckworth* south-east of Lizard
29.3.45

**Name** *U.247* **Built by** Germania Werft (Kiel) **Launched** 23.9.43
**Fate** Depth charged RCN frigates *St. John* and *Swansea* south of
Land's End 1.9.44

**Name** *U.248* **Built by** Germania Werft (Kiel) **Launched** 7.10.43
**Fate** Depth charged USN destroyer escorts *Hayter, Hubbard,
Otter* and *Varian* North Atlantic 16.1.45

**Name** *U.249* **Built by** Germania Werft (Kiel) **Launched** 23.10.43
**Fate** Surrendered off Lizard 8.5.45 and scuttled North Atlantic
1945/6

**Name** *U.250* **Built by** Germania Werft (Kiel) **Launched** 11.11.43
**Fate** Depth charged Russian sub-chasers *DS.910* and *MO.103*
and aircraft, Koivisto Straits 30.7.44

**Name** *U.251* **Built by** Bremer Vulkan (Vegesack) **Launched** 26.7.41
**Fate** Depth charged RAF aircraft (143, 235, 248 & 333 Norge
Sqns.) south of Gothenburg 19.4.45

**Name** *U.252* **Built by** Bremer Vulkan (Vegesack) **Launched** 14.8.41
**Fate** Depth charged RN sloop *Stork*, and corvette *Vetch* south-
west of Ireland 14.4.42

**Name** *U.253* **Built by** Bremer Vulkan (Vegesack) **Launched** 30.8.41 **Fate** Depth charged RAF aircraft (210 Sqn.) south of Jan Mayen Island 23.9.42

**Name** *U.254* **Built by** Bremer Vulkan (Vegesack) **Launched** 20.9.41 **Fate** Damaged collision German submarine *U.410,* and depth charged RAF aircraft (120 Sqn.) south of Cape Farewell 8.12.42

**Name** *U.255* **Built by** Bremer Vulkan (Vegesack) **Launched** 8.10.41 **Fate** Used for training. Surrendered UK port 5.45, and scuttled North Atlantic 1945/6

**Name** *U.256* **Built by** Bremer Vulkan (Vegesack) **Launched** 28.10.41 **Fate** Paid-off Bergen 5.10.44, surrendered 1945 and scuttled

**Name** *U.257* **Built by** Bremer Vulkan (Vegesack) **Launched** 19.11.41 **Fate** Depth charged RCN frigate *Waskesiu* North Atlantic 24.2.44

**Name** *U.258* **Built by** Bremer Vulkan (Vegesack) **Launched** 13.12.41 **Fate** Depth charged RAF aircraft (120 Sqn.) North Atlantic 20.5.43

**Name** *U.259* **Built by** Bremer Vulkan (Vegesack) **Launched** 30.12.41 **Fate** Depth charged RAF aircraft (500 Sqn.) north-west of Algiers 15.11.42

**Name** *U.260* **Built by** Bremer Vulkan (Vegesack) **Launched** 9.2.42 **Fate** Mined 50 m south-west of Kinsale 12.3.45

**Name** *U.261* **Built by** Bremer Vulkan (Vegesack) **Launched** 16.2.42 **Fate** Depth charged RAF aircraft (58 Sqn.) off Hebrides 15.9.42

**Name** *U.262* **Built by** Bremer Vulkan (Vegesack) **Launched** 10.3.42 **Fate** Paid-off French Atlantic port 8.44, surrendered 1945 and scuttled

**Name** *U.263* **Built by** Bremer Vulkan (Vegesack) **Launched** 18.3.42 **Fate** Mined off La Pallice 20.1.44

**Name** *U.264* **Built by** Bremer Vulkan (Vegesack) **Launched** 2.4.42 **Fate** Depth charged RN sloops *Starling* and *Woodpecker* west-south-west of Ireland 19.2.44

**Name** *U.265* **Built by** Bremer Vulkan (Vegesack) **Launched** 23.4.42 **Fate** Depth charged RAF aircraft (220 Sqn.) south of Iceland 3.2.43

**Name** *U.266* **Built by** Bremer Vulkan (Vegesack) **Launched** 11.5.42 **Fate** Depth charged RAF aircraft (86 Sqn.) south-west of Ireland 14.5.43

**Name** *U.267* **Built by** Bremer Vulkan (Vegesack) **Launched** 23.5.42 **Fate** Scuttled Flensburg 5.45

**Name** *U.268* **Built by** Bremer Vulkan (Vegesack)
**Launched** 9.6.42 **Fate** Depth charged RAF aircraft (172 Sqn.)
west of Nantes 19.2.43

**Name** *U.269* **Built by** Bremer Vulkan (Vegesack)
**Launched** 24.6.42 **Fate** Depth charged RN frigate *Bickerton*
north-east of Start Point 25.6.44

**Name** *U.270* **Built by** Bremer Vulkan (Vegesack)
**Launched** 11.7.42 **Fate** Depth charged RAAF aircraft (461 Sqn.)
west of La Rochelle 13.8.44

**Name** *U.271* **Built by** Bremer Vulkan (Vegesack)
**Launched** 29.7.42 **Fate** Depth charged USN aircraft (VB.103)
west of Limerick 28.1.44

**Name** *U.272* **Built by** Bremer Vulkan (Vegesack)
**Launched** 15.8.42 **Fate** Lost collision with German depot ship
*Hela* Baltic 12.11.42

**Name** *U.273* **Built by** Bremer Vulkan (Vegesack)
**Launched** 2.9.42 **Fate** Depth charged RAF aircraft (269 Sqn.)
south of Iceland 19.5.43

**Name** *U.274* **Built by** Bremer Vulkan (Vegesack)
**Launched** 19.9.42 **Fate** Depth charged RN destroyers *Duncan* and
*Vidette* and RAF aircraft (224 Sqn.) south-west of Iceland
23.10.43

**Name** *U.275* **Built by** Bremer Vulkan (Vegesack)
**Launched** 8.10.42 **Fate** Mined off Newhaven 10.3.45

**Name** *U.276* **Built by** Bremer Vulkan (Vegesack)
**Launched** 24.10.42 **Fate** Paid-off Neustadt 29.9.44, surrendered
1945 and scuttled

**Name** *U.277* **Built by** Bremer Vulkan (Vegesack)
**Launched** 7.11.42 **Fate** Depth charged RN aircraft of escort
carrier *Fencer* (842 Sqn.) south-west of Bear Island 1.5.44

**Name** *U.278* **Built by** Bremer Vulkan (Vegesack)
**Launched** 2.12.42 **Fate** Surrendered Narvik 19.5.45, and scuttled
North Atlantic 1945/6

**Name** *U.279* **Built by** Bremer Vulkan (Vegesack)
**Launched** 16.12.42 **Fate** Depth charged RAF aircraft (120 Sqn.)
south-west of Iceland 4.10.43

**Name** *U.280* **Built by** Bremer Vulkan (Vegesack)
**Launched** 4.1.43 **Fate** Depth charged RAF aircraft (86 Sqn.)
North Atlantic 16.11.43

**Name** *U.281* **Built by** Bremer Vulkan (Vegesack)
**Launched** 16.1.43 **Fate** Surrendered Christiansand 5.45, and
scuttled North Atlantic 1945/6

**Name** *U.282* **Built by** Bremer Vulkan (Vegesack)
**Launched** 8.2.43 **Fate** Depth charged RN destroyers *Duncan* and
*Vidette*, and corvette *Sunflower* North Atlantic 29.10.43

**Name** *U.283* **Built by** Bremer Vulkan (Vegesack)
**Launched** 17.2.43 **Fate** Depth charged RCAF aircraft (407 Sqn.) south-west of Faroes 11.2.44

**Name** *U.284* **Built by** Bremer Vulkan (Vegesack)
**Launched** 6.3.43 **Fate** Scuttled North Atlantic 21.12.43 following air attack

**Name** *U.285* **Built by** Bremer Vulkan (Vegesack)
**Launched** 3.4.43 **Fate** Depth charged RN frigates *Grindal* and *Keats* south-west of Ireland 15.4.45

**Name** *U.286* **Built by** Bremer Vulkan (Vegesack)
**Launched** 21.4.43 **Fate** Depth charged RN frigates *Anguilla, Cotton* and *Loch Shin* off Murmansk 29.4.45

**Name** *U.287* **Built by** Bremer Vulkan (Vegesack)
**Launched** 13.8.43 **Fate** Scuttled Elbe estuary 16.5.45

**Name** *U.288* **Built by** Bremer Vulkan (Vegesack)
**Launched** 15.5.43 **Fate** Depth charged RN aircraft of escort carriers *Activity* (819 Sqn.) and *Tracker* (846 Sqn.) south-east of Bear Island 3.4.44

**Name** *U.289* **Built by** Bremer Vulkan (Vegesack)
**Launched** 29.5.43 **Fate** Depth charged RN destroyer *Milne* Arctic 31.5.44

**Name** *U.290* **Built by** Bremer Vulkan (Vegesack)
**Launched** 16.6.43 **Fate** Scuttled Flensburg 5.45

**Name** *U.291* **Built by** Bremer Vulkan (Vegesack)
**Launched** 30.6.43 **Fate** Surrendered Wilhelmshaven 5.45 and scuttled North Atlantic 1945/6

**Name** *U.292* **Built by** Bremer Vulkan (Vegesack)
**Launched** 17.7.43 **Fate** Depth charged RAF aircraft (59 Sqn.) west of Aalsund 27.5.44

**Name** *U.293* **Built by** Bremer Vulkan (Vegesack)
**Launched** 30.7.43 **Fate** Surrendered Trondheim 5.45, and scuttled North Atlantic 1945/6

**Name** *U.294* **Built by** Bremer Vulkan (Vegesack)
**Launched** 27.8.43 **Fate** Surrendered Narvik 19.5.45, and scuttled North Atlantic 1945/6

**Name** *U.295* **Built by** Bremer Vulkan (Vegesack)
**Launched** 13.9.43 **Fate** Surrendered Narvik 19.5.45, and scuttled North Atlantic 1945/6

**Name** *U.296* **Built by** Bremer Vulkan (Vegesack)
**Launched** 25.9.43 **Fate** Depth charged RAF aircraft (120 Sqn.) North Channel 22.3.45

**Name** *U.297* **Built by** Bremer Vulkan (Vegesack)
**Launched** 9.10.43 **Fate** Depth charged RN frigates *Goodall* and *Loch Insh* 31 m north-east of Cape Wrath 6.12.44

**Name** *U.298* **Built by** Bremer Vulkan (Vegesack)
**Launched** 25.10.43 **Fate** Surrendered Bergen 5.45, and scuttled
North Atlantic 1945/6

**Name** *U.299* **Built by** Bremer Vulkan (Vegesack)
**Launched** 6.11.43 **Fate** Surrendered Bergen 5.45, and scuttled
North Atlantic 1945/6

**Name** *U.300* **Built by** Bremer Vulkan (Vegesack)
**Launched** 23.11.43 **Fate** Depth charged RN M/S sloops *Pincher*
and *Recruit*, and armed yacht *Evadne* south-west of Cadiz 22.2.45

**Name** *U.301* **Built by** Flenderwerft (Lübeck) **Launched** 21.3.42
**Fate** Torpedoed RN submarine *Sahib* west of Cape Bonifacio
21.1.43

**Name** *U.302* **Built by** Flenderwerft (Lübeck) **Launched** 25.4.42
**Fate** Depth charged RN frigate *Swale* off Azores 6.4.44

**Name** *U.303* **Built by** Flenderwerft (Lübeck) **Launched** 16.5.42
**Fate** Torpedoed RN submarine *Sickle* off Toulon 21.5.43

**Name** *U.304* **Built by** Flenderwerft (Lübeck) **Launched** 13.6.42
**Fate** Depth charged RAF aircraft (120 Sqn.) south of Cape
Farewell 28.5.43

**Name** *U.305* **Built by** Flenderwerft (Lübeck) **Launched** 25.7.42
**Fate** Depth charged RN destroyer *Wanderer* and frigate *Glenarm*
west-south-west of Ireland 17.i.44

**Name** *U.306* **Built by** Flenderwerft (Lübeck) **Launched** 29.8.42
**Fate** Depth charged RN destroyer *Whitehall*, and corvette
*Geranium* north-east of Azores 31.10.43

**Name** *U.307* **Built by** Flenderwerft (Lübeck) **Launched** 30.9.42
**Fate** Depth charged RN frigate *Loch Insh* off Murmansk 29.4.45

**Name** *U.308* **Built by** Flenderwerft (Lübeck) **Launched** 31.10.42
**Fate** Torpedoed RN submarine *Truculent* off Faroes 4.6.43

**Name** *U.309* **Built by** Flenderwerft (Lübeck) **Launched** 5.12.42
**Fate** Depth charged RCN frigate *St. John* 55 m north-east of
Cromarty 16.2.45

**Name** *U.310* **Built by** Flenderwerft (Lübeck) **Launched** 3.1.43
**Fate** Surrendered Trondheim 10.5.45 and scrapped there 3.47

**Name** *U.311* **Built by** Flenderwerft (Lübeck) **Launched** 20.1.43
**Fate** Depth charged RCAF aircraft (423 Sqn.) west of Ireland
24.4.44

**Name** *U.312* **Built by** Flenderwerft (Lübeck) **Launched** 27.2.43
**Fate** Surrendered Narvik 19.5.45, and scuttled North Atlantic
1945/6

**Name** *U.313* **Built by** Flenderwerft (Lübeck) **Launched** 27.3.43
**Fate** Surrendered Narvik 19.5.45, and scuttled North Atlantic
1945/6

**Name** *U.314* **Built by** Flenderwerft (Lübeck) **Launched** 17.4.43
**Fate** Depth charged RN destroyers *Meteor* and *Whitehall* Barents

**Name** *U.315* **Built by** Flenderwerft (Lübeck) **Launched** 29.5.43
**Fate** Surrendered Trondheim 1.5.45 and scrapped there 3.47

**Name** *U.316* **Built by** Flenderwerft (Lübeck) **Launched** 10.6.43
**Fate** Scuttled Travemünde 2.5.45

**Name** *U.317* **Built by** Flenderwerft (Lübeck) **Launched** 1.9.43
**Fate** Depth charged RAF aircraft (86 Sqn.) east of Shetlands
26.6.44

**Name** *U.318* **Built by** Flenderwerft (Lübeck) **Launched** 25.9.43
**Fate** Surrendered Narvik 19.5.45, and scuttled North Atlantic
1945/6

**Name** *U.319* **Built by** Flenderwerft (Lübeck) **Launched** 16.10.43
**Fate** Depth charged RAF aircraft (206 Sqn.) west-south-west of
The Naze 15.7.44

**Name** *U.320* **Built by** Flenderwerft (Lübeck) **Launched** 6.11.43
**Fate** Depth charged RAF aircraft (210 Sqn.) west of Bergen
7.5.45

**Name** *U.321* **Built by** Flenderwerft (Lübeck) **Launched** 27.11.43
**Fate** Depth charged RAF aircraft (304 Polish Sqn.) south-west
of Ireland 2.4.45

**Name** *U.322* **Built by** Flenderwerft (Lübeck) **Launched** 18.12.43
**Fate** Depth charged RN frigate *Ascension* and RAF aircraft
(330 Norge Sqn.) north-west of Orkneys 25.11.44

**Name** *U.323* **Built by** Flenderwerft (Lübeck) **Launched** 8.1.44
**Fate** Scuttled Nordenham 3.5.45

**Name** *U.324* **Built by** Flenderwerft (Lübeck) **Launched** 29.1.44
**Fate** Surrendered Bergen 5.45, and scrapped there 3.47

**Name** *U.325* **Built by** Flenderwerft (Lübeck) **Launched** 19.2.44
**Fate** Depth charged RN destroyers *Havelock* and *Hesperus* and
RAF aircraft (201 Sqn.) north of Anglesey 30.4.45

**Name** *U.326* **Built by** Flenderwerft (Lübeck) **Launched** 11.3.44
**Fate** Lost by unknown cause off UK coast 4.45

'**Name** *U.327* **Built by** Flenderwerft (Lübeck) **Launched** 1.4.44
**Fate** Depth charged RN sloop *Wild Goose*, frigates *Labuan* and
*Loch Fada*, and USN aircraft (VPB.112) south-west of Lizard
27.2.45

**Name** *U.328* **Built by** Flenderwerft (Lübeck) **Launched** 22.4.44
**Fate** Surrendered Bergen 5.45, and scuttled North Atlantic
1945/6

**Name** *U.239* **Built by** Flenderwerft (Lübeck) **Launched** 13.5.44
**Fate** Bombed USAAF aircraft Bremen 30.3.45

**Name** *U.330* **Built by** Flenderwerft (Lübeck) **Fate** Cancelled

U.331*'s deck gun.* (Drüppel)

**Name** *U.331* **Built by** Nordsee Werke (Emden) **Launched** 20.12.40
**Fate** Depth charged RN aircraft of fleet carrier *Formidable*
(820 Sqn.) and RAF aircraft (500 Sqn.) north-west of Algiers
17.11.42

**Name** *U.332* **Built by** Nordsee Werke (Emden) **Launched** 20.3.41
**Fate** Depth charged RAAF aircraft (461 Sqn.) off Scilly Isles
2.5.43

**Name** *U.333* **Built by** Nordsee Werke (Emden) **Launched** 14.6.41
**Fate** Depth charged RN sloop *Starling* and frigate *Loch Killin*
west of Scillies 31.7.44

**Name** *U.334* **Built by** Nordsee Werke (Emden) **Launched** 15.8.41
**Fate** Depth charged RN sloop *Pelican*, and frigate *Jed* south-west
of Ireland 14.6.43

**Name** *U.335* **Built by** Nordsee Werke (Emden) **Launched** 15.10.41
**Fate** Torpedoed RN submarine *Saracen* north-east of Shetlands
3.8.42

**Name** *U.336* **Built by** Nordsee Werke (Emden) **Launched** 1.12.41
**Fate** Depth charged USN aircraft (VB.128) south-west of Iceland
4.10.43

**Name** *U.337* **Built by** Nordsee Werke (Emden) **Launched** 25.3.42
**Fate** Depth charged RAF aircraft (206 Sqn.) south-west of
Iceland 15.1.43

**Name** *U.338* **Built by** Nordsee Werke (Emden) **Launched** 20.4.42
**Fate** Depth charged RAF aircraft (120 Sqn.) south-west of
Iceland 20.9.43

**Name** *U.339* **Built by** Nordsee Werke (Emden) **Launched** 30.6.42
**Fate** Scuttled Wilhelmshaven 5.45

**Name** *U.340* **Built by** Nordsee Werke (Emden) **Launched** 20.8.42
**Fate** Depth charged RN destroyers *Active* and *Witherington*,
sloop *Fleetwood*, and RAF aircraft (179 Sqn.) off Tangiers 1.11.43

**Name** *U.341* **Built by** Nordsee Werke (Emden) **Launched** 10.10.42
**Fate** Depth charged RCAF aircraft (10 Sqn.) south-west of
Iceland 19.9.43

**Name** *U.342* **Built by** Nordsee Werke (Emden) **Launched** 10.11.42
**Fate** Depth charged RCAF aircraft (162 Sqn.) south-west of
Iceland 17.4.44

**Name** *U.343* **Built by** Nordsee Werke (Emden) **Launched** 21.12.42
**Fate** Depth charged trawler *Mull* south-east of Sardinia 10.3.44

**Name** *U.344* **Built by** Nordsee Werke (Emden) **Launched** 29.1.43
**Fate** Depth charged RN destroyer *Keppel*, sloops *Mermaid* and
*Peacock*, frigate *Loch Dunvegan*, and RN aircraft of *Vindex*
(825 Sqn.) north-east of North Cape 24.8.44

**Name** *U.345* **Built by** Nordsee Werke (Emden) **Launched** 11.3.43
**Fate** Bombed Kiel 13.12.43, salved and paid-off 23.12.43;
surrendered and mined en-route Warnemünde/UK 27.12.45

**Name** *U.346* **Built by** Nordsee Werke (Emden) **Launched** 13.4.43
**Fate** Lost by accident off Hela 20.9.43

**Name** *U.347* **Built by** Nordsee Werke (Emden) **Launched** 24.5.43
**Fate** Depth charged RAF aircraft (210 Sqn.) west of Lofoten
17.7.44

**Name** *U.348* **Built by** Nordsee Werke (Emden) **Launched** 25.6.43
**Fate** Bombed USAAF aircraft Hamburg 30.3.45

**Name** *U.349* **Built by** Nordsee Werke (Emden) **Launched** 27.7.43
**Fate** Scuttled Flensburg 5.5.45

**Name** *U.350* **Built by** Flensburger Schiffsbau **Launched** 17.8.43
**Fate** Bombed USAAF aircraft Hamburg 30.3.45

**Name** *U.351* **Built by** Flensburger Schiffsbau **Launched** 27.3.41
**Fate** Scuttled Flensburg 5.5.45

**Name** *U.352* **Built by** Flensburger Schiffsbau **Launched** 7.5.41
**Fate** Depth charged USCG cutter *Icarus* off Raleigh Bay (N.C.)
9.5.42

**Name** *U.353* **Built by** Flensburger Schiffsbau **Launched** 11.11.41
**Fate** Depth charged RN destroyer *Fame* North Atlantic 16.10.42

**Name** *U.354* **Built by** Flensburger Schiffsbau **Launched** 6.1.42
**Fate** Depth charged RN aircraft of escort carrier *Vindex* (825
Sqn.) north-east of Bear Island 25.8.44

**Name** *U.355* **Built by** Flensburger Schiffsbau **Launched** 5.7.41
**Fate** Depth charged RN aircraft of escort carrier *Tracker* (846
Sqn.), and destroyer *Beagle* south-west of Bear Island 1.4.44

**Name** *U.356* **Built by** Flensburger Schiffsbau **Launched** 16.9.41
**Fate** Depth charged RCN destroyer *St. Laurent*, frigate *St. John*,
and corvettes *Battleford, Chilliwack* and *Napanee* north of Azores
27.12.42

**Name** *U.357* **Built by** Flensburger Schiffsbau **Launched** 31.3.42
**Fate** Depth charged RN destroyers *Hesperus* and *Vanessa* north-
west of Rockall 26.12.42

**Name** *U.358* **Built by** Flensburger Schiffsbau **Launched** 21.4.42
**Fate** Depth charged RN frigates *Affleck, Garlies, Gore* and *Gould*
north of Azores 1.3.44

**Name** *U.359* **Built by** Flensburger Schiffsbau **Launched** 11.6.42
**Fate** Depth charged USN aircraft (VP.32) south of San Domingo
28.7.43

**Name** *U.360* **Built by** Flensburger Schiffsbau **Launched** 28.7.42
**Fate** Depth charged RN destroyer *Keppel* north-west of
Hammerfest 2.4.44

**Name** *U.361* **Built by** Flensburger Schiffsbau **Launched** 9.9.41
**Fate** Depth charged RAF aircraft (86 Sqn.) west of Narvik
17.7.44

**Name** *U.362* **Built by** Flensburger Schiffsbau **Launched** 21.10.42
**Fate** Depth charged Russian minesweeper *T.116* Kara Sea 5.9.44

**Name** *U.363* **Built by** Flensburger Schiffsbau **Launched** 17.12.42
**Fate** Surrendered Narvik 19.5.45, and scuttled North Atlantic
1945/6

**Name** *U.364* **Built by** Flensburger Schiffsbau **Launched** 21.1.43
**Fate** Depth charged RAF aircraft (172 Sqn.) west of Bordeaux
30.1.44

**Name** *U.365* **Built by** Flensburger Schiffsbau **Launched** 9.3.43
**Fate** Depth charged RN aircraft of escort carrier *Campania*
(813 Sqn.) east of Jan Mayen Island 13.12.44

**Name** *U.366* **Built by** Flensburger Schiffsbau **Launched** 16.4.43
**Fate** Rocket fire RN aircraft of escort carrier *Chaser* (816 Sqn.)
north-west of Hammerfest 5.3.44

**Name** *U.367* **Built by** Flensburger Schiffsbau **Launched** 11.6.43
**Fate** Mined off Hela 15.3.45

**Name** *U.368* **Built by** Flensburger Schiffsbau **Launched** 16.11.43
**Fate** Surrendered Wilhelmshaven 5.45 and scuttled North Atlantic
1945/6

**Name** *U.369* **Built by** Flensburger Schiffsbau **Launched** 17.8.43
**Fate** Surrendered Christiansand 5.45, and scuttled North Atlantic
1945/6

**Name** *U.370* **Built by** Flensburger Schiffsbau **Launched** 24.9.43
**Fate** Scuttled Geltinger Bight 5.5.45

**Name** *U.371* **Built by** Howaldts Werke (Kiel) **Launched** 27.1.41
**Fate** Depth charged RN escort destroyer *Blankney*, French frigate
*Senegalais*, USN destroyer escorts *Pride* and *Joseph E. Campbell*
west of Bougie 4.5.44

**Name** *U.372* **Built by** Howaldts Werke (Kiel) **Launched** 8.3.41
**Fate** Depth charged RN destroyers *Sikh* and *Zulu*, escort
destroyers *Croome* and *Tetcott*, and RAF aircraft (221 Sqn.) off
Jaffa 4.8.42

**Name** *U.373* **Built by** Howaldts Werke (Kiel) **Launched** 5.4.41
**Fate** Depth charged RAF aircraft (224 Sqn.) off Brest 8.6.44

**Name** *U.374* **Built by** Howaldts Werke (Kiel) **Launched** 10.5.41
**Fate** Torpedoed RN submarine *Unbeaten* east of Catania 12.1.42

**Name** *U.375* **Built by** Howaldts Werke (Kiel) **Launched** 7.6.41
**Fate** Depth charged USN chaser *PC.624* north-west of Malta
30.7.43

**Name** *U.376* **Built by** Howaldts Werke (Kiel) **Launched** 10.7.41
**Fate** Depth charged RAF aircraft (172 Sqn.) west of Nantes
10.4.43

**Name** *U.377* **Built by** Howaldts Werke (Kiel) **Launched** 12.8.41
**Fate** Lost by unknown cause North Atlantic 1.44

**Name** *U.378* **Built by** Howaldts Werke (Kiel) **Launched** 13.9.41
**Fate** Depth charged USN aircraft of escort carrier *Core* (VC.13)
North Atlantic 20.10.43

**Name** *U.379* **Built by** Howaldts Werke (Kiel) **Launched** 16.10.41
**Fate** Depth charged RN corvette *Dianthus* North Atlantic 8.8.42

**Name** *U.380* **Built by** Howaldts Werke (Kiel) **Launched** 15.11.41
**Fate** Bombed USAAF aircraft Toulon 11.3.44

**Name** *U.381* **Built by** Howaldts Werke (Kiel) **Launched** 14.1.42
**Fate** Depth charged RN destroyer *Duncan*, and corvette
*Snowflake* south of Cape Farewell 19.5.43

**Name** *U.382* **Built by** Howaldts Werke (Kiel) **Launched** 21.3.42
**Fate** Lost by collision Baltic 1.45

**Name** *U.383* **Built by** Howaldts Werke (Kiel) **Launched** 22.4.42
**Fate** Depth charged RAF aircraft (228 Sqn.) west of Brest 1.8.43

**Name** *U.384* **Built by** Howaldts Werke (Kiel) **Launched** 28.5.42
**Fate** Depth charged RAF aircraft (201 Sqn.) south-west of
Iceland 20.3.43

**Name** *U.385* **Built by** Howaldts Werke (Kiel) **Launched** 8.7.42
**Fate** Depth charged RN sloop *Starling*, and RAAF aircraft
(461 Sqn.) west of La Rochelle 11.8.44

**Name** *U.386* **Built by** Howaldts Werke (Kiel) **Launched** 19.8.42
**Fate** Depth charged RN frigate *Spey* west-south-west of Ireland
19.2.44

**Name** *U.387* **Built by** Howaldts Werke (Kiel) **Launched** 1.10.42
**Fate** Depth charged RN corvette *Bamborough Castle* off
Murmansk 9.12.44

**Name** *U.388* **Built by** Howaldts Werke (Kiel) **Launched** 12.11.42
**Fate** Depth charged USN aircraft (VP.84) south of Cape Farewell
20.6.43

**Name** *U.389* **Built by** Howaldts Werke (Kiel) **Launched** 19.12.42
**Fate** Depth charged RAF aircraft (269 Sqn.) south-west of
Iceland 5.10.43

**Name** *U.390* **Built by** Howaldts Werke (Kiel) **Launched** 23.1.43
**Fate** Depth charged RN destroyer *Wanderer*, and frigate *Tavy*
Seine Bay 5.7.44

**Name** *U.391* **Built by** Howaldts Werke (Kiel) **Launched** 5.3.43
**Fate** Depth charged RAF aircraft (53 Sqn.) north-west of Cape
Ortegal 13.12.43

**Name** *U.392* **Built by** Howaldts Werke (Kiel) **Launched** 10.4.43
**Fate** Depth charged RN destroyer *Vanoc*, frigate *Affleck*, and
USN aircraft (VP.63) Straits of Gibraltar 16.3.44

**Name** *U.393* **Built by** Howaldts Werke (Kiel) **Launched** 15.5.43
**Fate** Depth charged RAF aircraft (236 & 254 Sqns.) north of Fyn
Island 4.5.45; and later scuttled

**Name** *U.394* **Built by** Howaldts Werke (Kiel) **Launched** 19.6.43
**Fate** Depth charged RN destroyers *Keppel* and *Whitehall*, sloops
*Mermaid* and *Peacock*, and aircraft of escort carrier *Vindex*
(825 Sqn.) south of Jan Mayen Island 2.9.44

**Name** *U.395* **Built by** Howaldts Werke (Kiel) **Launched** 17.7.43
**Fate** Cancelled

**Name** *U.396* **Built by** Howaldts Werke (Kiel) **Launched** 27.8.43
**Fate** Depth charged RAF aircraft (86 Sqn.) south-west of
Shetlands 23.4.45

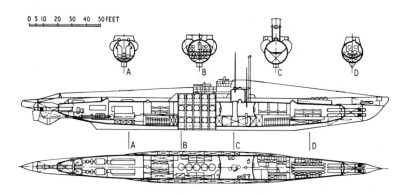

*Type VIID*

## *Type VIID:* **U.213–U.218**

Based on type VIIC with 32-foot section added abaft conning
tower to accommodate five free-flooding mine shafts stowing
fifteen mines. Bunkers and radius increased owing to extra
length, but with some loss of speed.

*Displacement:* 965/1,080 tons
*Dimensions:* $252\frac{1}{4}$ × 21 × $16\frac{1}{2}$ feet
*Machinery:* 2-shaft diesel/electric motors, B.H.P./S.H.P.
    2,800/750 = $16/7\frac{1}{4}$ knots
*Bunkers & Radius:* O.F. 170 tons; 8,100/69 miles at 12/4 knots
*Armament:* One 37mm A.A., two 20mm A.A. (2 × 1) guns;
    five 21inch torpedo tubes (four fwd and one aft—fourteen
    torpedoes and fifteen mines or thirty-nine mines)
*Complement:* 44
*Notes: Schnorchel* added

## VIIE Type

Was a design developed to examine the installation of a new
type of engine with which it was hoped to achieve considerable
economy in machinery weight. The development of this
engine, however, was subject to considerable delay and consequently progress with this type was later abandoned.

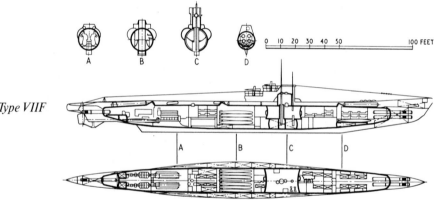

*Type VIIF*

## Type VIIF: U.1059–U.1062

Generally similar to type VIID, except that additional section
fitted with hatch and used to stow twenty-five torpedoes as
cargo to replenish operational boats at sea, and bunkers and
radius increased.

*Displacement:* 1,084/1,181 tons
*Dimensions:* $254\frac{3}{4}$ × 24 × 16 feet
*Machinery:* 2-shaft diesel/electric motors, B.H.P./S.H.P.
    2,800/750 = 17/8 knots
*Bunkers & Radius:* O.F. 199 tons; 9,500/75 miles at 12/4 knots
*Armament:* One 37mm A.A., two 20mm A.A. (2 × 1) guns;
    five 21inch torpedo tubes (four fwd and one aft—fourteen
    torpedoes plus twenty-five torpedoes as cargo)
*Complement:* 46

## Type VIII

Was a design study for which no details are available.

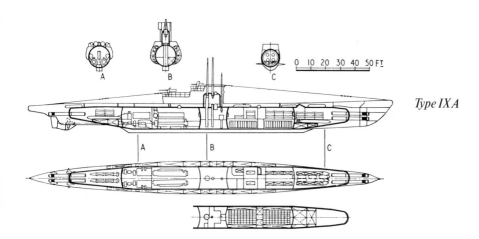

*Type IXA*

## Type IXA: **U.37–U.44**

Ocean-going boats, developed from *U.81* of the First World War, and enlarged from type IA, with higher surface speed and greater radius. Armament principally increased by stowing greater number of torpedo re-loads, and were frequently employed for distant minelaying.

*Displacement:* 1,032/1,153 tons
*Dimensions:* 251 × 21¼ × 15½ feet
*Machinery:* 2-shaft diesel/electric motors, B.H.P./S.H.P. 4,400/1,000 = 18¼/7¾ knots
*Bunkers & Radius:* 154 tons; 8,100/65 miles at 12/4 knots
*Armament:* One 4.1inch, one 37mm A.A., one 20mm A.A. guns; six 21inch torpedo tubes (four fwd and two aft—twenty-two torpedoes or six torpedoes and forty-two mines)
*Complement:* 48
*Notes: Schnorchel* added. A.A. armament increased by substituting twin for single 20mm guns

## Type IXB: **U.64, U.65, U.103–U.111, U.122–U.124**

Improved type IXA, with increased bunkers and radius.

*Displacement:* 1,051/1,178 tons
*Dimensions:* 251 × 22¼ × 15½ feet
*Machinery:* 2-shaft diesel/electric motors, B.H.P./S.H.P.
    4,400/1,000 = 18¼/7¼ knots
*Bunkers & Radius:* O.F. 166 tons; 8,700/64 miles at 12/4 knots
*Armament:* One 4.1inch, one 37mm A.A., one 20mm A.A. guns;
    six 21inch torpedo tubes (four fwd and two aft—twenty-two
    torpedoes or six torpedoes and forty-two mines)
*Complement:* 48
*Notes:* In 1942–43 the 4.1inch and 37mm A.A. deck guns were
    removed, and a second 20mm A.A. gun added on the conning
    tower. Later the A.A. armament was increased to eight 20mm
    (1 × 4 & 2 × 2) guns; and in some units the quadruple
    20mm mounting was replaced by a 37mm gun in 1943–44

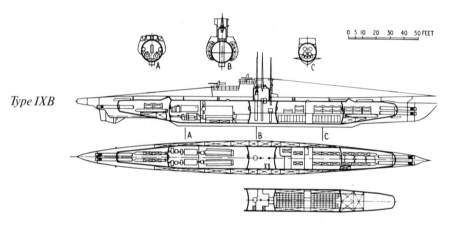

*Type IXB*

## TYPE VIIC

**Name** *U.397* **Built by** Howaldts Werke (Kiel) **Launched** 6.10.43
**Fate** Scuttled Flensburg 5.5.45

**Name** *U.398* **Built by** Howaldts Werke (Kiel) **Launched** 6.11.43
**Fate** Lost by unknown cause off east coast of Scotland 5.45

**Name** *U.399* **Built by** Howaldts Werke (Kiel) **Launched** 4.12.43
**Fate** Depth charged RN frigate *Duckworth* off The Lizard 26.3.45

**Name** *U.400* **Built by** Howaldts Werke (Kiel) **Launched** 8.1.44
**Fate** Depth charged RN frigate *Nyasaland* 38 m off Cork 17.12.44

**Name** *U.401* **Built by** Danziger Werft **Launched** 16.12.40
**Fate** Depth charged RN destroyers *St. Albans* and *Wanderer*, and
corvette *Hydrangea* south-west of Ireland 3.8.41

**Name** *U.402* **Built by** Danziger Werft **Launched** 28.12.40
**Fate** Depth charged USN aircraft of escort carrier *Card* (VC.9)
west-south-west of Iceland 13.10.43

**Name** *U.403* **Built by** Danziger Werft **Launched** 26.2.41
**Fate** Depth charged RAF aircraft (200 & 697 French Sqns.) off
Dakar 17.8.43

**Name** *U.404* **Built by** Danziger Werft **Launched** 4.6.41
**Fate** Depth charged RAF (224 Sqn.) & USAAF (4 Sqn.) aircraft
north-west of Cape Ortegal 28.7.43

**Name** *U.405* **Built by** Danziger Werft **Launched** 4.6.41
**Fate** Gunfire USN destroyer *Borie* North Atlantic 1.11.43

**Name** *U.406* **Built by** Danziger Werft **Launched** 16.6.41
**Fate** Depth charged RN frigate *Spey* North Atlantic 18.2.44

**Name** *U.407* **Built by** Danziger Werft **Launched** 16.8.41
**Fate** Depth charged RN destroyers *Garland, Terpsichore* and
*Troubridge* south of Mylos 19.9.44

**Name** *U.408* **Built by** Danziger Werft **Launched** 16.7.41
**Fate** Depth charged USN aircraft (VP.84) north of Iceland
5.11.42

**Name** *U.409* **Built by** Danziger Werft **Launched** 23.9.41
**Fate** Depth charged RN destroyer *Inconstant* north of Algiers
12.7.43

**Name** *U.410* **Built by** Danziger Werft **Launched** 14.10.41
**Fate** Bombed USAAF aircraft Toulon 11.3.44

**Name** *U.411* **Built by** Danziger Werft **Launched** 15.11.41
**Fate** Depth charged RN destroyer *Wrestler* off Bone 15.11.42

**Name** *U.412* **Built by** Danziger Werft **Launched** 15.12.41
**Fate** Depth charged RAF aircraft (179 Sqn.) north of Faroes
22.10.42

**Name** *U.413* **Built by** Danziger Werft **Launched** 15.1.42
**Fate** Depth charged RN destroyers *Forester* and *Vidette*, and
escort destroyer *Wensleydale* south of Brighton 20.8.44

**Name** *U.414* **Built by** Danziger Werft **Launched** 25.3.42
**Fate** Depth charged RN corvette *Vetch* north-east of Oran
25.5.43

**Name** *U.415* **Built by** Danziger Werft **Launched** 9.5.42
**Fate** Mined off Brest 14.7.44

**Name** *U.416* **Built by** Danziger Werft **Launched** 9.5.42
**Fate** Mined off Bornholm 30.3.43, salved and paid-off; lost in
collision west of Pillau 12.12.44

**Name** *U.417* **Built by** Danziger Werft **Launched** 6.6.42
**Fate** Depth charged RAF aircraft (206 Sqn.) south of Iceland
11.6.43

**Name** *U.418* **Built by** Danziger Werft **Launched** 11.7.42
**Fate** Depth charged RAF aircraft (236 Sqn.) north-west of Cape
Ortegal 1.6.43

**Name** *U.419* **Built by** Danziger Werft **Launched** 22.8.42
**Fate** Depth charged RAF aircraft (86 Sqn.) North Atlantic
8.10.43

**Name** *U.420* **Built by** Danziger Werft **Launched** 12.8.42
**Fate** Depth charged RCAF aircraft (10 Sqn.) North Atlantic
26.10.43

**Name** *U.421* **Built by** Danziger Werft **Launched** 24.9.42
**Fate** Bombed USAAF aircraft Toulon 29.4.44

**Name** *U.422* **Built by** Danziger Werft **Launched** 10.10.42
**Fate** Depth charged USN aircraft of escort carrier *Card* (VC.9)
north of Azores 4.10.43

U.426 *under air attack*. (IWM)

**Name** *U.423* **Built by** Danziger Werft **Launched** 7.11.42
**Fate** Depth charged RAF aircraft (333 Norge Sqn.) north-west
of Christiansand 17.6.44

**Name** *U.424* **Built by** Danziger Werft **Launched** 28.11.42
**Fate** Depth charged RN sloops *Wild Goose* and *Woodpecker*
south-west of Ireland 11.2.44

**Name** *U.425* **Built by** Danziger Werft **Launched** 19.12.42
**Fate** Depth charged RN sloop *Lark* and corvette *Alnwick Castle*
off Murmansk 17.2.45

**Name** *U.426* **Built by** Danziger Werft **Launched** 6.2.43
**Fate** Depth charged RAAF aircraft (10 Sqn.) west of Nantes
8.1.44

**Name** *U.427* **Built by** Danziger Werft **Launched** 6.2.43
**Fate** Surrendered Narvik 19.5.45, and scuttled North Atlantic
1945/6

**Name** *U.428* **Built by** Danziger Werft **Launched** 11.3.43
**Fate** Italian *S.1* (1943), German *U.428* (1943); scuttled Kiel Canal
5.45

**Name** *U.429* **Built by** Danziger Werft **Launched** 30.3.43
**Fate** Italian *S.4* (1943), German *U.429* (1943); bombed USAAF
aircraft Wilhelmshaven 30.3.45

**Name** *U.430* **Built by** Danziger Werft **Launched** 22.4.43
**Fate** Italian *S.6* (1943), German *U.430* (1943); bombed USAAF
aircraft Bremen 30.3.45

**Name** *U.431* **Built by** Schichau (Danzig) **Launched** 2.2.41
**Fate** Torpedoed RN submarine *Ultimatum* off Toulon 30.10.43

**Name** *U.432* **Built by** Schichau (Danzig) **Launched** 3.2.41
**Fate** Depth charged French corvette *Aconit* North Atlantic
11.3.43

**Name** *U.433* **Built by** Schichau (Danzig) **Launched** 15.3.41
**Fate** Depth charged RN corvette *Marigold* south of Malage
16.11.41

**Name** *U.434* **Built by** Schichau (Danzig) **Launched** 1.4.41
**Fate** Depth charged RN destroyer *Stanley*, and escort destroyer
*Blankney* south-west of Cape St. Vincent 18.12.41

**Name** *U.435* **Built by** Schichau (Danzig) **Launched** 31.5.41
**Fate** Depth charged RAF aircraft (179 Sqn.) west of Figueria
9.7.43

**Name** *U.436* **Built by** Schichau (Danzig) **Launched** 21.6.41
**Fate** Depth charged RN frigate *Test*, and corvette *Hyderabad* west
of Cape Ortegal 26.5.43

**Name** *U.437* **Built by** Schichau (Danzig) **Launched** 15.6.41
**Fate** Bombed RAF aircraft Bergen 4.10.44; paid-off 13.10.44

**Name** *U.438* **Built by** Schichau (Danzig) **Launched** 7.41
**Fate** Depth charged RN sloop *Pelican* North Atlantic 6.5.43

**Name** *U.439* **Built by** Schichau (Danzig) **Launched** 10.8.41
**Fate** Lost by collision with *U.659* west of Cape Ortegal 3.5.43

**Name** *U.440* **Built by** Schichau (Danzig) **Launched** 1.9.41
**Fate** Depth charged RAF aircraft (201 Sqn.) west of Cape
Ortegal 31.5.43

**Name** *U.441* **Built by** Schichau (Danzig) **Launched** 13.12.41
**Fate** Depth charged RAF aircraft (304 Polish Sqn.) 34 m
north-east of Ushant 18.6.44

**Name** *U.442* **Built by** Schichau (Danzig) **Launched** 12.1.42
**Fate** Depth charged RAF aircraft (48 Sqn.) south-west of Lisbon
12.2.43

**Name** *U.443* **Built by** Schichau (Danzig) **Launched** 31.1.42
**Fate** Depth charged RN escort destroyers *Bicester, Lamerton* and
*Wheatland* north-west of Algiers 23.2.43

**Name** *U.444* **Built by** Schichau (Danzig) **Launched** 1.1.42
**Fate** Depth charged RN destroyer *Harvester*, and French corvette
*Aconit* North Atlantic 11.3.43

**Name** *U.445* **Built by** Schichau (Danzig) **Launched** 1.2.42
**Fate** Depth charged RN frigate *Louis* west of St. Nazaire 24.8.44

**Name** *U.446* **Built by** Schichau (Danzig) **Launched** 11.4.42
**Fate** Mined Baltic 21.9.42, salved 8.11.43 and paid-off; scuttled
5.45

**Name** *U.447* **Built by** Schichau (Danzig) **Launched** 30.4.42
**Fate** Depth charged RAF aircraft (233 Sqn.) west of Gibraltar
7.5.43

**Name** *U.448* **Built by** Schichau (Danzig) **Launched** 5.42
**Fate** Depth charged RN sloop *Pelican*, and RCN frigate *Swansea*
north-west of Cape Finisterre 14.4.44

**Name** *U.449* **Built by** Schichau (Danzig) **Launched** 13.6.42
**Fate** Depth charged RN sloops *Kite, Wild Goose, Woodpecker*
and *Wren* north-west of Cape Ortegal 24.6.43

**Name** *U.450* **Built by** Schichau (Danzig) **Launched** 4.7.42
**Fate** Depth charged RN escort destroyers *Blankney, Blencathra,
Brecon* and *Exmoor* off Anzio 10.3.44

**Name** *U.451* **Built by** Deutsche Werke (Kiel) **Launched** 5.3.41
**Fate** Depth charged RN aircraft of escort carrier *Audacity*
(812 Sqn.) off Tangiers 21.12.41

**Name** *U.452* **Built by** Deutsche Werke (Kiel) **Launched** 29.3.41
**Fate** Depth charged RN trawler *Vascama*, and RAF aircraft
(209 Sqn.) south of Iceland 25.8.41

**Name** *U.453* **Built by** Deutsche Werke (Kiel) **Launched** 30.4.41
**Fate** Depth charged RN destroyers *Tenacious* and *Termagant*, and
escort destroyer *Liddesdale* east of Cape Spartivento 21.5.44

**Name** *U.454* **Built by** Deutsche Werke (Kiel) **Launched** 30.4.41
**Fate** Depth charged RAAF aircraft (10 Sqn.) north of Cape
Finisterre 1.8.43

**Name** *U.455* **Built by** Deutsche Werke (Kiel) **Launched** 21.6.41
**Fate** Lost by unknown cause off Spezia 6.4.44

**Name** *U.456* **Built by** Deutsche Werke (Kiel) **Launched** 21.6.41
**Fate** Depth charged RN destroyer *Pathfinder*, RN frigate *Lagan*,
RCN corvette *Drumheller*, and RAF aircraft (423 Sqn.) North
Atlantic 13.5.43

**Name** *U.457* **Built by** Deutsche Werke (Kiel) **Launched** 4.10.41
**Fate** Depth charged RN destroyer *Impulsive* north of Murmansk
16.9.42

**Name** *U.458* **Built by** Deutsche Werke (Kiel) **Launched** 4.10.41
**Fate** Depth charged RN escort destroyer *Easton* and RHN
*Pindos* off Pantellaria 22.8.43

## TYPE XIV

**Name** *U.459* **Built by** Deutsche Werke (Kiel) **Launched** 13.9.41
**Fate** Depth charged RAF aircraft (172 Sqn.) north-west of Cape
Ortega 24.7.43

**Name** *U.460* **Built by** Deutsche Werke (Kiel) **Launched** 13.9.41
**Fate** Depth charged USN aircraft of escort carrier *Card* (VC.9)
north of Azores 4.10.43

**Name** *U.461* **Built by** Deutsche Werke (Kiel) **Launched** 8.11.41
**Fate** Depth charged RAF aircraft (461 Sqn.) north of Cape
Finisterre 30.7.43

**Name** *U.462* **Built by** Deutsche Werke (Kiel) **Launched** 29.11.41
**Fate** Depth charged RAF aircraft (502 Sqn.) north-west of Cape
Ortegal 30.7.43

**Name** *U.463* **Built by** Deutsche Werke (Kiel) **Launched** 20.12.41
**Fate** Depth charged RAF aircraft (58 Sqn.) south-west of Scillies
15.5.43

**Name** *U.464* **Built by** Deutsche Werke (Kiel) **Launched** 20.12.41
**Fate** Depth charged USN aircraft (VP.73) north-west of Rockall
20.8.42

## TYPE VIIC

**Name** *U.465* **Built by** Deutsche Werke (Kiel) **Launched** 30.3.42
**Fate** Depth charged RAAF aircraft (10 Sqn.) north-west of Cape
Ortegal 7.5.43

**Name** *U.466* **Built by** Deutsche Werke (Kiel) **Launched** 30.3.42
**Fate** Scuttled Toulon 19.8.44

**Name** *U.467* **Built by** Deutsche Werke (Kiel) **Launched** 16.5.42
**Fate** Depth charged USN aircraft (VP.84) south-east of Iceland
25.5.43

**Name** *U.468* **Built by** Deutsche Werke (Kiel) **Launched** 16.5.42
**Fate** Depth charged RAF aircraft (200 Sqn.) west-south-west of
Bathurst 11.8.43

**Name** *U.469* **Built by** Deutsche Werke (Kiel) **Launched** 8.8.42
**Fate** Depth charged RAF aircraft (206 Sqn.) south of Iceland
25.3.43

**Name** *U.470* **Built by** Deutsche Werke (Kiel) **Launched** 8.8.42
**Fate** Depth charged RAF aircraft (59 & 120 Sqns.) south-west of
Iceland 16.10.43

**Name** *U.471* **Built by** Deutsche Werke (Kiel) **Launched** 6.3.43
**Fate** Bombed USAAF aircraft Toulon 6.8.44; salved and French
*Mille* (1945); decommissioned 8.63

**Name** *U.472* **Built by** Deutsche Werke (Kiel) **Launched** 6.3.43
**Fate** Rocket fire RN aircraft of escort carrier *Chaser* (816 Sqn.),
and depth charged destroyer *Onslaught* south-east of Bear Island
4.3.44

**Name** *U.473* **Built by** Deutsche Werke (Kiel) **Launched** 17.4.43
**Fate** Depth charged RN sloops *Starling, Wild Goose* and *Wren*
north-west of Palma 5.5.44

**Name** *U.474* **Built by** Deutsche Werke (Kiel) **Launched** 17.4.43
**Fate** Bombed Allied aircraft Kiel 1944 while building; scuttled
3.5.45

**Name** *U.475* **Built by** Deutsche Werke (Kiel) **Launched** 25.5.43
**Fate** Scuttled Kiel 3.5.45

**Name** *U.476* **Built by** Deutsche Werke (Kiel) **Launched** 5.6.43
**Fate** Depth charged RAF aircraft (210 Sqn.) north-east of
Trondheim 24.5.44

**Name** *U.477* **Built by** Deutsche Werke (Kiel) **Launched** 3.7.43
**Fate** Depth charged RCAF aircraft (162 Sqn.) north-west of
Christiansand 3.6.44

**Name** *U.478* **Built by** Deutsche Werke (Kiel) **Launched** 17.7.43
**Fate** Depth charged RAF (86 Sqn.) & RCAF (162 Sqn.) aircraft
north-west of Christiansand 30.6.44

**Name** *U.479* **Built by** Deutsche Werke (Kiel) **Launched** 14.8.43
**Fate** Mined Gulf of Finland 12.12.44

**Name** *U.480* **Built by** Deutsche Werke (Kiel) **Launched** 14.8.43
**Fate** Depth charged RN frigates *Duckworth* and *Rowley* south-
west of Land's End 24.2.45

**Name** *U.481* **Built by** Deutsche Werke (Kiel) **Launched** 25.9.43
**Fate** Surrendered Narvik 19.5.45, and scuttled North Atlantic
1945/6

**Name** *U.482* **Built by** Deutsche Werke (Kiel) **Launched** 25.9.43
**Fate** Depth charged RN sloops *Amethyst, Hart, Peacock* and
*Starling*, and frigate *Loch Craggie* 6 m north-west of
Machrihanish 16.1.45

**Name** *U.483* **Built by** Deutsche Werke (Kiel) **Launched** 30.10.43
**Fate** Surrendered Trondheim 5.45, and scuttled North Atlantic
1945/6

**Name** *U.484* **Built by** Deutsche Werke (Kiel) **Launched** 20.11.43
**Fate** Depth charged RCN frigate *Dunver,* corvette *Hespeler,* and
RCAF aircraft (423 Sqn.) off Inner Hebrides 9.9.44

**Name** *U.485* **Built by** Deutsche Werke (Kiel) **Launched** 15.1.44
**Fate** Surrendered Gibraltar 8.5.45, and scuttled North Atlantic
1945/6

**Name** *U.486* **Built by** Deutsche Werke (Kiel) **Launched** 11.2.44
**Fate** Torpedoed RN submarine *Tapir* west of Bergen 12.4.45

## TYPE XIV

**Name** *U.487* **Built by** Deutsche Werke (Kiel) **Launched** 24.10.42
**Fate** Depth charged USN aircraft of escort carrier *Core* (VC.13)
North Atlantic 13.7.43

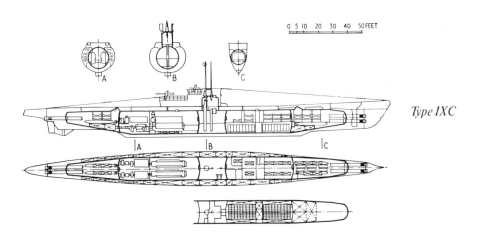

*Type IXC*

## *IXC: Type* **U.66–U.68, U.125–U.131, U.153–U.166, U.171–U.176, U.501–U.524, U.841–U.846, U.853–U.858, U.865–U.870, U.877–U.882, U.889–U.894, U.1221–U.1270, U.1501–U.1530**

Improved type IXB, with extended use of external tanks for
increased bunkers.

*Displacement:* 1,120/1,232 tons
*Dimensions:* 252 × $22\frac{1}{4}$ × $15\frac{1}{2}$ feet
*Machinery:* 2-shaft 9-cyl. diesel/electric motors, B.H.P./S.H.P.
     5,000/1,000 = $18\frac{1}{4}/7\frac{1}{4}$ knots
*Bunkers & Radius:* 208 tons; 11,000/63 miles at 12/4 knots
*Armament:* One 4.1inch, one 37mm A.A., one 20mm A.A. guns;
     six 21inch torpedo tubes (four fwd and two aft—twenty-two
     torpedoes)
*Complement:* 48
*Notes: Schnorchel* added. A.A. armament increased by
     substituting two twin for single 20mm guns, and 4.1inch gun
     removed. In 1942 *U.511* was experimentally fitted with six
     racks at a fixed angle of 45 deg. for launching rockets under-
     water, which were electrically discharged from as deep as
     75 ft. The *U.511* was transferred to Imperial Japanese Navy
     in 1943 and re-numbered *RO.500*, and *U.1224* in 1944 and
     renumbered *R.501. U.1231* had M.A.N.-9-2200 diesels, giving
     a total of 4,400 B.H.P.

## *Type IXC$_{40}$:* **U.167–U.170, U.183–U.194, U.525–U.550, U.801–U.820**

Generally similar to type IXC, except in details of equipment
fitted.

*Displacement:* 1,144/1,247 tons
*Dimensions:* 252 × $22\frac{3}{4}$ × $15\frac{1}{2}$ feet
*Machinery:* 2-shaft 9-cyl. diesel/electric motors, B.H.P./S.H.P.
     4,400/1,000 = $18\frac{1}{4}/7\frac{1}{4}$ knots
*Bunkers & Radius:* O.F. 214 tons; 11,400/63 miles at 12/4 knots
*Armament:* One 4.1inch, on 37mm A.A., two 20mm A.A. (2 × 1)
     guns; six 21inch torpedo tubes (four fwd and two aft—twenty-
     two torpedoes and forty-two mines)
*Complement:* 49
*Notes: Schnorchel* added. A.A. armament increased by sub-
     stituting twin for single 20mm guns, and 4.1inch gun removed.
     *U.541* was apparently fitted with automatic hydroplane
     depth-keeping gear

## *Type IXD$_1$:* **U.180 and U.195**

Ocean-going submarine tankers, developed from type IX but
larger and slower. Torpedo tubes and part of battery capacity
sacrificed to increase cargo deadweight, and only light
defensive A.A. armament mounted.

*Displacement:* 1,610/1,799 tons
*Dimensions:* $287\frac{1}{2} \times 24\frac{1}{2} \times 17\frac{3}{4}$ feet

*Machinery:* 2-shaft diesel/electric motors, B.H.P./S.H.P.
   2,800/1,100 = $15\frac{3}{4}$/7 knots
*Bunkers & Radius:* O.F. 203 tons, 9,900/115 miles at 12/4 knots.
   Cargo O.F. 252 tons
*Armament:* One 37mm A.A., four 20mm A.A. (2 × 2) guns
*Complement:* 57
*Notes:* Originally powered by six fast-running diesel engines
   (three per shaft) of total B.H.P. 9,000 for high surface speed of
   $20\frac{3}{4}$ knots, but these units did not prove satisfactory and were
   replaced by slower-running diesel engines of less power.
   *Schnorchel* added. *U.195* was transferred to the Imperial
   Japanese Navy in 1945 and re-named *I.506*

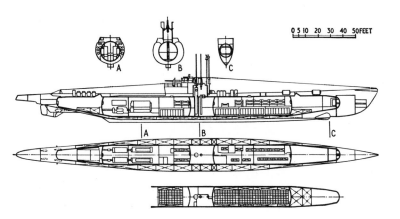

*Type IXD₁*

# Type IXD₂: U.177–U.179, U.181, U.182, U.196–U.200, U.847–U.852, U.859–U.864, U.871–U.876, U.883–U.888, U.895–U.900, U.1531–U.1600

Ocean-going boats developed from type IX with considerably increased bunkers and radius and higher surface speed. Following unsatisfactory experience with type IXD₁ the power output was increased by coupling two slow-running diesel engines per shaft, and not resorting to fast-running engines. Eight vertical mine shafts, each containing four mines, could be fitted as an alternative to torpedo reloads. They were the last conventional submarines put into production, as succeeding higher type numbers were put in hand at an earlier date.

*Displacement:* 1,616/1,804 tons
*Dimensions:* $287\frac{1}{2}$ × $24\frac{1}{2}$ × $17\frac{3}{4}$ feet
*Machinery:* 2-shaft 9-cyl. diesel (two per shaft)/electric motors,
   B.H.P./S.H.P. 4,400/1,100 = $19\frac{1}{4}$/7 knots
*Bunkers & Radius:* O.F. 442 tons; 23,700/57 miles at 12/4 knots
*Armament:* One 4.1inch, one 37mm A.A., one 20mm A.A. guns;
   six 21inch torpedo tubes (four fwd and two aft—twenty-four
   torpedoes or six torpedoes and thirty-two mines)
*Complement:* 57
*Notes: Schnorchel* added. A.A. armament increased by
   substituting two twin for single 20mm guns, and 4.1inch gun
   removed. *U.181* and *U.862* were transferred to the Imperial
   Japanese Navy in 1945 and were re-named *I.501* and *I.502*
   respectively. *U.861, U.874–5* and *U.883* were converted to
   stores carriers by 1945, with superstructure cut away and
   forward torpedo-tubes removed

*Type IXD₂*

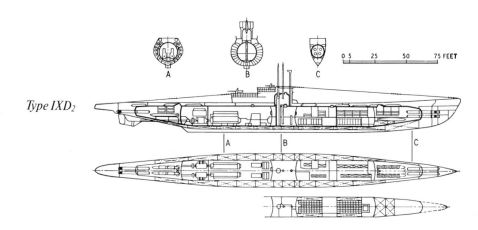

## TYPE XIV

**Name** *U.488* **Built by** Deutsche Werke (Kiel) **Launched** 29.10.42
**Fate** Depth charged USN destroyer escorts *Barber, Frost, Huse*
and *Snowden* north-west of Cape Verde Islands 26.4.44

**Name** *U.489* **Built by** Deutsche Werke (Kiel) **Launched** 19.12.42
**Fate** Depth charged RAF aircraft (423 Sqn.) south of Iceland
4.8.43

**Name** *U.490* **Built by** Deutsche Werke (Kiel) **Launched** 19.12.42
**Fate** Depth charged USN aircraft of escort carrier *Croatan*
(VC.25), and destroyer escorts *Frost, Huse* and *Inch* north-west
of the Azores 12.6.44

**Name** *U.491–U.493* **Built by** Deutsche Werke (Kiel)
**Fate** Cancelled

**Name** *U.494–U.496* **Built by** Germania Werft (Kiel)
**Fate** Cancelled

**Name** *U.497–U.500* **Built by** Deutsche Werke (Kiel)
**Fate** Cancelled

### TYPE IXC

**Name** *U.501* **Built by** Deutsche Werft (Hamburg)
**Launched** 25.1.41 **Fate** Depth charged RCN corvettes *Chambly* and *Moosejaw* south of Greenland 10.9.41

**Name** *U.502* **Built by** Deutsche Werft (Hamburg)
**Launched** 18.2.41 **Fate** Depth charged RAF aircraft (172 Sqn.) west of La Rochelle 5.7.42

**Name** *U.503* **Built by** Deutsche Werft (Hamburg)
**Launched** 5.4.41 **Fate** Depth charged USN aircraft (VP.82) off Newfoundland 15.3.42

**Name** *U.504* **Built by** Deutsche Werft (Hamburg)
**Launched** 26.4.41 **Fate** Depth charged RN sloops *Kite, Wild Goose, Woodpecker* and *Wren* north-west of Cape Ortegal 30.7.43

**Name** *U.505* **Built by** Deutsche Werft (Hamburg)
**Launched** 24.5.41 **Fate** Depth charged USN aircraft of escort carrier *Guadalcanal* (VC.8), and destroyer escorts *Chatelain, Jenks* and *Pillsbury* north-west of Dakar 4.6.44 and captured, USN *Nemo* (1944); naval relic at Chicago

**Name** *U.506* **Built by** Deutsche Werft (Hamburg)
**Launched** 20.6.41 **Fate** Depth charged USAAF aircraft 1st (A/S Sqn.) west of Vigo 12.7.43

**Name** *U.507* **Built by** Deutsche Werft (Hamburg)
**Launched** 15.7.41 **Fate** Depth charged USN aircraft (VP.83) off Parnahyba 13.1.43

**Name** *U.508* **Built by** Deutsche Werft (Hamburg)
**Launched** 30.7.41 **Fate** Depth charged USN aircraft (VB.103) north of Cape Ortegal 12.11.43

**Name** *U.509* **Built by** Deutsche Werft (Hamburg)
**Launched** 19.8.41 **Fate** Depth charged USN aircraft of escort carrier *Santee* (VC.29) south-east of Azores 15.7.43

**Name** *U.510* **Built by** Deutsche Werft (Hamburg)
**Launched** 4.9.41 **Fate** Surrendered St. Nazaire 8.5.45, and French *Bouan* (1945); scrapped (1958)

**Name** *U.511* **Built by** Deutsche Werft (Hamburg)
**Launched** 22.9.41 **Fate** IJN *RO.500* (1943); surrendered Maizuru 8.45 and sunk by USN in Maizura Gulf 30.4.46

**Name** *U.512* **Built by** Deutsche Werft (Hamburg)
**Launched** 9.10.41 **Fate** Depth charged USAAF aircraft (BomRon.99) north of Cayenne 2.10.42

**Name** *U.513* **Built by** Deutsche Werft (Hamburg)
**Launched** 29.10.41 **Fate** Depth charged USN aircraft (VP.74) off
Santos 19.7.43

**Name** *U.514* **Built by** Deutsche Werft (Hamburg)
**Launched** 18.11.41 **Fate** Depth charged RAF aircraft (224 Sqn.)
north-east of Cape Finisterre 8.7.43

**Name** *U.515* **Built by** Deutsche Werft (Hamburg)
**Launched** 2.12.41 **Fate** Depth charged USN aircraft of escort
carrier *Guadalcanal* (VC.58), destroyer *Pope*, and destroyer escorts
*Chatelain, Flaherty* and *Pillsbury* north of Madeira 9.4.44

**Name** *U.516* **Built by** Deutsche Werft (Hamburg)
**Launched** 16.12.41 **Fate** Surrendered UK port 5.45, and scuttled
North Atlantic 1945/6

**Name** *U.517* **Built by** Deutsche Werft (Hamburg)
**Launched** 30.12.41 **Fate** Depth charged RN aircraft of fleet carrier
*Victorious* (817 Sqn.) south-west of Iceland 21.11.42

**Name** *U.518* **Built by** Deutsche Werft (Hamburg)
**Launched** 11.2.42 **Fate** Depth charged USN destroyer escorts
*Carter* and *Neal A. Scott* north-west of Azores 22.4.45

**Name** *U.519* **Built by** Deutsche Werft (Hamburg)
**Launched** 12.2.42 **Fate** Depth charged USAAF aircraft (2 Sqn.)
north-east of Azores 10.2.43

**Name** *U.520* **Built by** Deutsche Werft (Hamburg)
**Launched** 2.3.42 **Fate** Depth charged RCAF aircraft (10 Sqn.)
east of Newfoundland 30.10.42

**Name** *U.521* **Built by** Deutsche Werft (Hamburg)
**Launched** 17.3.42 **Fate** Depth charged USN submarine chaser
*PC.565* south-east of Baltimore 2.6.43

**Name** *U.522* **Built by** Deutsche Werft (Hamburg)
**Launched** 1.4.42 **Fate** Depth charged RN cutter *Totland* south-
west of Madeira 23.2.43

**Name** *U.523* **Built by** Deutsche Werft (Hamburg)
**Launched** 15.4.42 **Fate** Depth charged RN destroyer *Wanderer*,
and corvette *Wallflower* west of Vigo 25.8.43

**Name** *U.524* **Built by** Deutsche Werft (Hamburg)
**Launched** 30.4.42 **Fate** Depth charged USAAF aircraft (1 Sqn.)
south of Madeira 22.3.43

**TYPE IXC$_{40}$**
**Name** *U.525* **Built by** Deutsche Werft (Hamburg)
**Launched** 20.5.42 **Fate** Depth charged USN aircraft of escort
carrier *Card* (VC.1) north-west of Azores 11.8.43

**Name** *U.526* **Built by** Deutsche Werft (Hamburg)
**Launched** 3.6.42 **Fate** Mined off Lorient 14.4.43

**Name** *U.527* **Built by** Deutsche Werft (Hamburg)
**Launched** 3.6.42 **Fate** Depth charged USN aircraft of escort
carrier *Bogue* (VC.9) south of Azores 23.7.43

**Name** *U.528* **Built by** Deutsche Werft (Hamburg)
**Launched** 1.7.42 **Fate** Depth charged RN sloop *Fleetwood*, and
RAF aircraft (58 Sqn.) south-west of Ireland 11.5.43

**Name** *U.529* **Built by** Deutsche Werft (Hamburg)
**Launched** 15.7.42 **Fate** Depth charged RAF aircraft (120 Sqn.)
south-east of Cape Farewell 15.2.43

**Name** *U.530* **Built by** Deutsche Werft (Hamburg)
**Launched** 28.7.42 **Fate** Surrendered Argentina 7.45; USN
experimental vessel (1945); torpedoed as target 28.11.47

**Name** *U.531* **Built by** Deutsche Werft (Hamburg)
**Launched** 12.8.42 **Fate** Gunfire RN corvette *Snowflake*, and
rammed destroyer *Oribi* north-east of Newfoundland 6.5.43

**Name** *U.532* **Built by** Deutsche Werft (Hamburg)
**Launched** 26.8.42 **Fate** Surrendered Liverpool 10.5.45, and
scuttled North Atlantic 1945/6

**Name** *U.533* **Built by** Deutsche Werft (Hamburg)
**Launched** 11.9.42 **Fate** Depth charged RAF aircraft (244 Sqn.)
Gulf of Oman 16.10.43

**Name** *U.534* **Built by** Deutsche Werft (Hamburg)
**Launched** 23.9.42 **Fate** Depth charged RAF aircraft (206 Sqn.)
Kattegat 5.5.45

**Name** *U.535* **Built by** Deutsche Werft (Hamburg)
**Launched** 8.10.42 **Fate** Depth charged RAF aircraft (53 Sqn.) off
Cape Finisterre 5.7.43

**Name** *U.536* **Built by** Deutsche Werft (Hamburg)
**Launched** 21.10.42 **Fate** Depth charged RN frigate *Nene*, and
RCN corvettes *Calgary* and *Snowbery* 20.11.43

**Name** *U.537* **Built by** Deutsche Werft (Hamburg)
**Launched** 7.11.42 **Fate** Torpedoed USN submarine *Flounder* east
of Surabaya 9.11.44

**Name** *U.538* **Built by** Deutsche Werft (Hamburg)
**Launched** 20.11.42 **Fate** Depth charged RN sloop *Crane*, and
frigate *Foley* south-west of Ireland 21.11.43

**Name** *U.539* **Built by** Deutsche Werft (Hamburg)
**Launched** 4.12.42 **Fate** Surrendered Bergen 5.45, and scuttled
North Atlantic 1945/6

**Name** *U.540* **Built by** Deutsche Werft (Hamburg)
**Launched** 18.12.42 **Fate** Depth charged RAF aircraft (59 & 120
Sqns.) east of Cape Farewell 17.10.43

**Name** *U.541* **Built by** Deutsche Werft (Hamburg)
**Launched** 5.1.43 **Fate** Surrendered Gibraltar 5.45, and scuttled
North Atlantic 1945/6

Facing page, top:
U.570 *running on the surface under the White Ensign.* (IWM)

Facing page, bottom: U.570 *after her capture, under a British crew.* (UPI)

**Name** *U.542* **Built by** Deutsche Werft (Hamburg) **Launched** 19.1.43 **Fate** Depth charged RAF aircraft (179 Sqn.) north of Madeira 28.11.43

**Name** *U.543* **Built by** Deutsche Werft (Hamburg) **Launched** 3.2.43 **Fate** Depth charged USN aircraft of escort carrier *Wake Island* (VC.58) south-west of Teneriffe 2.7.44

**Name** *U.544* **Built by** Deutsche Werft (Hamburg) **Launched** 17.2.43 **Fate** Depth charged USN aircraft of escort carrier *Guadalcanal* (VC.13) north-west of Azores 16.1.44

**Name** *U.545* **Built by** Deutsche Werft (Hamburg) **Launched** 3.3.43 **Fate** Depth charged RAF aircraft (612 Sqn.) west of Hebrides 10.2.44

**Name** *U.546* **Built by** Deutsche Werft (Hamburg) **Launched** 17.3.43 **Fate** Depth charged USN destroyer escorts *Chatelain, Flaherty, Harry E. Hubbard, Jansen, Keith, Neunzer, Pillsbury* and *Varian* north-west of Azores 24.4.45

**Name** *U.547* **Built by** Deutsche Werft (Hamburg) **Launched** 3.4.43 **Fate** Mined Baltic 11.44, salved and scrapped

**Name** *U.548* **Built by** Deutsche Werft (Hamburg) **Launched** 14.4.43 **Fate** Depth charged USN destroyer escorts *Bostwick, Coffman* and *Thomas,* and frigate *Natchez* east of Cape Hatteras 30.4.45

**Name** *U.549* **Built by** Deutsche Werft (Hamburg) **Launched** 28.4.43 **Fate** Depth charged USN destroyer escorts *Ahrens* and *Eugene E. Elmore* south-west of Madeira 29.5.44

**Name** *U.550* **Built by** Deutsche Werft (Hamburg) **Launched** 12.5.43 **Fate** Depth charged USN destroyer escorts *Gandy, Joyce* and *Peterson* east-south-east of New York 16.4.44

### TYPE VIIC

**Name** *U.551* **Built by** Blohm & Voss (Hamburg) **Launched** 14.9.40 **Fate** Depth charged RN trawler *Visenda* south of Iceland 23.3.41

**Name** *U.552* **Built by** Blohm & Voss (Hamburg) **Launched** 14.9.40 **Fate** Scuttled Wilhelmshaven 5.45

**Name** *U.553* **Built by** Blohm & Voss (Hamburg) **Launched** 7.11.40 **Fate** Lost by unknown cause North Atlantic 28.1.43

**Name** *U.554* **Built by** Blohm & Voss (Hamburg) **Launched** 7.11.40 **Fate** Scuttled Bremerhaven 3.5.45

**Name** *U.555* **Built by** Blohm & Voss (Hamburg) **Launched** 7.12.40 **Fate** Surrendered Hamburg 5.45 and scrapped

**Name** *U.556* **Built by** Blohm & Voss (Hamburg) **Launched** 7.12.40 **Fate** Depth charged RN corvettes *Celandine, Gladiolus* and *Nasturtium* south-west of Iceland 27.6.41

**Name** *U.557* **Built by** Blohm & Voss (Hamburg) **Launched** 22.12.40
**Fate** Lost collison Italian torpedo boat *Orione* south-west of
Crete 16.12.41

**Name** *U.558* **Built by** Blohm & Voss (Hamburg) **Launched** 23.12.40
**Fate** Depth charged USAAF aircraft (19 Sqn.) north-west of
Cape Ortegal 20.7.43

**Name** *U.559* **Built by** Blohm & Voss (Hamburg) **Launched** 8.1.41
**Fate** Depth charged RN destroyers *Hero, Pakenham* and *Petard*,
escort destroyers *Dulverton* and *Hurworth*, and RAF aircraft
(47 Sqn.) 60 m north-east of Port Said 30.10.42

**Name** *U.560* **Built by** Blohm & Voss (Hamburg) **Launched** 10.1.41
**Fate** Lost by collison off Memel 11.40; salved and scuttled Kiel
5.45

**Name** *U.561* **Built by** Blohm & Voss (Hamburg) **Launched** 23.1.41
**Fate** Torpedoed *MTB.81* off Lipari 12.7.43

**Name** *U.562* **Built by** Blohm & Voss (Hamburg) **Launched** 24.1.41
**Fate** Depth charged RN destroyer *Isis*, escort destroyer *Hursley*,
and RAF aircraft (38 Sqn.) north-east of Benghazi 19.2.43

**Name** *U.563* **Built by** Blohm & Voss (Hamburg) **Launched** 5.2.41
**Fate** Depth charged RAF (58 & 228 Sqns.) and RAAF (10 Sqn.)
aircraft south-west of Brest 31.5.43

**Name** *U.564* **Built by** Blohm & Voss (Hamburg) **Launched** 7.2.41
**Fate** Depth charged RAF aircraft (10 Sqn.) north-west of Cape
Ortegal 14.6.43

**Name** *U.565* **Built by** Blohm & Voss (Hamburg) **Launched** 20.2.41
**Fate** Bombed USAAF aircraft Salamis 24.9.44

**Name** *U.566* **Built by** Blohm & Voss (Hamburg) **Launched** 20.2.41
**Fate** Depth charged RAF aircraft (179 Sqn.) off Oporto 24.10.43

**Name** *U.567* **Built by** Blohm & Voss (Hamburg) **Launched** 6.3.41
**Fate** Depth charged RN sloop *Deptford*, and corvette *Samphire*
north of Azores 21.12.41

**Name** *U.568* **Built by** Blohm & Voss (Hamburg) **Launched** 6.3.41
**Fate** Depth charged RN destroyer *Hero,* and escort destroyers
*Eridge* and *Hurworth* off Tobruk 28.5.42

**Name** *U.569* **Built by** Blohm & Voss (Hamburg) **Launched** 20.3.41
**Fate** Depth charged USN aircraft of escort carrier *Bogue* (VC.9)
North Atlantic 22.5.43

**Name** *U.570* **Built by** Blohm & Voss (Hamburg) **Launched** 20.3.41
**Fate** Depth charged RAF aircraft (269 Sqn.) 80 m south of
Iceland 27.8.41 and captured, RN *Graph* (1941); wrecked en-route
Chatham/Clyde 20.3.44, salved and scrapped 1947

**Name** *U.571* **Built by** Blohm & Voss (Hamburg) **Launched** 4.4.41
**Fate** Depth charged RAAF aircraft (461 Sqn.) west of Galway
28.1.44

**Name** *U.572* **Built by** Blohm & Voss (Hamburg) **Launched** 5.4.41
**Fate** Depth charged USN aircraft (VP.205) north-east of
Georgetown 3.8.43

**Name** *U.573* **Built by** Blohm & Voss (Hamburg) **Launched** 17.4.41
**Fate** Interned Cartagena after being depth charged by RAF
aircraft (233 Sqn.) north-west of Algiers 1.5.42; Spanish *G 7*
(1943)

**Name** *U.574* **Built by** Blohm & Voss (Hamburg) **Launched** 18.4.41
**Fate** Rammed RN sloop *Stork* off Lisbon 19.12.41

**Name** *U.575* **Built by** Blohm & Voss (Hamburg) **Launched** 30.4.41
**Fate** Depth charged USN aircraft of escort carrier *Bogue* (VP.95),
destroyer escort *Haverfield,* M/S destroyer *Hobson,* RCN frigate
*Prince Rupert*, and RAF aircraft (172, 296 & 220 Sqns.) north of
Azores 13.3.44

**Name** *U.576* **Built by** Blohm & Voss (Hamburg) **Launched** 30.4.41
**Fate** Depth charged USN aircraft (VS.9), and gunfire auxiliary
*Unicoi* off Wilmington 15.7.42

**Name** *U.577* **Built by** Blohm & Voss (Hamburg) **Launched** 15.5.41
**Fate** Depth charged RAF aircraft (230 Sqn.) north-west of Mersa
Matruh 9.1.42

**Name** *U.578* **Built by** Blohm & Voss (Hamburg) **Launched** 15.5.41
**Fate** Depth charged RAF aircraft (311 Czech Sqn.) north of Cape
Ortegal 10.8.42

**Name** *U.579* **Built by** Blohm & Voss (Hamburg) **Launched** 28.5.41
**Fate** Depth charged RAF aircraft Little Belt 5.5.45

**Name** *U.580* **Built by** Blohm & Voss (Hamburg) **Launched** 28.5.41
**Fate** Lost by collision off Memel 11.11.41

## *Type XA*

Ocean-going minelayers of *ca.* 2,500 tons with mines carried
externally in shafts amidships, on each side, and internally
in shafts aft projecting above and below the pressure hull. The
internal disposition of space, however, was considered
uneconomical and the design was abandoned and the following fresh design (type XB) was prepared.

## *Type XB:* **U.116–U.119, U.219, U.220, U.233, U.234**

Much improved diminutives of type XA with increased mine
capacity and the addition of two stern torpedo tubes. The
mines were stowed three apiece in six internal shafts forward,
projecting above and below the pressure hull, and two apiece

in twenty-four external mine shafts, twelve a side. Torpedo re-loads were stowed both internally and externally. This type was more frequently employed as supply submarine than minelayer.

*Displacement:* 1,763/2,177 tons
*Dimensions:* $294\frac{3}{4}$ × $30\frac{1}{4}$ × $13\frac{1}{2}$ feet
*Machinery:* 2-shaft diesel/electric motors, B.H.P./S.H.P.
    4,200/1,100 = $16\frac{1}{2}$/7 knots
*Bunkers & Radius:* O.F. 368 tons; 14,550/93 miles at 12/4 knots
*Armament:* One 4.1inch, one 37mm A.A., one 20mm A.A. guns;
    two 21inch torpedo tubes (both aft—fifteen torpedoes and
    sixty-six mines)
*Complement:* 52
*Notes: Schnorchel* added. A.A. armament increased by sub-
    stituting two twins for single 20mm guns, and 4.1inch gun
    removed. *U.219* was transferred to the Imperial Japanese
    Navy in 1945 and re-named *I.505*

*Type XB*

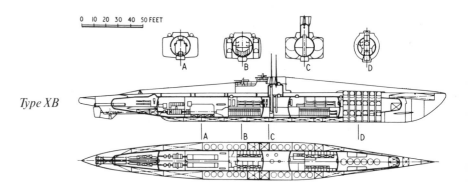

## *Type XI:* **U.113–U.115**

Design prepared in 1938 for submarine cruisers with a large radius of action, mainly intended to fight with guns on the surface, and with provision made to carry a seaplane to extend vision. As the role of this type was more limited than that of smaller submarines, and also a more combatant surface vessel could be built within its design parameter, the design which embraced a double cylinder pressure hull set one abreast the other, was not finally adopted. In fact, the German auxiliary cruisers did all, if not more, that these submarine-cruisers could have performed on the more distant trade routes. Their inception was probably accounted for by the restricted success achieved under more favourable conditions by their predecessors in the First World War.

*Displacement*: 3,140/3,630 tons
*Dimensions*: $377\frac{1}{4} \times 31\frac{1}{4} \times 20\frac{1}{4}$ feet
*Machinery*: 2-shaft diesel/electric motors, B.H.P./S.H.P.
   17,600/2,200 = 23/7 knots
*Armament*: Four 5inch (2 × 2), two 37mm A.A. (2 × 1), two
   20mm A.A. (1 × 2) guns; eight 21inch torpedo tubes (six fwd
   and two aft—twelve torpedoes); one aircraft
*Complement*: 110

## Type XII

Fleet submarines based on the type IX hull with a surface displacement of *ca.* 1,600 tons. Main propulsion was by diesel/electric motors of B.H.P./S.H.P. 7,000/1,680 coupled to two shafts for speeds of 22/10 knots, and the surface radius of action was 20,000 miles at 12 knots. The armament included eight 21inch torpedo tubes, disposed six forward and two aft.

## Type XIII

Coastal boats, based on the type II, with size and speed increased to 400 tons and 15 knots.

## Type XIV : U.459–464, U.487–500, U.2201–U.2204

Ocean-going submarine tankers which adopted a shorter and fuller hull form than the type $IXD_1$ and had a much improved cargo deadweight. Four externally stowed torpedoes were also carried for replenishing operational boats at sea.

*Displacement*: 1,688/1,932 tons
*Dimensions*: $220\frac{1}{4} \times 30\frac{3}{4} \times 21\frac{1}{4}$ feet
*Machinery*: 2-shaft diesel/electric motors, B.H.P./S.H.P.
   2,800/750 = $14\frac{1}{2}/6\frac{1}{4}$ knots
*Bunkers & Radius*: O.F. 203 tons; 9,300/53 miles at 12/4 knots.
   Cargo O.F. 432 tons
*Armament*: Two 37mm A.A. (2 × 1), one 20mm A.A. guns (four
   torpedoes as cargo)
*Complement*: 53
*Notes*: 37mm guns sited before and abaft the conning tower

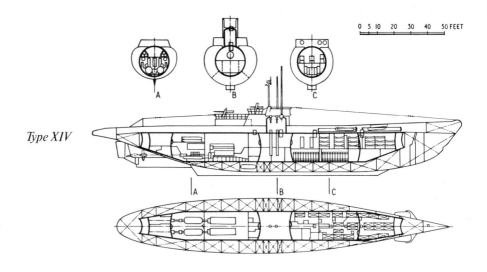

*Type XIV*

0  5  10    20    30    40    50 FEET

**TYPE VIIC**

**Name** *U.581* **Built by** Blohm & Voss (Hamburg) **Launched** 12.6.41
**Fate** Depth charged RN destroyer *Wetscott* south-west of Azores
2.2.42

**Name** *U.582* **Built by** Blohm & Voss (Hamburg) **Launched** 12.6.41
**Fate** Depth charged RAF aircraft (269 Sqn.) south-west of
Iceland 5.10.42

**Name** *U.583* **Built by** Blohm & Voss (Hamburg) **Launched** 26.6.41
**Fate** Lost by collision Baltic 15.11.41

**Name** *U.584* **Built by** Blohm & Voss (Hamburg) **Launched** 26.6.41
**Fate** Depth charged USN aircraft of escort carrier *Card* (VC.9)
North Atlantic 31.10.43

**Name** *U.585* **Built by** Blohm & Voss (Hamburg) **Launched** 9.7.41
**Fate** Depth charged RN destroyer *Fury* north-east of Vardo
29.3.42

**Name** *U.586* **Built by** Blohm & Voss (Hamburg) **Launched** 10.7.41
**Fate** Bombed USAAF aircraft Toulon 5.7.44

**Name** *U.587* **Built by** Blohm & Voss (Hamburg) **Launched** 23.7.41
**Fate** Depth charged RN destroyers *Volunteer* and *Leamington*,
and escort destroyers *Aldenham* and *Grove* south-west of Ireland
27.3.42

**Name** *U.588* **Built by** Blohm & Voss (Hamburg) **Launched** 23.7.41
**Fate** Depth charged RCN destroyer *Skeena*, and corvette
*Wetaskiwin* North Atlantic 31.7.42

**Name** *U.589* **Built by** Blohm & Voss (Hamburg) **Launched** 6.8.41
**Fate** Depth charged RN aircraft of escort carrier *Avenger*
(825 Sqn.), and destroyer *Onslow* Bear Island area 14.9.42

**Name** *U.590* **Built by** Blohm & Voss (Hamburg) **Launched** 6.8.41
**Fate** Depth charged USN aircraft (VP.94) off River Amazon
estuary 9.7.43

**Name** *U.591* **Built by** Blohm & Voss (Hamburg) **Launched** 20.8.41
**Fate** Depth charged USN aircraft (VB.127) off Pernambuco
30.7.43

**Name** *U.592* **Built by** Blohm & Voss (Hamburg) **Launched** 20.8.41
**Fate** Depth charged RN sloops *Magpie, Starling* and *Wild Goose*
west of Ireland 31.1.44

**Name** *U.593* **Built by** Blohm & Voss (Hamburg) **Launched** 3.9.41
**Fate** Depth charged USN destroyer *Wainwright* and RN escort
destroyer *Calpe* north-east of Djidjelli 13.12.43

**Name** *U.594* **Built by** Blohm & Voss (Hamburg) **Launched** 3.9.41
**Fate** Depth charged RAF aircraft (48 Sqn.) south-west of
Gibraltar 4.6.43

**Name** *U.595* **Built by** Blohm & Voss (Hamburg) **Launched** 17.9.41
**Fate** Depth charged RAF aircraft (500 Sqn.) north of Oran
14.11.42

**Name** *U.596* **Built by** Blohm & Voss (Hamburg) **Launched** 17.9.41
**Fate** Bombed USAAF aircraft Salamis 24.9.44

**Name** *U.597* **Built by** Blohm & Voss (Hamburg) **Launched** 11.10.41
**Fate** Depth charged RAF aircraft (120 Sqn.) south-south-west of
Iceland 12.10.42

**Name** *U.598* **Built by** Blohm & Voss (Hamburg) **Launched** 2.10.41
**Fate** Depth charged USN aircraft (VB.107) off Fernando
Norohna 23.7.43

**Name** *U.599* **Built by** Blohm & Voss (Hamburg) **Launched** 15.10.41
**Fate** Depth charged RAF aircraft (224 Sqn.) north of Azores
24.10.42

**Name** *U.600* **Built by** Blohm & Voss (Hamburg) **Launched** 15.10.41
**Fate** Depth charged RN frigates *Bazely* and *Blackwood* north of
Punta Delgada 25.11.43

**Name** *U.601* **Built by** Blohm & Voss (Hamburg) **Launched** 29.10.41
**Fate** Depth charged RAF aircraft (210 Sqn.) 250 m north-west
of Lofotens 25.2.44

**Name** *U.602* **Built by** Blohm & Voss (Hamburg) **Launched** 30.10.41
**Fate** Depth charged RAF aircraft (560 Sqn.) off Oran 23.4.43

**Name** *U.603* **Built by** Blohm & Voss (Hamburg) **Launched** 16.11.41
**Fate** Depth charged USN destroyer escort *Bronstein* North
Atlantic 1.3.44

**Name** *U.604* **Built by** Blohm & Voss (Hamburg) **Launched** 16.11.41
**Fate** Scuttled east of Pernambuco 11.8.43 after being depth
charged USN destroyer *Moffett*, and aircraft (VB.107 & 129)
3.8.43

**Name** *U.605* **Built by** Blohm & Voss (Hamburg) **Launched** 27.11.41
**Fate** Depth charged RN corvettes *Lotus* and *Poppy* off Algiers
13.11.42

**Name** *U.606* **Built by** Blohm & Voss (Hamburg) **Launched** 27.11.41
**Fate** Depth charged USCG cutter *Campbell*, and Polish destroyer
*Burza* North Atlantic 22.2.43

**Name** *U.607* **Built by** Blohm & Voss (Hamburg) **Launched** 11.12.41
**Fate** Depth charged RAF aircraft (228 Sqn.) north-west of Cape
Ortegal 13.7.43

**Name** *U.608* **Built by** Blohm & Voss (Hamburg) **Launched** 11.12.41
**Fate** Depth charged RN sloop *Wren* and RAF aircraft (53 Sqn.)
west of Ile d'Yeu 19.8.44

**Name** *U.609* **Built by** Blohm & Voss (Hamburg) **Launched** 23.12.41
**Fate** Depth charged French corvette *Lobelia* North Atlantic
7.2.43

**Name** *U.610* **Built by** Blohm & Voss (Hamburg) **Launched** 24.12.41
**Fate** Depth charged RCAF aircraft (423 Sqn.) North Atlantic
8.10.43

**Name** *U.611* **Built by** Blohm & Voss (Hamburg) **Launched** 8.1.42
**Fate** Depth charged USN aircraft (VP.84) south of Iceland
10.12.42

**Name** *U.612* **Built by** Blohm & Voss (Hamburg) **Launched** 9.1.42
**Fate** Scuttled Warnemunde 2.5.45

**Name** *U.613* **Built by** Blohm & Voss (Hamburg) **Launched** 29.1.42
**Fate** Depth charged USN destroyer *George E. Badger* south of
Azores 23.7.43

**Name** *U.614* **Built by** Blohm & Voss (Hamburg) **Launched** 29.1.42
**Fate** Depth charged RAF aircraft (172 Sqn.) off Cape Finisterre
29.7.43

**Name** *U.615* **Built by** Blohm & Voss (Hamburg) **Launched** 8.2.42
**Fate** Depth charged USN (VB.130, VP.204 & 205) and USAAF
(BomRon.10) aircraft south of Curacao 7.8.43

**Name** *U.616* **Built by** Blohm & Voss (Hamburg) **Launched** 8.2.42
**Fate** Depth charged USN destroyers *Ellyson*, *Emmons*, *Gleaves*,
*Hambleton*, *Hilary P. Jones*, *Macomb*, *Nields* and *Rodman*, and
RAF aircraft (36 Sqn.) north-east of Oran 14.5.44

**Name** *U.617* **Built by** Blohm & Voss (Hamburg) **Launched** 19.2.42
**Fate** Scuttled off Melilla 12.9.43, after being depth charged RN
corvette *Hyacinth*, RAN M/S sloop *Wollongong*, RN trawler
*Haarlem*, and RAF aircraft (179 Sqn.) off Oran 11.9.43

**Name** *U.618* **Built by** Blohm & Voss (Hamburg) **Launched** 20.2.42
**Fate** Depth charged RN frigates *Duckworth* and *Essington*, and
RAF aircraft (53 Sqn.) west of St. Nazaire 14.8.44

**Name** *U.619* **Built by** Blohm & Voss (Hamburg) **Launched** 9.3.42
**Fate** Depth charged RN destroyer *Viscount* North Atlantic
15.10.42

**Name** *U.620* **Built by** Blohm & Voss (Hamburg) **Launched** 9.3.42
**Fate** Depth charged RAF aircraft (202 Sqn.) north-west of Lisbon
14.2.43

**Name** *U.621* **Built by** Blohm & Voss (Hamburg) **Launched** 29.3.42
**Fate** Depth charged RCN destroyers *Chaudiere, Kootenay* and
*Ottawa* off La Rochelle 18.8.44

**Name** *U.622* **Built by** Blohm & Voss (Hamburg) **Launched** 29.3.42
**Fate** Bombed USAAF aircraft Trondheim 24.7.43, later salved;
surrendered 1945

**Name** *U.623* **Built by** Blohm & Voss (Hamburg) **Launched** 31.3.42
**Fate** Torpedoed RAF aircraft (120 Sqn.) North Atlantic 21.2.43

**Name** *U.624* **Built by** Blohm & Voss (Hamburg) **Launched** 31.3.42
**Fate** Depth charged RAF aircraft (220 Sqn.) North Atlantic
7.2.43

**Name** *U.625* **Built by** Blohm & Voss (Hamburg) **Launched** 15.4.42
**Fate** Depth charged and gunfire RCAF aircraft (422 Sqn.) west of
Ireland 10.3.44

**Name** *U.626* **Built by** Blohm & Voss (Hamburg) **Launched** 14.4.42
**Fate** Depth charged USCG cutter *Ingham* North Atlantic 15.12.42

**Name** *U.627* **Built by** Blohm & Voss (Hamburg) **Launched** 29.4.42
**Fate** Depth charged RAF aircraft (206 Sqn.) south of Iceland
27.10.42

**Name** *U.628* **Built by** Blohm & Voss (Hamburg) **Launched** 29.4.42
**Fate** Depth charged RAF aircraft (224 Sqn.) north-west of Cape
Ortegal 3.7.43

**Name** *U.629* **Built by** Blohm & Voss (Hamburg) **Launched** 12.5.42
**Fate** Depth charged RAF aircraft (224 Sqn.) off Brest 8.6.44

**Name** *U.630* **Built by** Blohm & Voss (Hamburg) **Launched** 12.5.42
**Fate** Depth charged RCAF aircraft (5 Sqn.) south of Cape
Farewell 4.5.43

**Name** *U.631* **Built by** Blohm & Voss (Hamburg) **Launched** 27.5.42
**Fate** Depth charged RN corvette *Sunflower* south of Cape
Farewell 17.10.43

**Name** *U.632* **Built by** Blohm & Voss (Hamburg) **Launched** 27.5.42
**Fate** Depth charged RAF aircraft (86 Sqn.) south of Iceland
6.4.43

**Name** *U.633* **Built by** Blohm & Voss (Hamburg) **Launched** 10.6.42
**Fate** Depth charged RAF aircraft (220 Sqn.) south of Iceland
7.3.43

**Name** *U.634* **Built by** Blohm & Voss (Hamburg) **Launched** 10.6.42
**Fate** Depth charged RN sloop *Stork,* and corvette *Stonecrop*
north-east of Azores 30.8.43

**Name** *U.635* **Built by** Blohm & Voss (Hamburg) **Launched** 24.6.42
**Fate** Depth charged RN frigate *Tay* south-west of Iceland
6.4.43

**Name** *U.636* **Built by** Blohm & Voss (Hamburg) **Launched** 25.6.42
**Fate** Depth charged RN frigates *Bazely, Bentinck* and *Drury*
90 m north-east of Donegal 21.4.45

**Name** *U.637* **Built by** Blohm & Voss (Hamburg) **Launched** 7.7.42
**Fate** Surrendered Stavanger 5.45, and scuttled North Atlantic
1945/6

**Name** *U.638* **Built by** Blohm & Voss (Hamburg) **Launched** 8.7.42
**Fate** Depth charged RN corvette *Loosestrife* off Newfoundland
6.5.43

**Name** *U.639* **Built by** Blohm & Voss (Hamburg) **Launched** 22.7.42
**Fate** Torpedoed Russian submarine *S.101* Kara Sea 30.8.43

**Name** *U.640* **Built by** Blohm & Voss (Hamburg) **Launched** 23.7.42
**Fate** Depth charged RN frigate *Swale* south-east of Cape
Farewell 17.5.43

**Name** *U.641* **Built by** Blohm & Voss (Hamburg) **Launched** 6.8.42
**Fate** Depth charged RN corvette *Violet* south-west of Ireland
19.1.44

**Name** *U.642* **Built by** Blohm & Voss (Hamburg) **Launched** 6.8.42
**Fate** Bombed USAAF Toulon 5.7.44

**Name** *U.643* **Built by** Blohm & Voss (Hamburg) **Launched** 20.8.42
**Fate** Depth charged RAF aircraft (86 & 120 Sqns.) North Atlantic
8.10.43

**Name** *U.644* **Built by** Blohm & Voss (Hamburg) **Launched** 20.8.42
**Fate** Torpedoed RN submarine *Tuna* south-east of Jan Mayen
Island 7.4.43

**Name** *U.645* **Built by** Blohm & Voss (Hamburg) **Launched** 3.9.42
**Fate** Depth charged USN destroyer *Schenck* 24.12.43

**Name** *U.646* **Built by** Blohm & Voss (Hamburg) **Launched** 3.9.42
**Fate** Depth charged RAF aircraft (269 Sqn.) south of Iceland
17.5.43

**Name** *U.647* **Built by** Blohm & Voss (Hamburg) **Launched** 16.9.42
**Fate** Mined Iceland/Faroes area 3.8.43

**Name** *U.648* **Built by** Blohm & Voss (Hamburg) **Launched** 17.9.42
**Fate** Depth charged RN frigates *Bazely, Blackwood* and *Drury*
north of Azores 23.11.43

**Name** *U.649* **Built by** Blohm & Voss (Hamburg) **Launched** 30.9.42
**Fate** Lost collision with German submarine *U.232* Baltic 24.2.43

**Name** *U.650* **Built by** Blohm & Voss (Hamburg) **Launched** 11.10.42
**Fate** Lost by unknown cause off north-east coast of Scotland
7.1.45

**Name** *U.651* **Built by** Howaldts Werke (Hamburg)
**Launched** 21.12.40 **Fate** Depth charged RN destroyers *Malcolm*
and *Scimitar*, M/S sloop *Speedwell*, and corvettes *Arabis* and
*Violet* south of Iceland 29.6.41

**Name** *U.652* **Built by** Howaldts Werke (Hamburg)
**Launched** 7.2.41 **Fate** Torpedoed German submarine *U.81* to
scuttle her after being depth charged RN (815 Sqn.) & RAF
(203 Sqn.) aircraft off Sollum 2.6.42

**Name** *U.653* **Built by** Howaldts Werke (Hamburg)
**Launched** 31.3.41 **Fate** Depth charged RN aircraft of escort
carrier *Vindex* (825 Sqn.), and sloops *Starling* and *Wild Goose*
North Atlantic 15.3.44

**Name** *U.654* **Built by** Howaldts Werke (Hamburg)
**Launched** 3.5.41 **Fate** Depth charged USAAF aircraft (45 Sqn.)
off Colon 22.8.42

**Name** *U.655* **Built by** Howaldts Werke (Hamburg)
**Launched** 9.6.41 **Fate** Rammed RN M/S sloop *Sharpshooter* north
of Hammerfest 24.3.42

**Name** *U.656* **Built by** Howaldts Werke (Hamburg)
**Launched** 1.7.41 **Fate** Depth charged USN aircraft (VP.82) east of
Newfoundland 1.3.42

**Name** *U.657* **Built by** Howaldts Werke (Hamburg)
**Launched** 12.8.41 **Fate** Depth charged USN aircraft (VP.84)
south-west of Iceland 14.5.43

**Name** *U.658* **Built by** Howaldts Werke (Hamburg)
**Launched** 11.9.41 **Fate** Depth charged RCAF aircraft (145 Sqn.)
east of Newfoundland 30.10.42

**Name** *U.659* **Built by** Howaldts Werke (Hamburg)
**Launched** 14.10.41 **Fate** Lost collision with German submarine
*U.439* west of Cape Finisterre 3.5.43

**Name** *U.660* **Built by** Howaldts Werke (Hamburg)
**Launched** 17.11.41 **Fate** Depth charged RN corvettes *Lotus* and
*Starwort* north-east of Oran 12.11.42

**Name** *U.661* **Built by** Howaldts Werke (Hamburg)
**Launched** 11.12.41 **Fate** Depth charged RAF aircraft (120 Sqn.)
North Atlantic 15.10.42

**Name** *U.662* **Built by** Howaldts Werke (Hamburg)
**Launched** 1.42 **Fate** Depth charged USN aircraft (VP.94) off Para
21.7.43

**Name** *U.663* **Built by** Howaldts Werke (Hamburg)
**Launched** 5.42 **Fate** Depth charged RAF aircraft (58 Sqn.) west
of Brest 7.5.43

**Name** *U.664* **Built by** Howaldts Werke (Hamburg)
**Launched** 1942 **Fate** Depth charged USN aircraft of escort carrier
*Card* (VC.1) west of Azores 9.8.43

**Name** *U.665* **Built by** Howaldts Werke (Hamburg)
**Launched** 1942 **Fate** Depth charged RAF aircraft (172 Sqn.) west
of Nantes 22.3.43

**Name** *U.666* **Built by** Howaldts Werke (Hamburg)
**Launched** 1942 **Fate** Depth charged RN aircraft of escort carrier
*Fencer* (842 Sqn.) west of Iceland 10.2.44

**Name** *U.667* **Built by** Howaldts Werke (Hamburg)
**Launched** 1942 **Fate** Mined off La Pallice 25.8.44

**Name** *U.668* **Built by** Howaldts Werke (Hamburg)
**Launched** 11.42 **Fate** Surrendered Narvik 19.5.45, and scuttled
North Atlantic 1945/6

**Name** *U.669* **Built by** Howaldts Werke (Hamburg)
**Launched** 12.42 **Fate** Depth charged RCAF aircraft (407 Sqn.)
north-west of Cape Ortegal 7.9.43

**Name** *U.670* **Built by** Howaldts Werke (Hamburg)
**Launched** 1943 **Fate** Lost by collision Baltic 21.8.43

**Name** *U.671* **Built by** Howaldts Werke (Hamburg)
**Launched** 1943 **Fate** Depth charged RN escort destroyer
*Wensleydale*, and frigate *Stayner* 25 m south-east of Brighton
4.8.44

**Name** *U.672* **Built by** Howaldts Werke (Hamburg)
**Launched** 1943 **Fate** Depth charged RN frigate *Balfour* 32 m
south of Portland Bill 18.7.44

**Name** *U.673* **Built by** Howaldts Werke (Hamburg)
**Launched** 1943 **Fate** Collision German mine-sweeper north of
Stavanger 16.10.44

**Name** *U.674* **Built by** Howaldts Werke (Hamburg)
**Launched** 6.43 **Fate** Depth charged RN aircraft of escort carrier
*Fencer* (842 Sqn.) north-west of Narvik 2.5.44

**Name** *U.675* **Built by** Howaldts Werke (Hamburg)
**Launched** 7.43 **Fate** Depth charged RAF aircraft (4 OTU) west of
Aalesund 24.5.44

**Name** *U.676* **Built by** Howaldts Werke (Hamburg)
**Launched** 1943 **Fate** Mined Gulf of Finland 19.2.45

**Name** *U.677* **Built by** Howaldts Werke (Hamburg)
**Launched** 1943 **Fate** Bombed RAF aircraft Hamburg 8.4.45

**Name** *U.678* **Built by** Howaldts Werke (Hamburg)
**Launched** 1943 **Fate** Depth charged RCN destroyers *Kootenay*
and *Ottawa*, and RN corvette *Statice* 23 m south-south-west of
Brighton 6.7.44

**Name** *U.679* **Built by** Howaldts Werke (Hamburg)
**Launched** 11.43 **Fate** Mined Baltic 10.1.45

**Name** *U.680* **Built by** Howaldts Werke (Hamburg)
**Launched** 11.43 **Fate** Surrendered Wilhelmshaven 5.45, and
scuttled North Atlantic 1945/6

**Name** *U.681* **Built by** Howaldts Werke (Hamburg)
**Launched** 1.44 **Fate** Bombed USN aircraft (VPB.103) after being
wrecked on Scillies 11.3.45

**Name** *U.682* **Built by** Howaldts Werke (Hamburg)
**Launched** 2.44 **Fate** Bombed RAF aircraft Hamburg 31.3.45

**Name** *U.683* **Built by** Howaldts Werke (Hamburg)
**Launched** 3.44 **Fate** Depth charged RN sloop *Wild Goose*, and
frigate *Loch Ruthven* south-west of Land's End 12.3.45

**Name** *U.684–U.686* **Built by** Howaldts Werke (Hamburg)
**Fate** Cancelled

**Name** *U.687–U.700* **Built by** Howaldts Werke (Hamburg)
**Fate** Projected

**Name** *U.701* **Built by** Stülcken Sohn (Hamburg) **Launched** 16.4.41
**Fate** Depth charged USAAF aircraft (396 Sqn.) off Cape
Hatteras 7.7.42

**Name** *U.702* **Built by** Stülcken Sohn (Hamburg) **Launched** 24.5.41
**Fate** Lost by unknown cause North Sea 4.4.42

**Name** *U.703* **Built by** Stülcken Sohn (Hamburg) **Launched** 16.7.41
**Fate** Mined off east coast of Iceland 30.9.44

**Name** *U.704* **Built by** Stülcken Sohn (Hamburg) **Launched** 29.8.41
**Fate** Scuttled Vegesack 3.5.45

**Name** *U.705* **Built by** Stülcken Sohn (Hamburg) **Launched** 1.10.41
**Fate** Depth charged RAF aircraft (77 Sqn.) west of Scillies 3.9.42

**Name** *U.706* **Built by** Stülcken Sohn (Hamburg) **Launched** 15.11.41
**Fate** Depth charged USAAF aircraft (4 Sqn.) off Cape Ortegal
2.8.43

**Name** *U.707* **Built by** Stülcken Sohn (Hamburg) **Launched** 18.12.41
**Fate** Depth charged RAF aircraft (220 Sqn.) 9.11.43

**Name** *U.708* **Built by** Stülcken Sohn (Hamburg) **Launched** 24.3.42
**Fate** Scuttled Wilhelmshaven 3.5.45

**Name** *U.709* **Built by** Stülcken Sohn (Hamburg) **Launched** 14.4.42
**Fate** Depth charged USN destroyer escorts *Bostwick*, *Bronstein*
and *Thomas* North Atlantic 1.3.44

**Name** *U.710* **Built by** Stülcken Sohn (Hamburg) **Launched** 11.5.42
**Fate** Depth charged RAF aircraft (206 Sqn.) south of Iceland
24.4.43

**Name** *U.711* **Built by** Stülcken Sohn (Hamburg) **Launched** 25.6.42 **Fate** Depth charged RN aircraft of escort carriers *Queen* (853 Sqn.), *Searcher* (882 Sqn.) and *Trumpeter* (846 Sqn.) off Harstad 4.5.45

**Name** *U.712* **Built by** Stülcken Sohn (Hamburg) **Launched** 10.8.42 **Fate** Surrendered Christiansand 5.45, RN (1946); scrapped 1949/50

**Name** *U.713* **Built by** Stülcken Sohn (Hamburg) **Launched** 23.9.42 **Fate** Depth charged RN destroyer *Keppel* off Narvik 24.2.44

**Name** *U.714* **Built by** Stülcken Sohn (Hamburg) **Launched** 12.11.42 **Fate** Depth charged RN destroyer *Wivern* and SAN frigate *Natal* 10 m north-east of Berwick 14.3.45

**Name** *U.715* **Built by** Stülcken Sohn (Hamburg) **Launched** 14.12.42 **Fate** Depth charged RCAF aircraft (162 Sqn.) east of Faroes 13.6.44

**Name** *U.716* **Built by** Stülcken Sohn (Hamburg) **Launched** 15.1.43 **Fate** Surrendered Narvik 19.5.45, and scuttled North Atlantic 1945/6

**Name** *U.717* **Built by** Stülcken Sohn (Hamburg) **Launched** 19.2.43 **Fate** Scuttled Flensburg 2.5.45 after being bombed by Allied aircraft

**Name** *U.718* **Built by** Stülcken Sohn (Hamburg) **Launched** 26.3.43 **Fate** Lost by collision Baltic 18.11.43

*U.660 was sunk on November 12, 1942 by the corvettes* HMS Starwort *and* HMS Lotus. *Note what appears to be camouflage on the conning-tower.* (IWM)

*U.754 (Type VIIC) seen running on the surface, probably during training in the Baltic.* (Drüppel)

**Name** *U.719* **Built by** Stülcken Sohn (Hamburg) **Launched** 24.4.43
**Fate** Depth charged RN destroyer *Bulldog* off north-west coast of
Ireland 26.6.44

**Name** *U.720* **Built by** Stülcken Sohn (Hamburg) **Launched** 5.6.43
**Fate** Surrendered Wilhelmshaven 5.45, and scuttled North
Atlantic 1945/6

**Name** *U.721* **Built by** Stülcken Sohn (Hamburg) **Launched** 22.7.43
**Fate** Scuttled Geltinger Bight 5.45

**Name** *U.722* **Built by** Stülcken Sohn (Hamburg) **Launched** 18.9.43
**Fate** Depth charged RN frigates *Byron, Fitzroy* and *Redmill*
23 m south-west of Dunvegan 27.3.45

**Name** *U.723–U.730* **Built by** Stülcken Sohn (Hamburg)
**Fate** Cancelled

**Name** *U.731* **Built by** Schichau (Danzig) **Launched** 1942
**Fate** Depth charged RN sloop *Kilmarnock*, trawler *Blackfly*, and
USN aircraft (VP.63) off Tangiers 15.5.44

**Name** *U.732* **Built by** Schichau (Danzig) **Launched** 1942
**Fate** Depth charged RN destroyer *Douglas*, and trawler
*Imperialist* off Tangiers 31.10.43

**Name** *U.733* **Built by** Schichau (Danzig) **Launched** 1942
**Fate** Scuttled Flensburg 5.5.45 after being bombed RAF aircraft

**Name** *U.734* **Built by** Schichau (Danzig) **Launched** 1942
**Fate** Depth charged RN sloop *Starling* and *Wild Goose* south-west
of Ireland 9.2.44

**Name** *U.735* **Built by** Schichau (Danzig) **Launched** 1942
**Fate** Bombed RAF aircraft Horten 28.12.44

**Name** *U.736* **Built by** Schichau (Danzig) **Launched** 1942
**Fate** Depth charged RN sloop *Starling*, and frigate *Loch Killin*
south-west of Belle Ile 6.8.44

**Name** *U.737* **Built by** Schichau (Danzig) **Launched** 1942
**Fate** Collision German minesweeper West Fjord 19.12.44

**Name** *U.738* **Built by** Schichau (Danzig) **Launched** 1940/3
**Fate** Lost by accident off Gdynia 14.2.44

**Name** *U.739* **Built by** Schichau (Danzig) **Launched** 1940/3
**Fate** Surrendered Wilhelmshaven 5.45, and scuttled North
Atlantic 1945/6

**Name** *U.740* **Built by** Schichau (Danzig) **Launched** 1943
**Fate** Depth charged RAF aircraft (120 Sqn.) west of Scillies
9.6.44

**Name** *U.741* **Built by** Schichau (Danzig) **Launched** 1943
**Fate** Depth charged RN corvette *Orchis* 32 m north-west of
Fecamp 15.8.44

**Name** *U.742* **Built by** Schichau (Danzig) **Launched** 1943
**Fate** Depth charged RAF aircraft (210 Sqn.) 18.7.44

**Name** *U.743* **Built by** Schichau (Danzig) **Launched** 1943
**Fate** Depth charged RN frigate *Helmsdale*, and corvette
*Portchester Castle* north-west of Ireland 9.9.44

**Name** *U.744* **Built by** Schichau (Danzig) **Launched** 1943
**Fate** Depth charged RN destroyer *Icarus* and RCN *Chaudière*
and *Gatineau*, RCN frigate *St. Catherines*, RCN corvettes
*Chilliwack* and *Fennel* and RN *Kenilworth Castle* 6.3.44

**Name** *U.745* **Built by** Schichau (Danzig) **Launched** 1943
**Fate** Lost by unknown cause Gulf of Finland 4.2.45

**Name** *U.746* **Built by** Schichau (Danzig) **Launched** 1943
**Fate** Italian *S.2* (1943), German *U.746* (1943); scuttled Geltinger
Bight 4.5.45 after being bombed RAF aircraft

**Name** *U.747* **Built by** Schichau (Danzig) **Launched** 1943
**Fate** Italian *S.3* (1943), German *U.747* (1943); bombed RAF
aircraft Hamburg 8.4.45

**Name** *U.748* **Built by** Schichau (Danzig) **Launched** 1943
**Fate** Italian *S.5* (1943), German *U.748* (1943); scuttled Rendsburg
3.5.45

**Name** *U.749* **Built by** Schichau (Danzig) **Launched** 1943
**Fate** Italian *S.7* (1943), German *U.749* (1943); bombed USAAF
aircraft Kiel 4.4.45

**Name** *U.750* **Built by** Schichau (Danzig) **Launched** 1943
**Fate** Italian *S.9* (1943), German *U.750* (1943); scuttled Flensburg
5.5.45

**Name** *U.751* **Built by** Naval Dockyard (Wilhelmshaven)
**Launched** 1940 **Fate** Depth charged RAF aircraft (61 & 502 Sqns.)
north-west of Cape Ortegal 17.7.42

**Name** *U.752* **Built by** Naval Dockyard (Wilhelmshaven)
**Launched** 1940/3 **Fate** Rocket fire of RN aircraft of escort carrier
*Archer* (819 Sqn.) 750 m west of Ireland 23.5.43

**Name** *U.753* **Built by** Naval Dockyard (Wilhelmshaven)
**Launched** 1940/3 **Fate** Lost by unknown cause North Atlantic
15.5.43

**Name** *U.754* **Built by** Naval Dockyard (Wilhelmshaven)
**Launched** 1941 **Fate** Depth charged RCAF aircraft (113 Sqn.)
south of Nova Scotia 31.7.42

**Name** *U.755* **Built by** Naval Dockyard (Wilhelmshaven)
**Launched** 1941 **Fate** Depth charged RAF aircraft (608 Sqn.)
north of Balearic Islands 28.5.43

**Name** *U.756* **Built by** Naval Dockyard (Wilhelmshaven)
**Launched** 1941 **Fate** Depth charged RAF aircraft south-west of
Iceland 3.9.42

**Name** *U.757* **Built by** Naval Dockyard (Wilhelmshaven)
**Launched** 1941 **Fate** Depth charged RN frigate *Bayntun*, and RCN
corvette *Camrose* south-west of Ireland 8.1.44

## *Type' XV*

Ocean-going boats for supplying submarines at sea with bunkers, torpedoes and stores, together with workshop facilities for undertaking limited repairs. With a triple cylinder pressure hull disposed abreast, size ran up to *ca.* 2,500 tons while conventional main propulsion was retained comprising diesel/electric motors of B.H.P./S.H.P. 2,800/750 coupled to two shafts. Such craft, while attending operational submarines, would have presented most vulnerable targets, unable to dive rapidly if detected, and the project was consequently abandoned.

## *Type XVI*

Was a similar project to the above type with size further increased to *ca.* 5,000 tons, but the design was not proceeded with as it possessed, to a larger degree, the inherent disadvantages associated with the type XV.

## *Experimental boat:* **VB.60**

When submarine construction was finally resumed in 1934 the first priority was for coastal boats (type II). Their limited size, however, emphasised the desirability of a closed-cycle engine which could be used for both surfaced and submerged propulsion in place of the separate diesel and electric systems. The most promising development under consideration at that time was for a Walter project for a small and fast submersible with closed-cycle diesel engines, but soon after Walter was proposing a closed-cycle turbine which showed greater promise.

An initial design was prepared for an unarmed 60-ton experimental boat—the *VB.60*—with a length of $68\frac{3}{4}$ feet, a beam of $6\frac{1}{2}$ feet, powered by a 2,000 S.H.P. turbine driving a single shaft, and manned by a crew of 3; and while the boat was not finally built it provided valuable design experience for larger follow-on boats. Although such development work was a closely guarded secret inevitably some news of it leaked out, and resulted in the ill-found rumour that the type II coastal submarines were powered by closed-cycle engines.

## Experimental boat: **V.80**

This craft was a slightly enlarged version of the *VB.60*, with the addition of a 10kW auxiliary electric motor drawing power from a battery. She was completed early in 1940, and employed under the State Service flag carried out trials to examine the feasability operational of the Walter system. Like the *VB.60* a figure-of-eight hull form was adopted amidships with a short second cylinder placed below the main pressure hull. The *V.80* was paid-off at the end of 1942 and placed in reserve.

*Displacement:* $73\frac{1}{4}$/76 tons
*Dimensions:* $72\frac{1}{4} \times 7 \times 10\frac{1}{2}$ feet
*Machinery:* 1-shaft Walter geared turbine S.H.P. 2,000 = 28 knots; and electric motor S.H.P. 14 = 4 knots
*Bunkers & Radius:* Perhydrol 20 tons, 50 miles at 28 knots
*Armament:* Nil
*Complement:* 4

## Experimental boat: **U.791 (ex-V.300)**

A sea-going prototype which adopted the Walter turbine for main propulsion but was not finally completed. Owing to the limited radius at full speed with the turbine, an auxiliary diesel/electric drive was added to extend the cruising range. Consequently, the ratio of machinery weight to displacement was high for this and all subsequent Walter boats, and was an inherent disadvantage of the system which was never completely overcome. A narrow casing was laid over the pressure hull, and was surmounted by a conning tower amidships; while the torpedo tubes were disposed vertically in the bows. The original draft was for a boat of about 360 tons, but this was twice modified and enlarged to improve operational capability.

*Displacement:* 610/655 tons
*Dimensions:* $156\frac{1}{4}$(pp)/171(oa) $\times 13\frac{1}{4} \times 18$ feet
*Machinery:* 1-shaft Walter geared turbines (two/shaft), S.H.P. 4,360 = 19 knots, and 6-cylinder MWM diesel (two/shaft)/electric motors (two/shaft), B.H.P./S.H.P. 300/150 = $9\frac{1}{4}$/$9\frac{1}{2}$ knots
*Bunkers & Radius:* Perhydrol 98 tons, 205 miles at 19 knots; O.F. 34 tons, 2,330/40 miles at $9$/$9\frac{1}{2}$ knots
*Armament:* Two 21inch torpedo tubes (both fwd—six torpedoes)
*Complement:* 25

## Type XVIIA : First group **U.792 & U.793.** Second group **U.794 & 795**

Coastal boats which formed the first production series powered by the Walter turbine, but were still largely experimental craft. The restricted range of the Walter system made it more suitable, in the first instance, for adoption by coastal boats until it could be further developed. Separate designs were developed for the first group (Wa.201) built by Blohm & Voss, and the second group (Wk.202) built by Germania; and there was a marked reduction in size compared with the prototype *U.791*. While the lead boat in each group had two turbines installed, this was reduced to one turbine in the follow-on boats.

## Wa.201

*Displacement:* 313/343 tons
*Dimensions:* $124\frac{3}{4}$ feet
*Machinery:* 1-shaft Walter geared turbines (two/shaft in *U.792* only) S.H.P. 5,000 (*U.792*)/2,500 (*U.793*) = 26/21 knots; and 8-cylinder Deutz diesel/electric motors B.H.P./S.H.P. 210/77 = 9/5 knots
*Bunkers & Radius:* Aurol 40 tons, 80 miles at 26 knots; and O.F. 17 tons, 1,840/76 at 9/2 knots
*Armament:* Two 21-inch (both fwd—four torpedoes) T.T.
*Complement:* 12

## Wk.202

*Displacement:* 236/259 tons
*Dimensions:* $111\frac{3}{4} \times 11\frac{1}{4} \times 15$ feet
*Machinery:* 1-shaft Walter geared turbines, S.H.P. 5,000 = 26 knots; and 8-cylinder Deutz diesel/electric motors B.H.P./ S.H.P. 210/77 = 9/5 knots
*Bunkers & Radius:* Perhydrol 40 tons, 80 miles at 26 knots; and O.F. 14 tons, 1,840/40 miles at $9/4\frac{1}{2}$ knots
*Armament:* Two 21inch torpedo tubes (both fwd—four torpedoes)
*Complement:* 12

## Deschimag project

As an alternative to turbines Deschimag A.G. Weser proposed diesel engines for a simpler closed-cycle system in 1943, and while the proposal was not new the design study they submitted appeared most feasible. Although no submersible was built to the Deschimag design the project was taken up in parallel with the type XVII turbine boats.

*Displacement:* 352 tons
*Dimensions:* $118 \times 13\frac{1}{4} \times 13\frac{3}{4}$ feet
*Machinery:* 1-shaft 20-cylinder Daimler-Benz diesel (two/shaft) motors B.H.P. 3,000 = $15\frac{3}{4}/22\frac{3}{4}$ knots; and electric motor S.H.P. 50 = 4 knots
*Bunkers:* O.F. 30 tons + oxygen $9\frac{1}{2}$ tons
*Armament:* Two 21inch (both fwd—four torpedoes) T.T.
*Complement:* Not known

## *Type XVIIB:* **U. 1405–1416**

Further coastal boats, rather precipitately embarked on considering the limited success achieved with the Walter system. The original provision was to fit two sets of turbines coupled to one shaft, but only one was finally installed with little loss of speed. The pressure hull was formed of two cylinders, disposed one over the other, and a periscopic *schnorchel* was provided.

*Displacement:* 312/337 tons
*Dimensions:* $136\frac{1}{4} \times 10\frac{3}{4} \times 14\frac{3}{4}$ feet

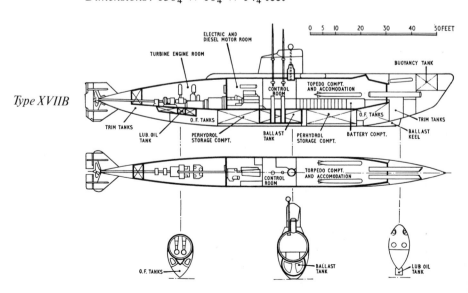

*Type XVIIB*

*Machinery:* 1-shaft Walter geared turbines, S.H.P. 2,500 =
  $21\frac{1}{2}$ knots; and 8-cylinder Deutz diesel/electric motors
  B.H.P./S.H.P. 210/77 = $8\frac{1}{2}$/5 knots
*Bunkers & Radius:* Aurol 55 tons, 150 miles at 20 knots; O.F.
  20 tons, 3,000/40 miles at 8/$4\frac{1}{2}$ knots
*Armament:* Two 21inch torpedo tubes (both fwd—four torpedoes)
*Complement:* 19

## *Types XVIIB$_2$ & XVIIB$_3$*

Modifications of type XVIIB to increase submerged radius
with turbine drive. The latter design omitted the diesel engine
but had two turbines coupled to the single shaft for higher
submerged speed.

*Displacement:* 306 tons
*Dimensions:* 144 × $10\frac{3}{4}$ × 14 feet
*Machinery:* 1-shaft Walter geared turbines (two/shaft in type
  XVIIB$_3$ only) S.H.P. 1,160 (XVIIB$_2$)/2,500 (XVIIB$_3$) =
  $15\frac{3}{4}$/20 knots; and diesel (in type XVIIB$_2$ only)/electric motors
  B.H.P./S.H.P. 210/$77\frac{1}{2}$ = 9/5 knots
*Bunkers & Radius:* Perhydrol 100 (XVIIB$_2$)/80 (XVIIB$_3$) tons,
  660 miles at $15\frac{3}{4}$ knots (XVIIB$_2$)/1,700 miles at 8 knots
  (XVIIB$_3$); and O.F. 20 tons (XVIIB$_2$ only)
*Armament:* Two 21inch (both fwd—two torpedoes) T.T.
*Complement:* 19

## TYPE VIIC

**Name** *U.758* **Built by** Naval Dockyard (Wilhelmshaven)
**Launched** 1942 **Fate** Surrendered Kiel 1945, and scrapped

**Name** *U.759* **Built by** Naval Dockyard (Wilhelmshaven)
**Launched** 1942 **Fate** Depth charged USN aircraft (VP.32) south-
east of Jamaica 26.7.43

**Name** *U.760* **Built by** Naval Dockyard (Wilhelmshaven)
**Launched** 1942 **Fate** Interned Vigo 8.9.43 after being damaged;
surrendered and scuttled North Atlantic 1945/6

**Name** *U.761* **Built by** Naval Dockyard (Wilhelmshaven)
**Launched** 1942 **Fate** Depth charged RN destroyers *Anthony* and
*Wishart,* and RAF (202 Sqn.) & USN (VP.63 & VB.127) aircraft
off Tangiers 24.2.44

**Name** *U.762* **Built by** Naval Dockyard (Wilhelmshaven)
**Launched** 1942 **Fate** Depth charged RN sloops *Wild Goose* and
*Woodpecker* south-west of Ireland 8.2.44

**Name** *U.763* **Built by** Naval Dockyard (Wilhelmshaven)
**Launched** 1942/3 **Fate** Bombed Russian aircraft Konigsberg
24.1.45

**Name** *U.764* **Built by** Naval Dockyard (Wilhelmshaven)
**Launched** 1943 **Fate** Surrendered UK port 5.45, and scuttled
North Atlantic 1945/6

**Name** *U.765* **Built by** Naval Dockyard (Wilhelmshaven)
**Launched** 1943 **Fate** Depth charged RN aircraft of escort carrier
*Vindex* (825 Sqn.), and frigates *Aylmer, Bickerton* and *Bligh*
North Atlantic 6.5.44

**Name** *U.766* **Built by** Naval Dockyard (Wilhelmshaven)
**Launched** 4.43 **Fate** Paid-off La Pallice 8.44, surrendered 1945;
French *Laubie* (1947); damaged in collision and scrapped
17.10.61

**Name** *U.767* **Built by** Naval Dockyard (Wilhelmshaven)
**Launched** 1943 **Fate** Depth charged RN destroyers *Fame,
Havelock* and *Inconstant* 10 m north-west Pte. de Talbat
18.6.44

**Name** *U.768* **Built by** Naval Dockyard (Wilhelmshaven)
**Launched** 1943 **Fate** Lost by collision Baltic 20.11.43

**Name** *U.769* & *U.770* **Built by** Naval Dockyard (Wilhelmshaven)
**Fate** Bombed Allied aircraft while building Wilhelmshaven
20.11.43, and construction abandoned

*Two views of the conning
tower of* U.776 *taken after her
surrender. Note the 3.7-cm AA
gun, the schnorchel and various
conning tower fittings.* (PPL)

**Name** *U.771* **Built by** Naval Dockyard (Wilhelmshaven)
**Launched** 1943 **Fate** Torpedoed RN submarine *Venturer* off
Harstadt 11.11.44

**Name** *U.772* **Built by** Naval Dockyard (Wilhelmshaven)
**Launched** 1943 **Fate** Depth charged RCAF aircraft (407 Sqn.)
30 m south of Portland Bill 30.12.44

**Name** *U.773* **Built by** Naval Dockyard (Wilhelmshaven)
**Launched** 1943 **Fate** Surrendered Trondheim 5.45, and scuttled
North Atlantic 1945/6

**Name** *U.774* **Built by** Naval Dockyard (Wilhelmshaven)
**Launched** 1943 **Fate** Depth charged RN frigates *Bentinck* and
*Calder* south-west of Ireland 8.4.45

**Name** *U.775* **Built by** Naval Dockyard (Wilhelmshaven)
**Launched** 1943/4 **Fate** Surrendered Trondheim 5.45, and scuttled
North Atlantic 1945/6

**Name** *U.776* **Built by** Naval Dockyard (Wilhelmshaven)
**Launched** 1943/4 **Fate** Surrendered UK port 5.45, RN *N.65*
(1945); scuttled North Atlantic 1945/6

**Name** *U.777* **Built by** Naval Dockyard (Wilhelmshaven)
**Launched** 1943/4 **Fate** Bombed RAF aircraft Wilhelmshaven
15.10.44

**Name** *U.778* **Built by** Naval Dockyard (Wilhelmshaven)
**Launched** 1943/4 **Fate** Surrendered Bergen 5.45, and scuttled
North Atlantic 1945/6

**Name** *U.779* **Built by** Naval Dockyard (Wilhelmshaven)
**Launched** 1943/4 **Fate** Surrendered Wilhelmshaven 5.45, and
scuttled North Atlantic 1945/6

**Name** *U.780–U.784* **Built by** Naval Dockyard (Wilhelmshaven)
**Fate** Cancelled

**Name** *U.785* **Built by** Naval Dockyard (Wilhelmshaven)
**Launched** 1944 **Fate** Bombed Allied aircraft Kiel 1945

**Name** *U.786–U.790* **Built by** Naval Dockyard (Wilhelmshaven)
**Fate** Cancelled

## EXPERIMENTAL

**Name** *V.80* **Built by** Germania Werft (Kiel) **Launched** 19.1.40
**Fate** Laid-up 1942; scuttled Danzig Bay 3.45

**Name** *U.791* (ex-*V.300*) **Built by** Germania Werft (Kiel)
LD 18.2.42 **Fate** Not completed and scrapped

## TYPE XVII

**Name** *U.792* **Built by** Blohm & Voss (Hamburg) **Launched** 28.9.43
**Fate** Scuttled Kiel 5.45, and later salved; RN (1947)

**Name** *U.793* **Built by** Blohm & Voss (Hamburg) **Launched** 4.3.44
**Fate** Scuttled Kiel 3.5.45, and later salved; RN (1947)

**Name** *U.794* **Built by** Germania Werft (Kiel) **Launched** 7.10.43
**Fate** Scuttled Geltinger Bight 3.5.45

**Name** *U.795* **Built by** Germania Werft (Kiel) **Launched** 21.3.44
**Fate** Scuttled incomplete Kiel 3.5.45, and later salved; RN (1947)

## TYPE XVIII

**Name** *U.796* & *U.797* **Built by** Germania Werft (Kiel)
**Fate** Cancelled 28.3.44 and scrapped on slip

## TYPE XVIIK

**Name** *U.798* **Built by** Germania Werft (Kiel) **Fate** Not completed
and scrapped

**Name** *U.799* & *U.800* **Built by** Germania Werft (Kiel)
**Fate** Cancelled

## TYPE IXC$_{40}$

**Name** *U.801* **Built by** Seebeckwerft (Bremerhaven)
**Launched** 1943 **Fate** Depth charged USN aircraft of escort carrier
*Block Island* (VC.6), destroyer *Corry*, and destroyer escort
*Bronstein* west of Cape Verde Islands 16.3.44

**Name** *U.802* **Built by** Seebeckwerft (Bremerhaven)
**Launched** 1943 **Fate** Surrendered UK port 5.45, and scuttled
North Atlantic 1945/6

*The Type IXC U.805 seen surrendering off US coast on May 15, 1945.* (Drüppel)

**Name** *U.803* **Built by** Seebeckwerft (Bremerhaven)
**Launched** 1943 **Fate** Mined Swinemünde 27.4.44

**Name** *U.804* **Built by** Seebeckwerft (Bremerhaven)
**Launched** 1943 **Fate** Rocket fire RAF aircraft (143, 235 & 248
Sqns.) Little Belt 9.4.45

**Name** *U.805* **Built by** Seebeckwerft (Bremerhaven)
**Launched** 1943 **Fate** Surrendered Portsmouth (N.H.) 14.5.45,
scuttled by USN 4.2.46

**Name** *U.806* **Built by** Seebeckwerft (Bremerhaven)
**Launched** 1940/2 **Fate** Surrendered Wilhelmshaven 5.45, and
scrapped

**Name** *U.807–U.816* **Built by** Seebeckwerft (Bremerhaven)
**Fate** Cancelled

**Name** *U.817–U.820* **Built by** Seebeckwerft (Bremerhaven)
**Fate** Projected

## TYPE VIIC

**Name** *U.821* **Built by** Oder Werke (Stettin) **Launched** 1943
**Fate** Depth charged RAF aircraft (206 & 248 Sqns.) off Brest
10.6.44

**Name** *U.822* **Built by** Oder Werke (Stettin) **Launched** 1944
**Fate** Scuttled Weser estuary 3.5.45

**Name** *U.823–U.824* **Built by** Oder Werke (Stettin) **Fate** Cancelled

**Name** *U.825* **Built by** Schichau (Danzig) **Launched** 1943
**Fate** Surrendered Wilhelmshaven 5.45, and scuttled North
Atlantic 1945/6

**Name** *U.826* **Built by** Schichau (Danzig) **Launched** 1943
**Fate** Surrendered UK port 5.45, and scuttled North Atlantic
1945/6

**Name** *U.827* **Built by** Schichau (Danzig) **Launched** 1943
**Fate** Scuttled Flensburg 5.5.45

**Name** *U.828* **Built by** Schichau (Danzig) **Launched** 1943
**Fate** Scuttled Weser estuary 3.5.45

**Name** *U.829–U.834* **Built by** Schichau (Danzig) **Fate** Cancelled

**Name** *U.835* **Built by** Schichau (Danzig) **Launched** 1944
**Fate** Scuttled Weser estuary 5.45

**Name** *U.836* **Built by** Schichau (Danzig) **Launched** 1944
**Fate** Scuttled Weser estuary 5.45

**Name** *U.837–U.840* **Built by** Schichau (Danzig) **Fate** Cancelled

### TYPE IXC

**Name** *U.841* **Built by** AG Weser (Bremen) **Launched** 21.10.42
**Fate** Depth charged RN frigate *Byard* east of Cape Farewell
17.10.43

**Name** *U.842* **Built by** AG Weser (Bremen) **Launched** 14.11.42
**Fate** Depth charged RN sloops *Starling* and *Wild Goose* North
Atlantic 6.11.43

**Name** *U.843* **Built by** AG Weser (Bremen) **Launched** 15.12.42
**Fate** Rocket fire RAF aircraft (143, 235 & 248 Sqns.) Kattegat
9.4.45

*Facing page: A view of* U.826
*showing the AA guns on the
conning tower and the exhaust
vents below the platforms.*
(IWM)

*A surrendered U-Boat comes
alongside her sister* U.826 *at
Loch Eriboll in May 1945.
The original caption
identified the left-hand boat as*
U.236 *but this cannot be
correct. Note the recess in the
deck casing of* U.826 *for the
schnorchel, and the connection.*
(British Official)

*The U-Boat Pens at Trondheim
after the Allied re-occupation
in 1945. Nearest the camera is
U.861 and furthest is U.953.*

**Name** *U.844* **Built by** AG Weser (Bremen) **Launched** 30.12.42
**Fate** Depth charged RAF aircraft (59 & 68 Sqns.) south-west of
Iceland 16.10.43

**Name** *U.845* **Built by** AG Weser (Bremen) **Launched** 22.1.43
**Fate** Depth charged RN destroyer *Forester* and RCN *St. Laurent*
and RCN frigates *Owen Sound* and *Swansea* North Atlantic
10.3.44

**Name** *U.846* **Built by** AG Weser (Bremen) **Launched** 17.2.43
**Fate** Depth charged RCAF aircraft (407 Sqn.) north of Cape
Ortegal 4.5.44

**TYPE IXD$_2$**

**Name** *U.847* **Built by** AG Weser (Bremen) **Launched** 5.9.42
**Fate** Depth charged USN aircraft of escort carrier *Card* (VC.1)
Saragossa Sea 27.8.43

**Name** *U.848* **Built by** AG Weser (Bremen) **Launched** 6.10.42
**Fate** Depth charged USAAF and USN (VB.107) aircraft 290 m
south-west of Ascension 5.11.43

**Name** *U.849* **Built by** AG Weser (Bremen) **Launched** 31.10.42
**Fate** Depth charged USN aircraft (VB.107) west of Congo
estuary 25.11.43

**Name** *U.850* **Built by** AG Weser (Bremen) **Launched** 7.12.42
**Fate** Depth charged USN aircraft of escort carrier *Bogue* (VC.19)
west of Madeira 20.12.43

**Name** *U.851* **Built by** AG Weser (Bremen) **Launched** 15.1.43
**Fate** Lost by unknown cause North Atlantic 3.44

**Name** *U.852* **Built by** AG Weser (Bremen) **Launched** 28.1.43
**Fate** Depth charged RAF aircraft (8 & 621 Sqns.) south-east of
Socotra 3.5.44

U.861 *and* U.953 *(nearest camera) seen from another angle.* (IWM)

## TYPE IXC

**Name** *U.853* **Built by** AG Weser (Bremen) **Launched** 11.3.43
**Fate** Depth charged USN destroyer escort *Atherton*, and frigate *Moberly* off Long Island 6.5.45

**Name** *U.854* **Built by** AG Weser (Bremen) **Launched** 5.4.43
**Fate** Mined off Swinemünde 4.2.44

**Name** *U.855* **Built by** AG Weser (Bremen) **Launched** 17.4.43
**Fate** Depth charged RAF aircraft (224 Sqn.) off Bergen 24.9.44

**Name** *U.856* **Built by** AG Weser (Bremen) **Launched** 11.5.43
**Fate** Depth charged USN destroyer *Champlin*, and destroyer escort *Huse* south of Sable Island 7.4.44

**Name** *U.857* **Built by** AG Weser (Bremen) **Launched** 23.5.43
**Fate** Depth charged USN destroyer escort *Gustafson* west of Cape Cod 7.4.45

**Name** *U.858* **Built by** AG Weser (Bremen) **Launched** 17.6.43
**Fate** Surrendered Portsmouth (N.H.) 14.5.45; to USN and torpedoed as target 11.47

## TYPE IXD$_2$

**Name** *U.859* **Built by** AG Weser (Bremen) **Launched** 2.3.43
**Fate** Torpedoed RN submarine *Trenchant* off Penang 23.9.44

**Name** *U.860* **Built by** AG Weser (Bremen) **Launched** 23.3.43
**Fate** Depth charged USN aircraft of escort carrier *Solomons* (VC.9) south-south-east of St. Helena 15.6.44

**Name** *U.861* **Built by** AG Weser (Bremen) **Launched** 29.4.33
**Fate** Surrendered Trondheim 5.45, and scuttled North Atlantic 1945/6

**Name** *U.862* **Built by** AG Weser (Bremen) **Launched** 5.6.43
**Fate** IJN *I.502* (1945), surrendered Singapore 8.45 and sunk off
Singapore 13.2.46

**Name** *U.863* **Built by** AG Weser (Bremen) **Launched** 29.6.43
**Fate** Depth charged USN aircraft (VB.107) Ascension area
29.9.44

**Name** *U.864* **Built by** AG Weser (Bremen) **Launched** 12.8.43
**Fate** Torpedoed RN submarine *Venturer* west of Bergen 9.2.45

## TYPE IXC

**Name** *U.865* **Built by** AG Weser (Bremen) **Launched** 11.7.43
**Fate** Depth charged RAF aircraft (206 Sqn.) north-east of
Shetlands 19.9.44

**Name** *U.866* **Built by** AG Weser (Bremen) **Launched** 29.7.43
**Fate** Depth charged USN destroyer escorts *Lowe, Menges,
Mosley* and *Pride* south-east of Sable Island 18.3.45

**Name** *U.867* **Built by** AG Weser (Bremen) **Launched** 24.8.43
**Fate** Depth charged RAF aircraft (224 Sqn.) north-east of
Shetlands 19.9.44

**Name** *U.868* **Built by** AG Weser (Bremen) **Launched** 18.9.43
**Fate** Surrendered Bergen 5.45, and scuttled North Atlantic 1945/6

**Name** *U.869* **Built by** AG Weser (Bremen) **Launched** 5.10.43
**Fate** Depth charged USN destroyer escort *Fowler*, and French
submarine chaser *L'Indiscret* off Casablanca 28.2.45

**Name** *U.870* **Built by** AG Weser (Bremen) **Launched** 29.10.43
**Fate** Bombed USAAF aircraft Bremen 30.3.45

## TYPE XD$_2$

**Name** *U.871* **Built by** AG Weser (Bremen) **Launched** 7.9.43
**Fate** Depth charged RAF aircraft (220 Sqn.) north-west of Azores
26.9.44

**Name** *U.872* **Built by** AG Weser (Bremen) **Launched** 20.10.43
**Fate** Bombed USAAF aircraft Bremen 29.7.44

**Name** *U.873* **Built by** AG Weser (Bremen) **Launched** 16.11.43
**Fate** Surrendered Portsmouth (N.H.) 16.5.45; USN (1945); sold
New York 10.3.48 for scrapping

**Name** *U.874* **Built by** AG Weser (Bremen) **Launched** 21.12.43
**Fate** Surrendered Horten 5.45, and scuttled North Atlantic 1945/6

**Name** *U.875* **Built by** AG Weser (Bremen) **Launched** 16.2.44
**Fate** Surrendered UK port 5.45, RN (1945); scuttled North
Atlantic 1945/6

**Name** *U.876* **Built by** AG Weser (Bremen) **Launched** 29.2.44
**Fate** Scuttled Eckernforde 5.5.45 after being bombed RAF
aircraft 4.5.45

*[Handwritten marginal note:]* U 869 – LOST 2/45? OFF COAST OF N.J. – CIRCLE RUN ON TORPEDO –

**TYPE IXC**

**Name** *U.877* **Built by** AG Weser (Bremen) **Launched** 10.12.43
**Fate** Depth charged RCN corvette *St. Thomas* north-west of
Azores 27.12.44

**Name** *U.878* **Built by** AG Weser (Bremen) **Launched** 6.1.44
**Fate** Depth charged RN destroyer *Vanquisher*, and corvette
*Tintagel Castle* south of Ireland 10.4.45

**Name** *U.879* **Built by** AG Weser (Bremen) **Launched** 11.1.44
**Fate** Depth charged USN destroyer escorts *Buckley* and *Rueben
James* 150 m south-south-east of Halifax 19.4.45

**Name** *U.880* **Built by** AG Weser (Bremen) **Launched** 10.2.44
**Fate** Depth charged USN destroyer escorts *Frost* and *Stanton*
North Atlantic 16.4.45

**Name** *U.881* **Built by** AG Weser (Bremen) **Launched** 4.3.44
**Fate** Depth charged USN destroyer escort *Farquar* south-east of
Cape Race 6.5.45

## Type XVIIE

Owing to technical problems encountered with the Walter
system this design adopted conventional propulsion with the
hull modified to accommodate it. Battery capacity was
doubled to power an electric motor whose output closely
approached that of the Walter turbine it supplanted. No boats
were finally built to this design, which formed the basis of the
later type XXIII.

*Displacement:* 340 tons
*Dimensions:* $144 \times 10\frac{3}{4} \times 14$ feet
*Machinery:* 1-shaft diesel/electric motors B.H.P./S.H.P. 900/1,160
  $= 11\frac{1}{2}/14\frac{1}{2}$ knots
*Bunkers & Radius:* O.F. 40 tons; 6,000/224 miles at 8/4 knots
*Armament:* Two 21inch (both fwd—four torpedoes) T.T.
*Complement:* Not known

## Type XVIIG: **U.1081–1092**

This design was a further modification of the preceding type
XVIIB which again reverted to two turbines coupled to a single
shaft, but all boats of this type were finally cancelled.

*Displacement:* 314/345 tons
*Dimensions:* $129\frac{3}{4} \times 11\frac{1}{4} \times 15\frac{1}{2}$ feet
*Machinery:* 1-shaft Walter geared turbines (two/shaft), S.H.P.
  2,500 = 25 knots; and 8-cylinder Deutz diesel/electric motors,
  B.H.P./S.H.P. 210/77 = $8\frac{1}{2}/5$ knots
*Bunkers & Radius:* Aurol 55 tons, 114 miles at 20 knots; O.F.
  20 tons, 3,000/40 miles $8/4\frac{1}{2}$ knots
*Armament:* Two 21inch torpedo tubes (both fwd—four torpedoes)
*Complement:* 19

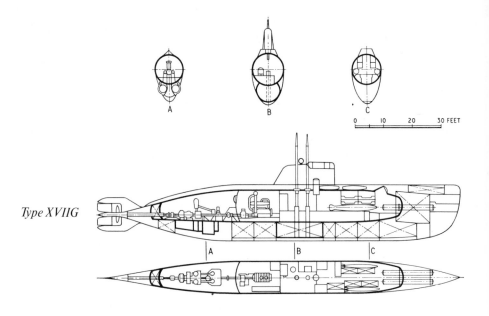

*Type XVIIG*

## Type XVIIG₂

Except that displacement was increased to 320 tons and dimensions enlarged to $141\frac{3}{4} \times 11\frac{3}{4} \times 14\frac{1}{2}$ feet this design was otherwise similar to type XVIIG.

## Type XVIIK: **U.798–800**

A further development of the Deschimag project for a coastal boat with closed-cycle diesel engines, and with the supply of compressed air cylinders considerably increased to widen the sphere of action. The provision of the latter, however, severely encroached on available space, and no reload torpedoes could be accommodated.

*Displacement:* 368 tons
*Dimensions:* $133\frac{1}{2} \times 11\frac{1}{4} \times 16$ feet
*Machinery:* 1-shaft diesel/electric motors, B.H.P./S.H.P.
 1,500/77 = 14/16 (diesel) or 5 (electric) knots
*Bunkers & Speed:* Oxygen $9\frac{1}{4}$ tons, 120 miles at 6 knots; and
 O.F. 3 tons, 1,600/45 miles at $12/4\frac{1}{2}$ knots
*Armament:* Two 21inch (both fwd—two torpedoes) T.T.
*Complement:* 19

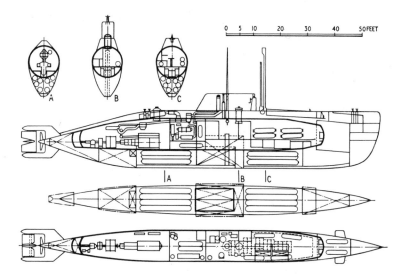

*Type XVIIK*

# Type XVIII: **U.796** and **U.797**

Ocean-going boats which adopted a two-shaft Walter system for main propulsion with auxiliary diesel/electric drive. They were in advance of development, however, and construction was halted in 1944 and not subsequently resumed. The pressure hull was of the double cylinder form, disposed one over the other, and was later adopted—with some modification—for the type XXI. This was a most advanced design which would have proved extremely effective had the problems associated with the Walter system been overcome.

*Displacement:* 1,485/1,652 tons
*Dimensions:* $235\frac{1}{4} \times 20\frac{1}{4} \times 21$ feet
*Machinery:* 2-shaft Walter geared turbines, S.H.P. 15,000 = 24 knots; and diesel/electric motors, B.H.P./S.H.P. 2,000/396 = $18\frac{1}{4}$/7 knots
*Bunkers & Radius:* Aurol 204 tons, 200 miles at 24 knots; and O.F. 124 tons, 5,200/40 miles at $12/4\frac{1}{2}$ knots
*Armament:* Four 30mm A.A. (2 × 2) guns; six 21inch torpedo tubes (all fwd—twenty-three torpedoes)
*Complement:* 52

# Type XIX.

Ocean-going submarine tankers of *ca.* 2,000 tons with double cylinder pressure hull, set abreast. Propulsion was to be by diesel engines of new design, but these never materialised and led to the abandonment of this type for the more conventional type XX that followed.

## *Type XX:* **U.1601–1800**

Ocean-going submarine transports for the Far Eastern trade and provided with eight cargo compartments for either dry, or oil, cargo. Their construction was abandoned in 1943 to meet deficiencies in the production of type XXI submarines.

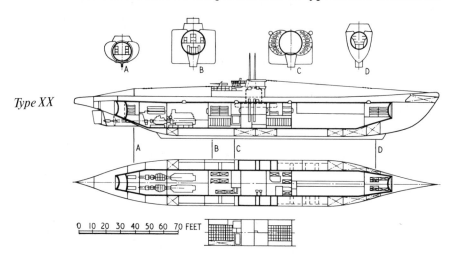

*Type XX*

*Displacement:* 2,708/2,962 tons
*Dimensions:* 255 × 30¼ × 21¾ feet
*Machinery:* 2-shaft diesel/electric motors, B.H.P./S.H.P. 2,800/940 = 12½/5¾ knots
*Bunkers & Radius:* O.F. 471 tons; 13,000/49 miles at 12/4 knots, Cargo O.F. 800 tons
*Armament:* One 37mm A.A., four 20mm A.A. (2 × 2) guns
*Complement:* 58

### TYPE IXC

**Name** *U.882* **Built by** AG Weser (Bremen) **Fate** Cancelled

### TYPE IXD₂

**Name** *U.883* **Built by** AG Weser (Bremen) **Launched** 28.4.44 **Fate** Surrendered Wilhelmshaven 5.45, and scuttled North Atlantic 1945/6

**Name** *U.884* **Built by** AG Weser (Bremen) **Launched** 17.5.44 **Fate** Bombed USAAF aircraft Bremen 30.3.45 while building and construction abandoned

**Name** *U.885* **Built by** AG Weser (Bremen) **Fate** Cancelled

**Name** *U.886* **Built by** AG Weser (Bremen) **Launched** 1942 **Fate** Bombed USAAF aircraft Bremen 30.3.45 while building and construction abandoned

**Name** *U.887* & *U.888* **Built by** AG Weser (Bremen) **Fate** Cancelled

## TYPE IXC

**Name** *U.889* **Built by** AG Weser (Bremen) **Launched** 1944
**Fate** Surrendered Halifax 5.45; RCN (1945); USN (1946)

**Name** *U.890–U.892* **Built by** AG Weser (Bremen) **Launched** 1944
**Fate** Bombed Allied aircraft Bremen 29.7.44 while building and construction abandoned

**Name** *U.893* & *U.894* **Built by** AG Weser (Bremen)
**Fate** Cancelled


## TYPE IXD₂

**Name** *U.895–U.900* **Built by** AG Weser (Bremen)
**Fate** Cancelled


## TYPE VIIC

**Name** *U.901* **Built by** Vulkan (Stettin) **Launched** 1943
**Fate** Surrendered Stavanger 5.45, and scuttled North Atlantic 1945/6

**Name** *U.902* **Built by** Vulkan (Stettin) **Fate** Cancelled

**Name** *U.903* **Built by** Flender Werft (Lübeck) **Launched** 1943
**Fate** Scuttled Kiel 3.5.45

**Name** *U.904* **Built by** Flender Werft (Lübeck) **Launched** 1943
**Fate** Scuttled Eckernforde 5.5.45 after being bombed RAF aircraft 4.5.45

**Name** *U.905* **Built by** Stülcken (Hamburg) **Launched** 20.11.43
**Fate** Depth charged RAF aircraft (86 Sqn.) 43 m north-west of Orkneys 20.3.45

**Name** *U.906* **Built by** Stülcken (Hamburg) **Launched** 28.6.43
**Fate** Bombed Allied aircraft Hamburg 31.12.44 while building and construction abandoned

**Name** *U.907* **Built by** Stülcken (Hamburg) **Launched** 1.3.44
**Fate** Surrendered Bergen 5.45, and scuttled North Atlantic 1945/6

**Name** *U.908* **Built by** Stülcken (Hamburg) **Launched** 27.4.44
**Fate** Bombed Allied aircraft Hamburg 31.12.44 while building and construction abandoned

**Name** *U.909–U.918* **Built by** Stülcken (Hamburg)
**Fate** Cancelled

**Name** *U.919–U.920* **Built by** Stülcken (Hamburg)
**Fate** Projected

**Name** *U.921* **Built by** Neptun Werft (Rostock) **Launched** 1943
**Fate** Depth charged RN aircraft of escort carrier *Camponia* (813 Sqn.) south-west of Bear Island 30.9.44

**Name** *U.922* **Built by** Neptun Werft (Rostock) **Launched** 1943
**Fate** Scuttled Kiel 3.5.45

**Name** *U.923* **Built by** Neptun Werft (Rostock) **Launched** 1943
**Fate** Mined Baltic 2.45; salved by E. Germany (DDR) and
scrapped 1954/55

**Name** *U.924* **Built by** Neptun Werft (Rostock) **Launched** 1943
**Fate** Scuttled Kiel 3.5.45

**Name** *U.925* **Built by** Neptun Werft (Rostock) **Launched** 1943
**Fate** Lost by unknown cause Faroes/Iceland area 18.9.44

**Name** *U.926* **Built by** Neptun Werft (Rostock) **Launched** 1944
**Fate** Surrendered Bergen 5.45; RNN *Kya* (1948) and
commissioned 10.1.49; decommissioned 3.64 for scrapping in
West Germany

**Name** *U.927* **Built by** Neptun Werft (Rostock) **Launched** 1944
**Fate** Depth charged RAF aircraft (179 Sqn.) south-west of
Lizard 24.2.45

**Name** *U.928* **Built by** Neptun Werft (Rostock) **Launched** 1944
**Fate** Surrendered Bergen 5.45, and scuttled North Atlantic 1945/6

**Name** *U.929* **Built by** Neptun Werft (Rostock) **Launched** 1944
**Fate** Scuttled Warnemünde 3.5.45

**Name** *U.930* **Built by** Neptun Werft (Rostock) **Launched** 1944
**Fate** Surrendered Bergen 5.45, and scuttled North Atlantic 1945/6

**Name** *U.931–U.942* **Built by** Neptun Werft (Rostock)
**Fate** Cancelled

**Name** *U.943–U.950* **Built by** Neptun Werft (Rostock)
**Fate** Projected

**Name** *U.951* **Built by** Blohm & Voss (Hamburg) **Launched** 14.10.42
**Fate** Depth charged USAAF aircraft (1st A/S Sqn.) north-west of
Cape St. Vincent 7.7.43

**Name** *U.952* **Built by** Blohm & Voss (Hamburg) **Launched** 4.10.42
**Fate** Bombed USAAF Toulon 6.8.44

**Name** *U.953* **Built by** Blohm & Voss (Hamburg) **Launched** 28.10.42
**Fate** Surrendered Trondheim 20.5.45; RN (1946) and scrapped
by Clayton & Davie at Dunston in 6.49

**Name** *U.954* **Built by** Blohm & Voss (Hamburg) **Launched** 28.10.42
**Fate** Depth charged RAF aircraft (120 Sqn.) south-east of Cape
Farewell 19.5.43

**Name** *U.955* **Built by** Blohm & Voss (Hamburg) **Launched** 13.11.42
**Fate** Depth charged RAF aircraft (201 Sqn.) north of Cape
Ortegal 7.6.44; salved 1971 and hulked as relic Kiel

**Name** *U.956* **Built by** Blohm & Voss (Hamburg) **Launched** 14.11.42
**Fate** Surrendered Trondheim 5.45, and scuttled 1945/6

**Name** *U.957* **Built by** Blohm & Voss (Hamburg) **Launched** 21.11.42
**Fate** Lost collision with German transport West Fjord 19.10.44,
salved and paid-off Narvik 21.10.44

**Name** *U.958* **Built by** Blohm & Voss (Hamburg) **Launched** 21.11.42
**Fate** Scuttled Kiel 3.5.45

**Name** *U.959* **Built by** Blohm & Voss (Hamburg) **Launched** 3.12.42
**Fate** Depth charged RN aircraft of escort carrier *Fencer* (842
Sqn.) south of Jan Mayen Island 2.5.44

**Name** *U.960* **Built by** Blohm & Voss (Hamburg) **Launched** 3.12.42
**Fate** Depth charged USN destroyers *Ludlow* and *Niblack*, and
RAF aircraft (36 & 500 Sqns.) north of Oran 19.5.44

**Name** *U.961* **Built by** Blohm & Voss (Hamburg) **Launched** 17.12.42
**Fate** Depth charged RN sloop *Starling* east-south-east of Faroes
29.3.44

**Name** *U.962* **Built by** Blohm & Voss (Hamburg) **Launched** 17.12.42
**Fate** Depth charged RN sloops *Crane* and *Cygnet* north-west of
Cape Finisterre 8.4.44

**Name** *U.963* **Built by** Blohm & Voss (Hamburg) **Launched** 30.12.42
**Fate** Wrecked off Lisbon 9.5.45

**Name** *U.964* **Built by** Blohm & Voss (Hamburg) **Launched** 30.12.42
**Fate** Depth charged RAF aircraft (86 Sqn.) south-west of
Iceland 16.10.43

**Name** *U.965* **Built by** Blohm & Voss (Hamburg) **Launched** 14.1.43
**Fate** depth charged RN frigate *Conn* 23 m west of Cape Wrath
27.3.45

**Name** *U.966* **Built by** Blohm & Voss (Hamburg) **Launched** 14.1.43
**Fate** Depth charged RAF (311 Czech Sqn.) & USN (VB.103 &
110 Sqns.) north-west of Cape Ortegal 10.11.43

**Name** *U.967* **Built by** Blohm & Voss (Hamburg) **Launched** 28.1.43
**Fate** Scuttled Toulon 11.8.44

**Name** *U.968* **Built by** Blohm & Voss (Hamburg) **Launched** 28.1.43
**Fate** Surrendered Narvik 19.5.45, and scuttled 1945/6

**Name** *U.969* **Built by** Blohm & Voss (Hamburg) **Launched** 11.2.43
**Fate** Bombed USAAF aircraft Toulon 6.8.44

**Name** *U.970* **Built by** Blohm & Voss (Hamburg) **Launched** 11.2.43
**Fate** Depth charged RAF aircraft (228 Sqn.) west of Bordeaux
7.6.44

**Name** *U.971* **Built by** Blohm & Voss (Hamburg) **Launched** 22.2.43
**Fate** Depth charged RN destroyer *Eskimo* and RCN *Haida*, and
RAF aircraft (311 Czech Sqn.) north of Ushant 24.6.44

**Name** *U.972* **Built by** Blohm & Voss (Hamburg) **Launched** 22.2.43
**Fate** Lost by unknown cause North Atlantic 1.44

**Name** *U.973* **Built by** Blohm & Voss (Hamburg) **Launched** 10.3.43
**Fate** Rocket fire of RN aircraft of escort carrier *Chaser* (816 Sqn.)
north-west of Narvik 6.3.44

**Name** *U.974* **Built by** Blohm & Voss (Hamburg) **Launched** 11.3.43
**Fate** Torpedoed RNN submarine *Ula* off Stavanger 19.4.44

**Name** *U.975* **Built by** Blohm & Voss (Hamburg) **Launched** 24.3.43
**Fate** Surrendered Horten 5.45, and scuttled North Atlantic 1945/6

**Name** *U.976* **Built by** Blohm & Voss (Hamburg) **Launched** 25.3.43
**Fate** Depth charged RAF aircraft (248 Sqn.) off Charente estuary
25.3.44

**Name** *U.977* **Built by** Blohm & Voss (Hamburg) **Launched** 31.3.43
**Fate** Surrendered La Plata 17.8.45; torpedoed by USS *Atule* as
target 13.11.46

**Name** *U.978* **Built by** Blohm & Voss (Hamburg) **Launched** 1.4.43
**Fate** Surrendered Trondheim 5.45, and scuttled North Atlantic
1945/6

**Name** *U.979* **Built by** Blohm & Voss (Hamburg) **Launched** 15.4.43
**Fate** Scuttled off Amrum 5.45

**Name** *U.980* **Built by** Blohm & Voss (Hamburg) **Launched** 15.4.43
**Fate** Depth charged RCAF aircraft (162 Sqn.) north-west of
Bergen 11.6.44

**Name** *U.981* **Built by** Blohm & Voss (Hamburg) **Launched** 29.4.33
**Fate** Depth charged RAF aircraft (502 Sqn.) Gironde estuary
12.8.44

**Name** *U.982* **Built by** Blohm & Voss (Hamburg) **Launched** 29.4.43
**Fate** Bombed RAF aircraft Hamburg 8.4.45

**Name** *U.983* **Built by** Blohm & Voss (Hamburg) **Launched** 12.5.43
**Fate** Lost collision with German submarine *U.988* north of Loba
8.9.43

**Name** *U.984* **Built by** Blohm & Voss (Hamburg) **Launched** 12.5.43
**Fate** Depth charged RCN destroyers *Chaudière*, *Kootenay* and
*Ottawa* south-west of Ushant 20.8.44

**Name** *U.985* **Built by** Blohm & Voss (Hamburg) **Launched** 20.5.43
**Fate** Mined off Lister 23.10.44, salved and paid-off 15.11.44;
surrendered Christiansand 1945, and scuttled North Atlantic
1945/6

**Name** *U.986* **Built by** Blohm & Voss (Hamburg) **Launched** 20.5.43
**Fate** Depth charged USN minesweeper *Swift*, and submarine
chaser *PC.619* south-west of Ireland 17.4.44

**Name** *U.987* **Built by** Blohm & Voss (Hamburg) **Launched** 2.6.43
**Fate** Torpedoed RN submarine *Satyr* south-east of Jan Mayen
Island 5.6.44

**Name** *U.988* **Built by** Blohm & Voss (Hamburg) **Launched** 3.6.43
**Fate** Depth charged RN frigates *Cooke*, *Duckworth*, *Domett* and
*Essington*, and RAF aircraft (224 Sqn.) off Lorient 29.6.44

**Name** *U.989* **Built by** Blohm & Voss (Hamburg) **Launched** 16.6.43
**Fate** Depth charged RN frigates *Bayntun*, *Braithwaite*, *Loch
Dunvegan* and *Loch Eck* east of Shetlands 14.2.45

**Name** *U.990* **Built by** Blohm & Voss (Hamburg) **Launched** 16.6.43
**Fate** Depth charged RAF aircraft (59 Sqn.) north-west of
Trondheim 25.5.44

**Name** *U.991* **Built by** Blohm & Voss (Hamburg) **Launched** 24.6.43
**Fate** Surrendered Bergen 5.45, and scuttled North Atlantic 1945/6

**Name** *U.992* **Built by** Blohm & Voss (Hamburg) **Launched** 24.6.43
**Fate** Surrendered Narvik 19.5.45, and scuttled North Atlantic
1945/6

**Name** *U.993* **Built by** Blohm & Voss (Hamburg) **Launched** 5.7.43
**Fate** Paid-off Bergen 4.10.44 after being bombed RAF aircraft;
surrendered 1945

**Name** *U.994* **Built by** Blohm & Voss (Hamburg) **Launched** 6.7.43
**Fate** Surrendered Trondheim 5.45, and scuttled North Atlantic
1945/6

**Name** *U.995* **Built by** Blohm & Voss (Hamburg) **Launched** 22.7.43
**Fate** Surrendered Trondheim 8.5.45; RN (1947), RNN *Kaura*
(1948) and recomm. 6.12.52; 1.63 decommissioned for scrapping
in West Germany; preserved as memorial at Laboe (Kiel)

**Name** *U.996* **Built by** Blohm & Voss (Hamburg) **Launched** 22.7.43
**Fate** Bombed RAF aircraft Hamburg 8.44 while building and
construction abandoned

**Name** *U.997* **Built by** Blohm & Voss (Hamburg) **Launched** 18.8.43
**Fate** Surrendered Narvik 19.5.45, and scuttled North Atlantic
1945/6

**Name** *U.998* **Built by** Blohm & Voss (Hamburg) **Launched** 18.8.43
**Fate** Paid-off Bergen 27.6.44 after being depth charged RAF
aircraft (333 Norge Sqn.) east of Shetlands 16.6.44

**Name** *U.999* **Built by** Blohm & Voss (Hamburg) **Launched** 17.9.43
**Fate** Scuttled Flensburg 5.5.45

**Name** *U.1000* **Built by** Blohm & Voss (Hamburg) **Launched** 17.9.43
**Fate** Mined Baltic 25.8.44, salved and paid-off 29.9.44

**Name** *U.1001* **Built by** Blohm & Voss (Hamburg) **Launched** 6.10.43
**Fate** Depth charged RN frigates *Byron* and *Fitzroy* 150 m west of
Scillies 8.4.45

**Name** *U.1002* **Built by** Blohm & Voss (Hamburg)
**Launched** 27.10.43 **Fate** Surrendered Bergen 5.45, and scuttled
North Atlantic 1945/6

**Name** *U.1003* **Built by** Blohm & Voss (Hamburg) **Launched** 6.10.43
**Fate** Abandoned 23.3.45 off Donegal after being rammed RCN
frigate *New Glasgow* off Lough Foyle 20.3.45

**Name** *U.1004* **Built by** Blohm & Voss (Hamburg)
**Launched** 27.10.43 **Fate** Surrendered Bergen 5.45, and scuttled
North Atlantic 1945/6

**Name** *U.1005* **Built by** Blohm & Voss (Hamburg) **Launched** 1943
**Fate** Surrendered Bergen 5.45, and scuttled North Atlantic 1945/6

**Name** *U.1006* **Built by** Blohm & Voss (Hamburg)
**Launched** 17.11.43 **Fate** Depth charged RCN frigate *Annan* west of
Shetlands 16.10.44

**Name** *U.1007* **Built by** Blohm & Voss (Hamburg)
**Launched** 17.11.43 **Fate** Bombed RAF aircraft and mined off
Wismar 2.5.45

**Name** *U.1008* **Built by** Blohm & Voss (Hamburg) **Launched** 8.12.43
**Fate** Depth charged RAF aircraft (86 Sqn.) Kattegat 6.5.45

**Name** *U.1009* **Built by** Blohm & Voss (Hamburg) **Launched** 8.12.43
**Fate** Surrendered UK port 5.45, and scuttled North Atlantic
1945/6

**Name** *U.1010* **Built by** Blohm & Voss (Hamburg) **Launched** 5.1.44
**Fate** Surrendered UK port 5.45, and scuttled North Atlantic
1945/6

**Name** *U.1011* **Built by** Blohm & Voss (Hamburg) **Launched** 5.1.44
**Fate** Bombed Allied aircraft Hamburg 1944 while building and
construction abandoned

**Name** *U.1012* **Built by** Blohm & Voss (Hamburg) **Launched** 1943/4
**Fate** Bombed Allied aircraft Hamburg 1944 while building and
construction abandoned

**Name** *U.1013* **Built by** Blohm & Voss (Hamburg) **Launched** 19.1.44
**Fate** Lost by collision Baltic 17.3.44

**Name** *U.1014* **Built by** Blohm & Voss (Hamburg) **Launched** 30.1.44
**Fate** Depth charged RN frigates *Loch Scavaig, Loch Shin,
Nyasaland* and *Papua* North Channel 4.2.45

**Name** *U.1015* **Built by** Blohm & Voss (Hamburg) **Launched** 7.2.44
**Fate** Lost by collision west of Pillau 19.5.44

**Name** *U.1016* **Built by** Blohm & Voss (Hamburg) **Launched** 8.2.44
**Fate** Scuttled Great Belt 5.5.45

**Name** *U.1017* **Built by** Blohm & Voss (Hamburg) **Launched** 1.3.44
**Fate** Depth charged RAF aircraft (120 Sqn.) north-west of
Ireland 29.4.45

**Name** *U.1018* **Built by** Blohm & Voss (Hamburg) **Launched** 1.3.44
**Fate** Depth charged RN frigate *Loch Fada* south of The Lizard
27.2.45

**Name** *U.1019* **Built by** Blohm & Voss (Hamburg) **Launched** 22.3.44
**Fate** Surrendered Trondheim 5.45, and scuttled North Atlantic
1945/6

**Name** *U.1020* **Built by** Blohm & Voss (Hamburg) **Launched** 22.3.44
**Fate** Lost by unknown cause Moray Firth 1.45

**Name** *U.1021* **Built by** Blohm & Voss (Hamburg) **Launched** 13.4.44
**Fate** Depth charged RN frigates *Conn* and *Rupert* 30.3.45

**Name** *U.1022* **Built by** Blohm & Voss (Hamburg) **Launched** 13.3.44
**Fate** Surrendered Bergen 5.45, and scuttled North Atlantic 1945/6

**Name** *U.1023* **Built by** Blohm & Voss (Hamburg) **Launched** 3.5.44
**Fate** Surrendered Weymouth 5.45, RN *N.83* (1945); scuttled
North Atlantic 1945/6

**Name** *U.1024* **Built by** Blohm & Voss (Hamburg) **Launched** 24.5.44
**Fate** Sank in tow 23 m north-west of Holyhead 12.4.45 after
being depth charged RN frigate *Loch Glendhu*

**Name** *U.1025* **Built by** Blohm & Voss (Hamburg) **Launched** 1944
**Fate** Scuttled Flensburg 5.5.45

**Name** *U.1026* **Built by** Blohm & Voss (Hamburg) **Launched** 25.5.44
**Fate** Scuttled incomplete 5.45

**Name** *U.1027* **Built by** Blohm & Voss (Hamburg)
**Launched** 27.11.44 **Fate** Scuttled incomplete 3.5.45

## *Type XXI:* **U.2501–4000**

Ocean-going boats capable of fully submerged operation using
improved *schnorchel* technique and conventional diesel/
electric propulsion, and met requirements for a production
series until the closed-cycle system of propulsion was further
developed. Compared with earlier types battery capacity was
trebled, but full speed with electric motors was still restricted
to one hour when running fully submerged. When using the
*schnorchel* and diesel engines, however, they could proceed at
more than double the limitation of 6 knots which applied
to earlier boats which had the *schnorchel* added, and so
recovered the mobility which had been previously sacrificed.
The hull was streamlined to aid submerged performance, and
the pressure hull was formed of two flattened cylinders placed
one over the other. To speed production the hull was of all-
welded construction and was prefabricated in eight sections.

*Displacement:* 1,621/1,819 tons
*Dimensions:* $251\frac{3}{4} \times 21\frac{3}{4} \times 20\frac{3}{4}$ feet
*Machinery:* 2-shaft 6-cylinder M.A.N. diesel/electric motors,
  B.H.P./S.H.P. 4,000/5,000 = $15\frac{1}{2}/17\frac{1}{4}$ knots; and silent
  creeping electric motors, S.H.P. 226 = 6 knots
*Bunkers & Radius:* O.F. 234 tons; 11,150/285 miles at 12/6 knots
*Armament:* Four 30mm A.A. (2 × 2) guns; six 21inch torpedo
  tubes (all fwd—twenty torpedoes or fourteen torpedoes and
  eighteen small/twelve large mines)
*Complement:* 58
*Notes:* Owing to production difficulties most, if not all, mounted
  four 20mm A.A. (2 × 2) guns. *U.2502* was fitted with automatic hydroplane depth-keeping gear, and carried out the first
  trials of the class. *U.2511* and *U.3017* were similarly fitted

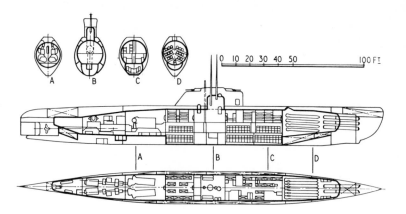

*Type XXI*

## Types XXIB and XXIC

Variations in basic design to increase number of torpedo
tubes. Type XXIB had a second torpedo compartment forward with six fixed tubes but trained aft and angled 10 deg.
from the centre line. With type XXIC this second compartment was lengthened to accommodate twelve tubes.

## Type XXIB

*Displacement:* 1,620 tons
*Dimensions:* $251\frac{3}{4} \times 21\frac{3}{4} \times 20\frac{1}{4}$ feet
*Machinery:* 2-shaft 6-cylinder M.A.N. diesel/electric motors,
    B.H.P./S.H.P. 4,000/4,200 = $15\frac{1}{2}/15\frac{1}{2}$ knots; and creeping
    silent electric motors S.H.P. 220 = 5 knots
*Bunkers & Radius:* O.F. Not known
*Armament:* Four 30mm A.A. (2 × 2) guns; twelve 21inch
    torpedo tubes (six bow and six broadside fwd—twelve
    torpedoes)
*Complement:* Not known

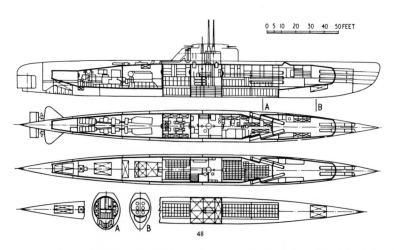

*Type XXIB*

# Type XXIC

*Displacement:* Not known
*Dimensions:* $272\frac{1}{4} \times 21\frac{3}{4} \times 20\frac{1}{4}$ feet
*Machinery:* 2-shaft 6-cylinder M.A.N. diesel/electric motors
B.H.P./S.H.P. 4,000/4,200 = $15\frac{1}{2}/15\frac{1}{2}$ knots; and creeping silent
electric motors S.H.P. 220 = 5 knots
*Bunkers & Radius:* O.F. Not known
*Armament:* Four 30mm A.A. (2 × 2) guns; eighteen 21inch
torpedo tubes (six bow and twelve broadside fwd)
*Complement:* Not known

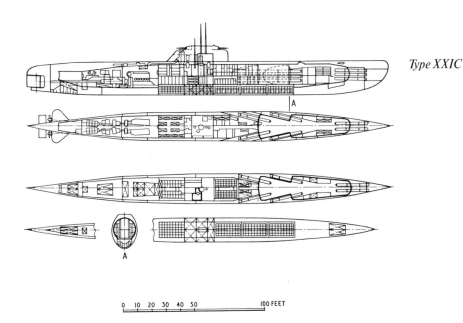

*Type XXIC*

0  10  20  30  40  50        100 FEET

# Types XXID₁ & XXID₂

Supply submarines based on the type XXI design and able to
stow 430 tons of cargo oil fuel. While the former design was
unarmed two 21inch torpedo tubes were added to the latter.

*Displacement:* 1,949 tons
*Dimensions:* $251\frac{3}{4} \times 21\frac{3}{4}$ $20\frac{1}{4}$ feet
*Machinery:* 2-shaft 6-cylinder M.A.N. diesel/electric motors
B.H.P./S.H.P. 4,000/4,200 = $15\frac{1}{2}/16$ knots; and creeping silent
electric motors S.H.P. 220 = $5\frac{1}{2}$ knots
*Bunkers & Radius:* O.F.; 11,300/155 miles at 10/6 knots
*Armament:* Two 21inch torpedo tubes (both fwd—two torpedoes
—in type XXID₂ only)
*Complement:* Not known

## Types XXIV & XXIT

Further supply submarines based on the type XXI design but intended for any cargo and with the battery capacity halved to increase stowage capacity. Up to 275 tons d.w. could be accommodated.

*Displacement:* Not known
*Dimensions:* $251\frac{3}{4} \times 21\frac{3}{4} \times 20\frac{1}{4}$ feet
*Machinery:* 2-shaft 6-cylinder M.A.N. diesel/electric motors
   B.H.P./S.H.P. 4,000/4,200 = $15\frac{1}{4}/15\frac{1}{2}$ knots; and creeping silent
   electric motors S.H.P. 220 = 5 knots
*Bunkers & Radius:* O.F. not known
*Armament:* Two 21 inch torpedo tubes (both fwd—two torpedoes)
*Complement:* Not known

## Types XXIE$_1$ & XXIE$_2$

Transport submarines based on the type XXI design and able to stow 800 tons d.w. of cargo, but with the hull lengthened some $4\frac{1}{2}$ feet and full battery capacity restored. The latter design only differed in that two 21 inch torpedo tubes were added.

   While modifications to all type XXI supply/transport submarine designs were kept to a minimum, the overall effect was to severely slow type XXI production, and consequently all these projects were abandoned. In addition, replenishing submarines at sea had—by this time—become impracticable, and ran counter to the current basic philosophy of a fully submerged operational patrol.

*Displacement:* 2,809 tons
*Dimensions:* $256 \times 21\frac{3}{4}$ feet
*Machinery:* 2-shaft 6-cylinder M.A.N. diesel/electric motors
   B.H.P./S.H.P. 4,000/4,200 = $10\frac{1}{2}/14$ knots
*Bunkers & Radius:* O.F.; 20,000/110 miles at 4/4 knots
*Armament:* Two 21 inch torpedo tubes (both fwd—two torpedoes)
*Complement:* Not known

## Type XXII

The principal modification with these coastal boats was the addition of an external torpedo tube aft, and again reverting to only a single turbine; but construction was halted at an early stage and production was switched to the type XXIII.

*Displacement:* 155/200 tons
*Dimensions:* 89 × 9¾ × 12¾ feet
*Machinery:* 1-shaft Walter geared turbines, S.H.P. 1,750 = 20
   knots; and diesel/electric motors, B.H.P./S.H.P. 210/77 =
   7/7 knots
*Bunkers & Radius:* Aurol 30 tons, 95 miles at 20 knots; O.F.
   12 tons, 1,550/40 miles at 6½/4½ knots
*Armament:* Three 21inch torpedo tubes (two fwd and one aft—
   three torpedoes) T.T.
*Complement:* 12

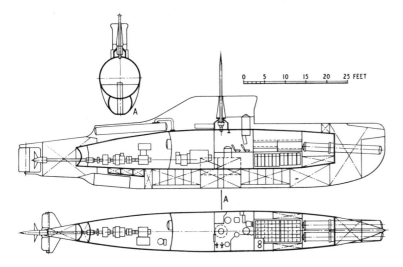

*Type XXII*

## Type XXIII: **U.2321–2500, U.4500, U.4701–5000.**

Coastal counterparts of type XXI which were similarly
prefabricated in four all-welded sections, and had the pressure
hull formed of two flattened cylinders, vertically disposed,
but not fitted with a deck casing. Space was so restricted that
the torpedoes had to be loaded externally into the bow tubes.

*Displacement:* 234/258 tons
*Dimensions:* 113¾ × 9¾ × 12¼ feet
*Machinery:* 1-shaft 6-cylinder M.W.M. diesel-electric motors,
   B.H.P./S.H.P. 575/600 = 9¾/12½ knots; and silent creeping
   electric motor, S.H.P. 35 = 4½ knots
*Bunkers & Radius:* O.F. 18 tons; 1,350/175 miles at 9¾/4 knots
*Armament:* Two 21inch torpedo tubes (both fwd)
*Complement:* 14
*Note:* U.2326 carried out first trials for the class. These boats
   had the same type of telescopic *schnorchel* mast as the
   type XXI

### TYPE VIIC$_{42}$
**Name** *U.1093–U.1100* **Built by** Germania Werft (Kiel)
**Fate** Cancelled

### TYPE VIIC$_{41}/_2$
**Name** *U.1101* **Built by** Nordsee Werke (Emden) **Launched** 1943
**Fate** Scuttled Flensburg 5.5.45

**Name** *U.1102* **Built by** Nordsee Werke (Emden) **Launched** 1943
**Fate** Surrendered Wilhelmshaven 5.45, and scuttled North
Atlantic 1945/6

**Name** *U.1103* **Built by** Nordsee Werke (Emden) **Launched** 1943
**Fate** Surrendered Wilhelmshaven 5.45, and scuttled North
Atlantic 1945/6

**Name** *U.1104* **Built by** Nordsee Werke (Emden) **Launched** 1942/4
**Fate** Surrendered Bergen 5.45 and scrapped

**Name** *U.1105* **Built by** Nordsee Werke (Emden) **Launched** 1942/4
**Fate** Surrendered 5.45; RNN16 (1945); USN (1946); expended
18.11.48

**Name** *U.1106* **Built by** Nordsee Werke (Emden) **Launched** 1944
**Fate** Depth charged RAF aircraft (224 Sqn) north-west of
Shetlands 29.3.45

**Name** *U.1107* **Built by** Nordsee Werke (Emden) **Launched** 1944
**Fate** Depth charged USN aircraft (VPB.103) south-west of
Ushant 25.4.45

**Name** *U.1108* **Built by** Nordsee Werke (Emden) **Launched** 1944
**Fate** Surrendered Horten 5.45; R.N. (1946) and scrapped 1949

**Name** *U.1109* **Built by** Nordsee Werke (Emden) **Launched** 1944
**Fate** Surrendered Horten 5.45; R.N. (1947) and scrapped;
arrived Bicton Ferry 12.5.49 for scrapping by Ward

**Name** *U.1110* **Built by** Nordsee Werke (Emden) **Launched** 1944
**Fate** Surrendered Wilhelmshaven 5.45, and scuttled North
Atlantic 1945/6

**Name** *U.1111–U.1120* **Built by** Nordsee Werke (Emden)
**Fate** Cancelled

**Name** *U.1121–U.1130* **Built by** Nordsee Werke (Emden)
**Fate** Projected

**Name** *U.1131* **Built by** Howaldts Werke (Kiel) **Launched** 1944
**Fate** Bombed RAF aircraft Kiel 9.4.45

**Name** *U.1132* **Built by** Howaldts Werke (Kiel) **Launched** 1944
**Fate** Scuttled Flensburg 5.5.45

**Name** *U.1133–U.1152* **Built by** Howaldts Werke (Kiel)
**Fate** Cancelled

**Name** *U.1153–U.1160* **Built by** Howaldts Werke (Kiel)
**Fate** Projected

**Name** *U.1161* **Built by** Danziger Werft **Launched** 1943
**Fate** Italian *S.8* (1943), German *U.1161* (1943); scuttled
Flensburg 5.5.45

**Name** *U.1162* **Built by** Danziger Werft **Launched** 1943
**Fate** Italian *S.10* (1943), German *U.1162* (1943); scuttled
Flensburg 5.5.45

**Name** *U.1163* **Built by** Danziger Werft **Launched** 1943
**Fate** Surrendered Christiansand 5.45, and scuttled North Atlantic
1945/6

**Name** *U.1164* **Built by** Danziger Werft **Launched** 1943
**Fate** Paid-off Kiel 24.7.44 after being bombed RAF aircraft
23.7.44

**Name** *U.1165* **Built by** Danziger Werft **Launched** 1943
**Fate** Surrendered Narvik 19.5.45, and scuttled North Atlantic
1945/6

**Name** *U.1166* **Built by** Danziger Werft **Launched** 1943
**Fate** Paid-off Kiel 28.8.44 following internal explosion 22.7.44

**Name** *U.1167* **Built by** Danziger Werft **Launched** 1943
**Fate** Bombed USAAF aircraft Hamburg 30.3.45

**Name** *U.1168* **Built by** Danziger Werft **Launched** 1943
**Fate** Scuttled Flensburg 5.5.45

**Name** *U.1169* **Built by** Danziger Werft **Launched** 1943
**Fate** Mined 20 m south-east of Carnsore Pt. 5.4.45

**Name** *U.1170* **Built by** Danziger Werft **Launched** 1943
**Fate** Scuttled Travemünde 3.5.45

**Name** *U.1171* **Built by** Danziger Werft **Launched** 1943
**Fate** Surrendered Stavanger 5.45; RN *N.19* (1947); sold 4.49 to
Young & Co., Sunderland for scrapping

**Name** *U.1172* **Built by** Danziger Werft **Launched** 1943
**Fate** Depth charged RN frigates *Aylmer, Bentinck, Calder* and
*Manners* 32 m north-east of Dublin 26.1.45

**Name** *U.1173* **Built by** Danziger Werft **Fate** Cancelled

**Name** *U.1174* **Built by** Danziger Werft **Fate** Completed as Russian

**Name** *U.1175* **Built by** Danziger Werft **Fate** Cancelled

**Name** *U.1176* **Built by** Danziger Werft **Fate** Completed as Russian

**Name** *U.1177* **Built by** Danziger Werft **Fate** Russian

**Name** *U.1178–U.1190* **Built by** Danziger Werft **Fate** Cancelled

**Name** *U.1191* **Built by** Schichau (Danzig) **Launched** 1943
**Fate** Depth charged RN frigates *Affleck* and *Balfour* 25 m
south-east of Start Pt. 25.6.44

**Name** *U.1192* **Built by** Schichau (Danzig) **Launched** 1943
**Fate** Scuttled Kiel 3.5.45

*Type XXIII*

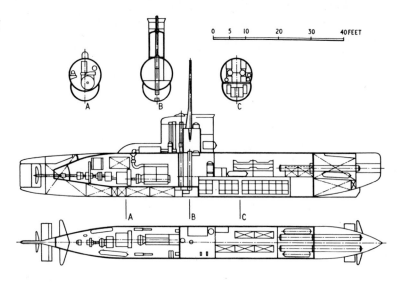

0  5  10  20  30  40 FEET

## TYPE VIIC

**Name** *U.1028* **Built by** Blohm & Voss (Hamburg)
**Launched** 28.11.44 **Fate** Scuttled incomplete 5.45

**Name** *U.1029* **Built by** Blohm & Voss (Hamburg) **Launched** 5.7.44
**Fate** Scuttled incomplete 5.45

**Name** *U.1030* **Built by** Blohm & Voss (Hamburg) **Launched** 5.7.44
**Fate** Scuttled incomplete 5.45

**Name** *U.1031* **Built by** Blohm & Voss (Hamburg) **Launched** 12.7.44
**Fate** Scuttled incomplete 3.5.45

**Name** *U.1032* **Built by** Blohm & Voss (Hamburg) **Launched** 12.7.44
**Fate** Cancelled incomplete

**Name** *U.1033–U.1046* **Built by** Blohm & Voss (Hamburg)
**Fate** Cancelled

**Name** *U.1047* **Built by** Blohm & Voss (Hamburg) **Launched** 1944
**Fate** Scuttled 1945 but later salved; RN (1947)

**Name** *U.1048–U.1050* **Built by** Blohm & Voss (Hamburg)
**Fate** Cancelled

**Name** *U.1051* **Built by** Germania Werft (Kiel) **Launched** 3.2.44
**Fate** Depth charged RN frigates *Bligh, Keats* and *Tyler* 26 m
east-north-east of Wexford 27.1.45

**Name** *U.1052* **Built by** Germania Werft (Kiel) **Launched** 16.12.43
**Fate** Surrendered Bergen 5.45, and scuttled North Atlantic 1945/6

**Name** *U.1053* **Built by** Germania Werft (Kiel) **Launched** 17.2.44
**Fate** Lost by accident off Bergen 15.2.45

**Name** *U.1054* **Built by** Germania Werft (Kiel) **Launched** 24.1.44
**Fate** Surrendered Rostock 1945 and scrapped

**Name** *U.1055* **Built by** Germania Werft (Kiel) **Launched** 9.3.44
**Fate** Depth charged USN aircraft (VPB.63) south-west of Ushant
30.4.45

**Name** *U.1056* **Built by** Germania Werft (Kiel) **Launched** 30.3.44
**Fate** Scuttled Flensburg 5.5.45

**Name** *U.1057* **Built by** Germania Werft (Kiel) **Launched** 20.4.44
**Fate** Surrendered Flensburg 5.5.45, to USSR (11.45) and renamed
*S.81*: scrapped 1963

**Name** *U.1058* **Built by** Germania Werft (Kiel) **Launched** 11.4.44
**Fate** Surrendered Flensburg 5.5.45, to USSR (11.45) and renamed
*S.82*; scrapped 1963

## TYPE VIIF

**Name** *U.1059* **Built by** Germania Werft (Kiel) **Launched** 12.3.43
**Fate** Depth charged USN aircraft of escort carrier *Block Island*
(VC.6) south-west of Cape Verde Islands 19.3.44

**Name** *U.1060* **Built by** Germania Werft (Kiel) **Launched** 8.4.43
**Fate** Depth charged RN aircraft of fleet carrier *Implacable* (1771
Sqn.), and RAF aircraft (311 Czech & 502 Sqns.) north-west of
Namsos 27.10.44

**Name** *U.1061* **Built by** Germania Werft (Kiel) **Launched** 22.4.43
**Fate** Surrendered Bergen 5.5.45, and scuttled North Atlantic
1945/6

**Name** *U.1062* **Built by** Germania Werft (Kiel) **Launched** 8.5.43
**Fate** Depth charged USN destroyer escort *Fessenden* south-west
of Cape Verde Islands 30.9.44

## TYPE VIIC

**Name** *U.1063* **Built by** Germania Werft (Kiel) **Launched** 8.6.44
**Fate** Depth charged RN frigate *Loch Killin* west of Land's End
15.4.45

**Name** *U.1064* **Built by** Germania Werft (Kiel) **Launched** 22.6.44
**Fate** Surrendered Trondheim 5.45, to USSR (11.45) and renamed
*S.83*; scrapped 1963

**Name** *U.1065* **Built by** Germania Werft (Kiel) **Launched** 3.8.44
**Fate** Cannon fire RAF aircraft (235 Sqn.) Skagerrak 9.4.45

**Name** *U.1066–U.1080* **Built by** Germania Werft (Kiel)
**Fate** Cancelled

## TYPE XVIIG

**Name** *U.1081–U.1086* **Built by** Germania Werft (Kiel)
**Fate** Cancelled 14.8.44

**Name** *U.1087–U.1092* **Built by** Germania Werft (Kiel)
**Fate** Cancelled 12.10.43

**Name** *U.1193* **Built by** Schichau (Danzig) **Launched** 1943
**Fate** Scuttled Flensburg 5.5.45

**Name** *U.1194* **Built by** Schichau (Danzig) **Launched** 1943
**Fate** Surrendered Wilhelmshaven 5.45, and scuttled North
Atlantic 1945/6

**Name** *U.1195* **Built by** Schichau (Danzig) **Launched** 1943
**Fate** Depth charged RN destroyer *Watchman* 12 m south-east
of Sandown 6.4.45

**Name** *U.1196* **Built by** Schichau (Danzig) **Launched** 1943
**Fate** Paid-off 8.44 following internal explosion; scuttled
Travemünde 3.5.45

**Name** *U.1197* **Built by** Schichau (Danzig) **Launched** 1943
**Fate** Badly damaged by air attack at Wesermunde 25.4.45;
surrendered at Wilhelmshaven 5.45 and scrapped there

**Name** *U.1198* **Built by** Schichau (Danzig) **Launched** 1943
**Fate** Surrendered Wilhelmshaven 5.45, and scuttled North
Atlantic 1945/6

**Name** *U.1199* **Built by** Schichau (Danzig) **Launched** 1943
**Fate** Depth charged RN destroyer *Icarus*, and corvette *Mignonette*
16 m south of Land's End 21.1.45

**Name** *U.1200* **Built by** Schichau (Danzig) **Launched** 1943
**Fate** Depth charged RN corvettes *Kenilworth Castle, Launceston
Castle, Pevensey Castle* and *Portchester Castle* west of Scillies
11.11.44

**Name** *U.1201* **Built by** Schichau (Danzig) **Launched** 1943
**Fate** Surrendered Hamburg 5.45 and scrapped

**Name** *U.1202* **Built by** Schichau (Danzig) **Launched** 1943
**Fate** Surrendered Bergen 10.5.45, RN (1947), RNN *Kynn* (1948)
and recommissioned 1.7.51; decommissioned 1.6.61 for scrapping
in West Germany

**Name** *U.1203* **Built by** Schichau (Danzig) **Launched** 1943
**Fate** Surrendered Trondheim 5.45, and scuttled North Atlantic
1945/6

**Name** *U.1204* **Built by** Schichau (Danzig) **Launched** 1943
**Fate** Scuttled Flensburg 5.5.45

**Name** *U.1205* **Built by** Schichau (Danzig) **Launched** 1943
**Fate** Scuttled Kiel 3.5.45

**Name** *U.1206* **Built by** Schichau (Danzig) **Launched** 1943
**Fate** Lost by accident 30 m north-east Aberdeen 14.4.45

**Name** *U.1207* **Built by** Schichau (Danzig) **Launched** 1943
**Fate** Scuttled Flensburg 5.5.45

**Name** *U.1208* **Built by** Schichau (Danzig) **Launched** 1943
**Fate** Depth charged RN sloop *Amethyst* 46 m east-south-east of
Cork 20.2.45

**Name** *U.1209* **Built by** Schichau (Danzig) **Launched** 1943
**Fate** Wrecked Wolf Rock 18.12.44

**Name** *U.1210* **Built by** Schichau (Danzig) **Launched** 1943
**Fate** Bombed RAF aircraft off Eckernforde 3.5.45

**Name** *U.1211–U.1216* **Built by** Schichau (Danzig) **Fate** Cancelled

**Name** *U.1217* **Built by** Schichau (Danzig) **Launched** 1944
**Fate** Surrendered Bremen 1945 and scrapped

**Name** *U.1218–U.1220* **Built by** Schichau (Danzig) **Fate** Cancelled


## TYPE IXC

**Name** *U.1221* **Built by** Deutsche Werft (Hamburg)
**Launched** 2.5.43 **Fate** Bombed USAAF aircraft (7 Sqn.) Kiel
3.4.45.

**Name** *U.1222* **Built by** Deutsche Werft (Hamburg)
**Launched** 9.6.43 **Fate** Depth charged RAF aircraft (201 Sqn.)
west of La Rochelle 11.7.44

**Name** *U.1223* **Built by** Deutsche Werft (Hamburg)
**Launched** 16.6.43 **Fate** Bombed Allied aircraft off Weser estuary
28.4.45

**Name** *U.1224* **Built by** Deutsche Werft (Hamburg)
**Launched** 7.7.43 **Fate** IJN *RO.501* (1944); depth charged USN
destroyer escort *Francis M. Robertson* north-west of Cape Verde
Islands 13.5.44

**Name** *U.1225* **Built by** Deutsche Werft (Hamburg)
**Launched** 21.7.43 **Fate** Depth charged RCAF aircraft (162 Sqn.)
north-west of Bergen 24.6.44

**Name** *U.1226* **Built by** Deutsche Werft (Hamburg)
**Launched** 21.8.43 **Fate** Lost by unknown cause North Atlantic
28.10.44

**Name** *U.1227* **Built by** Deutsche Werft (Hamburg)
**Launched** 18.9.43 **Fate** Bombed RAF aircraft Kiel 9.4.45

**Name** *U.1228* **Built by** Deutsche Werft (Hamburg)
**Launched** 2.10.43 **Fate** Surrendered USA port 5.45, and scuttled
USN 5.2.46

**Name** *U.1229* **Built by** Deutsche Werft (Hamburg)
**Launched** 22.10.43 **Fate** Depth charged USN aircraft of escort
carrier *Bogue* (VC.42) south-east of Newfoundland 20.8.44

**Name** *U.1230* **Built by** Deutsche Werft (Hamburg)
**Launched** 8.11.43 **Fate** Surrendered Wilhelmshaven 5.45, and
scuttled North Atlantic 1945/6

**Name** *U.1231* **Built by** Deutsche Werft (Hamburg)
**Launched** 18.11.43 **Fate** Surrendered UK port 5.45; Russian as
*N.25* (11.45), scrapped 1960

**Name** *U.1232* **Built by** Deutsche Werft (Hamburg)
**Launched** 20.12.43 **Fate** Surrendered Weser estuary 5.45 and
scrapped

**Name** *U.1233* **Built by** Deutsche Werft (Hamburg)
**Launched** 23.12.43 **Fate** Surrendered Wilhelmshaven 5.45,
and scuttled North Atlantic 1945/6

**Name** *U.1234* **Built by** Deutsche Werft (Hamburg)
**Launched** 7.1.44 **Fate** Lost by collision off Gydnia 15.5.44, and
later salved; scuttled Flensburg 5.5.45

**Name** *U.1235* **Built by** Deutsche Werft (Hamburg)
**Launched** 25.1.44 **Fate** Depth charged USN destroyer escorts
*Frost* and *Stanton* North Atlantic 15.4.45

**Name** *U.1236* **Built by** Deutsche Werft (Hamburg)
**Launched** 7.2.44 **Fate** Scuttled Hamburg 5.45

**Name** *U.1237* **Built by** Deutsche Werft (Hamburg)
**Launched** 22.2.44 **Fate** Scuttled Hamburg 5.45

**Name** *U.1238* **Built by** Deutsche Werft (Hamburg)
**Launched** 23.2.44 **Fate** Scuttled Hamburg 5.45

**Name** *U.1239–U.1262* **Built by** Deutsche Werft (Hamburg)
**Fate** Cancelled

**Name** *U.1263–U.1270* **Built by** Deutsche Werft (Hamburg)
**Fate** Projected

**TYPE VIIC$_{41/2}$**
**Name** *U.1271* **Built by** Bremer Vulkan (Vegesack) **Launched** 1943
**Fate** Surrendered Bergen 5.45 and scrapped

**Name** *U.1272* **Built by** Bremer Vulkan (Vegesack) **Launched** 1943
**Fate** Surrendered Bergen 5.45 and scrapped

**Name** *U.1273* **Built by** Bremer Vulkan (Vegesack) **Launched** 1943/4
**Fate** Mined off Horten 17.2.45

**Name** *U.1274* **Built by** Bremer Vulkan (Vegesack) **Launched** 1944
**Fate** Depth charged RN destroyer *Viceroy* 6 m east of Sunderland
16.4.45

## Type XXIV

Ocean-going boats with double cylinder pressure hull, disposed one over the other and main propulsion by Walter
geared turbines. The torpedo armament was arranged in a
new manner, and the after torpedo compartment was moved
further forward—but remained in the after half-length—with
the tubes angled 10 deg. from the centre line. The original
provision was for eighteen tubes, but this was reduced to

twelve by halving the number of angled tubes. The arrangement was principally to secure the maximum number of torpedoes instantly available for action use, and to eliminate the lengthy process of reloading the tubes with spare torpedoes stowed either internally or externally. Besides which, for the fully submerged operations now contemplated, externally stowed torpedoes were of little further use. This project was not advanced but influenced the later types XXVI.

*Displacement:* 1,800 tons
*Dimensions:* $234\frac{1}{2} \times 20\frac{1}{4} \times 21\frac{3}{4}$ feet
*Machinery:* 2-shaft Walter geared turbines, S.H.P. 15,000 = 22 knots; diesel/electric motors, B.H.P./S.H.P. 4,000/550 = 15/7 knots; and silent creeping electric motors, S.H.P. 226 = 5 knots
*Bunkers:* Perhydrol
*Armament:* Four 30mm A.A. (2 × 2) guns; twelve 21inch torpedo tubes (six fwd and six aft angled from the centre line—fourteen torpedoes)
*Complement:* Not known

## Type XXV

Few details are available on this small coastal all-electric boat, whose operational scope appeared limited to coast defence duties only.

*Displacement:* 160 tons
*Dimensions:* $92 \times 9\frac{3}{4}$ feet
*Machinery:* 1-shaft electric motor S.H.P. 160 = 9 knots
*Bunkers & Radius:* 400 miles at 6 knots
*Armament:* Two 21inch (both fwd—two torpedoes) T.T.
*Complement:* Not known

## Type XXVI: U.4501–4700

Sea-going boats that were single-shaft diminutives of type XXIV using the Walter system for main propulsion, with the addition of diesel/electric auxiliary drive, and *schnorchel* fitted. As a result of this one-shaft arrangement, a diesel generator was provided so that the batteries could be kept charged while diesel propelled. The original design was for a dimensionally smaller hull ($176\frac{1}{2} \times 17\frac{1}{2} \times 18\frac{1}{4}$ feet and 720/772 tons) powered by a 12-cylinder Deutz diesel engine of 1,200 B.H.P. for a speed of about $14\frac{1}{2}$ knots; but as this speed was in excess of that permissible with the *schnorchel* a lower rated engine was finally installed.

*Displacement:* 842/926 tons

*Dimensions:* $184\frac{1}{2} \times 18 \times 19\frac{1}{2}$ feet

*Machinery:* 1-shaft Walter geared turbines, S.H.P. 7,500 = 24 knots; 6-cylinder MWM diesel/electric motors B.H.P./S.H.P. 580 + 265/580 = 11/10 knots; and silent creeping electric motor S.H.P. 70 = 5 knots

*Bunkers & Radius:* Perhydrol 97 tons, 160 miles at 24 knots (submerged); O.F. 65 tons, 7,300/100 miles at 10/4 knots (surfaced)

*Armament:* Ten 21inch torpedo tubes (four bow and six broadside fwd—ten torpedoes)

*Complement:* 35

*Type XXVI*

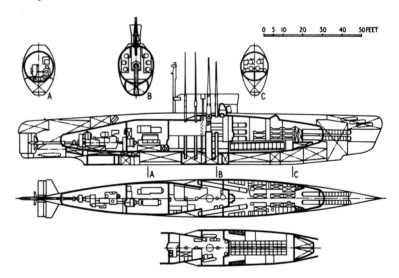

## *Types XXVIA & XXVIB*

Variants of the type XXVI design with dimensions enlarged to incorporate a more powerful diesel engine and heavier armament. The latter design was made some $13\frac{1}{4}$ feet longer to provide additional accommodation forward.

## Type XXVIA

*Displacement:* 950 tons

*Dimensions:* $190\frac{1}{4} \times 21 \times 21\frac{1}{4}$ feet

*Machinery:* 1-shaft Walter geared turbines S.H.P. 7,500 = $22\frac{1}{2}$ knots; and diesel/electric motors B.H.P./S.H.P. 2,000 + 265/580 = $15\frac{1}{2}$/12 knots

*Bunkers & Radius:* Not known

*Armament:* Four 30mm A.A. (2 × 2) guns; twelve 21inch torpedo tubes (six bow and six broadside fwd—twelve torpedoes)

*Complement:* Not known

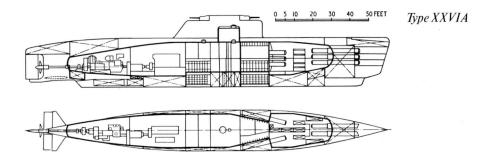

*Type XXVIA*

# Type XXVIB

*Displacement:* 1,150 tons
*Dimensions:* $203\frac{1}{2} \times 21 \times 21\frac{1}{4}$ feet
*Machinery:* 1-shaft Walter geared turbines S.H.P. 7,500 = $21\frac{1}{4}$
 knots; and diesel/electric motors B.H.P./S.H.P. 2,000 + 265/
 580 = 15/11 knots
*Bunkers & Radius:* Aurol 130 tons, 21 miles; O.F. 160 miles at
 4 knots
*Armament:* Four 30mm A.A. (2 × 2) guns; twelve 21inch
 torpedo tubes (six bow and six broadside fwd—twelve
 torpedoes)
*Complement:* Not known

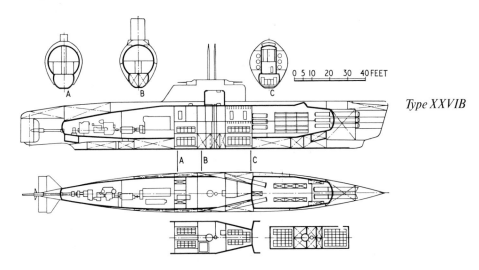

*Type XXVIB*

# Types XXVIE$_2$, XXVIF & XXVIG

These design projects incorporated the type XXVI hull form
but had conventional diesel/electric propulsion with a large
battery capacity for submerged speed and endurance.

Dimensions were varied to suit the different propulsion systems, but adhered to the short and deep hull most suitable for operating continuously submerged. Surfaced speed was now generally assumed to be that attained using the *schnorchel* air mast which imposed a restriction of about 12 knots. All the torpedo tubes were placed forward, and while four were angled-out from the centreline and arranged to discharge aft in types XXVIE$_2$ and XXVIF, only two were so arranged in the type XXVIG.

## Type XXVIE$_2$

*Displacement:* 830 tons
*Dimensions:* $180\frac{1}{2} \times 18 \times 21$ feet
*Machinery:* 1-shaft 6-cylinder M.A.N. diesel/electric motors
  B.H.P./S.H.P. $1,400 + 265/2,400 = 14\frac{1}{2}/16$ knots; and creeping
  silent electric motor S.H.P. 120 = 5 knots
*Bunkers & Radius:* O.F. 8,500 miles at 10 knots
*Armament:* Eight 21 inch torpedo tubes (four bow and four
  broadside fwd)
*Complement:* 31

## Type XXVIF

*Displacement:* 880 tons
*Dimensions:* $187 \times 17\frac{3}{4} \times 21$ feet
*Machinery:* 1-shaft 6-cylinder M.W.M. diesel (two/shaft)/electric
  (two/shaft) motors B.H.P./S.H.P. $1,500/1,800 = 13\frac{1}{2}/15\frac{1}{2}$ knots
*Bunkers & Radius:* O.F. 6,500 miles at 10 knots
*Armament:* Eight 21 inch torpedo tubes (four bow and four
  broadside fwd)
*Complement:* Not known

## Type XXVIG

*Displacement:* 800 tons
*Dimensions:* $174 \times 18 \times 21$ feet
*Machinery:* 1-shaft 6-cylinder M.W.M. diesel/electric motors
  B.H.P./S.H.P. $750 + 265/2,800 = 12/16\frac{1}{2}$ knots; and creeping
  silent electric motor S.H.P. 140 = 5 knots
*Bunkers & Radius:* O.F. 8,400/400 miles at 10/6 knots
*Armament:* Eight 21 inch torpedo tubes (six bow and two
  broadside fwd)
*Complement:* Not known

## Types 126W, 1260, 126K & 126E

These were all private design projects incorporating four alternative systems of propulsion, and embraced a standard armament of eight bow torpedo tubes and high underwater speed. Types 126W and 1260 were both powered by Walter turbines but secured their oxygen by the decomposition of hydrogen peroxide or extraction from sea water respectively, type 126K utilised closed-cycle diesel engines, and type 126E had electric propulsion.

## Type 126W

*Displacement:* 863 tons
*Dimensions:* $163\frac{1}{2} \times 16\frac{1}{2} \times 21$ feet
*Machinery:* 1-shaft Walter geared turbines S.H.P. 7,500 = 23 knots; diesel/electric motors B.H.P./S.H.P. 580 + 265/536; and creeping silent electric motor S.H.P. 71 = 4 knots
*Bunkers & Radius:* Perhydrol 120 tons, 240 miles at 20 knots; O.F. 115 tons
*Armament:* Eight 21inch torpedo tubes (all fwd—ten torpedoes)
*Complement:* Not known

## Type 1260

*Displacement:* 870 tons
*Dimensions:* $163\frac{1}{2} \times 17\frac{3}{4} \times 21$ feet
*Machinery:* 1-shaft Walter geared turbines S.H.P. 7,500 = 23 knots; diesel/electric motors B.H.P./S.H.P. 580 + 265/536; and creeping silent electric motor S.H.P. 71 = 4 knots
*Bunkers & Radius:* Oxygen 40 tons, 140 miles at 20 knots; O.F. 110 tons
*Armament:* Eight 21inch torpedo tubes (all fwd—ten torpedoes)
*Complement:* Not known

## Type 126K

*Displacement:* 864 tons
*Dimensions:* $155\frac{3}{4} \times 17 \times 21$ feet
*Machinery:* 1-shaft diesel (three/shaft)/electric motors B.H.P./ S.H.P. 4,500 = 20 (diesel) knots; and creeping silent electric motor S.H.P. 200 = 6 knots
*Bunkers & Radius:* Oxygen 40 tons, 160 miles at 20 knots; O.F. 100 tons
*Armament:* Eight 21inch (all fwd—ten torpedoes) T.T.
*Complement:* Not known

# Type 126E

*Displacement:* 894 tons
*Dimensions:* 164 × 19¾ × 21 feet
*Machinery:* 1-shaft diesel (two/shaft)-electric motors B.H.P.
   3,600/4,000 = 20 knots; and creeping silent electric motor
   S.H.P. 200 = 6 knots
*Bunkers & Radius:* O.F. 90 tons, 27 at 20 knots
*Armament:* Eight 21inch (all torpedo tubes fwd—ten torpedoes)
*Complement:* Not known

**TYPE VIIC$_{41/2}$**

**Name** *U.1275* **Built by** Bremer Vulkan (Vegesack) **Launched** 1944
**Fate** Surrendered Bergen 5.45 and scrapped

**Name** *U.1276* **Built by** Bremer Vulkan (Vegesack) **Launched** 1944
**Fate** Depth charged RAF aircraft (224 Sqn.) north-east of
Shetlands 3.4.45

**Name** *U.1277* **Built by** Bremer Vulkan (Vegesack) **Launched** 1944
**Fate** Scuttled west of Oporto 3.6.45

**Name** *U.1278* **Built by** Bremer Vulkan (Vegesack) **Launched** 1944
**Fate** Depth charged RN frigates *Bayntun* and *Loch Eck* north-
north-west of Shetlands 17.2.45

**Name** *U.1279* **Built by** Bremer Vulkan (Vegesack) **Launched** 1944
**Fate** Depth charged RN frigates *Bayntun, Braithwaite* and *Loch
Eck* north-west of Shetlands 3.2.45

**Name** *U.1280–U.1297* **Built by** Bremer Vulkan (Vegesack)
**Fate** Cancelled

**Name** *U.1298–U.1300* **Built by** Bremer Vulkan (Vegesack)
**Fate** Projected

**Name** *U.1301* **Built by** Flensburger Schiffbau **Launched** 22.12.43
**Fate** Surrendered Bergen 5.45, and scuttled North Atlantic 1945/6

**Name** *U.1302* **Built by** Flensburger Schiffbau **Launched** 4.4.44
**Fate** Depth charged RCN frigates *La Hulloise, Strathadam* and
*Thetford Mines* 25 m north-west of St. David's Head 7.3.45

**Name** *U.1303* **Built by** Flensburger Schiffbau **Launched** 10.2.44
**Fate** Scuttled Flensburg 5.5.45

**Name** *U.1304* **Built by** Flensburger Schiffbau **Launched** 4.8.44
**Fate** Scuttled Flensburg 5.5.45

**Name** *U.1305* **Built by** Flensburger Schiffbau **Launched** 10.7.44
**Fate** Surrendered UK port 5.45; to USSR (11.45) and renamed
*S.84*; scrapped 1963

**Name** *U.1306* **Built by** Flensburger Schiffbau **Launched** 25.10.44
**Fate** Scuttled Flensburg 5.5.45

**Name** *U.1307* **Built by** Flensburger Schiffbau **Launched** 29.9.44
**Fate** Surrendered Bergen 5.45, and scuttled North Atlantic 1945/6

**Name** *U.1308* **Built by** Flensburger Schiffbau **Launched** 22.11.44
**Fate** Scuttled Warnemünde 2.5.45

**Name** *U.1309–U.1318* **Built by** Flensburger Schiffbau
**Fate** Cancelled

**Name** *U.1319–U.1330* **Built by** Flensburger Schiffbau
**Fate** Projected

## TYPE VIIC$_{42}$

**Name** *U.1331–U.1350* **Built by** Flender Werft (Lübeck)
**Fate** Cancelled

**Name** *U.1351–U.1400* **Built by** Blohm & Voss (Hamburg)
**Fate** Projected

**Name** *U.1401–U.1404* **Built by** Blohm & Voss (Hamburg)
**Fate** Cancelled

## TYPE XVIIB

**Name** *U.1405* **Built by** Blohm & Voss (Hamburg) **Launched** 1.12.44
**Fate** Scuttled Flensburg 5.5.45

**Name** *U.1406* **Built by** Blohm & Voss (Hamburg) **Launched** 2.1.45
**Fate** Scuttled Cuxhaven 2.5.45, and later salved; USN (1946);
sold New York 18.5.48 for scrapping

**Name** *U.1407* **Built by** Blohm & Voss (Hamburg) **Launched** 2.45
**Fate** Scuttled Cuxhaven 2.5.45, and later salved; RN *Meteorite*
(*N.25*–1946), scrapped by Wards in Vickers' yard, Barrow from
12.49

**Name** *U.1408* **Built by** Blohm & Voss (Hamburg) **Launched** 1944
**Fate** Cancelled and scrapped 1.2.45

**Name** *U.1409* **Built by** Blohm & Voss (Hamburg) **Launched** 1944
**Fate** Cancelled and scrapped 15.2.45

*The Walther-engined* U.1407
*(Type XVIIB) became HM
Submarine* Meteorite *post-war
and is seen here under the
White Ensign some time
between 1948 and 1950.*
(MoD)

**Name** *U.1410* **Built by** Blohm & Voss (Hamburg)
**Fate** Cancelled and scrapped on slip 10.3.44

**Name** *U.1411–U.1416* **Built by** Blohm & Voss (Hamburg)
**Fate** Cancelled 14.8.43

### TYPE VIIC$_{42}$
**Name** *U.1417–U.1463* **Built by** Blohm & Voss (Hamburg)
**Fate** Cancelled

**Name** *U.1464–U.1500* **Built by** Blohm & Voss (Hamburg)
**Fate** Projected

### TYPE IXC

**Name** *U.1501–U.1530* **Built by** AG Weser (Bremen)
**Fate** Cancelled

### TYPE IXD$_2$
**Name** *U.1531–U.1542* **Built by** AG Weser (Bremen)
**Fate** Cancelled

**Name** *U.1543–U.1600* **Built by** AG Weser (Bremen)
**Fate** Projected

### TYPE XX

**Name** *U.1601–U.1615* **Built by** AG Weser (Bremen)
**Fate** Cancelled

**Name** *U.1616–U.1700* **Built by** AG Weser (Bremen)
**Fate** Projected

**Name** *U.1701–U.1715* **Built by** AG Weser (Bremen)
**Fate** Cancelled

**Name** *U.1716–U.1800* **Built by** AG Weser (Bremen)
**Fate** Projected

### TYPE VIIC$_{42}$
**Name** *U.1801–U.1828* **Built by** AG Weser (Bremen)
**Fate** Cancelled

**Name** *U.1829–U.1900* **Built by** AG Weser (Bremen)
**Fate** Projected

**Name** *U.1901–U.1904* **Built by** AG Weser (Bremen)
**Fate** Cancelled

**Name** *U.1905–U.2000* **Built by** AG Weser (Bremen)
**Fate** Projected

**Name** *U.2001–U.2004* **Built by** AG Weser (Bremen)
**Fate** Cancelled

**Name** *U.2005–U.2100* **Built by** AG Weser (Bremen)
**Fate** Projected

**Name** *U.2101–U.2104* **Built by** Germania Werft (Kiel)
**Fate** Cancelled

**Name** *U.2105–U.2110* **Built by** Germania Werft (Kiel)
**Fate** Projected

## TYPE XXVIIA

**Name** *U.2111–U.2113* **Built by** Germania Werft (Kiel)
**Fate** Completed (*Hecht*)

**Name** *U.2114–U.2200* **Built by** Germania Werft (Kiel)
**Fate** Cancelled (*Hecht*)

## TYPE XIV

**Name** *U.2201–U.2204* **Built by** Germania Werft (Kiel)
**Fate** Cancelled

## TYPE XXVIIA

**Name** *U.2205–U.2250* **Built by** Germania Werft (Kiel)
**Fate** Cancelled (*Hecht*)

**Name** *U.2251–U.2295* **Built by** Simmering, Graz & Pauker
(Vienna) **Fate** Completed (*Hecht*)

**Name** *U.2296–U.2300* **Built by** Simmering, Graz & Pauker
(Vienna) **Fate** Cancelled (*Hecht*)

## TYPE VIIC$_{42}$

**Name** *U.2301–U.2318* **Built by** Schichau (Danzig)
**Fate** Cancelled but some subsequently completed as Russian

**Name** *U.2319 & U.2320* **Built by** Schichau (Danzig)
**Fate** Projected

## TYPE XXIII

**Name** *U.2321* **Built by** Deutsche Werft (Hamburg)
**Launched** 17.4.44 **Fate** Surrendered Christiansand 5.45, and
scuttled North Atlantic 1945/6

**Name** *U.2322* **Built by** Deutsche Werft (Hamburg)
**Launched** 30.4.44 **Fate** Surrendered Stavanger 5.45, and scuttled
North Atlantic 1945/6

**Name** *U.2323* **Built by** Deutsche Werft (Hamburg)
**Launched** 31.5.44 **Fate** Mined Strander Bight 29.7.44

**Name** *U.2324* **Built by** Deutsche Werft (Hamburg)
**Launched** 16.6.44 **Fate** Surrendered Stavanger 5.45, and scuttled
North Atlantic 1945/6

**Name** *U.2325* **Built by** Deutsche Werft (Hamburg)
**Launched** 13.7.44 **Fate** Surrendered Christiansand 5.45, and
scuttled North Atlantic 1945/6

**Name** *U.2326* **Built by** Deutsche Werft (Hamburg)
**Launched** 17.7.44 **Fate** Surrendered UK port 5.45; RN *N.35*
(1945), French (1946) and lost by accident 6.12.46

**Name** *U.2327* **Built by** Deutsche Werft (Hamburg)
**Launched** 29.7.44 **Fate** Scuttled Hamburg 2.5.45

**Name** *U.2328* **Built by** Deutsche Werft (Hamburg)
**Launched** 17.8.44 **Fate** Surrendered Bergen 5.45, and scuttled
North Atlantic 1945/6

**Name** *U.2329* **Built by** Deutsche Werft (Hamburg)
**Launched** 11.8.44 **Fate** Surrendered Stavanger 5.45, and scuttled
North Atlantic 1945/6

**Name** *U.2330* **Built by** Deutsche Werft (Hamburg)
**Launched** 19.8.44 **Fate** Scuttled Kiel 3.5.45

**Name** *U.2331* **Built by** Deutsche Werft (Hamburg)
**Launched** 28.8.44 **Fate** Lost by accident off Hela 10.44

**Name** *U.2332* **Built by** Germania Werft (Kiel) **Launched** 18.10.44
**Fate** Scuttled Hamburg 2.5.45

**Name** *U.2333* **Built by** Germania Werft (Kiel) **Launched** 16.11.44
**Fate** Scuttled Flensburg 5.5.45

**Name** *U.2334* **Built by** Deutsche Werft (Hamburg)
**Launched** 26.8.44 **Fate** Surrendered Christiansand 5.45, and
scuttled North Atlantic 1945/6

**Name** *U.2335* **Built by** Deutsché Werft (Hamburg)
**Launched** 31.8.44 **Fate** Surrendered Christiansand 5.45, and
scuttled North Atlantic 1945/6

**Name** *U.2336* **Built by** Deutsche Werft (Hamburg)
**Launched** 10.9.44 **Fate** Surrendered Kiel 5.45, and scuttled North
Atlantic 1945/6

**Name** *U.2337* **Built by** Deutsche Werft (Hamburg)
**Launched** 15.9.44 **Fate** Surrendered Christiansand 5.45,

**Name** *U.2338* **Built by** Deutsche Werft (Hamburg)
**Launched** 18.9.44 **Fate** Depth charged RAF aircraft (236 & 254
Sqns.) Little Belt 4.5.45

**Name** *U.2339* **Built by** Deutsche Werft (Hamburg)
**Launched** 22.9.44 **Fate** Scuttled Flensburg 5.45

**Name** *U.2340* **Built by** Deutsche Werft (Hamburg)
**Launched** 28.9.44 **Fate** Bombed USAAF aircraft Hamburg
30.3.45

**Name** *U.2341* **Built by** Deutsche Werft (Hamburg)
**Launched** 3.10.44 **Fate** Surrendered Wilhelmshaven 5.45, and
scuttled North Atlantic 1945/6

**Name** *U.2342* **Built by** Deutsche Werft (Hamburg)
**Launched** 13.10.44 **Fate** Mined east of Swinemünde 26.12.44

**Name** *U.2343* **Built by** Deutsche Werft (Hamburg)
**Launched** 18.10.44 **Fate** Scuttled Flensburg 5.45

**Name** *U.2344* **Built by** Deutsche Werft (Hamburg)
**Launched** 24.10.44 **Fate** Lost by collision off Heiligenhaven
18.2.45, later salved by E. Germany (DDR) and scrapped 1954/5

**Name** *U.2345* **Built by** Deutsche Werft (Hamburg)
**Launched** 28.10.44 **Fate** Surrendered Stavanger 5.45, and scuttled
North Atlantic 1945/6

**Name** *U.2346* **Built by** Deutsche Werft (Hamburg)
**Launched** 31.10.44 **Fate** Scuttled Flensburg 5.5.45

**Name** *U.2347* **Built by** Deutsche Werft (Hamburg)
**Launched** 6.11.44 **Fate** Scuttled Flensburg 5.5.45

**Name** *U.2348* **Built by** Deutsche Werft (Hamburg)
**Launched** 11.11.44 **Fate** Surrendered Stavanger 5.45, RN (1945);
sold 4.49 to Leigh & Co., Belfast for scrapping

**Name** *U.2349* **Built by** Deutsche Werft (Hamburg)
**Launched** 20.11.44 **Fate** Scuttled Flensburg 5.5.45

**Name** *U.2350* **Built by** Deutsche Werft (Hamburg)
**Launched** 22.11.44 **Fate** Surrendered Christiansand 5.45, and
scuttled North Atlantic 1945/6

**Name** *U.2351* **Built by** Deutsche Werft (Hamburg)
**Launched** 25.11.44 **Fate** Surrendered Kiel 5.45, and scrapped

**Name** *U.2352* **Built by** Deutsche Werft (Hamburg)
**Launched** 5.12.44 **Fate** Scuttled Flensburg 5.5.45

**Name** *U.2353* **Built by** Deutsche Werft (Hamburg)
**Launched** 6.12.44 **Fate** Surrendered Christiansand 5.45; to USSR
(11.45) as *N.31*; scrapped 1963

**Name** *U.2354* **Built by** Deutsche Werft (Hamburg)
**Launched** 10.12.44 **Fate** Surrendered Christiansand 5.45, and
scuttled North Atlantic 1945/6

**Name** *U.2355* **Built by** Deutsche Werft (Hamburg)
**Launched** 13.12.44 **Fate** Scuttled Kiel 3.5.45

**Name** *U.2356* **Built by** Deutsche Werft (Hamburg)
**Launched** 19.12.44 **Fate** Surrendered Wilhelmshaven 5.45, and
scrapped

**Name** *U.2357* **Built by** Deutsche Werft (Hamburg)
**Launched** 19.12.44 **Fate** Scuttled Flensburg 5.5.45

**Name** *U.2358* **Built by** Deutsche Werft (Hamburg)
**Launched** 20.12.44 **Fate** Scuttled Flensburg 5.5.45

**Name** *U.2359* **Built by** Deutsche Werft (Hamburg)
**Launched** 23.12.44 **Fate** Bombed RAF (143, 235, 248 & 303
Norge Sqns.) & RCAF (404 Sqn.) aircraft Kattegat 2.5.45

**Name** *U.2360* **Built by** Deutsche Werft (Hamburg)
**Launched** 29.12.44 **Fate** Scuttled Flensburg 5.5.45

**Name** *U.2361* **Built by** Deutsche Werft (Hamburg)
**Launched** 3.1.45 **Fate** Surrendered Christiansand 5.45, and
scuttled North Atlantic 1945/6

**Name** *U.2362* **Built by** Deutsche Werft (Hamburg)
**Launched** 11.1.45 **Fate** Scuttled Flensburg 5.5.45

**Name** *U.2363* **Built by** Deutsche Werft (Hamburg)
**Launched** 18.1.45 **Fate** Surrendered Christiansand 5.45, and
scuttled North Atlantic 1945/6

**Name** *U.2364* **Built by** Deutsche Werft (Hamburg)
**Fate** 23.1.45 **Fate** Scuttled Flensburg 5.5.45

**Name** *U.2365* **Built by** Deutsche Werft (Hamburg)
**Launched** 26.1.45 **Fate** Scuttled Skagerrak 8.5.45 after being
bombed RAF aircraft (311 Czech Sqn.) 5.5.45; salved 1956 and
renamed *Hai*

**Name** *U.2366* **Built by** Deutsche Werft (Hamburg)
**Launched** 17.2.45 **Fate** Scuttled Flensburg 5.5.45

**Name** *U.2367* **Built by** Deutsche Werft (Hamburg)
**Launched** 23.2.45 **Fate** Lost in collision with German submarine
while under air attack Great Belt 5.5.45; salved 1956 and renamed
*Hecht*

**Name** *U.2368* **Built by** Deutsche Werft (Hamburg)
**Launched** 19.3.45 **Fate** Scuttled Flensburg 5.5.45

**Name** *U.2369* **Built by** Deutsche Werft (Hamburg)
**Launched** 24.3.45 **Fate** Scuttled Flensburg 5.5.45

**Name** *U.2370* **Built by** Deutsche Werft (Hamburg)
**Launched** 3.45 **Fate** Scuttled Hamburg 2.5.45

**Name** *U.2371* **Built by** Deutsche Werft (Hamburg)
**Launched** 18.4.45 **Fate** Scuttled Hamburg 2.5.45

**Name** *U.2372* **Built by** Deutsche Werft (Toulon) **Fate** Scrapped
incomplete

**Name** *U.2373* **Built by** Deutsche Werft (Toulon) **Fate** Scrapped
incomplete

**Name** *U.2374* **Built by** Deutsche Werft (Toulon) **Fate** Scrapped
incomplete

**Name** *U.2375* **Built by** Deutsche Werft (Toulon) **Fate** Scrapped
incomplete

**Name** *U.2376* **Built by** Deutsche Werft (Toulon) **Fate** Scrapped
incomplete

**Name** *U.2377* **Built by** Deutsche Werft (Toulon) **Fate** Scrapped
incomplete

**Name** *U.2378–U.2400* **Built by** Deutsche Werft (Toulon)
**Fate** Cancelled

**Name** *U.2401–U.2430* **Built by** Deutsche Werft (Genoa)
**Fate** Cancelled

**Name** *U.2431–U.2445* **Built by** Deutsche Werft (Monfalcone)
**Fate** Cancelled

**Name** *U.2446–U.2460* **Built by** Deutsche Werft (Nicolaiev & Linz)
**Fate** Cancelled

**Name** *U.2461–U.2500* **Built by** Deutsche Werft (Nicolaiev & Linz)
**Fate** Projected

## TYPE XXI

**Name** *U.2501* **Built by** Blohm & Voss (Hamburg) **Launched** 12.5.44
**Fate** Scuttled Hamburg 2.5.45

**Name** *U.2502* **Built by** Blohm & Voss (Hamburg) **Launched** 15.6.44
**Fate** Surrendered Horten 5.45, and scrapped

**Name** *U.2503* **Built by** Blohm & Voss (Hamburg) **Launched** 29.6.44
**Fate** Cannon and rocket fire of RAF aircraft (236 & 254 Sqns.)
Little Belt 4.5.45

**Name** *U.2504* **Built by** Blohm & Voss (Hamburg) **Launched** 18.7.44
**Fate** Scuttled Hamburg 2.5.45

**Name** *U.2505* **Built by** Blohm & Voss (Hamburg) **Launched** 27.7.44
**Fate** Scuttled Hamburg 2.5.45

**Name** *U.2506* **Built by** Blohm & Voss (Hamburg) **Launched** 5.8.44
**Fate** Surrendered Bergen 5.45, and scrapped

**Name** *U.2507* **Built by** Blohm & Voss (Hamburg) **Launched** 14.8.44
**Fate** Scuttled Flensburg 5.5.45

**Name** *U.2508* **Built by** Blohm & Voss (Hamburg) **Launched** 19.8.44
**Fate** Scuttled Kiel 3.5.45

**Name** *U.2509* **Built by** Blohm & Voss (Hamburg) **Launched** 27.8.44
**Fate** Bombed RAF aircraft Hamburg 8.4.45

**Name** *U.2510* **Built by** Blohm & Voss (Hamburg) **Launched** 29.8.44
**Fate** Scuttled Travemünde 2.5.45

**Name** *U.2511* **Built by** Blohm & Voss (Hamburg) **Launched** 2.9.44
**Fate** Surrendered Bergen 5.45, and scrapped

**Name** *U.2512* **Built by** Blohm & Voss (Hamburg) **Launched** 7.9.44
**Fate** Scuttled Eckernforde 3.5.45

**Name** *U.2513* **Built by** Blohm & Voss (Hamburg) **Launched** 14.9.44
**Fate** Surrendered Horten 5.45; USN (1946) and sunk as target
for rockets 7.10.51

**Name** *U.2514* **Built by** Blohm & Voss (Hamburg) **Launched** 17.9.44
**Fate** Bombed RAF aircraft Hamburg 8.4.45

**Name** *U.2515* **Built by** Blohm & Voss (Hamburg) **Launched** 22.9.44
**Fate** Bombed USAAF aircraft Hamburg 11.3.45

**Name** *U.2516* **Built by** Blohm & Voss (Hamburg) **Launched** 27.9.44
**Fate** Bombed RAF aircraft Hamburg 8.4.45

**Name** *U.2517* **Built by** Blohm & Voss (Hamburg) **Launched** 4.10.44
**Fate** Scuttled Flensburg 4.5.45

**Name** *U.2518* **Built by** Blohm & Voss (Hamburg) **Launched** 4.10.44
**Fate** Surrendered Horten 5.45; RN (1946), French *Roland
Morillot* (1947)

**Name** *U.2519* **Built by** Blohm & Voss (Hamburg) **Launched** 18.10.44
**Fate** Scuttled Kiel 3.5.45

**Name** *U.2520* **Built by** Blohm & Voss (Hamburg) **Launched** 16.10.44
**Fate** Scuttled Kiel 3.5.45

**Name** *U.2521* **Built by** Blohm & Voss (Hamburg) **Launched** 18.10.44
**Fate** Bombed RAF aircraft (547 sqn.) south-east of Aarhus 5.5.45

**Name** *U.2522* **Built by** Blohm & Voss (Hamburg) **Launched** 22.10.44
**Fate** Scuttled Flensburg 5.5.45

**Name** *U.2523* **Built by** Blohm & Voss (Hamburg) **Launched** 25.10.44
**Fate** Bombed Allied aircraft Hamburg 17.1.45

## *Type XXVIIA* (*Hecht*): **U.2111–2200** and **U.2205–2300.**

The original design was for a 7-ton midget submarine mine-layer, able to stow one limpet mine, with electric drive and a radius of action of 90 miles. As no suitable small compass was available and standard gyro equipment had to be utilised size had perforce to be increased with a corresponding reduction in radius. Difficulties then arose in providing and fitting a suitable mine, and the idea to use them operationally was abandoned prior to their completion and they were all relegated to training duties. Consequently, the type XXVIIA building programme was considerably cut back and only a very few were finally completed. Modifications extended to some units were:

    (*a*) Mine replaced by an externally stowed torpedo slung underneath the hull.

    (*b*) The fore compartment, which originally housed the mine, was used for additional battery space to increase radius,

or (*c*) was fitted as a "wet and dry" compartment from which frogmen could leave or enter the craft.

*Displacement:* $11\frac{3}{4}$ tons
*Dimensions:* $34 \times 5\frac{1}{2} \times 5$ feet
*Machinery:* 1-shaft electric motor, S.H.P. $13 = 5\frac{3}{4}/6$ knots
*Radius:* 38 miles at 4 knots (69 miles at 4 knots with addl. battery capacity)
*Armament:* One mine or 21 inch torpedo
*Complement:* 2

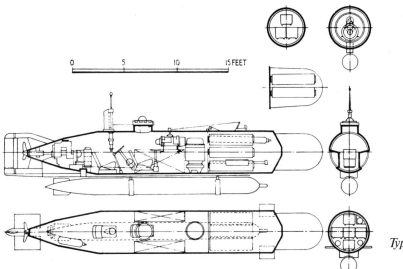

*Type XXVIIA*

# Type XXVIIB (Seehund): U.5001–6351.

This type was a logical development from the type XXVIIA and was the most successful of the German midget submarines. Armament was increased to two torpedoes, both externally stowed below the hull, and propulsion was by a conventional diesel/electric arrangement coupled to a single shaft with the screw turning in a Kort nozzle rudder.

*Displacement:* 15 tons
*Dimensions:* $39 \times 5\frac{1}{2} \times 5$ feet
*Machinery:* 1-shaft diesel/electric motors, B.H.P./S.H.P. $60/25 = 7\frac{3}{4}/6$ knots
*Bunkers & Radius:* O.F. $\frac{1}{2}$ ton; 300/63 miles at 7/3 knots (with addl. external tanks surface radius was increased to 500 miles at 7 knots)
*Armament:* Two 21 inch torpedoes
*Complement:* 2

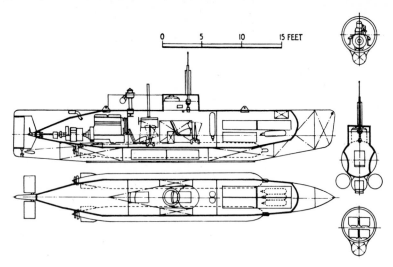

The types **XXVIIA** (*Hecht*) and **XXVIIB** (*Seehund*) submarines were the highest type numbers put into production. Subsequent type numbers were only projected design studies—none of which progressed further than the drawing board—which concentrated on craft capable of undertaking a completely submerged war patrol by either using the *schnorchel* or a closed-cycle type of engine.

## *Type XXVIII*

Coastal boat design project in which speed was subjugated to radius so that the diesel engine could be eliminated.

*Displacement:* 200 tons
*Dimensions:* 105 feet
*Machinery:* 1-shaft Walter geared turbines S.H.P. 250 = 8/10 knots; and silent creeping electric motor S.H.P. 35 = 5 knots
*Bunkers & Radius:* Durol; 2,000/250 miles at 6/5 knots
*Armament:* Four 21inch torpedo tubes (all fwd—four torpedoes)
*Complement:* Not known

## *Types XXIXA, XXIXB, XXIXB$_2$, XXIXC, XXIXD, XXIXG & XXIXH*

This was a diverse series of conventionally powered sea-going boats which progressively increased in size only to revert back to the tonnage originally projected.

Type XXIXA adopted the now standard short and deep hull and single screw, and was armed with eight torpedo tubes in the bow; and the succeeding type XXIXB was closely similar except that battery capacity was increased by 50% with a corresponding rise in electric motor output and speed. With the type XXIXB$_2$ the hull was lengthened and made deeper, and while there was only a slight increase in power with the electric motor that of the diesel engine was practically doubled.

Length was again increased with type XXIXC to accommodate yet greater battery capacity, and a reversion made back to the smaller diesel engine. All round increases were incorporated by type XXIXD except that battery capacity was now reduced by 25%; while four additional torpedo tubes were added forward, angled out from the centreline and arranged to discharge aft. This process was again reversed for type XXIXG where the output of the diesel engine was reduced and that of the electric motors increased, and the torpedo tubes were arranged in two banks of six in a beamier and deeper hull.

Finally, the type XXIXH while retaining a shorter and fuller hull form had the same machinery as was first proposed for the type XXIXA, but had two less torpedo tubes in the bow.

# Type XXIXA

*Displacement:* 681 tons
*Dimensions:* $176\frac{1}{4} \times 15\frac{3}{4} \times 16\frac{3}{4}$ feet
*Machinery:* 1-shaft diesel/electric motors B.H.P. 750 + 265/1,400
    = $12/13\frac{3}{4}$ knots; and creeping silent electric motor S.H.P.
    70 = 5 knots
*Bunkers & Radius:* O.F.; 7,100/125 miles at 10/6 knots
*Armament:* Eight 21inch (all fwd) T.T.
*Complement:* Not known

# Type XXIXB

*Displacement:* 753 tons
*Dimensions:* $188\frac{3}{4} \times 15\frac{3}{4} \times 16\frac{3}{4}$ feet
*Machinery:* 1-shaft diesel/electric motors B.H.P./S.H.P.
    750 + 265/2,100 = $12/15\frac{1}{2}$ knots; and creeping silent electric
    motor S.H.P. 110 = 5 knots
*Bunkers & Radius:* O.F.; 7,100/175 miles at 10/6 knots
*Armament:* Eight 21inch torpedoes (all fwd) T.T.
*Complement:* Not known

## Type XXIXB₂

*Displacement:* 790 tons
*Dimensions:* 187 × 15¾ × 19¾ feet
*Machinery:* 1-shaft 6-cylinder M.A.N. diesel/electric motors
B.H.P./S.H.P. 1,500 + 265/2,400 = 15¼/16½ knots; and
creeping silent electric motor S.H.P. 120 = 5 knots
*Bunkers & Radius:* O.F.; torpedoes 7,100/235 miles at 10/6 knots
*Armament:* Eight 21inch torpedoes (all fwd) T.T.
*Complement:* Not known

## Type XXIXC

*Displacement:* 825 tons
*Dimensions:* 201 × 15¾ × 16¾ feet
*Machinery:* 1-shaft 6-cylinder M.W.M. diesel/electric motors
B.H.P./S.H.P. 750 + 265/2,800 = 11¾/16¾ knots; and creeping
silent electric motor S.H.P. 140 = 5 knots
*Bunkers & Radius:* O.F.; 7,100/250 miles at 10/6 knots
*Armament:* Eight 21inch torpedoes (all fwd) T.T.
*Complement:* Not known

## Type XXIXD

*Displacement:* 1,035 tons
*Dimensions:* 218¾ × 17¾ × 17½ feet
*Machinery:* 1-shaft 6-cylinder M.A.N. diesel/electric motors
B.H.P./S.H.P. 1,200 + 265/2,100 = 15/14¾ knots; and creeping
silent eletric motor S.H.P. 110 = 5 knots
*Bunkers & Radius:* O.F.; 7,100/150 miles at 10/6 knots
*Armament:* Twelve 21inch (eight bow and six broadside fwd—
twelve torpedoes) T.T.
*Complement:* Not known

## Type XXIXG

*Displacement:* 1,122 tons
*Dimensions:* 189¾ × 22 × 19¾ feet
*Machinery:* 1-shaft 6-cylinder M.W.M. diesel/electric motors
B.H.P./S.H.P. 750 + 750/2,800 = 12/16½ knots; and creeping
silent electric motor S.H.P. 140 = 5 knots
*Bunkers & Radius:* O.F.; 10,000/225 miles at 10/6 knots
*Armament:* Twelve 21inch (six bow and four broadside fwd—
twelve torpedoes) T.T.
*Complement:* Not known

## Type XXIXH

*Displacement:* 715 tons
*Dimensions:* 170½ × 21 × 15 feet
*Machinery:* 1-shaft 6-cylinder M.W.M. diesel/electric motors

B.H.P./S.H.P. 580 + 580/1,400 = 13/15½ knots
*Bunkers & Radius:* O.F.; 9,000/120 miles at 10/6 knots
*Armamanet:* Six 21inch torpedoes (all fwd) T.T.
*Complement:* Not known

## TYPE XXI

**Name** *U.2524* **Built by** Blohm & Voss (Hamburg)
**Launched** 30.10.44 **Fate** Scuttled east of Samso after cannon and rocket fire attack RAF aircraft (236 & 254 Sqns.) south-east of Aarhus 3.5.45

**Name** *U.2525* **Built by** Blohm & Voss (Hamburg)
**Launched** 30.10.44 **Fate** Scuttled Flensburg 5.5.45

**Name** *U.2526* **Built by** Blohm & Voss (Hamburg)
**Launched** 30.11.44 **Fate** Scuttled Travemünde 2.5.45

**Name** *U.2527* **Built by** Blohm & Voss (Hamburg)
**Launched** 30.11.44 **Fate** Scuttled Travemünde 2.5.45

**Name** *U.2528* **Built by** Blohm & Voss (Hamburg)
**Launched** 18.11.44 **Fate** Scuttled Travemünde 2.5.45

**Name** *U.2529* **Built by** Blohm & Voss (Hamburg)
**Launched** 18.11.44 **Fate** Surrendered Christiansand 5.45; to USSR (11.45); renamed *N.27* and scrapped 1963

**Name** *U.2530* **Built by** Blohm & Voss (Hamburg)
**Launched** 23.11.44 **Fate** Bombed USAAF aircraft 11.3.45

**Name** *U.2531* **Built by** Blohm & Voss (Hamburg)
**Launched** 5.12.44 **Fate** Scuttled Travemünde 2.5.45

**Name** *U.2532* **Built by** Blohm & Voss (Hamburg)
**Launched** 7.12.44 **Fate** Bombed Allied aircraft Hamburg 31.12.44

**Name** *U.2533* **Built by** Blohm & Voss (Hamburg)
**Launched** 7.12.44 **Fate** Scuttled Travemünde 3.5.45

**Name** *U.2534* **Built by** Blohm & Voss (Hamburg)
**Launched** 11.12.44 **Fate** Bombed RAF aircraft (86 Sqn.) Kattegat 6.5.45

**Name** *U.2535* **Built by** Blohm & Voss (Hamburg)
**Launched** 16.12.44 **Fate** Scuttled Travemünde 2.5.45

**Name** *U.2536* **Built by** Blohm & Voss (Hamburg)
**Launched** 16.12.44 **Fate** Scuttled Travemünde 2.5.45

**Name** *U.2537* **Built by** Blohm & Voss (Hamburg)
**Launched** 22.12.44 **Fate** Bombed Allied aircraft Hamburg 8.4.45

**Name** *U.2538* **Built by** Blohm & Voss (Hamburg)
**Launched** 6.1.45 **Fate** Mined off south-west coast of Aero bei Marstal 9.5.45

**Name** *U.2539* **Built by** Blohm & Voss (Hamburg)
**Launched** 6.1.45 **Fate** Scuttled Kiel 3.5.45

**Name** *U.2540* **Built by** Blohm & Voss (Hamburg)

**Launched** 13.1.45 **Fate** Scuttled off Flensburg 4.5.45 after being attacked RAF aircraft (2.TAF) Great Belt 3.5.45; salved and renamed *Wilhelm Bauer*

**Name** *U.2541* **Built by** Blohm & Voss (Hamburg) **Launched** 13.1.45 **Fate** Scuttled Flensburg 5.5.45

**Name** *U.2542* **Built by** Blohm & Voss (Hamburg) **Launched** 22.1.45 **Fate** Bombed USAAF aircraft Kiel 3.4.45

**Name** *U.2543* **Built by** Blohm & Voss (Hamburg) **Launched** 9.2.45 **Fate** Scuttled Kiel 3.5.45

**Name** *U.2544* **Built by** Blohm & Voss (Hamburg) **Launched** 9.2.45 **Fate** Scuttled off Aarhus 5.5.45

**Name** *U.2545* **Built by** Blohm & Voss (Hamburg) **Launched** 12.2.45 **Fate** Scuttled Kiel 3.5.45

**Name** *U.2546* **Built by** Blohm & Voss (Hamburg) **Launched** 19.2.45 **Fate** Scuttled Kiel 3.5.45

**Name** *U.2547* **Built by** Blohm & Voss (Hamburg) **Launched** 19.3.45 **Fate** Bombed Allied aircraft Hamburg 8.4.45 while building and construction abandoned

**Name** *U.2548* **Built by** Blohm & Voss (Hamburg) **Launched** 9.3.45 **Fate** Scuttled Kiel 3.5.45

**Name** *U.2549* **Built by** Blohm & Voss (Hamburg) **Launched** 1945 **Fate** Bombed Allied aircraft Hamburg 8.4.45 while building and construction abandoned

**Name** *U.2550* **Built by** Blohm & Voss (Hamburg) **Launched** 1945 **Fate** Bombed Allied aircraft Hamburg 8.4.45 while building and construction abandoned

**Name** *U.2551* **Built by** Blohm & Voss (Hamburg) **Launched** 1945 **Fate** Scuttled Flensburg 5.5.45

**Name** *U.2552* **Built by** Blohm & Voss (Hamburg) **Launched** 1945 **Fate** Bombed Allied aircraft Hamburg 8.4.45 while building

**Name** *U.2553* **Built by** Blohm & Voss (Hamburg) **Fate** Scrapped incomplete

**Name** *U.2554* **Built by** Blohm & Voss (Hamburg) **Fate** Scrapped incomplete

**Name** *U.2555* **Built by** Blohm & Voss (Hamburg) **Fate** Scrapped incomplete

**Name** *U.2556* **Built by** Blohm & Voss (Hamburg) **Fate** Scrapped incomplete

**Name** *U.2557* **Built by** Blohm & Voss (Hamburg) **Fate** Scrapped incomplete

**Name** *U.2558* **Built by** Blohm & Voss (Hamburg) **Fate** Scrapped incomplete

**Name** *U.2559* **Built by** Blohm & Voss (Hamburg) **Fate** Scrapped incomplete

**Name** *U.2560* **Built by** Blohm & Voss (Hamburg) **Fate** Scrapped incomplete

**Name** *U.2561* **Built by** Blohm & Voss (Hamburg) **Fate** Scrapped incomplete

**Name** *U.2562* **Built by** Blohm & Voss (Hamburg) **Fate** Scrapped incomplete

**Name** *U.2563* **Built by** Blohm & Voss (Hamburg) **Fate** Scrapped incomplete

**Name** *U.2564* **Built by** Blohm & Voss (Hamburg) **Fate** Scrapped incomplete

**Name** *U.2565–U.2761* **Built by** Blohm & Voss (Hamburg) **Fate** Cancelled

**Name** *U.2762–***U.***3000* **Built by** Blohm & Voss (Hamburg) **Fate** Projected

**Name** *U.3012* **Built by** AG Weser (Bremen) **Launched** 13.10.44 **Fate** Scuttled Travemünde 3.5.45

**Name** *U.3013* **Built by** AG Weser (Bremen) **Launched** 19.10.44 **Fate** Scuttled Travemünde 3.5.45

**Name** *U.3001* **Built by** AG Weser (Bremen) **Launched** 30.5.44 **Fate** Scuttled Weser estuary 1.5.45

**Name** *U.3002* **Built by** AG Weser (Bremen) **Launched** 9.7.44 **Fate** Scuttled Travemünde 2.5.45

**Name** *U.3003* **Built by** AG Weser (Bremen) **Launched** 18.7.44 **Fate** Bombed USAAF aircraft Kiel 4.4.45

**Name** *U.3004* **Built by** AG Weser (Bremen) **Launched** 26.7.44 **Fate** Scuttled Hamburg 2.5.45

**Name** *U.3005* **Built by** AG Weser (Bremen) **Launched** 18.8.44 **Fate** Scuttled Weser estuary 1.5.45

**Name** *U.3006* **Built by** AG Weser (Bremen) **Launched** 25.3.44 **Fate** Scuttled Wilhelmshaven 1.5.45

**Name** *U.3007* **Built by** AG Weser (Bremen) **Launched** 4.9.44 **Fate** Bombed USAAF aircraft Bremen 24.2.45

**Name** *U.3008* **Built by** AG Weser (Bremen) **Launched** 15.9.44 **Fate** Surrendered Kiel 5.45; USN (1946) and sold Puerto Rico late in 1954 for scrapping

**Name** *U.3009* **Built by** AG Weser (Bremen) **Launched** 30.9.44 **Fate** Scuttled Weser estuary 1.5.45

**Name** *U.3010* **Built by** AG Weser (Bremen) **Launched** 20.10.44 **Fate** Scuttled Kiel 3.5.45

**Name** *U.3011* **Built by** AG Weser (Bremen) **Launched** 20.10.44 **Fate** Scuttled Travemünde 3.5.45

**Name** *U.3014* **Built by** AG Weser (Bremen) **Launched** 25.10.44
**Fate** Scuttled off Neustadt 3.5.45

**Name** *U.3015* **Built by** AG Weser (Bremen) **Launched** 27.10.44
**Fate** Scuttled Flensburg 5.5.45

**Name** *U.3016* **Built by** AG Weser (Bremen) **Launched** 2.11.44
**Fate** Scuttled Travemünde 2.5.45

**Name** *U.3017* **Built by** AG Weser (Bremen) **Launched** 5.11.44
**Fate** Surrendered Horten 5.45, RN *N.41* (1947); scrapped 11.49

**Name** *U.3018* **Built by** AG Weser (Bremen) **Launched** 29.11.44
**Fate** Scuttled Travemünde 2.5.45

**Name** *U.3019* **Built by** AG Weser (Bremen) **Launched** 15.11.44
**Fate** Scuttled Travemünde 2.5.45

**Name** *U.3020* **Built by** AG Weser (Bremen) **Launched** 16.11.44
**Fate** Scuttled Travemünde 2.5.45

**Name** *U.3021* **Built by** AG Weser (Bremen) **Launched** 27.11.44
**Fate** Scuttled Travemünde 2.5.45

**Name** *U.3022* **Built by** AG Weser (Bremen) **Launched** 30.11.44
**Fate** Scuttled Flensburg 5.5.45

**Name** *U.3023* **Built by** AG Weser (Bremen) **Launched** 2.12.44
**Fate** Scuttled Travemünde 3.5.45

**Name** *U.3024* **Built by** AG Weser (Bremen) **Launched** 6.12.44
**Fate** Scuttled Neustadt 3.5.45

**Name** *U.3025* **Built by** AG Weser (Bremen) **Launched** 9.12.44
**Fate** Scuttled Travemünde 3.5.45

**Name** *U.3026* **Built by** AG Weser (Bremen) **Launched** 14.12.44
**Fate** Scuttled Travemünde 3.5.45

**Name** *U.3027* **Built by** AG Weser (Bremen) **Launched** 18.12.44
**Fate** Scuttled Travemünde 3.5.45

**Name** *U.3028* **Built by** AG Weser (Bremen) **Launched** 22.12.44
**Fate** Bombed Allied aircraft Great Belt 3.5.45

**Name** *U.3029* **Built by** AG Weser (Bremen) **Launched** 28.12.44
**Fate** Scuttled Kiel 3.5.45

**Name** *U.3030* **Built by** AG Weser (Bremen) **Launched** 31.12.44
**Fate** Depth charged RAF aircraft (2. TAF) Little Belt 3.5.45

**Name** *U.3031* **Built by** AG Weser (Bremen) **Launched** 6.1.45
**Fate** Scuttled Kiel 3.5.45

**Name** *U.3032* **Built by** AG Weser (Bremen) **Launched** 10.1.45
**Fate** Depth charged RAF aircraft (2 TAF) Little Belt 3.5.45

**Name** *U.3033* **Built by** AG Weser (Bremen) **Launched** 20.1.45
**Fate** Scuttled Flensburg 3.5.45

**Name** *U.3034* **Built by** AG Weser (Bremen) **Launched** 21.1.45
**Fate** Scuttled Flensburg 3.5.45

**Name** *U.3035* **Built by** AG Weser (Bremen) **Launched** 24.1.45
**Fate** Surrendered Stavanger 5.45; to USSR (11.45) as *N.28*;
scrapped 1963

**Name** *U.3036* **Built by** AG Weser (Bremen) **Launched** 27.1.45
**Fate** Bombed Allied aircraft Bremen 4.45 while building and
construction abandoned

**Name** *U.3037* **Built by** AG Weser (Bremen) **Launched** 31.1.45
**Fate** Scuttled Travemünde 3.5.45

**Name** *U.3038* **Built by** AG Weser (Bremen) **Launched** 7.2.45
**Fate** Scuttled Kiel 3.5.45

**Name** *U.3039* **Built by** AG Weser (Bremen) **Launched** 14.2.45
**Fate** Scuttled Kiel 3.5.45

*The conning tower of an
incomplete Type XXI boat
post-war, showing the enclosed
AA gun-mounting.* (IWM)

**Name** *U.3040* **Built by** AG Weser (Bremen) **Launched** 10.2.45
**Fate** Scuttled Kiel 3.5.45

**Name** *U.3041* **Built by** AG Weser (Bremen) **Launched** 23.2.45
**Fate** Surrendered Horten 5.45; to USSR (11.45) as *N.29*;
scrapped 1963

**Name** *U.3042* **Built by** AG Weser (Bremen) **Launched** 1945
**Fate** Bombed Allied aircraft Bremen 4.45 while building and
construction abandoned

**Name** *U.3043* **Built by** AG Weser (Bremen) **Launched** 1945
**Fate** Bombed Allied aircraft Bremen 4.45 while building and
construction abandoned

**Name** *U.3044* **Built by** AG Weser (Bremen) **Launched** 1.3.45
**Fate** Scuttled Flensburg 5.5.45

**Name** *U.3045* **Built by** AG Weser (Bremen) **Launched** 6.3.45
**Fate** Scrapped

**Name** *U.3046* **Built by** AG Weser (Bremen) **Launched** 10.3.45
**Fate** Scrapped

**Name** *U.3047* **Built by** AG Weser (Bremen) **Launched** 11.4.45
**Fate** Scuttled Bremen 5.45

**Name** *U.3048* **Built by** AG Weser (Bremen) **Launched** 1945
**Fate** Scrapped

**Name** *U.3049* **Built by** AG Weser (Bremen) **Launched** 1945
**Fate** Scrapped

**Name** *U.3050* **Built by** AG Weser (Bremen) **Launched** 18.4.45
**Fate** Scuttled Bremen 5.45

**Name** *U.3051* **Built by** AG Weser (Bremen) **Launched** 20.4.45
**Fate** Scuttled Bremen 5.45

**Name** *U.3052* **Built by** AG Weser (Bremen) **Fate** Scrapped

**Name** *U.3053* **Built by** AG Weser (Bremen) **Fate** Scrapped

**Name** *U.3054* **Built by** AG Weser (Bremen) **Fate** Scrapped

**Name** *U.3055* **Built by** AG Weser (Bremen) **Fate** Scrapped

**Name** *U.3056* **Built by** AG Weser (Bremen) **Fate** Scrapped

**Name** *U.3057* **Built by** AG Weser (Bremen) **Fate** Scrapped

**Name** *U.3058* **Built by** AG Weser (Bremen) **Fate** Scrapped

**Name** *U.3059* **Built by** AG Weser (Bremen) **Fate** Scrapped

**Name** *U.3060* **Built by** AG Weser (Bremen) **Fate** Scrapped

**Name** *U.3061* **Built by** AG Weser (Bremen) **Fate** Scrapped

**Name** *U.3062–U.3500* **Built by** AG Weser (Bremen)
**Fate** Projected

**Name** *U.3501* **Built by** Schichau (Danzig) **Launched** 1944
**Fate** Scuttled Weser estuary 1.5.45

**Name** *U.3502* **Built by** Schichau (Danzig) **Launched** 1944
**Fate** Scuttled Hamburg 2.5.45

**Name** *U.3503* **Built by** Schichau (Danzig) **Launched** 1944
**Fate** Scuttled off Gothenburg 8.5.45 after being attacked RAF
aircraft (86 Sqn.) Kattegat 5.5.45

**Name** *U.3504* **Built by** Schichau (Danzig) **Launched** 1944
**Fate** Scuttled Wilhelmshaven 1.5.45

**Name** *U.3505* **Built by** Schichau (Danzig) **Launched** 1944
**Fate** Bombed USAAF aircraft Kiel 3.5.45; salved RSw.N

**Name** *U.3506* **Built by** Schichau (Danzig) **Launched** 1944
**Fate** Scuttled Hamburg 2.5.45

**Name** *U.3507* **Built by** Schichau (Danzig) **Launched** 1944
**Fate** Scuttled Travemünde 3.5.45

**Name** *U.3508* **Built by** Schichau (Danzig) **Launched** 1944
**Fate** Bombed USAAF aircraft Wilhelmshaven 30.3.45

**Name** *U.3509* **Built by** Schichau (Danzig) **Launched** 1944
**Fate** Bombed Allied aircraft Bremen 9.44 while building and
construction abandoned. Fore part later salved and scuttled
Bremen 3.5.45

**Name** *U.3510* **Built by** Schichau (Danzig) **Launched** 1944
**Fate** Scuttled Flensburg 5.5.45

**Name** *U.3511* **Built by** Schichau (Danzig) **Launched** 1944
**Fate** Scuttled Travemünde 3.5.45

**Name** *U.3512* **Built by** Schichau (Danzig) **Launched** 1944
**Fate** Bombed RAF aircraft Kiel 8.4.45

**Name** *U.3513* **Built by** Schichau (Danzig) **Launched** 1944
**Fate** Scuttled Travemünde 3.5.45

**Name** *U.3514* **Built by** Schichau (Danzig) **Launched** 1944
**Fate** Surrendered Bergen 5.45, and scuttled North Atlantic
1945/6

**Name** *U.3515* **Built by** Schichau (Danzig) **Launched** 1944
**Fate** Surrendered Horten 5.45; to USSR (11.45) as *N.30*;
scrapped 1963

**Name** *U.3516* **Built by** Schichau (Danzig) **Launched** 1944
**Fate** Scuttled Travemünde 2.5.45

**Name** *U.3517* **Built by** Schichau (Danzig) **Launched** 1944
**Fate** Scuttled Travemünde 2.5.45

**Name** *U.3518* **Built by** Schichau (Danzig) **Launched** 1944
**Fate** Scuttled Kiel 3.5.45

**Name** *U.3519* **Built by** Schichau (Danzig) **Launched** 1944
**Fate** Mined off Warnemünde 2.3.45

**Name** *U.3520* **Built by** Schichau (Danzig) **Launched** 1944
**Fate** Mined off Eckernforde 31.1.45

**Name** *U.3521* **Built by** Schichau (Danzig) **Launched** 1944
**Fate** Scuttled Travemünde 2.5.45

**Name** *U.3522* **Built by** Schichau (Danzig) **Launched** 1944
**Fate** Scuttled Travemünde 2.5.45

**Name** *U.3523* **Built by** Schichau (Danzig) **Launched** 1944
**Fate** Bombed RAF aircraft (224 Sqn.) off Aarhus 5.5.45

**Name** *U.3524* **Built by** Schichau (Danzig) **Launched** 1945
**Fate** Scuttled Flensburg 5.5.45

**Name** *U.3525* **Built by** Schichau (Danzig) **Launched** 1945
**Fate** Scuttled Kiel 1.5.45 after being attacked Allied aircraft 4.45

**Name** *U.3526* **Built by** Schichau (Danzig) **Launched** 1945
**Fate** Scuttled Flensburg 5.5.45

**Name** *U.3527* **Built by** Schichau (Danzig) **Launched** 1945
**Fate** Scuttled Weser estuary 1.5.45

**Name** *U.3528* **Built by** Schichau (Danzig) **Launched** 1945
**Fate** Scuttled Weser estuary 1.5.45

**Name** *U.3529* **Built by** Schichau (Danzig) **Launched** 1945
**Fate** Scuttled Flensburg 5.5.45

**Name** *U.3530* **Built by** Schichau (Danzig) **Launched** 1945
**Fate** Scuttled Kiel 3.5.45

**Name** *U.3531* **Built by** Schichau (Danzig) **Launched** 1944/5
**Fate** Scrapped Bremerhaven 1946

**Name** *U.3532* **Built by** Schichau (Danzig) **Launched** 1944/5
**Fate** Scrapped Bremerhaven 1946

**Name** *U.3533* **Built by** Schichau (Danzig) **Launched** 1944/5
**Fate** Scrapped Bremerhaven 1946

**Name** *U.3534* **Built by** Schichau (Danzig) **Launched** 1944/5
**Fate** Scrapped Bremerhaven 1946

**Name** *U.3535* **Built by** Schichau (Danzig) **Launched** 1944/5
**Fate** Scrapped Bremerhaven 1946

**Name** *U.3536* **Built by** Schichau (Danzig) **Launched** 1944/5
**Fate** Scrapped Bremerhaven 1946

**Name** *U.3537* **Built by** Schichau (Danzig) **Launched** 1944/5
**Fate** Scrapped Bremerhaven 1946

**Name** *U.3538* **Built by** Schichau (Danzig) **Fate** Completed as
Russian

**Name** *U.3539* **Built by** Schichau (Danzig) **Fate** Completed as
Russian

**Name** *U.3540* **Built by** Schichau (Danzig) **Fate** Completed as
Russian

**Name** *U.3541* **Built by** Schichau (Danzig) **Fate** Completed as
Russian

**Name** *U.3542* **Built by** Schichau (Danzig) **Fate** Completed as Russian

**Name** *U.3543–U.3695* **Built by** Schichau (Danzig) **Fate** Scrapped incomplete except for an unknown number completed as Russian

**Name** *U.3696–U.4000* **Built by** Schichau (Danzig) **Fate** Projected

## XXIII

**Name** *U.4001–U.4120* **Built by** Deutsche Werft (Hamburg) **Fate** Scrapped incomplete

**Name** *U.4121–U.4500* **Built by** Deutsche Werft (Hamburg) **Fate** Projected

## XXVI

**Name** *U.4501–U.4600* **Built by** Deutsche Werft (Hamburg) **Fate** Scrapped incomplete

**Name** *U.4601–U.4700* **Built by** Deutsche Werft (Hamburg) **Fate** Cancelled

## XXIII

**Name** *U.4701* **Built by** Germania Werft (Kiel) **Launched** 14.12.44 **Fate** Scuttled Flensburg 5.5.45

**Name** *U.4702* **Built by** Germania Werft (Kiel) **Launched** 20.12.44 **Fate** Scuttled Flensburg 5.5.45

**Name** *U.4703* **Built by** Germania Werft (Kiel) **Launched** 3.1.45 **Fate** Scuttled Flensburg 5.5.45

**Name** *U.4704* **Built by** Germania Werft (Kiel) **Launched** 13.2.45 **Fate** Scuttled Flensburg 5.5.45

**Name** *U.4705* **Built by** Germania Werft (Kiel) **Launched** 11.1.45 **Fate** Scuttled Kiel 3.5.45

**Name** *U.4706* **Built by** Germania Werft (Kiel) **Launched** 19.1.45 **Fate** Surrendered Christiansand 5.45; RN (1947, RNN *Knerter* (1948)

**Name** *U.4707* **Built by** Germania Werft (Kiel) **Launched** 25.1.45 **Fate** Scuttled Flensburg 5.5.45

**Name** *U.4708* *Built by* Germania Werft (Kiel) **Launched** 26.3.45 **Fate** Bombed Allied aircraft Kiel 4.5.45 while building and construction abandoned; scrapped

**Name** *U.4709* **Built by** Germania Werft (Kiel) **Launched** 8.2.45 **Fate** Bombed Allied aircraft Kiel 4.5.45 while building and construction abandoned

**Name** *U.4710* **Built by** Germania Werft (Kiel) **Launched** 14.4.45 **Fate** Scuttled Flensburg 5.5.45

**Name** *U.4711* **Built by** Germania Werft (Kiel) **Launched** 21.2.45
**Fate** Bombed Allied aircraft Kiel 4.5.45 while building and
construction abandoned

**Name** *U.4712* **Built by** Germania Werft (Kiel) **Launched** 1.3.45
**Fate** Bombed Allied aircraft Kiel 4.5.45 while building and
construction abandoned

**Name** *U.4713–U.4891* **Built by** Germania Werft (Kiel)
**Fate** Cancelled. Scrapped incomplete

**Name** *U.4892–U.5000* **Built by** Germania Werft (Kiel)
**Fate** Projected

### XXVIIB

**Name** *U.5001–U.5003* **Built by** Howaldts Werke (Kiel)
**Fate** Completed (*Seehund*)

**Name** *U.5004–U.5100* **Built by** Germania Werft (Kiel)
**Fate** Completed (*Seehund*)

**Name** *U.5101–U.5250* **Built by** Germania Werft (Kiel)
**Fate** Cancelled

**Name** *U.5251–U.5350* **Built by** Schichau (Elbing)
**Fate** Completed (*Seehund*)

**Name** *U.5351–U.5750* **Built by** Schichau (Elbing) **Fate** Cancelled

**Name** *U.5751–U.5800* **Built by** Klockner (Ulm) **Fate** Completed
(*Seehund*)

**Name** *U.5801–U.6170* **Built by** Klockner (Ulm) **Fate** Cancelled

**Name** *U.6171–U.6200* **Built by** Klockner (Ulm) **Fate** Projected

**Name** *U.6201–U.6245* **Built by** Germania Werft (Kiel)
**Fate** Scrapped incomplete

**Name** *U.6246–U.6250* **Built by** Germania Werft (Kiel)
**Fate** Cancelled

*A heavily censored view of the
U.A (ex-Turkish* Batiray)
*which was building in Germany
pre-war.* (Keystone Press)

*A closeup of the conning-tower. of* U.A *showing how the 10.5-cm was built up and enclosed, as in British submarines.* (Wohbild)

**Name** *U.6251 & U.6252* **Built by** Schichau (Elbing)
**Fate** Completed

**Name** *U.6253–U.6300* **Built by** Schichau (Elbing)
**Fate** Scrapped incomplete

**Name** *U.6301–U.6351* **Built by** Schichau (Elbing) **Fate** Cancelled

**ex-TURKISH**

**Name** *UA* (ex-*Batiray*) **Built by** Germania Werft **Launched** 28.9.38
**Fate** Scuttled Kiel 3.5.45

**ex-RN**

**Name** *UB* (ex-*Seal*) **Built by** H.M. Dockyard (Chatham)
**Launched** 27.9.38 **Fate** Scuttled Kiel 3.5.45

**ex-RNN**

**Name** *UC.1* (ex-*B.5*) **Built by** Naval Dockyard (Horten)
**Launched** 17.6.29 **Fate** Scrapped 1942

**Name** *UC.2* (ex-*B.6*) **Built by** Naval Dockyard (Horten)
**Launched** 4.8.29 **Fate** Paid-off Bergen 10.44

**ex-RNeth.N**

**Name** *UD.1* (ex-*0.8,* ex-*R.N. H.6*) **Built by** Canadian Vickers
(Montreal) **Launched** 8.15 **Fate** Scuttled Willemsoord 14.5.40
and salved; scuttled Kiel 3.5.45

**Name** *UD.2* (ex-*0.12*) **Built by** De Schelde (Flushing)
**Launched** 8.11.30 **Fate** Scuttled Willemsoord 14.5.40 and salved;
paid-off Bergen 6.7.44

**Name** *UD.3* (ex-*0.25*) **Built by** Wilton-Fijenoord (Schiedam)
**Launched** 1.5.40 **Fate** Scuttled Kiel 3.5.45

**Name** *UD.4* (ex-*0.26*) **Built by** Rotterdam D.D. **Launched** 23.11.40
**Fate** Scuttled Kiel 3.5.45

**Name** *UD.5* (ex-*0.27*) **Built by** Rotterdam D.D. **Launched** 26.9.41
**Fate** Surrendered 5.45, and retroceded RNeth.N 13.7.45;
*0.27*; stricken 14.11.59 and scrapped

### ex-French

**Name** *UF.1* (ex-*L'Africaine*) **Built by** Worms (Rouen)
**Fate** Retroceded incomplete French *L'Africaine* (1948), stricken
(1.7.61)

**Name** *UF.2* (ex-*La Favorite*) **Built by** Worms (Rouen)
**Launched** 1940 **Fate** Paid-off Gdynia 5.7.44; scuttled 5.45

**Name** *UF.3* (ex-*L'Astree*) **Built by** Dubigeon (Nantes)
**Fate** Retroceded incomplete French *L'Astree* (1949), stricken
and scrapped 12.65

### ex-Italian

**Name** *UIT.1* (ex-*R.10*) **Built by** Odero-Terni-Orlando (Muggiano)
**Launched** 13.7.43 **Fate** Bombed Allied aircraft Genoa 4.9.44;
salved 1947 and scrapped

**Name** *UIT.2* (ex-*R.11*) **Built by** Odero-Terni-Orlando (Muggiano)
**Launched** 6.7.44 **Fate** Scuttled Genoa 24.4.45

**Name** *UIT.3* (ex-*R.12*) **Built by** Odero-Terni-Orlando (Muggiano)
**Launched** 29.9.44 **Fate** Scuttled Genoa 24.4.45, salved 1947 and
scrapped

**Name** *UIT.4* (ex-*R.7*) **Built by** Cant. Riuniti dell'Adriatico
(Monfalcone) **Launched** 31.10.43 **Fate** Bombed Allied aircraft
Monfalcone 20.4.44 and scuttled; salved 31.5.45 and scrapped

**Name** *UIT.5* (ex-*R.8*) **Built by** Cant. Riuniti dell'Adriatico
(Monfalcone) **Launched** 28.12.43 **Fate** Bombed Allied aircraft
Monfalcone 20.4.44 and scuttled; salved 3.6.46 and scrapped

**Name** *UIT.6* (ex-*R.9*) **Built by** Cant. Riuniti dell'Adriatico
(Monfalcone) **Launched** 27.2.44 **Fate** Bombed Allied aircraft
Monfalcone 16.3.45 and scuttled 1.5.45; salved 1946 and scrapped

**Name** *UIT.7* (ex-*Bario*) **Built by** Cant. Riuniti dell'Adriatico
(Monfalcone) **Launched** 23.1.44 **Fate** Bombed Allied aircraft
Monfalcone 16.3.45 and scuttled 1.5.45; salved 1945, *Pietro
Calvi* (1961)

**Name** *UIT.8* (ex-*Litio*) **Built by** Cant. Riuniti dell'Adriatico
(Monfalcone) **Launched** 19.2.44 **Fate** Bombed Allied aircraft
Monfalcone 16.3.45 and scuttled 1.5.45

**Name** *UIT.9* (ex-*Sodio*) **Built by** Cant. Riuniti dell'Adriatico
(Monfalcone) **Launched** 16.3.44 **Fate** Bombed Allied aircraft
Monfalcone 16.3.45, and construction abandoned

**Name** *UIT.10*. (ex-*Potassio*) **Built by** Cant. Riuniti dell'Adriatico
**Launched** 22.11.43 **Fate** Laid-up incomplete 22.11.43

**Name** *UIT.11* (ex-*Rame*) **Built by** Cant. Riuniti dell'Adriatico
(Monfalcone) **Launched** 4.11.43 **Fate** Laid-up incomplete 4.11.43

UIT.21 *was the ex-Italian* Giuseppe Finzi *of the* Calvi Class. *This view of her conning tower was taken while still under the Italian flag.* (Drüppel)

**Name** *UIT.12* (ex-*Ferro*) **Built by** Cant. Riuniti dell'Adriatico (Monfalcone) **Launched** 22.11.43 **Fate** Laid-up incomplete 22.11.43

**Name** *UIT.13* (ex-*Piombo*) **Built by** Cant. Riuniti dell'Adriatico (Monfalcone) **Launched** 4.11.43 **Fate** Laid-up incomplete 4.11.43

**Name** *UIT.14* (ex-*Zinco*) **Built by** Cant. Riuniti dell'Adriatico (Monfalcone) **Launched** 4.11.43 **Fate** Laid-up incomplete 4.11.43

**Name** *UIT.15* (ex-*Sparide*) **Built by** Odero-Terni-Orlando (Muggiano) **Launched** 21.2.43 **Fate** Scuttled Spezia 9.9.43 and salved; bombed RAF aircraft Genoa 4.9.44

**Name** *UIT.16* (ex-*Murena*) **Built by** Odero-Terni-Orlando (Muggiano) **Launched** 11.4.43 **Fate** Scuttled Spezia 9.9.43 and salved; bombed RAF aircraft Genoa 4.9.44

**Name** *UIT.17* (ex-*CM.1*) **Built by** Cant. Riuniti dell'Adriatico (Monfalcone) **Launched** 5.9.43 **Fate** Scuttled Monfalcone 1.5.45

**Name** *UIT.18* (ex-*CM.2*) **Built by** Cant. Riuniti dell'Adriatico (Monfalcone) **Launched** 2.44 **Fate** Scuttled Monfalcone 1.5.45; salved and retained as naval relic Trieste War museum

**Name** *UIT.19* (ex-*Nautilo*) **Built by** Cant. Riuniti dell'Adriatico (Monfalcone) **Launched** 20.3.43 **Fate** Bombed USAAF aircraft Pola 9.1.44; salved and Yugoslavian *Sava* (1949)

**Name** *UIT.20* (ex-*Grongo*) **Built by** Odero-Terni-Orlando (Muggiano) **Launched** 6.5.43 **Fate** Scuttled Spezia 9.9.43 and salved; bombed RAF aircraft Genoa 4.9.44

**Name** *UIT.21* (ex-*Giuseppe Finzi*) **Built by** Odero-Terni-Orlando (Muggiano) **Launched** 29.6.35 **Fate** Scuttled Bordeaux 25.8.44

**Name** *UIT.22* (ex-*Alpino Bagnolini*) **Built by** Tosi (Taranto) **Launched** 28.10.39 **Fate** Bombed SAAF aircraft (226 & 279 Sqns.) south of Cape of Good Hope 11.3.44

**Name** *UIT.23* (ex-*Reginaldo Giuliani*) **Built by** Tosi (Taranto) **Launched** 3.12.39 **Fate** Torpedoed RN submarine *Tallyho* Straits of Malacca 14.2.44

**Name** *UIT.24* (ex-*Comandante Cappellini*) **Built by** Odero-Terni-Orlando (Muggiano) **Launched** 14.5.39 **Fate** IJN *RO.503* (1945); surrendered Kobe 8.45, taken over by USN 2.9.45 and sunk at Kii Suido 15.4.46

**Name** *UIT.25* (ex-*Luigi Torelli*) **Built by** Odero-Terni-Orlando (Muggiano) **Launched** 6.1.40 **Fate** IJN *RO.504* (1945); surrendered Kobe 8.45, taken over by USN 2.9.45 and scuttled at Kii Suido 15.4.46

## Type XXIXK$_{1/4}$

Few details are available of this type except that a closed-cycle diesel engine of B.H.P. 1,500, coupled to a single shaft, was adopted for main propulsion, together with diesel/electric motors of B.H.P. S.H.P. 580/375 for auxiliary drive.

## Type XXX

Ocean-going boat of *ca.* 1,180 tons armed with twelve 21 inch torpedo tubes, eight forward and four aft. Main propulsion was by diesel/electric motors of B.H.P./S.H.P. 2,000/2,800 coupled to a single shaft for speeds of $12/14\frac{1}{2}$ knots, with the addition of a silent running electric motor of S.H.P. 113 for a creep speed of aout 2 knots. The radius of action, with the *schnorchel*, was 15,000 miles.

## Types XXXA & XXXB

These ocean-going design projects had one shaft powered by half the type XXI machinery, but as the *pro-rata* battery capacity was higher there was a corresponding increase in the output of the electric motor. The type XXXA had 12 torpedo tubes forward, eight in the bows and four angled out from the centre line and arranged to discharge aft; but the latter tubes were omitted from the type XXXB, which was shorter in consequence.

## Type XXXI

A design project for an ocean-going boat with a short and full double cylinder (disposed one over the other) hull form for improved performance and manoeuvrability while submerged; but which was otherwise powered and armed as the type XXXA above.

## Type XXXII

Midget craft of *ca.* 90 tons powered by a fast-running MTB type closed-cycle diesel engine of B.H.P. 1,500, coupled to a single shaft, for a speed of 22 knots. Drawing on 6 tons of stored oxygen the radius of action was 80 miles at 21 knots, which was extended to 200 miles at 12 knots. Armament comprised two externally stowed 21 inch torpedoes secured below the hull, and the design was reminiscent of the Italian "CM" class except in the matter of the propulsion system.

## Type XXXIII

Coastal boat design project which adopted a closed-cycle diesel engine for propulsion and stored its oxygen in a large pressure vessel placed amidships in the pressure hull. A short second hull cylinder was also placed over the main pressure hull amidships to provide access to the fore end, and to serve as a command attack station.

## Type XXXIV

Midget craft design project powered by a closed-cycle fast-running diesel engine and capable of high submerged speed. As in the above design oxygen was stored in a large pressure vessel but positioned at the fore end of the pressure hull. Two torpedoes were carried externally over the pressure hull.

## Type XXXV

A design study for a sea-going boat powered by Walter turbines, and armed with eight bow torpedo tubes.

## Type XXXVI

An alternative design study to the above for a sea-going boat powered by four fast-running closed-cycle diesel engines.

## Type XXXA

*Displacement:* 1,180 tons
*Dimensions:* 226 × 17¾ × 20¼ feet
*Machinery:* 1-shaft 6-cylinder M.A.N. diesel/electric motors, B.H.P./S.H.P. 2,000+265/2,800=14½/15½ knots; and creeping silent electric motor, S.H.P. 140 = 5 knots
*Bunkers & Radius:* O.F.; 15,500/210 miles @ 10/6 knots

*Armament:* Twelve 21-inch torpedo tubes (eight bow & four broadside fwd – twelve torpedoes)
*Complement:* Not known.

## Type XXXB

*Displacement:* 1,170 tons
*Dimensions:* $215\frac{1}{2} \times 17\frac{3}{4} \times 20\frac{1}{4}$ feet
*Machinery:* 1-shaft 6-cylinder M.A.N. diesel/electric motors, B.H.P./S.H.P. 2,000 + 265/2,800 = $14\frac{1}{2}/15\frac{3}{4}$ knots; and silent creeping electric motor, S.H.P. 140 = 5 knots
*Bunkers & Radius:* O.F.; 15,500/210 miles @ 10/6 knots
*Armament:* Eight 21-inch torpedo tubes (all forward)
*Complement:* Not known

## Type XXXI

*Displacement:* 1,200 tons
*Dimensions:* $177\frac{1}{4} \times 20\frac{1}{4} \times 23$ feet
*Machinery:* 1-shaft 6-cylinder M.A.N. diesel/electric motors, B.H.P./S.H.P. 2,000 + 265/2,800 = $14\frac{1}{4}/16\frac{1}{2}$ knots.
*Bunkers & Radius:* O.F.; 15,500/245 miles @ 10/6 knots
*Armament:* Twelve 21-inch torpedo tubes (eight bow & four broadside fwd – twelve torpedoes).
*Complement:* Not known

## Type XXXIII

*Displacement:* 360 tons
*Dimensions:* $131\frac{1}{4} \times 13\frac{1}{4} \times 13\frac{3}{4}$ feet
*Machinery:* 1-shaft diesel engine, B.H.P. 580 = $9\frac{1}{2}/11\frac{1}{2}$ knots; and silent creeping electric motor, S.H.P. 50 = 5 knots
*Bunkers & Radius:* O.F.; $23\frac{1}{2}$ tons + oxygen $25\frac{1}{2}$ tons; 4,500/1,600 miles @ 8/6 knots
*Armament:* Four 21-inch torpedo tubes (all fwd – six torpedoes)
*Complement:* Not known

## Type XXXIV

*Displacement:* 90 tons
*Dimensions:* $78 \times 8\frac{1}{4} \times 8\frac{1}{2}$ feet
*Machinery:* 1-shaft 11-cylinder M.A.N. diesel engine, B.H.P. 1,500 = 10/22 knots; and silent creeping electric motor, S.H.P. 35 = 6 knots
*Bunkers & Radius:* O.F.; $5\frac{1}{4}$ tons + oxygen $6\frac{1}{2}$ tons; 1,200/90 miles @ 11/22 knots
*Armament:* Two 21-inch torpedoes
*Complement:* 3

# Type XXXV

*Displacement:* 850 tons
*Dimensions:* 164 feet
*Machinery:* 1-shaft Walter geared turbines, S.H.P. 7,500 = 22 knots; and diesel/electric motors, B.H.P./S.H.P. 2,000/175 = 15/6 knots
*Bunkers & Radius:* Aurol 40 tons + oxygen 25 tons, O.F. 160 miles @ 22 knots
*Armament:* Eight 21-inch torpedo tubes (all fwd – twelve torpedoes)
*Complement:* Not known

The following foreign submarines were incorporated into the German Navy after being either acquired, or captured, after the outbreak of the Second World War. Their maintenance, as a result of non-standard equipment, posed difficulties which were not easily overcome, and resulted in only a few being operationally employed, and then only for a short period. After the Italian surrender in September, 1943, Italian submarines lying, or under construction in German-held ports were seized, but again only a relatively few were placed in service.

As these foreign units form no part of German submarine evolution they are only briefly described, and are principally included for historical completeness.

## Ex-Turkish minelaying type: UA

*Displacement:* 1,044/1,357 tons
*Dimensions:* $282\frac{1}{4} \times 22\frac{1}{4} \times 14$ feet
*Machinery:* 2-shaft diesel/electric motors, B.H.P./S.H.P. 4,800/1,100 = 20/9 knots
*Bunkers & Radius:* O.F.
*Armament:* One 4.1inch, one 20mm A.A. gun, six 21inch torpedo tubes (four fwd and two aft)
*Complement:* 47

## Ex-RN "Porpoise" class: UB

*Displacement* 1,520/2,157 tons
*Dimensions:* $289 \times 25\frac{1}{2} \times 15\frac{1}{2}$ feet
*Machinery:* 2-shaft diesel/electric motors, B.H.P./S.H.P. 3,300/1,630 = $15/8\frac{3}{4}$ knots
*Bunkers & Radius:* O.F. 136 tons
*Armament:* One 4inch, two machine guns, six 21inch torpedo tubes (all fwd), fifty mines
*Complement:* 55

## Ex-RNN "B" class: **UC.1** *and* **2**

*Displacement:* 420/545 tons
*Dimensions:* $167\frac{1}{4} \times 17\frac{1}{2} \times 11\frac{1}{2}$ feet
*Machinery:* 2-shaft diesel/electric motors, B.H.P./S.H.P.
900/700 = $14\frac{3}{4}$/11 knots
*Bunkers & Radius:* O.F.
*Armament:* One 3inch gun, four 18inch torpedo tubes (all fwd)
*Complement:* 23

## Ex-RNeth.N "H" class: **UD.1**

*Displacement:* 343/433 tons
*Displacement:* $151\frac{1}{2} \times 15\frac{1}{4} \times 12\frac{3}{4}$ feet
*Machinery:* 2-shaft diesel/electric motors, B.H.P./S.H.P.
480/320 = 13/$8\frac{1}{2}$ knots
*Bunkers & Radius:* O.F. 16 tons (1,350 miles at 12 knots)
*Armament:* One 37mm AA gun, four 18inch torpedo tubes
(all fwd)
*Complement:* 26

## Ex-RNeth.N "O.12" class: **UD.2**

*Displacement:* 546/704 tons
*Dimensions:* $198\frac{1}{4} \times 17\frac{3}{4} \times 11\frac{3}{4}$ feet
*Machinery:* 2-shaft diesel/electric motors, B.H.P./S.H.P.
1,800/620 = 15/8 knots
*Bunkers & Radius:* O.F. (3,500/26 miles at 10/8 knots)
Two 40mm A.A. (2 × 1) guns, five 21inch torpedo tubes (four
fwd and one aft)
*Complement:* 31

## Ex-RNeth.N "O.21" class: **UD.3–5**

*Displacement:* 888/1,380 tons
*Dimensions:* 255 × $21\frac{1}{2}$ × 13 feet
*Machinery:* 2-shaft diesel/electric motors, B.H.P./S.H.P.
5,200/1,000 = $19\frac{1}{2}$/9 knots
*Bunkers & Radius:* 135 tons
*Armament:* One 3.5inch, one 20mm A.A. guns, eight 21inch
torpedo tubes (six fwd and two aft)
*Complement:* 60

## Ex-French "Aurore" class: **UF.1–3**

*Displacement:* 910/1,180 tons
*Dimensions:* 241 × $21\frac{1}{4}$ × $11\frac{1}{2}$ feet
*Machinery:* 2-shaft diesel/electric motors, B.H.P./S.H.P.
3,000/1,400 = $17\frac{1}{4}$/10 knots

*Bunkers & Radius:* O.F. 101 tons (8,800 miles at 10 knots)
*Armament:* One 3.5inch, four 20mm A.A. (2 × 2) guns, ten
   21inch torpedo tubes (eight fwd and two aft)
*Complement:* 65

## *Ex-RIt.N "Romolo" class:* **UIT.1–6**

*Displacement:* 1,300/2,600 tons
*Dimensions:* $285\frac{1}{2}$ × $25\frac{1}{2}$ × 20 feet
*Machinery:* 2-shaft diesel/electric motors, B.H.P./S.H.P.
   2,600/900 = $14/6\frac{1}{2}$ knots
*Bunkers & Radius:* O.F. 12,000/90 miles at 9/4 knots)
*Armament:* Six 20mm A.A. (3 × 2) guns, cargo capacity 610 d.w.
*Complement:* 63

## *Ex-RIt.N "Tritone" class (second group):* **UIT.9–14**

*Displacement:* 928/1,131 tons
*Dimensions* $210\frac{3}{4}$ × 23 × $16\frac{1}{4}$ feet
*Machinery:* 2-shaft diesel/electric motors, B.H.P./S.H.P.
   2,400/800 = 16/8 knots
*Bunkers & Radius:* OF (5,400/80 miles at 8/4 knots)
*Armament:* One 3.9inch, four 20mm A.A. (2 × 2) guns, six
   21inch torpedo tubes (four fwd and two aft)
*Complement:* 59

## *Ex-RIt.N "Tritone" class (first group):* **UIT.15 and 16, UIT.19 and 20**

*Displacement:* 905/1,070 tons
*Dimensions:* $207\frac{1}{4}$ × 23 × 16 feet
*Machinery:* 2-shaft diesel/electric motors, B.H.P./S.H.P.
   2,400/800 = 16/8 knots
*Bunkers & Radius:* (5,400/80 miles at 8/4 knots)
*Armament:* One 3.9inch, four 13mm A.A. (2 × 2) guns, six
   21inch torpedo tubes (four fwd and two aft)
*Complement:* 49

## *Ex-RIt.N "CM" class:* **UIT.17 and 18**

*Displacement:* 92/114 tons
*Dimensions:* 108 × $9\frac{1}{2}$ × 9 feet
*Machinery:* 2-shaft diesel/electric motors, B.H.P./S.H.P.
   660/120 = 14/6 knots
*Bunkers & Radius:* O.F. (2,000/70 miles at 9/4 knots)
*Armament:* Two 18inch torpedo tubes (both fwd)
*Complement:* 8

### Ex-RIt.N "Calvi" class: **UIT.21**

*Displacement:* 1,550/2,060 tons
*Dimensions:* 276½ × 25¼ × 17 feet
*Machinery:* 2-shaft diesel/electric motors, B.H.P./S.H.P.
  4,400/1,800 = 17/8 knots
*Bunkers & Radius:* O.F. (11,400/80 miles at 8/4 knots)
*Armament:* Two 4.7inch (2 × 1), four 13mm A.A. (2 × 2) guns,
  eight 21inch torpedo tubes (four fwd and four aft)
*Complement:* 72

### Ex-RIt.N "Luzzi" class: **UIT.22** and **23**

*Displacement:* 1,166/1,484 tons
*Dimensions:* 249¾ × 23 × 15 feet
*Machinery:* 2-shaft diesel/electric motors, B.H.P./S.H.P.
  3,500/1,500 = 18/8 knots
*Bunkers & Radius:* O.F. (9,500/80 miles at 9/4 knots)
*Armament:* One 3.9inch, four 13mm A.A. (2 × 2) guns, eight
  21inch torpedo tubes (four fwd and four aft)
*Complement:* 57

### Ex-RIt.N "Marcello" class: **UIT.24**

*Displacement:* 1,060/1,313 tons
*Dimensions:* 239½ × 23¾ × 16¾ feet
*Machinery:* 2-shaft diesel/electric motors, B.H.P./S.H.P.
  3,000/1,100 = 17½/8 knots
*Bunkers & Radius:* O.F. (7,500/80 miles at 9/4 knots)
*Armament:* Two 3.9inch (2 × 1), four 13mm A.A. (2 × 2) guns,
  eight 21inch torpedo tubes (four fwd and four aft)
*Complenent:* 57

### Ex-RIt.N "Marconi" class: **UIT.25**

*Displacement:* 1,191/1,489 tons
*Dimensions:* 249¼ × 22¼ × 15½ feet
*Machinery:* 2-shaft diesel/electric motors, B.H.P./S.H.P.
  3,600/1,500 = 18/8 knots
*Bunkers & Radius:* O.F. (10,500/80 miles at 8/4 knots)
*Armament:* One 3.9inch, four 13mm A.A. (2 × 2) guns, eight
  21inch torpedo tubes (four fwd and four aft)
*Complement:* 57

# Midget Submarines

The principal use midget submarine craft were put to was in an anti-invasion role against the mass of shipping that was bound to concentrate in a restricted area for such an operation. Their limited radius of action rather circumscribed their employment, and the smaller units were transported by road, or rail, to beach areas close to the scene of operations. The German Navy was rather late in this field, but nevertheless devoted considerable effort towards the production of these craft from which optimistically good results were expected, although the Naval Staff did not contribute to this view. The various types of craft are only briefly summarised below as their development was quite divorced from that of the larger submarines.

## Type Neger

One man torpedo with G7E torpedo underslung. The open cockpit was later covered with plexiglass dome but no breathing apparatus was provided. About 200 were placed in operational service.

*Displacement:* 5 tons
*Dimensions:* $26\frac{1}{4} \times 1\frac{3}{4} \times 3\frac{1}{2}$ feet
*Machinery:* 1-shaft electric motor, S.H.P. 12 = 20 knots (30 miles at 3 knots)
*Armament:* One 21inch torpedo
*Complement:* 1

## Type Marder

Except that they were capable of running submerged were otherwise similar to the *Neger* type above. About 300 were placed in operational service.

## Type Biber

One-man midget submarines built by A. G. Weser (Bremen), of which 324 were placed in operational service.

*Displacement:* $6\frac{1}{4}$ tons
*Dimensions:* $29\frac{1}{2} \times 5\frac{1}{4} \times 4\frac{3}{4}$ feet
*Machinery:* 1-shaft petrol/electric motors, B.H.P./S.H.P. 32/13
$= 6\frac{1}{2}/5\frac{1}{4}$ knots (125/10 miles at 6/5 knots)
*Armament:* Two 21inch torpedoes
*Complement:* 1

*Type "BIBER"*

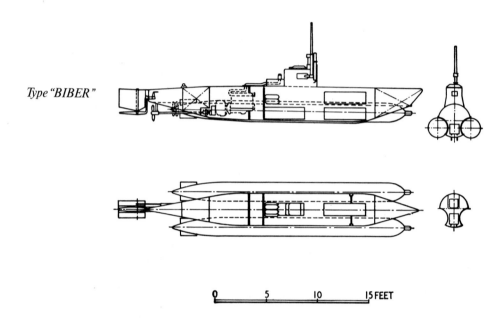

*Displacement:* 5 tons

## Type Hai

One-man torpedo of which only the prototype was completed.

*Displacement:* 5 tons
*Dimensions:* $26\frac{1}{4} \times 1\frac{3}{4} \times 1\frac{3}{4}$ feet
*Machinery:* 1-shaft electric motor, S.H.P. 12 = 20 knots
   (30 miles at 3 knots)
*Armament:* One 21inch torpedo
*Complement:* 1

## Type Delphin

Two-man torpedo of 5 tons powered by an electric motor of S.H.P. 12 coupled to a single shaft for a speed of 20 knots, and with a submerged radius of 30 miles at 3 knots. Only two units were completed, and particulars of armament are not available.

*A U-Boat with two "Bibers" on the casing, in the same manner as "Kaiten" carried by Japanese submarines.* (Drüppel)

*The "Adam" was the prototype "Biber" produced by Fkenderwerke, Lübeck.* (Drüppel)

*"Delphin" Type 2-man torpedo, seen after a collision with a tender.* (Drüppel)

# Summary of German Submarine Losses

## 1939

| | |
|---|---|
| *September:* | *U.27, U.39* |
| *October:* | *U.12, U.16, U.40, U.42, U.45* |
| *November:* | *U.35* |
| *December:* | *U.36* |

## 1940

| | |
|---|---|
| *January:* | *U.55* |
| *February:* | *U.15, U.33, U.41, U.53, U.63* |
| *March:* | *U.31\*, U.44* |
| *April:* | *U.1, U.22, U.49, U.50, U.54, U.64* |
| *May:* | *U.13* |
| *June:* | *U.122* |
| *July:* | *U.26* |
| *August:* | *U.25, U.51, U.102* |
| *September:* | *U.57\** |
| *October:* | *U.32* |
| *November:* | *U.31\*, U.104, U.560\** |
| *December:* | Nil |

## 1941

| | |
|---|---|
| *January:* | Nil |
| *February:* | Nil |
| *March:* | *U.47, U.70, U.99, U.100, U.551* |
| *April:* | *U.65, U.76* |
| *May:* | *U.110* |
| *June:* | *U.138, U.147, U.556, U.651* |
| *July:* | Nil |
| *August:* | *U.144, U.401, U.452, U.570* |
| *September:* | *U.207, U.501* |
| *October:* | *U.111, U.204* |
| *November:* | *U.95, U.206, U.433, U.580, U.583* |
| *December:* | *U.75, U.79, U.127, U.131, U.208, U.434, U.451, U.557, U.567, U.574* |

## 1942

| | |
|---|---|
| *January:* | *U.93, U.374, U.577* |
| *February:* | *U.82, U.581* |
| *March:* | *U.133, U.503, U.585, U.587, U.655, U.656* |
| *April:* | *U.85, U.252, U.702* |

| | |
|---|---|
| *May:* | *U.74, U.352, U.568, U.573* |
| *June:* | *U.157, U.158, U.652* |
| *July:* | *U.90, U.136, U.153, U.213, U.215, U.502, U.576,* |
| | *U.588, U.701, U.751, U.754* |
| *August:* | *U.94, U.166, U.210, U.335, U.372, U.379, U.464,* |
| | *U.578, U.654* |
| *September:* | *U.88, U.162, U.165, U.222, U.253, U.261, U.446*,* |
| | *U.457, U.589, U.705, U.756* |
| *October:* | *U.171, U.179, U.216, U.353, U.412, U.512, U.520,* |
| | *U.559, U.582, U.597, U.599, U.619, U.627, U.658,* |
| | *U.661* |
| *November:* | *U.98, U.132, U.173, U.184, U.259, U.272, U.331,* |
| | *U.408, U.411, U.517, U.595, U.605, U.660* |
| *December:* | *U.254, U.356, U.357, U.611, U.626, UC.1* |

## 1943

| | |
|---|---|
| *January:* | *U.164, U.224, U.301, U.337, U.507, U.553* |
| *February:* | *U.69, U.187, U.201, U.205, U.225, U.265, U.268,* |
| | *U.442, U.443, U.519, U.522, U.529, U.562, U.606,* |
| | *U.609, U.620, U.621, U.623, U.624, U.649* |
| *March:* | *U.5, U.77, U.83, U.87, U.130, U.156, U.163, U.169,* |
| | *U.384, U.416*, U.432, U.444, U.469, U.524, U.633,* |
| | *U.665* |
| *April:* | *U.123, U.167, U.174, U.175, U.189, U.191, U.203,* |
| | *U.227, U.376, U.526, U.602, U.632, U.635, U.644,* |
| | *U.710* |
| *May:* | *U.89, U.109, U.125, U.128, U.176, U.182, U.186,* |
| | *U.192, U.209, U.258, U.266, U.273, U.303, U.304,* |
| | *U.332, U.381, U.414, U.436, U.438, U.439, U.440,* |
| | *U.447, U.456, U.463, U.465, U.467, U.528, U.531,* |
| | *U.563, U.569, U.630, U.638, U.640, U.646, U.657,* |
| | *U.659, U.663, U.752, U.753, U.755, U.954* |
| *June:* | *U.97, U.105, U.118, U.119, U.194, U.200, U.202,* |
| | *U.217, U.308, U.334, U.388, U.417, U.418, U.449,* |
| | *U.521, U.564, U.594* |
| *July:* | *U.43, U.67, U.126, U.135, U.159, U.160, U.199,* |
| | *U.232, U.359, U.375, U.404, U.409, U.435, U.459,* |
| | *U.461, U.462, U.487, U.504, U.506, U.509, U.513,* |
| | *U.514, U.527, U.535, U.558, U.561, U.590, U.591* |
| | *U.598, U.607, U.613, U.614, U.622*, U.628, U.662,* |
| | *U.759, U.951* |
| *August:* | *U.34*, U.84, U.106, U.117, U.134, U.185, U.197,* |
| | *U.383, U.403, U.454, U.458, U.468, U.489, U.523,* |
| | *U.525, U.572, U.604, U.615, U.634, U.639, U.647,* |
| | *U.664, U.670, U.706, U.847* |
| *September:* | *U.161, U.221, U.229, U.338, U.341, U.346, U.617,* |
| | *U.669, U.760*, U.983* |
| *October:* | *U.220, U.274, U.279, U.282, U.306, U.336, U.378,* |
| | *U.389, U.402, U.419, U.420, U.422, U.431, U.460,* |
| | *U.470, U.533, U.540, U.566, U.584, U.610, U.631,* |
| | *U.643, U.732, U.841, U.844, U.964* |

| | |
|---|---|
| *November:* | *U.86, U.211, U.226, U.280, U.340, U.405, U.508, U.536, U.538, U.542, U.600, U.648, U.707, U.718, U.768, U.769, U.770, U.842, U.848, U.849, U.966* |
| *December:* | *U.73, U.172, U.284, U.345\*, U.391, U.593, U.645, U.850* |

**1944**

| | |
|---|---|
| *January:* | *U.81, U.231, U.263, U.271, U.305, U.314, U.364, U.377, U.426, U.544, U.571, U.592, U.641, U.757, U.972, UIT.19* |
| *February:* | *U.7, U.91, U.177, U.238, U.257, U.264, U.283, U.380, U.386, U.406, U.424, U.545, U.601, U.666, U.713, U.734, U.738, U.761, U.762, U.854, UIT.23* |
| *March:* | *U.28, U.223, U.343, U.358, U.366, U.392, U.410, U.450, U.472, U.575, U.603, U.625, U.653, U.709, U.744, U.801, U.845, U.851, U.961, U.973, U.976, U.1013, U.1059, UIT.22* |
| *April:* | *U.2, U.68, U.108\*, U.193, U.288, U.302, U.311, U.342, U.355, U.360, U.421, U.448, U.455, U.488, U.515, U.550, U.803, U.856, U.962, U.974, U.986, UIT.4\*, UIT.5* |
| *May:* | *U.66, U.240, U.241, U.277, U.289, U.292, U.371, U.453, U.473, U.476, U.549, U.616, U.674, U.675, U.731, U.765, U.846, U.852, U.959, U.960, U.990, U.1015, U.1224 (=IJN RO.501), U.1234\** |
| *June:* | *U.269, U.317, U.373, U.423, U.441, U.477, U.478, U.490, U.505, U.629, U.715, U.719, U.740, U.767, U.821, U.860, U.955, U.970, U.971, U.980, U.987, U.988, U.998, U.1191, U.1225* |
| *July:* | *U.3\*, U.4\*, U.6\*, U.129, U.154, U.212, U.214, U.233, U.239\*, U.243, U.250, U.319, U.333, U.347, U.361, U.390, U.415, U.543, U.586, U.642, U.672, U.678, U.742, U.872, U.890, U.891, U.892, U.1164, U.1166, U.1222, U.2323* |
| *August:* | *U.9, U.107, U.178, U.180, U.188, U.198, U.230, U.270, U.344, U.354, U.385, U.413, U.445, U.466, U.471\*, U.608, U.618, U.667, U.671, U.736, U.741, U.952, U.967, U.969, U.981, U.984, U.996, U.1000, U.1196\*, U.1229, UIT.21* |
| *September:* | *U.18, U.19, U.20, U.23, U.24, U.247, U.362, U.394, U.407, U.484, U.565, U.596, U.703, U.743, U.855, U.859, U.863, U.865, U.867, U.871, U.921, U.925, U.1062, U.3509, UIT.1, UIT.15, UIT.16, UIT.20* |
| *October:* | *U.92\*, U.116, U.168, U.228\*, U.437, U.673, U.777, U.957\*, U.958\*, U.993\*, U.1006, U.1060, U.1226, U.2331* |
| *November:* | *U.80, U.196, U.322, U.537, U.547\*, U.771, U.1200* |
| *December:* | *U.11\*, U.297, U.365, U.387, U.400, U.416†, U.479, U.735, U.737, U.772, U.877, U.906, U.908, U.1011, U.1012, U.1209, U.2342, U.2532* |

**1945**

| | |
|---|---|
| *January:* | *U.92†, U.248, U.382, U.482, U.650, U.679, U.763,* |

|            |                                                                          |
|------------|--------------------------------------------------------------------------|
|            | *U.1020, U.1051, U.1172, U.1199, U.2523, U.3520*                        |
| *February:* | *U.21, U.300, U.309, U.327, U.425, U.480, U.676,*                       |
|            | *U.745, U.864, U.869, U.923, U.927, U.989, U.1014,*                     |
|            | *U.1018, U.1053, U.1208, U.1273, U.1278, U.1279,*                       |
|            | *U.2344\*, U.3007*                                                       |
| *March:*   | *U.72, U.96, U.246, U.260, U.275, U.296, U.329,*                        |
|            | *U.348, U.350, U.367, U.399, U.429, U.430, U.681,*                      |
|            | *U.682, U.683, U.714, U.722, U.866, U.870, U.884,*                      |
|            | *U.886, U.905, U.965, U.1103, U.1021, U.1106,*                         |
|            | *U.1167, U.1302, U.2340, U.2515, U.2530, U.3508,*                      |
|            | *U.3519, UIT.9*                                                          |
| *April:*   | *U.56, U.78, U.103, U.183, U.235, U.237, U.242,*                       |
|            | *U.251, U.285, U.286, U.307, U.321, U.325, U.326,*                     |
|            | *U.396, U.486, U.518, U.546, U.548, U.636, U.677,*                     |
|            | *U.747, U.749, U.774, U.804, U.843, U.857, U.878,*                     |
|            | *U.879, U.880, U.982, U.1001, U.1017, U.1024,*                         |
|            | *U.1055, U.1063, U.1065, U.1107, U.1131, U.1169,*                      |
|            | *U.1195, U.1206, U.1221, U.1223, U.1227, U.1235,*                      |
|            | *U.1274, U.1276, U.2509, U.2514, U.2516, U.2537,*                      |
|            | *U.2542, U.2547, U.2549, U.2550, U.2552, U.3003,*                      |
|            | *U.3036, U.3042, U.3043, U.3512*                                        |
| *May:*     | *U.236, U.320, U.393, U.398, U.534, U.579, U.711,*                     |
|            | *U.717, U.733, U.746, U.785, U.853, U.876, U.881,*                     |
|            | *U.904, U.963, U.1007, U.1008, U.1210, U.2338,*                        |
|            | *U.2359, U.2365, U.2367, U.2503, U.2521, U.2524,*                      |
|            | *U.2534, U.2538, U.2540, U.3028, U.2030, U.3032,*                      |
|            | *U.3503, U.3505, U.3523, U.3525, U.4708, U.4709,*                      |
|            | *U.4711, U.4712*                                                        |
|            |                                                                          |
| *Scuttled,* | *U.8, U.14, U.17, U.29, U.30, U.37, U.38, U.46, U.48,*                  |
| *salved and* | *U.52, U.57†, U.58, U.60, U.61, U.62, U.71, U.108†,*                   |
| *scrapped* | *U.120, U.121, U.137, U.139, U.140, U.141, U.142,*                     |
| *1947/53*  | *U.146, U.148, U.151, U.152, U.267, U.287, U.290,*                     |
|            | *U.316, U.323, U.339, U.349, U.351, U.370, U.397,*                     |
|            | *U.428, U.446†, U.474, U.475, U.552, U.554, U.560†,*                   |
|            | *U.612, U.704, U.708, U.721, U.748, U.750, U.792,*                     |
|            | *U.793, U.794, U.795, U.822, U.827, U.828, U.835,*                     |
|            | *U.836, U.903, U.922, U.924, U.929, U.958, U.979,*                     |
|            | *U.999, U.1016, U.1025, U.1047, U.1056, U.1101,*                       |
|            | *U.1132, U.1161, U.1162, U.1168, U.1170, U.1192,*                      |
|            | *U.1193, U.1196†, U.1204, U.1205, U.1207, U.1234†,*                    |
|            | *U.1236, U.1237, U.1238, U.1277, U.1303, U.1304,*                      |
|            | *U.1306, U.1308, U.1405, U.1406, U.1407, U.2327,*                      |
|            | *U.2330, U.2332, U. 2333, U.2339, U.2343, U.2346,*                     |
|            | *U.2347, U.2349, U.2352, U.2355, U.2357, U.2358,*                      |
|            | *U.2360, U.2362, U.2364, U.2366, U.2368, U.2369,*                      |
|            | *U.2370, U.2371, U.2501, U.2504, U.2505, U.2507,*                      |
|            | *U.2508, U.2510, U.2512, U.2517, U.2519, U.2520,*                      |
|            | *U.2522, U.2525, U.2526, U.2527, U.2528, U.2531,*                      |
|            | *U.2533, U.2535, U.2536, U.2539, U.2541, U.2543,*                      |
|            | *U.2544, U.2545, U.2546, U.2548, U.2551, U.3001,*                      |
|            | *U.3002, U.3004, U.3005, U.3006, U.3009, U.3010,*                      |

U.3011, U.3012, U.3013, U.3014, U.3015, U.3016,
U.3018, U.3019, U.3020, U.3021, U.3022, U.3023,
U.3024, U.3025, U.3026, U.3027, U.3029, U.3031,
U.3033, U.3034, U.3037, U.3038, U.3039, U.3040,
U.3044, U.3047, U.3050, U.3051, U.3501, U.3502,
U.3504, U.3506, U.3507, U.3510, U.3511, U.3513,
U.3516, U.3517, U.3518, U.3521, U.3522, U.3524,
U.3526, U.3527, U.3528, U.3529, U.3530, U.4701,
U.4702, U.4703, U.4704, U.4705, U.4707, U.4710,
UA, UB, UD.1, UD.3, UD.4, UF.2, UIT.2, UIT.3,
UIT.6, UIT.7, UIT.8, UIT.17, UIT.18

*Surrendered:* U.3, U.4, U.6, U.10, U.11, U.59, U.101, U.123,
U.143, U.145, U.149, U.150, U.155, U.170, U.181
(=IJN *I.501*), U.190, U.195 (=IJN *I.506*), U.218,
U.219 (=IJN *I.505*), U.228, U.234, U.244, U.245,
U.249, U.255, U.256, U.262, U.276, U.278, U.281,
U.291, U.293, U.294, U.295, U.298, U.299, U.310,
U.312, U.313, U.315, U.318, U.324, U.328, U.345,
U.363, U.368, U.369, U.427, U.481, U.483, U.485,
U.510, U.511 (=IJN *RO.500*), U.516, U.530, U.532,
U.539, U.541, U.555, U.622, U.637, U.668, U.680,
U.708, U.712, U.716, U.720, U.739, U.758, U.760,
U.764, U.766, U.773, U.775, U.776, U.778, U.779,
U.802, U.805, U.806, U.825, U.826, U.858, U.861,
U.862, (=IJN *1.502*), U.868, U.873, U.874, U.875,
U.883, U.889, U.901, U.907, U.927, U.928, U.930,
U.953, U.956, U.968, U.975, U.977, U.978, U.985,
U.991, U.992, U.993, U.994, U.995, U.997, U.1002,
U.1004, U.1005, U.1009, U.1010, U.1019, U.1022,
U.1023, U.1052, U.1054, U.1057, U.1058, U.1061,
U.1064, U.1102, U.1103, U.1104, U.1105, U.1108,
U.1109, U.1110, Y.1163, U.1165, U.1171, U.1194,
U.1197, U.1198, U.1201, U.1202, U.1203, U.?217,
U.1228, U.1230, U.1231, U.1232, U.1233, U.1271,
U.1272, U.1275, U.1301, U.1305, U.1307, U.2321,
U.2322, U.2324, U.2325, U.2326, U.2328, U.2329,
U.2334, U.2335, U.2336, U.2337, U.2341, U.2344,
U.2345, U.2348, U.2350, U.2351, U.2353, U.2354,
U.2356, U.2361, U.2363, U.2502, U.2506, U.2511,
U.2513, U.2518, U.2529, U.3008, U.3017, U.3035,
U.3041, U.3514, U.3515, U.4706, UC.2, UD.2, UD.5,
UF.1, UF.3, UIT.4, UIT.24, (=IJN *1.503*), UIT.25
(=IJN *1.504*)

*Fate*          U.34, U.239, U.547, U.957, U.1000
  *unknown*

*Not*            U.330, U.395, U.491–500, U.684–686, U.723–730,
*completed*      U.780–784, U.786–791, U.796–800, U.807–816,
*or cancelled:*  U.823, U.824, U.829–834, U.837–840, U.882, U.885,
                 U.887, U.888, U.893–900, U.902, U.909–918,
                 U.931–942, U.1026–1046, U.1048–1050, U.1066–
                 1100, U.1111–1120, U.1133–1152, U.1173–1190,

## 1945

*January:*       U.92†, U.248, U.382, U.482, U.650, U.679, U.763,
               U.1020, U.1051, U.1172, U.1199, U.2523, U.3520

*February:*      U.21, U.300, U.309, U.327, U.425, U.480, U.676,
               U.745, U.864, U.869, U.923, U.927, U.989, U.1014,
               U.1018, U.1053, U.1208, U.1273, U.1278, U.1279,
               U.2344*, U.3007

*March:*         U.72, U.96, U.246, U.260, U.275, U.296, U.329,
               U.348, U.350, U.367, U.399, U.429, U.430, U.681,
               U.682, U.683, U.714, U.722, U.866, U.870, U.884,
               U.886, U.905, U.965, U.1103, U.1021, U.1106,
               U.1167, U.1302, U.2340, U.2515, U.2530, U.3508,
               U.3519, UIT.9

*April:*         U.56, U.78, U.103, U.183, U.235, U.237, U.242,
               U.251, U.285, U.286, U.307, U.321, U.325, U.326,
               U.396, U.486, U.518, U.546, U.548, U.636, U.677,
               U.747, U.749, U.774, U.804, U.843, U.857, U.878,
               U.879, U.880, U.982, U.1001, U.1017, U.1024,
               U.1055, U.1063, U.1065, U.1107, U.1131, U.1169,
               U.1195, U.1206, U.1221, U.1223, U.1227, U.1235,
               U.1274, U.1276, U.2509, U.2514, U.2516, U.2537,
               U.2542, U.2547, U.2549, U.2550, U.2552, U.3003,
               U.3036, U.3042, U.3043, U.3512

*May:*           U.236, U.320, U.393, U.398, U.534, U.579, U.711,
               U.717, U.733, U.746, U.785, U.853, U.876, U.881,
               U.904, U.963, U.1007, U.1008, U.1210, U.2338,
               U.2359, U.2365, U.2367, U.2503, U.2521, U.2524,
               U.2534, U.2538, U.2540, U.3028, U.2030, U.3032,
               U.3503, U.3505, U.3523, U.3525, U.4708, U.4709,
               U.4711, U.4712

*Scuttled,*      U.8, U.14, U.17, U.29, U.30, U.37, U.38, U.46, U.48,
*salved and*     U.52, U.57†, U.58, U.60, U.61, U.62, U.71, U.108†,
*scrapped*       U.120, U.121, U.137, U.139, U.140, U.141, U.142,
*1947/53*        U.146, U.148, U.151, U.152, U.267, U.287, U.290,
               U.316, U.323, U.339, U.349, U.351, U.370, U.397,
               U.428, U.446†, U.474, U.475, U.552, U.554, U.560†,
               U.612, U.704, U.708, U.721, U.748, U.750, U.792,
               U.793, U.794, U.795, U.822, U.827, U.828, U.835,
               U.836, U.903, U.922, U.924, U.929, U.958, U.979,
               U.999, U.1016, U.1025, U.1047, U.1056, U.1101,
               U.1132, U.1161, U.1162, U.1168, U.1170, U.1192,
               U.1193, U.1196†, U.1204, U.1205, U.1207, U.1234†,
               U.1236, U.1237, U.1238, U.1277, U.1303, U.1304,
               U.1306, U.1308, U.1405, U.1406, U.1407, U.2327,
               U.2330, U.2332, U. 2333, U.2339, U.2343, U.2346,
               U.2347, U.2349, U.2352, U.2355, U.2357, U.2358,
               U.2360, U.2362, U.2364, U.2366, U.2368, U.2369,
               U.2370, U.2371, U.2501, U.2504, U.2505, U.2507,
               U.2508, U.2510, U.2512, U.2517, U.2519, U.2520,
               U.2522, U.2525, U.2526, U.2527, U.2528, U.2531,
               U.2533, U.2535, U.2536, U.2539, U.2541, U.2543,
               U.2544, U.2545, U.2546, U.2548, U.2551, U.3001,

U.3002, U.3004, U.3005, U.3006, U.3009, U.3010,
U.3011, U.3012, U.3013, U.3014, U.3015, U.3016,
U.3018, U.3019, U.3020, U.3021, U.3022, U.3023,
U.3024, U.3025, U.3026, U.3027, U.3029, U.3031,
U.3033, U.3034, U.3037, U.3038, U.3039, U.3040,
U.3044, U.3047, U.3050, U.3051, U.3501, U.3502,
U.3504, U.3506, U.3507, U.3510, U.3511, U.3513,
U.3516, U.3517, U.3518, U.3521, U.3522, U.3524,
U.3526, U.3527, U.3528, U.3529, U.3530, U.4701,
U.4702, U.4703, U.4704, U.4705, U.4707, U.4710,
UA, UB, UD.1, UD.3, UD.4, UF.2, UIT.2, UIT.3,
UIT.6, UIT.7, UIT.8, UIT.17, UIT.18

*Surrendered:* U.3, U.4, U.6, U.10, U.11, U.59, U.101, U.123,
U.143, U.145, U.149, U.150, U.155, U.170, U.181
(=IJN *I.501*), U.190, U.195 (=IJN *I.506*), U.218,
U.219 (=IJN *I.505*), U.228, U.234, U.244, U.245,
U.249, U.255, U.256, U.262, U.276, U.278, U.281,
U.291, U.293, U.294, U.295, U.298, U.299, U.310,
U.312, U.313, U.315, U.318, U.324, U.328, U.345,
U.363, U.368, U.369, U.427, U.481, U.483, U.485,
U.510, U.511 (=IJN *RO.500*), U.516, U.530, U.532,
U.539, U.541, U.555, U.622, U.637, U.668, U.680,
U.708, U.712, U.716, U.720, U.739, U.758, U.760,
U.764, U.766, U.773, U.775, U.776, U.778, U.779,
U.802, U.805, U.806, U.825, U.826, U.858, U.861,
U.862, (=IJN *I.502*), U.868, U.873, U.874, U.875,
U.883, U.889, U.901, U.907, U.927, U.928, U.930,
U.953, U.956, U.968, U.975, U.977, U.978, U.985,
U.991, U.992, U.993, U.994, U.995, U.997, U.1002,
U.1004, U.1005, U.1009, U.1010, U.1019, U.1022,
U.1023, U.1052, U.1054, U.1057, U.1058, U.1061,
U.1064, U.1102, U.1103, U.1104, U.1105, U.1108,
U.1109, U.1110, Y.1163, U.1165, U.1171, U.1194,
U.1197, U.1198, U.1201, U.1202, U.1203, U.?217,
U.1228, U.1230, U.1231, U.1232, U.1233, U.1271,
U.1272, U.1275, U.1301, U.1305, U.1307, U.2321,
U.2322, U.2324, U.2325, U.2326, U.2328, U.2329,
U.2334, U.2335, U.2336, U.2337, U.2341, U.2344,
U.2345, U.2348, U.2350, U.2351, U.2353, U.2354,
U.2356, U.2361, U.2363, U.2502, U.2506, U.2511,
U.2513, U.2518, U.2529, U.3008, U.3017, U.3035,
U.3041, U.3514, U.3515, U.4706, UC.2, UD.2, UD.5,
UF.1, UF.3, UIT.4, UIT.24, (=IJN *I.503*), UIT.25
(=IJN *I.504*)

*Fate
unknown*  U.34, U.239, U.547, U.957, U.1000

> *U.1211–1216, U.1218–1220, U.1239–1262, U.1280–1297, U.1309–1318, U.1331–1350, U.1401–1404, U.1408–1463, U.1501–1542, U.1601–1615, U.1701–1715, U.1801–1828, U.1901–1904, U.2001–2004, U.2101–2104, U.2201–2204, U.2301–2318, U.2372–2460, U.2553–2761, U.3045, U.3046, U.3048, U.3409, U.3052–3061, U.3531–3695, U.4001–4120, U.4501–4600, U.4713–4891, UIT.10–14*

*Projected:*     *U.112–115, U.687–700, U.817–820, U.919, U.920, U.943–950, U.1121–1130, U.1153–1160, U.1263–1270, U.1298–1300, U.1319–1330, U.1351–1400, U.1464–1500, U.1543–1600, U.1616–1700, U.1716–1800, U.1829–1900, U.1905–2000, U.2005–2100, U.2105–2110, U.2319, U.2320, U.2461–2500, U.2762–3000, U.3062–3500, U.3696–4000, U.4121–4500, U.4601–4700, U.4892–5000*

Of the submarines surrendered to the Allied powers the greater number were scuttled in the North Atlantic between November, 1945 and January, 1946; a smaller number were scrapped; one was lost on passage to the UK; and the remainder allocated between the Allied navies as follows:—

*Royal Navy:*     *U.249, U.712, U.926, U.953, U.995, U.1105, U.1108, U.1171, U.1202, U.2326, U.2518, U.3017, U.4706*

*Royal Canadian Navy:*     *U.190*

*United States Navy:*     *U.234, U.530, U.858, U.873, U.889, U.977, U.2513, U.3008*

*Russian Navy:*     *U.1057, U.1058, U.1064, U.1231, U.1305, U.2529, U.3035, U.3041, U.3515*

*French Navy:*     *U.123, U.471, U.510, U.766*

In addition to these, the Russian Navy also completed a number of uncompleted hulls that were lying, or were towed to, East German yards, while the United States Navy also had in their possession the *U.505* which they had captured during the war. Whereas the French and Russian navies incorporated these ex-German units into their fleets, the Royal and United States navies only retained them briefly for experimental purposes after which they were scrapped, except the *U.926*, *U.995*, *U.1202* and *U.4706* which were transferred to the Royal Norwegian Navy, and the *U.2326* and *U.2518* which were transferred to France, from the Royal Navy. Two submarines which had been scuttled, the *U.1406* and *U.1407*, were salved respectively by the United States and Royal navies, but were also only retained for a brief experimental period.

NOTE. In the above summary of German submarine losses and construction, no account is taken of the midget types XXVIIA and XXVIIB (U. 2111–2200, U.2205–2300, U.5001–6351).

# Sloops and Corvettes

### Fleet sloops: **F.1–10**

Essential qualities for an escort vessel, such as ample A.A. armament, large endurance and good seakeeping qualities, were needlessly sacrificed in these vessels for high speed of little practical use, but they were provided with active fin stabilisation. During 1938–9 *F.2* and *F.4* were lengthened forward, increasing their length(oa) to 262½ feet and displacement to 1,768 tons (1,147 tons full), and *F.1, F.3,* and *F.6* were similarly altered and also had the fo'c'sle deck extended right to the stern, and the side plated in, to provide additional accommodation as senior officer's ships for flotilla craft. War modifications were limited to the addition of a quadruple 20mm A.A. mounting, while some were later disarmed. The design was not further proceeded with as they were unsuited to rapid war construction.

*The fast escort or fleet sloop F.1 pre-war.* (Drüppel)

*Displacement:* 712 tons (1,028 tons full)
*Dimensions:* 239½(pp) 249¼(oa) × 28¾ × 8¼/10½ feet
*Machinery:* Two Lamont (pressure 1,616 lb.) except *F.7* and *8*
   Benson and *F9* and *10* Velox (pressure 1,028 lb.) boilers;
   two shafts; Wagner geared turbines, S.H.P. 14,000 = 28 knots
*Bunkers & Radius:* O.F. 216 tons; 1,500 miles at 20 knots
*Armament:* Two 4.1inch (2 × 1), four 37mm A.A. (2 × 2),
   four 20mm A.A. (1 × 4) guns
*Complement:* 121
*Notes:* Also fitted for minelaying

**Name** *F.1* **Built by** Germania Werft (Kiel) **Launched** 1.3.35
**Fate** *Libelle* (1944), *Jagd* (1945), USN (1945); scrapped France
1947

**Name** *F.2* **Built by** Germania Werft (Kiel) **Launched** 2.4.35
**Fate** RN (1945); scrapped

**Name** *F.3* **Built by** Germania Werft (Kiel) **Launched** 1.6.35
**Fate** *Hai* (1941); bombed RAF aircraft Kiel 3.5.45, salved and
scrapped

**Name** *F.4* **Built by** Germania Werft (Kiel) **Launched** 2.7.35
**Fate** RN (1945); scrapped

**Name** *F.5* **Built by** Germania Werft (Kiel) **Launched** 14.8.35
**Fate** Mined Baltic 29.1.45

**Name** *F.6* **Built by** Germania Werft (Kiel) **Launched** 1.10.35
**Fate** *Königin Luise* (1944); bombed USAAF aircraft
Wilhelmshaven 30.3.45

**Name** *F.7* **Built by** Blohm & Voss (Hamburg) **Launched** 25.5.35
**Fate** Russian (1947)

**Name** *F.8* **Built by** Blohm & Voss (Hamburg) **Launched** 25.7.35
**Fate** USN (1945); scrapped Holland 1950

**Name** *F.9* **Built by** Naval Dockyard (Wilhelmshaven)
**Launched** 11.5.35 **Fate** Torpedoed RN submarine *Ursula* off
Heligoland 14.12.39

**Name** *F.10* **Built by** Naval Dockyard (Wilhelmshaven)
**Launched** 11.5.35 **Fate** USN (1945); scrapped Holland 1950

## *Escort sloops:* **G.1–24**

These vessels were developed from a *type 1938 gunboat* project,
and although the lead yard was German the bulk were to be
constructed in the Netherlands which influenced design con-
siderations. Their dimensions were enlarged to accommodate
bulkier and lower powered machinery which resulted in a
25 per cent loss of speed, as compared with the preceding
class, but they were better seaboats in consequence. The

armament was augmented by pairing the forward and after 4.1inch A.A. guns, but the latter was later removed in order that a helicopter could be carried. Work only proceeded on the initial unit of the class and the remainder were cancelled.

*Displacement:* 1,324 tons (1,739 tons full)
*Dimensions:* $275\frac{1}{2}$(pp) $285\frac{1}{2}$(oa) $\times$ $32\frac{3}{4}$ $\times$ $10\frac{1}{4}/12\frac{3}{4}$ feet
*Machinery:* Three Benson boilers (pressure 411 lb.); two shafts; reciprocating (VTE) and exhaust turbine, I.H.P. 6,750 = 21 knots
*Bunkers & Radius:* I.F. 402 tons; 6,000 miles at 20 knots
*Armament:* Four 4.1 inch A.A. (2 $\times$ 2, four 37mm A.A. (1 $\times$ 2 and 2 $\times$ 1), eight 20mm A.A. (4 $\times$ 2) guns; one aircraft
*Complement:* 158

**Name** *G.1* **Built by** Stulcken (Hamburg) **Fate** Bombed Allied aircraft while building 27.7.43, and construction abandoned
**Name** *G2–4* **Built by** Stulcken (Hamburg) **Fate** Cancelled
**Name** *G5–24* **Built by** Netherlands **Fate** Cancelled

## *Ex-French sloops:* **SG.1–4**

*Displacement:* 1,372 tons (1,760 tons full)
*Dimensions:* $301\frac{3}{4}$(pp) $311\frac{1}{4}$(oa) $\times$ 40 $\times$ $10\frac{1}{4}/11\frac{3}{4}$ feet
*Machinery:* Two-shaft diesel motors, B.H.P. 4,140 = 16 knots
*Bunkers & Radius:* O.F. 256 tons; 6,000 miles at 16 knots
*Armament:* Three 4.1inch A.A. (3 $\times$ 1), four 37mm A.A. (2 $\times$ 2), ten 20mm A.A. (2 $\times$ 4 and 1 $\times$ 2) guns
*Complement:* 178
*Notes:* Four 20mm A.A. (1 $\times$ 4) replaced one 4.1inch gun in some units

SG.1 *was the ex-French aircraft tender* Sans Pareil, *later renamed* Jupiter. (Drüppel)

**Name** *SG.1* (ex-*Sans Pareil*) **Built by** At. & Ch. de la Loire
(St. Nazaire) **Launched** 1940 **Fate** *Jupiter* (1942); scuttled Gironde
8.44 after being bombed Allied aircraft 6.8.44

**Name** *SG.2* (ex-*Sans Reproche*) **Built by** At. & Ch. de la Loire
(St. Nazaire) **Launched** 1940 **Fate** *Saturn* (1942); bombed Allied
aircraft north-west of Gironde estuary 6.8.44

**Name** *SG.3* (ex-*Sans Souci*) **Built by** At. & Ch. de la Mediterranee)
**Launched** 1941 **Fate** *Uranus* (1942); retroceded incomplete 1945;
French surveying vessel *Beautemps-Beaupré* (1947)

**Name** *SG.4* (ex-*Sans Peur*) **Built by** At. & Ch. de la Mediterranee
(St. Nazaire) **Launched** 1941 **Fate** *Merkur* (1942); retroceded
incomplete 1945; French surveying vessel *La Pérouse* (1947)

## *Corvettes:* **MZ.1–12**

These versatile small craft were styled as multi-purpose vessels,
and could undertake a wide variety of coastal duties for which
they were well-armed. Their fire power was exceptional for
their size, and their limited radius acceptable for their inshore
employment. Only the initial unit was completed and the
remainder were cancelled.

*Displacement:* 285 tons (318 tons full)
*Dimensions:* 164(wl) 170½(oa) × 27¼ × 6½/7½ feet
*Machinery:* One shaft; Deutz diesel motor, B.H.P. 1,000 = 14
   knots
*Bunkers & Radius:* O.F. 17½ tons; 1,000 miles at 14 knots
*Armament:* Two 3.5inch A.A. (2 × 1), one 37mm A.A., eight
   20mm A.A. (1 × 4 and 2 × 2) guns; two 21inch (2 × 1)
   torpedo tubes
*Complement:* 52

**Name** *MZ.1* **Built by** C. Stülcken (Hamburg) **Launched** 1944
**Fate** RN (1945); scrapped

**Name** *MZ.2–12* **Built by** C. Stülcken (Hamburg) **Fate** Cancelled

## *Ex-RDN sloop:* **NERGER**

*Displacement:* 705 tons
*Dimensions:* 175(oa) × 30 × 12 feet
*Machinery:* Two cylinder boilers; one-shaft reciprocating
   (VTE) I.H.P. 800 = 13 knots
*Bunkers & Radius:* O.F. 100 tons; 4,000 miles at 12 knots
*Armament:* Two 3inch (2 × 1), two 40mm A.A. (2 × 1),
   two 8mm A.A. (2 × 1) guns
*Complement:* 40

## Ex-RDN sloop: **SUDPOL**

*Displacement:* 322 tons
*Dimensions:* $124\frac{3}{4}$(pp) 134(oa) × $25\frac{1}{4}$ × $7\frac{1}{4}$ feet
*Machinery:* One cylinder boiler; one-shaft reciprocating (VTE)
 I.H.P. 300 = $10\frac{1}{2}$ knots
*Bunkers:* O.F. 15 tons
*Armament:* Two 3inch (2 × 1), two 20mm A.A. (2 × 1) guns
*Complement:* 40

## Ex-RDN sloop: **Vs.1401**

*Displacement:* 614 tons
*Dimensions:* $167\frac{1}{4}$(pp) $175\frac{1}{2}$(oa) × 29 × 8 feet
*Machinery:* Two Thornycroft boilers; two-shafts reciprocating
 (VTE) I.H.P. 1,200 = 14 knots
*Bunkers:* O.F. 35 tons
*Armament:* Two 3inch (2 × 1), three 20mm A.A. (3 × 1) guns
*Complement:* 58
*Notes:* Former minelayer which could stow 150 mines

**Name** *Nerger* (ex-*Hejmdal*) **Built by** Naval Dockyard
(Copenhagen) **Launched** 1.2.35 **Fate** Scuttled Copenhagen
29.8.43, salved and German; retroceded 1945

**Name** *Südpol* (ex-*Freja*) **Built by** Naval Dockyard (Copenhagen)
**Launched** 22.12.38 **Fate** Scuttled Copenhagen 29.8.43, salved and
German; navigation school tender *Freya* (1944); retroceded 1945

**Name** *Vs.1401* (ex-*Lindormen*) **Built by** Naval Dockyard
(Copenhagen) **Launched** 30.3.40 **Fate** Scuttled Copenhagen
29.8.43, salved and German; retroceded 1945

## Ex-French sloops: **SG.14–17** and **21** (*first group*), **SG.19, 22, 23** and **25** (*second group*)

*Displacement:* 590 tons (830 tons full)
*Dimensions:* $249\frac{1}{4}$(wl) 257(oa) × 28 × $7\frac{3}{4}/10\frac{1}{2}$ feet
*Machinery:* Two-shaft Sulzer diesel motors (two per shaft)
 B.H.P. 4,000 = 20 knots
*Bunkers & Radius:* O.F. 105 tons; 10,000 miles at 9 knots
*Armament:* Two 4.1inch A.A. (2 × 1 *first group*, 1 × 2 *second
 group*), two 37mm A.A. (2 × 1), five/six 20mm A.A. (1 × 4
 and 1/2 × 1 *first group*, 1 × 2 and 3/4 × 1 *second group*) guns
*Complement:* 103
*Notes:* First group with foc's'le, second group without foc's'le,
 and were classed as colonial and mine-sweeping sloops
 respectively by the French Navy

**Name** *SG.14* (ex-*Matelot Leblanc*) **Built by** Ch. & At. de la Provence (Port de Bouc) **Launched** 10.7.42 **Fate** Scuttled Toulon 27.11.42, salved and German; bombed south of Capri Allied aircraft 28.8.44

**Name** *SG.15* (ex-*Rageot de la Touche*) **Built by** Ch. & At. de la Provence (Port de Bouc) **Launched** 3.9.42 **Fate** Scuttled Toulon 27.11.42, salved and German; scuttled Genoa 26.4.45

**Name** *SG.16* (ex-*Admiral Sénés*) **Built by** Ch. & At. de la Provence (Port de Bouc) **Launched** 1942 **Fate** Scuttled Toulon 27.11.42, salved and German; scuttled Marseilles 21.8.44

**Name** *SG.17* (ex-*Enseigne Ballande*) **Built by** Ch. & At. de la Provence (Port de Bouc) **Launched** 1942 **Fate** Scuttled incomplete· Toulon 27.11.42; salved and German; retroceded incomplete 1945 and scrapped

**Name** *SG.19* (ex-*Elan*) **Built by** Naval Dockyard (Lorient) **Launched** 27.7.38 **Fate** Scuttled Toulon 27.11.42, salved and German; interned Erdek (Turkey) 8.9.43; retroceded 1945

**Name** *SG.21* (ex-*Chamois*) **Built by** Naval Dockyard (Lorient) **Launched** 19.4.38 **Fate** Scuttled Toulon 27.11.42, salved and RIt.N *FR.53*, German (1943); bombed Allied aircraft Toulon 15.8.44

**Name** *SG.22* (ex-*Commandant Rivière*) **Built by** Ch. & At. de la Provence (Port de Bouc) **Launched** 16.2.39 **Fate** Scuttled Bizerta 30.11.42, salved and RIt.N *FR.52,* German (1943); bombed Allied aircraft Leghorn 28.5.43

**Name** *SG.23* (ex-*La Batailleuse*) **Built by** Ch. & At. de la Provence (Port de Bouc) **Launched** 22.8.39 **Fate** Scuttled Bizerta 30.11.42, salved and RIt.N *FR.51*, German (1943); scuttled Genoa 23.4.45

**Name** *SG.25* (ex-*La Curieuse*) **Built by** Naval Dockyard (Lorient) **Launched** 11.11.39 **Fate** Scuttled Toulon 27.11.42, salved and RIt.N *FR.55*, German (1943); retroceded incomplete 1945

*SG.26 was formerly the elderly French sweeper* Granit, *salvaged at Toulon in 1943.* (Drüppel)

## Ex-French corvettes: **PA.1–4**

*Displacement:* 930 tons
*Dimensions:* $190\frac{1}{4}$(pp) $203\frac{1}{2}$(oa) × $32\frac{3}{4}$ × $11\frac{1}{2}$/14 feet
*Machinery:* Two S.E. cyl. boilers (pressure 235 lb.); one-shaft
    reciprocating (VTE) I.H.P. 2,700 = 16 knots
*Bunkers & Radius:* O.F. 480 tons; 7,000 miles at 10 knots
*Armament:* one 4.1inch, four 37mm A.A. (2 × 2), four 20mm
    A.A. (4 × 1) guns
*Complement:* 80
*Notes:* Design RN "Flower" class corvette

**Name** *PA.1* (ex-*Arquebuse*) **Built by** Fges & Ch. de la Mediterranée
(St. Nazaire) **Launched** 16.10.40 **Fate** Bombed RAF aircraft
Le Havre 6.44

**Name** *PA.2* (ex-*Hallebarde*) **Built by** Fges & Ch. de la
Mediterranée (St. Nazaire) **Launched** 27.11.40 **Fate** Lost English
Channel 15.6.44

**Name** *PA.3* (ex-*Sabre*) **Built by** Fges & Ch. de la Mediterranée
(St. Nazaire) **Launched** 29.11.40 **Fate** Bombed RAF aircraft
Le Havre 6.44

**Name** *PA.4* (ex-*Poignard*) **Built by** Fges & Ch. de la Mediterranée
(St. Nazaire) **Launched** 29.11.40 **Fate** Expended blockship off
Nantes 25.8.44


## Ex-RNeth.N sloops: **K.1–3**

*Displacement:* 1,200 tons (1,420 tons full)
*Dimensions:* 246(pp) 256(oa) × $33\frac{1}{2}$ × $9\frac{1}{2}$ /$12\frac{3}{4}$ feet
*Machinery:* Two-shaft diesel motors, B.H.P. 2,770 = $14\frac{1}{2}$ knots
    except *K.3* B.H.P. 3,500 = 18 knots
*Bunkers & Radius:* O.F. 157 tons; 6,900 miles at 12 knots
*Protection:* Main belt $1\frac{1}{2}$–$2\frac{1}{4}$ inches, deck $\frac{3}{4}$–$1\frac{1}{4}$ inches, turrets $2\frac{1}{4}$
    inches
*Armament:* Four 4.7inch (2 × 2), four 37mm A.A. (2 × 2),
    twelve 20mm A.A. (2 × 4 and 2 × 2) guns, 200 mines
*Complement:* 161


## Ex-RBN sloops: **K.4**

*Displacement:* 1,640 tons (2,270 tons full)
*Dimensions:* 292(pp) 323(oa) × $34\frac{1}{2}$ × $10\frac{3}{4}$ /$12\frac{1}{2}$ feet
*Machinery:* Two Babcock & Wilcox boilers (pressure 500 lb.);
    two-shaft Parsons-Rateau geared turbines, S.H.P. 21,700 = $28\frac{1}{2}$
    knots
*Bunkers & Radius:* O.F. 680 tons; 2,600 miles at 19 knots
*Protection:* Turrets $1\frac{1}{2}$ inches
*Armament:* Three 4.1inch A.A. (3 × 1), four 37mm A.A. (2 × 2),
    ten 20mm A.A. (2 × 4 and 1 × 2) guns, 120 mines
*Complement:* 180

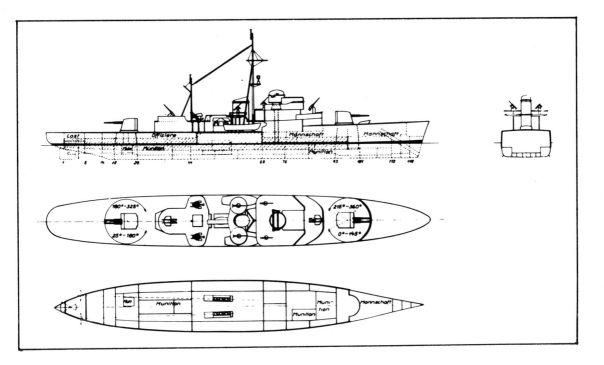

**Name** *K.1* **Built by** P. Smit (Rotterdam) **Launched** 23.11.40
**Fate** Bombed RAF aircraft Aarhus 5.4.45

**Name** *K.2* **Built by** Werft Gusto (Schiedam) **Launched** 28.6.41
**Fate** Foundered Delfzijl 1945 after being torpedoed Allied
aircraft west of Egersund 28.9.44; salved 26.7.46 and scrapped

**Name** *K.3* **Built by** P. Smit (Rotterdam) **Launched** 22.3.41
**Fate** Retroceded RNeth.N *Van Speijk* (1945)

**Name:** *K.4 (ex-Artevelde)* **Built by** Cockerill (Antwerp)
**Launched** 28.8.40 **Fate** *Lorele* (1943), completed Wilton-Fijenoord
(Schiedam); retroceded 1945; scrapped Brugge 22.11.54

*General Arrangement of the
ex-Dutch gunboats* K.1–3.

**K.3** *was an ex-Dutch gunboat
captured on the stocks in 1940.*
(Drüppel)

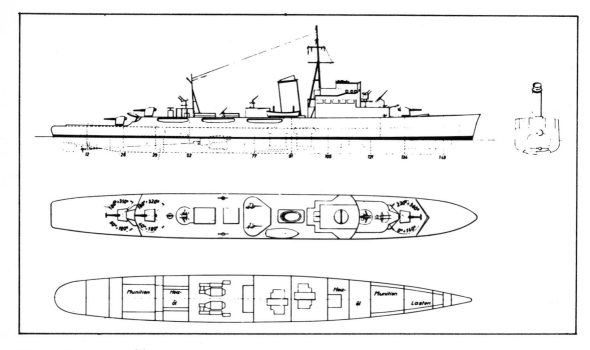

*General Arrangement of the gunboat* K.4, *formerly the Belgian* Artevelde. *She was renumbered* Lorelei *in 1943.*

## *Ex-RIt.N corvettes:* **Uj.201–209, 2221–2228, 6081–6088**

*Displacement:* 642 tons (738 tons full)
*Dimensions:* 196¾(pp) 210(oa) × 28½ × 8¼/00 feet
*Machinery:* Two-shafts Fiat diesel motor, B.H.P. 3,500 = 19 knots; and electric motors (for cruising) S.H.P. 150 = 6 knots
*Bunkers & Radius:* O.F. 64 tons; 3,000 miles at 15 knots
*Armament:* One 3.9inch, seven 20mm A.A. (7 × 1) guns
*Complement:* 100
*Notes:* Electric motors not fitted in *Uj.206* and *207,* and the former had a modified bridge and light armoured plating over the machinery spaces

**Name** *Uj.201* (ex-*Egeria*) **Built by** Cant. Riuniti dell'Adriatico (Monfalcone) **Launched** 3.7.43 **Fate** Bombed Allied aircraft Monfalcone 29.2.44

**Name** *Uj.202* (ex-*Melpomene*) **Built by** Cant. Riuniti dell'Adriatico (Monfalcone) **Launched** 29.8.43 **Fate** Gunfire RN escort destroyers *Avon Vale* and *Wheatland* off Zara 1.11.44

**Name** *Uj.203* (ex-*Tersicore*) **Built by** Cant. Riuniti dell'Adriatico (Monfalcone) **Launched** 16.10.43 **Fate** Bombed Allied aircraft Monfalcone 20.4.44 while building and construction abandoned

**Name** *Uj.204* (ex-*Euridice*) **Built by** Cant. Riuniti dell'Adriatico (Monfalcone) **Launched** 12.3.44 **Fate** Bombed Allied aircraft Monfalcone 25.5.44 while building and construction abandoned

**Name** *Uj.205* (ex-*Columbrina*) **Built by** Breda (Porto Maghera) **Launched** 7.12.42 **Fate** Bombed Allied aircraft off Venice 27.3.44

**Name** *Uj.206* (ex-*Bombarda*) **Built by** Breda (Porto Maghera) **Launched** 10.2.44 **Fate** Scuttled incomplete Venice after being bombed Allied aircraft 25.4.45; salved

**Name** *Uj.207* (ex-*Carabina*) **Built by** Breda (Porto Maghera) **Launched** 31.8.43 **Fate** Bombed Allied aircraft Breda 2.44 while building and construction abandoned

**Name** *Uj.208* (ex-*Spingarda*) **Built by** Breda (Porto Maghera) **Launched** 22.5.43 **Fate** Gunfire RN escort destroyers *Avon Vale* and *Wheatland* off Zara 1.11.44

**Name** *Uj.209* (ex-*Scure*) **Built by** Breda (Porto Maghera) **Fate** Scuttled incomplete Breda 25.4.45 after being bombed Allied aircraft

**Name** *Uj.2221* (ex-*Vespa*) **Built by** Navalmeccanica (Castellammare) **Launched** 22.11.42 **Fate** Scuttled Genoa 24.4.45

**Name** *Uj.2222* (ex-*Tuffeto*) **Built by** Ansaldo (Genoa) **Launched** 25.8.43 **Fate** Scuttled Genoa 24.4.45 following gunfire RN surface forces 23.4.45

**Name** *Uj.2223* (ex-*Maragone*) **Built by** Ansaldo (Genoa) **Launched** 16.9.43 **Fate** Bombed Allied aircraft Genoa 16.8.44

**Name** *Uj.2224* (ex-*Strolaga*) **Built by** Ansaldo (Genoa) **Fate** Expended incomplete as blockship Genoa 24.4.45

**Name** *Uj.2225* (ex-*Ardea*) **Built by** Ansaldo (Genoa) **Fate** Scuttled incomplete Genoa 24.4.45

**Name** *Uj.2226* (ex-*Artemide*) **Built by** Cant. Riuniti dell'Adriatico (Monfalcone) **Launched** 10.8.42 **Fate** Scuttled Monfalcone 24.4.45

**Name** *Uj.2227* (ex-*Persefone*) **Built by** Cant. Riuniti dell'Adriatico (Monfalcone) **Launched** 21.9.42 **Fate** Scuttled Monfalcone 9.9.43, salved and German; scuttled Monfalcone 24.4.45

**Name** *Uj.2228* (ex-*Euterpe*) **Built by** Cant. Riuniti dell'Adriatico (Monfalcone) **Launched** 22.10.42 **Fate** Scuttled Monfalcone 9.9.43, salved and German; scuttled Monfalcone 24.4.45

**Name** *Uj.6081* (ex-*Camoscio*) **Built by** Odero-Terni-Orlando (Leghorn) **Launched** 9.5.42 **Fate** Gunfire RN surface forces south of Toulon 17.8.44

**Name** *Uj.6082* (ex-*Antilope*) **Built by** Odero-Terni-Orlando (Leghorn) **Launched** 9.5.42 **Fate** Gunfire RN surface forces south of Casines 16.8.44

**Name** *Uj.6083* (ex-*Capriolo*) **Built by** Odero-Terni-Orlando (Leghorn) **Launched** 5.12.42 **Fate** Scuttled Genoa 24.4.45

**Name** *Uj.6084* (ex-*Alce*) **Built by** Odero-Terni-Orlando (Leghorn) **Launched** 5.12.42 **Fate** Scuttled Genoa 24.4.45

**Name** *Uj.6085* (ex-*Renna*) **Built by** Odero-Terni-Orlando (Leghorn) **Launched** 5.12.42 **Fate** Bombed Allied aircraft Genoa 4.9.44

**Name** *Uj.6086* (ex-*Cervo*) **Built by** Odero-Terni-Orlando (Leghorn) **Fate** Scuttled incomplete Genoa 24.4.45

**Name** *Uj.6087* (ex-*Daino*) **Built by** Odero-Terni-Orlando (Leghorn) **Fate** Bombed Allied aircraft Leghorn while building and construction abandoned

**Name** *Uj.6088* (ex-*Stambercco*) **Built by** Odero-Terni-Orlando (Leghorn) **Fate** Bombed Allied aircraft Leghorn while building and construction abandoned

# MTBs

*An unidentified S-Boat with the older type of bridge en route to surrender in May 1945.* (MoD)

Picture on previous page: *Two surrendered S-Boats coming alongside the jetty at* HMS Hornet, *the Coastal Forces base at Portsmouth. Note the "skullcap" bridge.*

## *MTB:* **S.1**

*Displacement:* 39¾ tons (51½ tons full)
*Dimensions:* 88½(oa) × 13¾ × 3½ feet
*Machinery:* Three-shaft Daimler-Benz petrol motors, B.H.P. 2,700/2,400=34/32 knots
*Bunkers & Radius:* Petrol 8½ tons; 582 miles at 22 knots
*Armament:* One 20mm A.A. gun, two 19.7inch (2 × 1 fixed) T.T.
*Complement:* 18
*Notes:* Built 1930 and discarded pre-war

## *MTBs:* **S.2–5**

*Displacement:* 46½ tons (52½ tons full)
*Dimensions:* 91¾(oa) × 13¾ × 3½ feet
*Machinery:* Three-shaft Daimler-Benz petrol motors, B.H.P. 3,300/2,400 = 36/34 knots
*Bunkers & Radius:* Petrol 9 tons; 582 miles at 22 knots
*Armament:* One 20mm A.A., one 8mm A.A., guns, two 19.7inch (2 × 1 fixed) T.T.
*Complement:* 18
*Notes:* Built 1932. Sold to Spanish Navy 1938 and renumbered *LT. 11, 12, 14* and *15* respectively.

*S.4 was an early type of S-Boat which had been sold to Spain in 1936.* Drüppel)

## *MTB:* **S.6**

*Displacement:* $60\frac{1}{2}$ tons (85 tons full)
*Dimensions:* $106\frac{1}{4}$(oa) × 16 × 4 feet
*Machinery:* Three-shaft M.A.N. diesel motors, B.H.P. 3,960/2,880
 = 35/32 knots
*Bunkers & Radius:* O.F. 13 tons; 758 miles at 22 knots
*Armament:* One 20mm A.A. gun, two 21inch (2 × 1 fixed—four
 torpedoes) T.T.
*Complement:* 21
*Notes:* Built 1933

## *MTBs:* **S.7–9**

*Displacement:* $75\frac{3}{4}$ tons (86 tons full)
*Dimensions:* $106\frac{1}{4}$(oa) × 16 × 4 feet
*Machinery:* Three-shaft M.A.N. diesel motors, B.H.P. 3,960/2,880
 = $36\frac{1}{2}$/34 knots
*Bunkers & Radius:* O.F. 13 tons; 758 miles at 22 knots
*Armament:* One 20mm A.A. gun, two 21inch (2 × 1 fixed—four
 torpedoes) T.T.
*Complement:* 21
*Notes:* Built 1933–4

## *MTBs:* **S.10–13**

*Displacement:* $75\frac{3}{4}$ tons (86 tons full)
*Dimensions:* $106\frac{1}{4}$(oa) × 16 × 4 feet
*Machinery:* Three-shaft Daimler-Benz diesel motors, B.H.P.
 3,960/3,600 = 35/34 knots
*Bunkers & Radius:* O.F. 13 tons; 758 miles at 22 knots
*Armament:* One 20mm A.A. gun, two 21inch (2 × 1 fixed—four
 torpedoes) T.T.
*Complement:* 21
*Notes:* Built 1934–5

*Motor torpedo boat* S.8
*pre-war.* (Drüppel)

S.13 *pre-war*. (Drüppel)

## *MTBs:* **S.14–17**

*Displacement:* 92½ tons (105½ tons full)
*Dimensions:* 113½(oa) × 16¾ × 4¾ feet
*Machinery:* Three-shaft M.A.N. diesel motors, B.H.P. 6,150/4,200
    = 37/35 knots
*Bunkers & Radius:* O.F. 16½ tons; 500 miles at 32 knots
*Armament:* One 20mm A.A. gun, two 21inch (2 × 1 fixed—four
    torpedoes) T.T.
*Complement:* 21
*Notes:* Built 1935–8

## *MTBs:* **S.18–25**

*Displacement:* 92½ tons (104½ tons full)
*Dimensions:* 113½(oa) × 16¾ × 4¾ feet
*Machinery:* Three-shaft Daimler-Benz diesel motors, B.H.P.
    6,000/4,500 = 38½/35 knots
*Bunkers & Radius:* O.F. 16½ tons; 700 miles at 35 knots
*Armament:* Two 20mm A.A. (2 × 1) guns, two 21inch (2 × 1
    fixed—four torpedoes)
*Complement:* 21
*Notes:* Built 1938–9

## *MTBs:* **S.26–39, 38–53, 62–138, 159–166**

*Displacement:* 92½ tons (104½ tons full)
*Dimensions:* 114¾(oa) × 16¾ × 5 feet
*Machinery:* Three-shaft Daimler-Benz diesel motors, B.H.P.
    6,000/4,500 = 39/35 knots
*Bunkers & Radius:* O.F. 16¾ tons; 700 miles at 35 knots
*Armament:* Two 20mm A.A. (2 × 1) guns, two 21inch (2 × 1
    fixed—four torpedoes)
*Complement:* 21

*Port broadside view of* S.18 *at speed.* (Drüppel)

*The motor torpedo boat* S.18 *was one of the last group of flush-decked S-Boats.* (Drüppel)

*Notes:* Built 1939–43. *S.100, 136* and *138* had supercharged engines of B.H.P. 7,500/6,000 = 41/38 knots. Most had one 37mm A.A. and one 20mm A.A. (twin in lieu of single) guns added. *S.73, 78, 124–126* transferred to Spanish Navy and renumbered *L.T.21–25* (1943)

## *MTBs:* S.30–37, 54–61

*Displacement:* 81 tons (88 tons full)
*Dimensions:* 107½(oa) × 16 × 4 feet
*Machinery:* Three-shaft Daimler-Benz diesel motors, B.H.P. 3,960/3,600 = 36/34 knots
*Bunkers & Radius:* O.F. 13 tons; 800 miles at 30 knots
*Armament:* Two 20mm A.A. (2 × 1) guns, two 21inch (2 × 1 fixed—four torpedoes) T.T.
*Complement:* 16
*Notes:* Built 1939–40

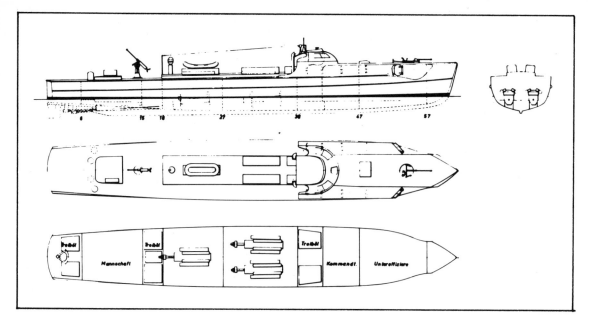

Above: *General Arrangement
of* S.67 *group of S-Boats.*

Right: S.128 *was one of
the* S.38 *type of S-Boat with an
enclosed forecastle.*

S.81 *had the older type of
wheelhouse.* (Drüppel)

## *MTBs:* **S.139–150, S.167, S.200, S.201(ii), S.202(ii), S.203–500**

*Displacement:* 92½ tons (105½ tons full)
*Dimensions:* 114¾(oa) × 16¾ × 4¾ feet
*Machinery:* Three-shaft Daimler-Benz diesel motors, B.H.P.
   7,500/6,000 = 41/38 knots
*Bunkers & Radius:* O.F. 16¾ tons; 700 miles at 35 knots
*Armament:* One 37mm A.A., three 20mm A.A. (1 × 2 and 1 × 1)
   except *S.219* up six 20mm A.A. (3 × 2) guns, two 21inch
   (2 × 1 fixed—four torpedoes)
*Complement:* 21
*Notes:* Built 1942–4. *S.170* and *S.228* had supercharged engines
   of B.H.P. 9,000/7,500 = 44/41 knots. *S.145* transferred to
   Spanish Navy and renumbered *LT.26* (1943)

## *MTBs:* **S.701–800**

*Displacement:* 99 tons (112 tons full)
*Dimensions:* 114½(oa) × 16¾ × 7 feet
*Machinery:* Three-shaft Daimler-Benz diesel motors, B.H.P.
   7,500/6,000 = 42/38 knots
*Bunkers & Radius:* O.F. 17 tons; 700 miles at 30 knots
*Armament:* Six 20mm A.A. (3 × 2) guns, four 21inch (4 × 1
   fixed) T.T.
*Complement:* 23
*Notes:* Built 1944–5

## *Ex-RBul.N MTB:* **S.1(ii)**; *ex-RYN MTBs:* **S.2(ii)–5(ii)**

*Displacement:* 49 tons (56½ tons full)
*Dimensions:* 91¾(oa) × 14 × 4 feet
*Machinery:* Three-shaft Daimler-Benz diesel motors, B.H.P.
   2,850/2,100 = 35½/34 knots
*Bunkers & Radius:* O.F. 9 tons; 350 miles at 30 knots
*Armament:* One 40mm A.A. and one 15mm A.A. guns except
   *S.1* one 20mm A.A. gun, two 21.7inch except *S.1*
   21inch (2 × 1 fixed) T.T.
*Complement:* 14 except *S.1* 12
*Notes:* Built 1938–9. *S.1* was former *No. 1* and sister boat *No. 2*
   was cannibalised for spares. *S.2–5* were former *Velebit, Dinara,
   Triglav* and *Rudnik* and were numbered *MS. 42–44* and *46*
   while serving in RIt.N 1941–3

## *Ex-RNeth.N MTBs:* **S.151–158**

*Displacement:* 57 tons (64 tons full)
*Dimensions:* $91\frac{3}{4}$(oa) × 14 × 4 feet
*Machinery:* Three-shaft Daimler-Benz diesel motors, B.H.P.
   2,850/2,100 = 34/30 knots
*Bunkers & Radius:* O.F. $9\frac{1}{4}$ tons; 350 miles at 30 knots
*Armament:* One 20mm A.A. gun, two 21inch (2 × 1 fixed) T.T.
*Complement:* 21
*Notes:* Built 1940 and former *TM.54–61* seized incomplete.
   *S.154–158* believed transferred to RRoum.N and re-numbered
   Nos. *10–13* and *S.155–158* to Bulgarian Navy and re-numbered
   Nos. *5–8* (1942)

## *Ex-RNeth.N MTBs:* **S.201** *and* **202**

*Displacement:* $30\frac{3}{4}$ tons ($38\frac{1}{2}$ tons full)
*Dimensions:* $70\frac{1}{4}$(oa) × $19\frac{1}{2}$ × $4\frac{1}{4}$ feet
*Machinery:* Three-shaft Rolls-Royce petrol motors, B.H.P.
   3,300/3,000 = $42\frac{1}{2}$/39 knots
*Bunkers:* Petrol
*Armament:* One 20mm A.A. gun, two 19.7inch (2 × 1 fixed) T.T.
*Complement:* 12
*Notes:* Built 1940 and former *TM.52* and *53* seized incomplete.
   Engines were obtained from RAF aircraft shot down over
   Europe. Transferred RBul.N and renumbered Nos. *3* and *4*
   (1942)

## *Experimental MTB*

*Displacement:* 94 tons (117 tons full)
*Dimensions:* $114\frac{1}{2}$(oa) × $17\frac{1}{4}$ × $6\frac{1}{2}$ feet
*Machinery:* Three-shaft Daimler-Benz diesel motors, B.H.P.
   9,000/7,500 = 49/44 knots
*Bunkers & Radius:* O.F. $16\frac{3}{4}$ tons; 690 miles at 35 knots
*Armament:* One 37mm A.A., three 20mm A.A. (1 × 2
   and 1 × 1), two 8mm A.A. (2 × 1) guns, four 21inch (4 × 1
   fixed) T.T.
*Complement:* 24
*Notes:* 1945 project for hard chine boat and not completed

## *Experimental MTB*

*Displacement:* $92\frac{1}{2}$ tons ($124\frac{1}{4}$ tons full)
*Dimensions:* $114\frac{3}{4}$(oa) × $16\frac{3}{4}$ × $5\frac{1}{2}$ feet
*Machinery:* Three-shaft Daimler-Benz diesel motors, B.H.P.
   9,000/7,500 = 44/37 knots

*Bunkers & Radius:* O.F. 16¾ tons; 700 miles at 35 knots
*Armament:* One 30mm A.A., three 20mm A.A. (1 × 2 and 1 × 1),
  two 8mm A.A. (2 × 1) guns, four 21inch (4 × 1 fixed) T.T.
*Complement:* 24
*Notes:* 1945 project for armoured boat with welded steel deck,
  low bridge, and of round bilge form generally similar to *S.170*
  but not completed

## *Ex-RIt.N MTBs:* **S.501–507, 510–512, 621, 623** *and* **629, SA.15–21**

*Displacement:* 28 tons
*Dimensions:* 69(oa) × 14¾ × 4½ feet
*Machinery:* Two-shaft Isotta-Fraschini petrol motors, B.H.P.
  2,000 = 40 knots
*Bunkers & Radius:* Petrol 1¼ tons; 260 miles
*Armament:* One 20mm A.A. or three 13mm A.A. (3 × 1) guns,
  two 18inch torpedoes
*Complement:* 12
*Notes:* Built 1940–4 and former *MAS.566–570, 574, 575, 551,
  557, 553, 561, 554, 558, 604, 624, 625, 629, 622, 623*; others
  not known

## *Ex-RIt.N MTBs:* **S.508, 509, 601, 622, 626–628, SA.11–14**

*Displacement:* 20 tons
*Dimensions:* 69(oa) × 14¾ × 4½ feet
*Machinery:* Two-shaft Isotta-Fraschini petrol motors, B.H.P.
  2,000 = 47 knots
*Bunkers & Radius:* Petrol 1¼ tons; 260 miles
*Armament:* One/two 13mm A.A. (2 × 1) guns, two 18inch
  torpedoes
*Complement:* 12
*Notes:* Built 1938–40 and former *MAS.525, 549, 524, 550, 502,
  504, 505, 508–510* and *512*

## *Ex-RIt.N MTBs:* **S.602–604, 624** *and* **625**

*Displacement:* 13 tons
*Dimensions:* 52½(oa) × 10½ × 3½ feet
*Machinery:* Three-shaft petrol motors, B.H.P. 1,500 = 40 knots
*Bunkers:* Petrol
*Armament:* two 8mm A.A. (2 × 1) guns, two 18inch torpedoes
*Complement:* 12
*Notes:* Built 1935–6 and former *MAS.430, 431, 423, 424* and *437*

## *Ex-RIt.N:* **SA.1–3** *(first group)*, **4–7** *(second group)*

*Displacement:* 63 tons (*first group*), 66 tons (*second group*)
    (75 tons full)
*Dimensions:* $91\frac{3}{4}$(oa) × 14 × 5 feet
*Machinery:* Three-shaft Isotta-Fraschini petrol motors, B.H.P.
    3,450/3,000 = 33/31 knots
*Bunkers & Radius:* Petrol 9 tons; 300 miles at 30 knots
*Armament:* Two 20mm A.A. (2 × 1) guns, two 21inch (2 × 1
    fixed) T.T., two 18inch torpedoes (*second group* only)
*Complement:* 14
*Notes:* Built 1941–3. Former *MS.16, 34, 36, 51, 63, 71* and *76*,
    and design generally similar to German MTBs except that the
    T.T. forward were not enclosed by a fo'c'sle deck

## *Ex-RN MTB:* **RA.10**

*Displacement:* 45 tons (52 tons full)
*Dimensions:* 77(oa) × 20 × $5\frac{1}{2}$ feet
*Machinery:* Three-shaft Packard petrol motors, B.H.P. 4,050/
    3,600 = 45/40 knots
*Bunkers:* Petrol 8 tons
*Armament:* One 20mm A.A., four .5inch A.A. (1 × 2 and 2 × 1)
    guns, two 21inch (2 × 1 fixed) T.T.
*Complement:* 12
*Notes:* Built 1942 and former *MTB.314* (ex-*BPT.8*, ex-USN
    *PT.56*)

## *MTBs:* **LS.1–20**

*Displacement:* $11\frac{1}{2}$ tons
*Dimensions:* $41\frac{1}{4}$(oa) × $10\frac{3}{4}$ × $2\frac{3}{4}$ feet
*Machinery:* Two-shaft Daimler-Benz diesel motors, B.H.P. 1,400
    except *LS.1, 5* and *6* Junkers diesel motors, B.H.P. 1,700 =
    $42\frac{1}{2}$ knots
*Bunkers & Radius:* O.F.; 300 miles at 30 knots
*Armament:* One 20mm A.A. gun, two 17.7inch (2 × 1 fixed) T.T.
    except *LS.2* and *3* three/four mines
*Complement:* 6
*Notes:* Built 1940–5

## *MTBs:* **KS.201–220**

*Displacement:* 13 tons
*Dimensions:* $43\frac{3}{4}$(oa) × $11\frac{1}{2}$ × $2\frac{3}{4}$ feet
*Machinery:* Two-shaft petrol motors, B.H.P. 1,500 = 33 knots
*Bunkers & Radius:* Petrol; 100 miles at 30 knots
*Armament:* Two 21inch (2 × 1 fixed) T.T.
*Complement:* 6
*Notes:* Built 1945

# *Motor Torpedo Boats—Summary of Losses and Fates*

*Lost:*

**1940**    *S.21\*, S.32*
**1941**    *S.38, S.41, S.43, S.106, LS.2, LS.3*
**1942**    *S.1(ii), S.27, S.31, S.35, S.37, S.53, S.111, LS.7–11*
**1943**    *S.29, S.34, S.46, S.56, S.59, S.63, S.74, S.75, S.88, S.96,*
         *S.102, S.104, S.121, S.172, S.603, S.623, LS.4, RA.10*
**1944**    *S.2(ii)–5(ii), S.14, S.17, S.18, S.22, S.23, S.26, S.28,*
         *S.33, S.40, S.42, S.44, S.45, S.47, S.49, S.51, S.52, S.54,*
         *S.55, S.57, S.66, S.70–72, S.77, S.80, S.84, S.87, S.90,*
         *S.91, S.94, S.100, S.108, S.112, S.114, S.119, S.128, S.129,*
         *S.131, S.134, S.136–144, S.146–150, S.153, S.158,*
         *S.169–171, S.173, S.178, S.179, S.182–185, S.187–190,*
         *S.192, S.194, S.198, S.200, S.501–507, S.601, S.602, S.604,*
         *S.624–629, S.702, SA.11, SA.12*
**1945**    *S.36, S.58, S.60, S.61, S.93, S.103, S.116, S.154, S.157,*
         *S.167, S.176, S.177, S.180, S.181, S.186, S.191, S.193,*
         *S.199, S.201(ii), S.202(ii), S.203, S.213, S.220, S.223,*
         *S.224, S.226, S.301, S.508–512, S.621, S.701, S.703*

*Transferred:*

**Spanish Navy**    *S.2–5 (1936), S.73, S.78, S.124, S.125, S.126,*
                  *S.145 (1943)*
**RBul.N**    *S.155–158, S.201, S.202 (1942)*
**RRoum.N**    *S.151–154 (1942)*

*Uncompleted:*    *S.229–243, S.308–328, S.622, S.710–715, SA.1–7,*
               *SA.13–21, LS.1, KS.203–211, KS.214, KS.216–218*

*Cancelled:*    *S.159–166, S.244–266, S.329–425, S.716–748*

*Projected:*    *S.267–300, S.426–500, S.749–800*

*Surrendered:*

**RN**    *S.6–8, S.13, S.19, S.20, S.25, S.39, S.62, S.67,*
       *S.69, S.83, S.89, S.92, S.95, S.105, S.115, S.120,*
       *S.130, S.168, S.195 (= RNN, RDN Lommen),*
       *S.196, S.204, S.205, S.207 (= RDN, T.61,*
       *Skaden), S.208 (= MTB.5208), S.212 (=*
       *MTB.5212), S.215, S.217, S.221, S.228, S.303*
       *(= RNN, RDN Taarnfalken), S.304, S.307,*
       *S.705*
**USN**    *S.9 (= RNN Blink), S.10 (= RNN Brand),*
        *S.12 (= RNN Kjekk), S.15 (= RDN T.60),*
        *S.21, S.48 (= RNN Kvikk (ii) ), S.64 (= RNN*
        *Lynn, RDN Stormfuglen), S.68 (= RDN T.62,*
        *Viven), S.76 (RNN Lynn), S.79 (= RDN T.58,*
        *Musyaagen), S.85 (= RNN Storm, RDN*
        *Trannen), S.97 (= RDN T.63, Ravnen), S.98*
        *(= RNN, Kvikk (i) ), S.107 (= RDN T.52,*
        *Gribben), S.117 (= RNN Tross, RDN Hejren),*
        *S.122 (= RDN T.64), S.127 (= RDN T.56,*

|  |  |
|---|---|
|  | *Isfuglen), S.133 (= RDN T.54, Haerfuglen), S.174 (= RDN Rap), S.197 (= RDN T.59, Raagen), S.206 (= RDN T.55, Hogen), S.210 (= RNN Snar), S.216 (= RDN T.53, Havornen), S.218, S.225, S.302 (= RNN, RDN Falken), S.305 (= RDN T.57, Jagtfalken), S.306 (= RDN T.51, Glenten), S.706* |
| **Russian Navy** | *S.11, S.16, S.24, S.50, S.65, S.81, S.82, S.86, S.99, S.101, S.109, S.110, S.113, S.118, S.123, S.132, S.135, S.175, S.209, S.211, S.214, S.219, S.222, S.227, S.704, S.707–709, LS.12* |
| **French Navy** | *LS.14–20* |
| **Unallocated** | *S.30, S.151, S.152, S.155, S.146, LS.5, LS.6, LS.13, KS.201, KS.202, KS.212, KS.213, KS.215, KS.219, KS.220* |
| *Scrapped:* | *S.1* (pre-war) |

* Later salved.

# Motor Minesweepers

*MMSs:* **R.1–16**

*Displacement:* 60 tons
*Dimensions:* 85¼(oa) × 14½ × 4 feet
*Machinery:* Two-shaft MWM diesel motors, B.H.P. 700 =
    17 knots
*Bunkers & Radius:* O.F. 6 tons; 800 miles at 13 knots
*Armament:* One 20mm A.A. gun
*Complement:* 18
*Notes:* Launched 1929–34. *R.8* fitted with two Voith Schneider
    propellers and electric motors. Armament later increased to
    four 20mm A.A. (2 × 2) guns

*Minesweepers of the* R.1–16
*group in Norwegian waters.*
(Drüppel)

R.19 *was a later flush-decked type of minesweeper. Note the black patch over the diesel exhaust.* (Drüppel)

## *MMSs:* **R.17–24**

*Displacement:* 115 tons
*Dimensions:* 121½(oa) × 18 × 4¼ feet
*Machinery:* Two-shaft M.A.N. or MWM diesel motors, B.H.P.
1,800 = 21 knots
*Bunkers & Radius:* O.F. 10 tons; 1,100 miles at 15 knots
*Armament:* Two 20mm A.A. (2 × 1) guns
*Complement:* 34
*Notes:* Launched 1934–38. All fitted with two Voith Schneider
propellers and electric motors. Armament later increased to
four 20mm A.A. (2 × 2) guns

## *MMSs:* **R.25–40**

*Displacement:* 110 tons
*Dimensions:* 116¼(oa) × 18¼ × 4½ feet
*Machinery:* Two-shaft M.A.N. diesel motors, B.H.P. 1,800 =
21 knots
*Bunkers & Radius:* O.F. 10 tons; 1,100 miles at 15 knots
*Armament:* Two 20mm A.A. (2 × 1) guns
*Complement:* 34
*Notes:* Launched 1938–39. All fitted with two Voith Schneider
propellers and electric motors. Armament later increased to
four 20mm A.A. (2 × 2) guns

## *MMSs:* **R.41–129**

*Displacement:* 125 tons
*Dimensions:* 124(oa) × 19 × 4½ feet
*Machinery:* Two-shaft M.A.N. diesel motors, B.H.P. 1,800 =
20 knots
*Bunkers & Radius:* O.F. 10 tons; 1,100 miles at 15 knots
*Armament:* One 37mm A.A. gun
*Complement:* 34
*Notes:* Launched 1939–43. All fitted with two Voith Schneider
propellers and electric motors. Three/six 20mm A.A. (3 × 1/2)
guns added

*Motor minesweeper* R.34.
(Drüppel)

*Motor minesweeper* R.48.
(Drüppel)

## *MMSs:* **R.130–150**

*Displacement:* 150 tons
*Dimensions:* 134¾(oa) × 19 × 5¼ feet
*Machinery:* Two-shaft M.A.N. diesel motors, B.H.P. 1,800 =
  19 knots
*Bunkers & Radius:* O.F. 11 tons; 1,000 miles at 15 knots
*Armament:* One 37mm A.A. gun
*Complement:* 38
*Notes:* Launched 1943–44. Three/six 20mm A.A. (3 × 1/2) guns
  added

## *MMSs:* **R.151–172**

*Displacement:* 125 tons
*Dimensions:* 116¼(oa) × 18¼ × 4½ feet
*Machinery:* Two-shaft M.A.N. diesel motors, B.H.P. 1,800 =
  21 knots
*Bunkers & Radius:* O.F. 10 tons; 1,100 miles at 15 knots
*Armament:* One 37mm A.A. gun
*Complement:* 34
*Notes:* Launched 1940–43. Three/six 20mm A.A. (3 × 1/2) guns
  added

## *MMSs:* **R.182–300**

*Displacement:* 140 tons
*Dimensions:* $128\frac{1}{2}$(oa) × $18\frac{3}{4}$ × 5 feet
*Machinery:* Two-shaft M.A.N. diesel motors, B.H.P. 2,550 =
    21 knots
*Bunkers & Radius:* O.F. 15 tons; 1,000 miles at 15 knots
*Armament:* One 37mm A.A. gun
*Complement: 38*
*Notes:* Launched 1943–45. Three/six 20mm A.A. (3 × 1/2)
    guns


## *MMSs:* **R.301–400**

*Displacement:* 175 tons
*Dimensions:* $134\frac{1}{2}$(oa) × $19\frac{3}{4}$ × 6 feet
*Machinery:* Two-shaft M.A.N. diesel motors, B.H.P. 2,550 =
    24 knots
*Bunkers & Radius:* O.F. $16\frac{1}{2}$ tons; 1,100 miles at 15 knots
*Armament:* One 37mm A.A., three/six 20mm A.A. (3 × 1/2)
    guns
*Complement:* 38
*Notes:* Launched 1942–45. Were later re-classed as *GR.301* up
    and two 21inch (2 × 1) T.T. were added


## *MMSs:* **R.401–448**

*Displacement:* 140 tons
*Dimensions:* $128\frac{1}{2}$(oa) × $18\frac{3}{4}$ × 5 feet
*Machinery:* Two-shaft M.A.N. diesel motors, B.H.P. 2,550 =
    21 knots
*Bunkers & Radius:* O.F. $16\frac{1}{2}$ tons; 1,100 miles at 15 knots
*Armament:* One 37mm A.A., six 20mm A.A. (3 × 2) guns
*Complement:* 38
*Notes:* Launched 1943–45


## *Ex-RNeth.N MMSs:* **RA.51–56**

*Displacement:* 125 tons
*Dimensions:* 124(oa) × 19 × $4\frac{1}{2}$ feet
*Machinery:* Two-shaft M.A.N. diesel motors, B.H.P. 1,800 =
    20 knots
*Bunkers & Radius:* O.F. 10 tons; 1,100 miles at 15 knots
*Armament:* One 37mm A.A., three 20mm A.A. (3 × 1) guns
*Complement:* 34
*Notes:* Launched 1940 and were former *Mv.I–VI*

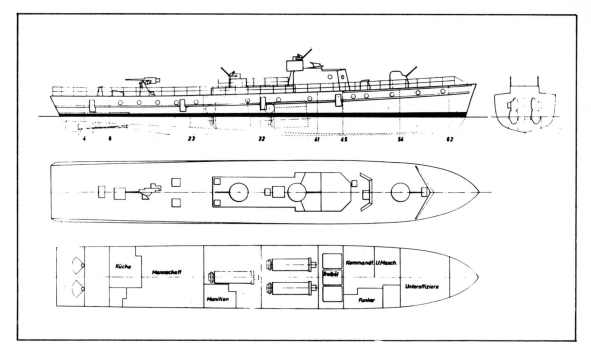

*General Arrangement of Escort Motor Launches GR.301–312, formerly R.301–312.*

## *MMSs:* **FR.1–12**

*Displacement:* 21 tons
*Dimensions:* 57(oa) × 10½ × 2¼ feet
*Machinery:* Two-shaft Kamper diesel motors, B.H.P.
    300 = 13 knots
*Bunkers:* O.F. 1 ton
*Armament:* One 20mm A.A. gun
*Complement:* 10
*Notes:* Launched 1938–39

## *MMSs:* **MR.1–10**

*Displacement:* 23 tons
*Dimensions:* 60¾(oa) × 13¾ × 3¼ feet
*Machinery:* Two-shaft diesel motors, B.H.P. 300 = 12 knots
*Armament:* One 20mm A.A. gun
*Complement:* 8
*Notes:* Launched 1939–40

# *Motor Minesweepers—Summary of Losses and Fates*

*Lost:*

**1939**  *R.5*

**1940**  *R.17*

**1941**  *R.60–62, R.158, R.169, FR.5, FR.6, FR.12, MR.7, RA.53, RA.55*

**1942**  *R.11, R.41, R.42, R.45, R.66, R.77, R.78, R.82, R.86, R.106, R.109, R.184*

**1943**  *R.1\*, R.6, R.7, R.9, R.13, R.19, R.30, R.33, R.36, R.40, R.44, R.54, R.56, R.64, R.74, R.84, R.93, R.94, R.114, R.186, R.306\**

**1944**  *R.12, R.20, R.27, R.29, R.34, R.35, R.37, R.38, R.39, R.43\*, R.46, R.50, R.51, R.70, R.73, R.75, R.79–81, R.89, R.92, R.95, R.97, R.108, R.110, R.111, R.116, R.119, R.123, R.125, R.129, R.131, R.139, R.141, R.151, R.161, R.163–166, R.171, R.178–180, R.182, R.185, R.187\*, R.188, R.190–197, R.200, R.201, R.203–211, R.213, R.215–219, R.221, R.222, R.224\*, R.232, R.235, R.237, R.248, R.250, R.301, R.304, R.402, FR.2, FR.11, RA.51, RA.52, RA.54, RA.56*

**1945**  *R.3, R.8\*, R.14, R.15, R.57, R.59, R.69, R.72, R.85, R.88, R.104, R.112, R.126, R.145, R.159, R.162, R.177, R.183, R.189, R.198, R.199, R.202, R.212, R.224, R.227, R.228, R.239, R.243, R.247, R.256, R.260, R.261, R.272–276, FR.8*

| | |
|---|---|
| *Scuttled:* | *R.112, R.228* |
| *Uncompleted:* | *R.271, R.291–300, R.425–427* |
| *Cancelled:* | *R.277–287, R.313–320, R.428–448, MR.8–10* |
| *Projected:* | *R.321–400* |

*Surrendered:*

**R.N.**          *R.18* (= RDN), *R.21, R.25, R.26* (= RDN), *R.31, R.32* (= RDN), *R.47–49, R.83, R.115* (= *ML.6115*), *R.118, R.143* (= RDN), *R.152–157* (= all RDN), *R.160* (= RDN), *R.167* (= RDN), *R.168* (= RDN), *R.170* (= RDN), *R.173–176* (= all RDN), *R.181* (= RDN), *R.124* (= RDN), *R.220* (= RNeth.N *Walcheren*), *R.225* (= RDN), *R.226* (= RDN), *R.229–231* (= all RDN), *R.233* (= RDN), *R.236* (= RDN), *R.240* (= RNeth.N *Goeree*), *R.242* (= RDN), *R.244* (= RNeth.N *Schouwen*), *R.246* (= RNeth.N *Schiermonnikoog*), *R.251* (= RNeth.N *Urk*), *R.252* (= RNeth.N *Stortemelk*), *R.255* (= RNeth.N *Schulpengat*), *R.259* (= RDN), *R.268* (= RNeth.N *Malzwin*), *R.290* (= RNeth.N. *Vlieter*), *R.424* (= RNeth.N *Roompot*)

| | |
|---|---|
| **USN** | *R.22, R.24, R.43, R.52, R.55, R.67* (= W. German *R.130*), *R.68* (= W. German *R.143*), *R.71, R.76* (= W. German *R.145*), *R.91* (= W. German *R.131*), *R.96, R.98, R.99* (= W. German *R.148*), *R.100, R.101* (= W. German *R.149*), *R.102, R.117, R.120* (= W. German *R.139*), *R.127* (= W. German *R.141*), *R.128* (= W. German *R.151*), *R.130, R.132, R.132–138* (= W. German *R.132–138*), *R.140* (= W. German *R.140*), *R.142* (= W. German *R.142*), *R.144* (= W. German *R.144*), *R.146* (= W. German *R.146*), *R.147* (= W. German *R.147*), *R.148, R.150* (= W. German *R.150*), *R.241, R.249, R.253, R.264, R.266* (= W. German *R.152*), *R.267, R.401, R.403* (= W. German *Rewo I*), *R.404* (= W. German *Rewo II*), *R.405, R.406* (= W. German *R.154*), *R.407* (= W. German *R.153*), *R.408* (= W. German *R.155*) |
| **Russian Navy** | *R.23, R.28, R.53, R.58, R.63, R.65, R.87, R.90, R.103, R.105, R.107, R.113, R.121, R.122, R.124, R.149, R.234, R.238, R.245, R.254, R.257, R.258, R.262, R.263, R.265, R.269, R.270, R.288, R.289, R.302, R.303, R.305, R.307, R.308, R.310–312, R.409–423* |
| **RYN** | *R.4, R.8, R.10, R.16, R.187* |
| **Unallocated** | *R.2, R.172, R.223, R.306, R.309, FR.1, FR.3, FR.7, FR.9, FR.10, MR.1–6* |

\* Later salved.

# Minelayers and Miscellaneous Small Craft

## *Ex-French MLs:* **RA.1–8**

*Displacement:* 107 tons (135 tons full)
*Dimensions:* $121\frac{1}{4}$(pp) $139\frac{1}{2}$(oa) $\times$ 17 $\times$ 2 feet
*Machinery:* Two-shaft M.A.N. diesel motors, B.H.P. 1,100 =
   16 knots
*Bunkers & Radius:* O.F. $4\frac{1}{2}$ tons; 1,200 miles at 9 knots
*Armament:* One 37mm A.A., three 20mm A.A. (3 × 1) guns
*Complement:* 39
*Notes:* Former submarine chasers *CH.17–23* and *44–46* built
   1939–40. Armament later increased to one 37mm or 40mm
   A.A., six 20mm A.A. (1 × 4 and 2 × 1) guns

## *Ex-RN ML:* **RA.9**

*Displacement:* 65 tons
*Dimensions:* 112(oa) × 8 × 5 feet
*Machinery:* Two-shaft Hall-Scott petrol motors, B.H.P. 1,200 =
   20 knots
*Bunkers & Radius:* Petrol 11 tons; 2,000 miles at 10 knots
*Armament:* One 40mm A.A., three 20mm A.A. (3 × 1) guns
*Complement:* 18
*Notes:* Former *ML.306* built 1941

## *Danish type MLs:* **RA.101–105**

*Displacement:* 70 tons
*Dimension:* $94\frac{3}{4}$(oa) × $14\frac{1}{2}$ × $9\frac{1}{4}$ feet
*Machinery:* Two-shaft MWM diesel motors, B.H.P. 700 =
   16 knots
*Bunkers & Radius:* O.F. 6 tons; 1,000 miles at 13 knots
*Armament:* Two 15mm A.A. (2 × 1) guns
*Complement:* 18

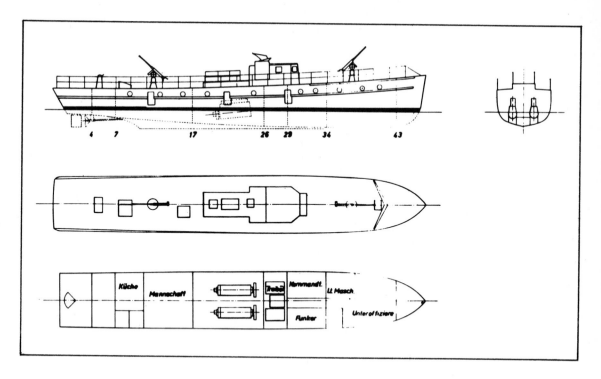

*General Arrangement of Danish type Motor Launches RA.101–102.*

## Danish type MLs: **RA. 106–112**

*Displacement:* 80 tons
*Dimensions:* $98\frac{1}{2}$(oa) × $15\frac{1}{2}$ × $9\frac{1}{4}$ feet
*Machinery:* Two-shaft MWM diesel motors, B.H.P. 700 = 16 knots
*Bunkers & Radius:* O.F. 6 tons; 1,000 miles at 13 knots
*Armament:* Two 15mm A.A. (2 × 1) guns
*Complement:* 18
*Notes:* Built 1942–3 (*RA.101–105*), and built 1943–5 (*RA.106–112*)

## Norwegian type MLs: **RA.201–204**

*Displacement:* ca. 30 tons
*Dimensions:* 82(oa) × $14\frac{3}{4}$ × $4\frac{1}{2}$ feet
*Machinery:* Two-shaft MWM diesel motors, B.H.P. 700 = 14 knots
*Bunkers & Radius:* O.F. 6 tons; 1,000 miles at 13 knots
*Armament:* Two 20mm A.A. (2 × 1) guns
*Complement:* 18
*Notes:* Built 1940–1

## *Ex-RIt.N MLs:* **RA.251–268**

*Displacement:* 69 tons
*Dimensions:* $91\frac{3}{4}$(oa) × $15\frac{1}{2}$ × 4 feet
*Machinery:* Three-shaft Fiat (wing shafts) and Carraro (centre shaft) petrol motors, B.H.P. 1,850 = 19 knots
*Bunkers & Radius:* Petrol $11\frac{3}{4}$ tons; 1,000 miles at 10 knots
*Armament:* Three 20mm A.A. (3 × 1) guns
*Complement:* 26
*Notes:* Former MA/SBs *VAS. 306, 305, 307, 301, 304, 303, 302, 309, 311, 312, 236, 239, 308, 310, 240–243* built 1944–5

## *Italian type MLs:* **RD.101–149**

*Displacement:* 101 tons
*Dimensions:* $111\frac{1}{2}$(oa) × 19 × $4\frac{1}{2}$ feet
*Machinery:* Two-shaft Isotta-Fraschini petrol motors, B.H.P. 2,300 except *RD.113* and *149* Fiat diesel motors (two per shaft), B.H.P. 2,000 = 20 knots
*Bunkers & Radius:* Petrol or O.F. $11\frac{3}{4}$ tons; 1,000 miles at 10 knots except *RD.113* and *149* 2,000 miles at 13 knots
*Armament:* One 20mm A.A. gun
*Complement:* 30
*Notes:* Built 1944–6

## *MMLs:* **KM.1–36**

*Displacement: ca.* 16 tons
*Dimensions:* $52\frac{1}{2}$(oa) × $10\frac{1}{2}$ × $3\frac{1}{2}$ feet
*Machinery:* Two-shaft BMW petrol motors, B.H.P. 1,300 = 32 knots
*Bunkers & Radius:* Petrol $2\frac{1}{4}$ tons; 280 miles at 24 knots
*Armament:* Two 8mm A.A. (2 × 1) guns, four mines
*Complement:* 8
*Notes:* Built 1942. Later reclassed as MTBs and re-numbered *KS.1–36* when mines replaced by two 18inch (2 × 1) T.T.

## *Hydrofoils:* **TS.1–6**

*Displacement:* $6\frac{1}{4}$ tons (full)
*Dimensions:* $39\frac{1}{4}$(oa) × $12\frac{1}{2}$ × 3 feet
*Machinery:* One-shaft Lorrain petrol motor, B.H.P. 380 = 40 knots
*Armament:* One 15mm A.A. gun
*Complement: 4*
*Notes:* Built 1940–1

# *Experimental boats:* **VS.1–5**

Cancelled projects for which no details are available

# *Hydrofoils:* **VS.6** *and* **7**

*Displacement:* 17 tons (full)
*Dimensions:* $51\frac{1}{2}$(oa) × $17\frac{1}{2}$ × $3\frac{1}{4}$ feet
*Machinery:* One-shaft Avia petrol motor, B.H.P. 1,400 =
   47 knots
*Armament:* Four mines
*Complement:* 8
*Notes:* Built 1941 and used as patrol craft

# *Hydrofoils:* **VS.8** *and* **9**

*Displacement:* 80 tons (full)
*Dimensions:* $104\frac{3}{4}$(oa) × $33\frac{3}{4}$ × $6\frac{1}{2}$ feet
*Machinery:* Two-shaft Daimler-Benz diesel motors, B.H.P.
   5,000 = 45 knots
*Bunkers & Radius:* O.F.; 200 miles at 45 knots
*Armament.:* Four 20mm A.A. (4 × 1) guns, one 26-ton tank
   *Complement:* 12
*Notes:* Built 1943 as fast transports for the Mediterranean

# *Hydrofoils:* **VS.10** *and* **14**

*Displacement:* 40 tons (full)
*Dimensions:* $80\frac{3}{4}$(oa) feet
*Machinery:* Two-shaft Isotta-Faschini petrol motors (two per
   shaft), B.H.P. 6,000 = 60 knots in *VS.10,* two-shaft Daimler-
   Benz diesel motors, B.H.P. 5,000 = 55 knots in *VS.14*
*Armament:* six 20mm A.A. (3 × 2) guns, two 18inch or 21inch
   (2 × 1 fixed) T.T.
*Complement:* 12

# *Experimental boats:* **VS.11** *and* **12**

Explosive motor boats of 3 tons

# *Experimental boat:* **VS.13**

Cancelled project for which no details are available

## Miscellaneous Small Craft—Summary of Losses and Fates

*Lost:*
**1943**   *KM.7, KM.27, KM.28, KM.30*
**1944**   *RA.2–9, RA.251, RA.255–257, RA.259, RD.110, KM.5\**
**1945**   *RA.252–254, RA.258, RA.260–264, RD.101, RD.109,*
         *RD.111–114, RD.147, VS.10*

*Uncompleted:*   *RA.265–268, RD.102–108, RD.116–122, RD.127–*
              *136, RD.148, RD.149, VS.14*

*Cancelled:*     *RD.123–126, RD.137–146, VS.1–5, VS.9, VS.13*

*Surrendered:*
**RN**           *TS.1–6*
**USN**          *RA.106, RA.107*
**Russian Navy** *RA.111, RA.112, KM.1–6, KM.9–12, KM.17–19,*
              *KM.20–29, VS.8*
**French Navy**  *RA.1, RA.2*
**RNN**          *RA.201–204*
**RYN**          *RD.115*
**Unallocated**  *RA.101–105, RA.108–110, KM.8, KM.13–16,*
              *KM.31–36, VS.6, VS.7, VS.11, VS.12*

## Builders

Abeking & Rasmussen (Lemwerder): *R.2–7, 9–14, 18–23, 25–37,*
   *44–150, 301–312, 401–424; MR.1–4, 8–10*
Ansaldo (Genoa): *RA.251–268*
Binnenwerften: *KS.201, 202, 212, 213, 215, 219, 220*
Burmester (Lessum): *R.151–193, 200–233, 238–247, 254–263*
      (Swinemünde): *R.194–199, 234–237, 248–253, 264–288*
Cant. Riuniti dell' Adriatico (Monfalcone): *S.501–507, 510–512,*
   *621, 623, 629; SA.1–7*
Danziger Waggonfabrik: *S.701–708*
De Vries Lentsch (Amsterdam): *RA.51–56*
Dornier (Friedrichshafen): *LS.2–20*
Electric Boat (Bayonne): *RA.10*
Fges. & Ch. de la Mediterranée (St. Nazaire): *RA.6–8*
Gusto (Schiedam): *S.151–166, 201, 202*
Italian yards: *S.508, 509, 601–604, 622, 624–628; SA.11–21;*
   *RA.251–268; RD.101–149*
Lürssen (Vegesack): *S.1–100, 134–148, 150, 167–186, 195–218,*
   *301–307, S.1(ii)–5(ii); R.1, 8; FR.1–12*
Mjellen & Karlsen (Bergen): *RA.201–204*
Naglo (Berlin): *LS.1*
Ch. de la Normandie (Fecamp): *RA.1–5*
Rasmussen (Svendborg): *RA.101–112*
Rolandwerft (Hemelingen): *MR.5–7; KM.1–36*

Gebr. Saschenberg (Harburg): *TS.1–6; VS.8–14*
Schiffswerft (Donau and Linz): *S.149*
Schlichting (Travemünde): *S.101–133, 187–194, 219–228; R.15–17, 24, 38–43, 289, 290*
Solent Shipyard (Sarisbury Green): *RA.9*
Vertens (Schleswig): *VS.7*
AG Weser (Bremerhaven): *VS.5*
Builders unknown: *VS.1–5, KS.203–211, 214, 216, 218*


\* Later salved.

# Motor Fishing Vessels

*A typical* KFK *or drifter.*
(Drüppel)

## *MFVs:* **KFK.1–1000**

A very large programme of MFVs, based on their commercial counterpart, was embarked on for the many and varied tasks these vessels could undertake—principally patrol, anti submarine, minesweeping, and coastal escort work. Building contracts were placed all over the Continent as well as in Germany for these craft, and large numbers remained incomplete at the end of the war.

*Displacement:* ca. 110 tons
*Dimensions:* 78¾(wl) × 21 × 8¾ feet
*Machinery:* One shaft diesel motor, B.H.P. 150 = 9 knots
*Bunkers & Radius:* O.F.; 1,200 miles at 7 knots
*Armament:* One 37mm A.A., four 20mm A.A. (4 × 1) guns
*Notes:*Built 1943–5. A total of one hundred and seventy-five were lost, one interned in Sweden, eighty-two were not completed, and three hundred and sixty cancelled. On the termination of hostilities one hundred and one were allocated to the USN, one hundred and forty-seven to the Russian Navy, fifty-six to other Allied navies, and one hundred and forty-six remained in German hands–seven as naval vessels and the remainder sold out commercially

# Summary of War Losses

*Lost:*
**1941**   KFK.175‡
**1943**   KFK.2, 4–30, 31,*32–49, 196, 200, 249, 262–268, 270
**1944**   KFK.3, 52, 81, 83–93, 99, 102, 155, 156‡,*163‡, 164–166,
174, 177, 190, 193‡, 197, 201, 202, 209, 218, 255, 261, 273,
275, 276, 278‡, 279, 280, 288, 290, 303, 307, 324, 330, 331,
355, 357, 358, 368,*375‡, 393, 427, 477, 482, 493, 494,
496, 506, 510‡, 512‡, 515‡, 540
**1945**   KFK.61, 128, 140, 152, 169, 181, 182, 191, 298 (interned),
299, 300, 309‡, 325, 333, 390, 398, 532, 541‡, 543, 546‡,
547–550, 553‡, 677 (incomplete), 679 (incomplete),
689 (incomplete), 683–699 (incomplete), 744

**Date unknown**
KFK.53, 54, 58, 115, 136, 137, 167, 203, 204, 295, 296, 334,
346, 412

*Uncompleted:*   KFK.418–423, 437, 438, 562–600, 604–611, 637,
642–655, 657, 660, 661, 669–673, 675, 678, 681,
682

*Cancelled:*   KFK.700–739, 753–1072

*Transferred:*
**RRoum.N**   KFK.198, 199, 270

*Surrendered:*
**USN**   KFK.1*, 50*, 51*, 60*, 63*, 64*, 104*, 125*, 131*,
133*, 142*–147*, 159*, 175*, 184*, 185*, 186
187*, 188*, 213*, 215*, 216*, 219*, 227*, 232*,
233*, 235*, 238*, 246*–248*, 250*, 252*, 253*,
256*, 257*, 259*, 281*–287*, 291*, 293*, 294
(=W. German), 301*, 326*, 338, 363*, 365*,
366*, 368*, 370*, 375, 376 (= W. German), 377
(= W. German), 387, 395*–397*, 411*, 413*,
416*, 431*, 465*, 468, 469*, 472*, 478*, 480*,
481*, 483*–486*, 488*, 510*, 513*, 515, 525*,
529*, 534*, 544*, 545*, 554*, 612*, 614*, 621*,
622*, 626*, 627*, 633*, 639*–641*

**Russian Navy**   KFK.55–57, 67–71, 73, 75, 80, 97, 98, 106, 111,
113, 114, 116, 118–122, 126, 130, 132, 134, 139,
141, 148, 149, 151, 154, 160, 161, 168, 170–173,
176, 178, 179, 194, 205, 206, 211, 212, 221, 222,
225, 226, 229–231, 243, 245, 254, 271, 272, 302,
304–306, 308, 310–314, 339, 341–345, 347–349,
352–354, 361, 362, 367, 374, 378, 383–386, 391,
399–402, 404, 408, 415, 424, 426, 428–430, 439,
440, 442, 444, 445, 448, 452–456, 471, 475, 489,
490, 497, 498, 501, 507, 509, 511, 514, 516, 520,
527, 528, 535, 536, 542, 546, 548–550, 556–559,
601, 603, 636, 659, 663, 664, 676, 749

**RN**   KFK.94*, 105*, 108*, 153*, 157*, 158*, 228*,
236*, 240*, 309* (= W. German W.1), 321*,
336*, 337*, 356*, 382*, 389*, 392*, 394*, 406*,

|  |  |
|---|---|
|  | *462\*, 464\*, 474\*, 495\*, 499\*, 500\*, 503\*, 526\*, 537\*, 541\*, 561\* (= W. German W.3), 613\*, 615\*, 617\*, 623\*, 625\*, 743\** |
| **RDN** | *KFK.751* |
| **RNN** | *KFK.96, 100, 101, 103, 112, 117, 123, 192, 466* |
| **French Navy** | *KFK.59, 62, 65, 66, 72, 74, 76–79* |
| **Unallocated** | *KFK.95, 107, 109, 110, 124, 127, 129, 135, 138, 150, 162, 180, 183, 189\*, 195, 196, 201, 207, 208, 210, 214 (= W. German Atair), 217 (= W. German Vega), 220, 223, 224, 234, 237, 239, 241, 242, 244, 251, 258, 260, 269\*, 274, 277, 278, 289, 292, 297, 315, 316, 318, 319, 322, 323, 327–329, 332, 334, 335, 340, 350, 351, 359, 360\*, 369, 373\*, 379–381, 403, 405, 407, 409 (= W. German), 410, 417\*, 425, 432–436, 441, 443, 446, 447, 449–451, 457, 459–461, 463, 467, 470, 473, 476, 479, 487, 491 (= W. German Südfall), 492 (= W. German Uthorn), 502, 504, 505, 508, 512, 517–519, 522–524, 530, 531 = W. German, 533, 538, 539, 551\*, 552, 553, 555, 560, 602, 616 (= W. German), 618–620, 624, 629–632, 635, 638, 656, 658, 662, 665–668, 674, 740–742, 745–748, 750–752* |
| *Scuttled:* | *KFK.325* |
| **Fate unknown:** | *KFK.82, 317, 320, 364, 371, 372, 388, 414, 458, 521, 628, 634* |

\* Later mercantile.

\* Later salved.

## Builders

Abrahamson (Ramsö): *KFK.104, 105*
Aegean Sea yards: *KFK. 2–16*
Gebr. Baas (Onderkerk): *KFK.62, 63*
Black Sea yards: *KFK.81–92*
Belgian & Netherlands yards: *KFK.412–438, 563, 573–612, 913–972*
Gebr. Burmester (Swinemünde): *KFK.138–137, 243–261, 263–411, 462–561, 613–641, 656–668, 674–699, 740–752*
Constr. Werkfl. (Enkuizen): *KFK.54–56*
Davidsonns (Sandvikshamn): *KFK.99*
De Haan & Orlemans (Heusden): *KFK.60, 61*
Sch. De Hoop (Amsterdam): *KFK.66, 67*
Jul. Deny (Ostend): *KFK.70, 71*
De Vries Lentsch (Amsterdam): *KFK.64, 65*
Eckmanns Werft (Hamburg): *KFK.1*
Fisksats (Saltsjobäden): *KFK.128–130*
E. Grabsels (Ostend): *KFK.68, 69*
Gustavson (Lidingö): KFK.114–116
Tore Holms (Gambleby): KFK.131–134
B.S. Jachtwerft (Zaandam): KFK.76–80

Karlshamns Skeepvarv: *KFK.135*
W. Kater (Amsterdam): *KFK.238–241*
Kerstholt (Groningen): *KFK.57–59*
Kherson yards: *KFK.38–49*
Kungsörs (Batvary): *KFK.117–120*
Larssons (Kristinehamn): *KFK.121–124*
Loy (Ostend): *KFK.75*
Lunds Skefs (Ekenes): *KFK.95–97*
Meyer (Papenburg): *KUj.13–18*
Neglingsvarvet (Saltsjobäden): *KFK.125–127*
Nobiskrug (Rendsburg): *KUj.7–12*
A/B Norköpping: *KFK.106, 107*
Ottenser Eisenwerk: *KUj.19, 20*
Provoost (Nieuport): *KFK.242*
Reihersteig (Hamburg): *KUj.21–25, 41, 42*
Rödesunts (Karlsborg): *KFK.111–113*
Saltviks (Oskarshamn): *KFK.98*
Sjötorps (Mariestad): *KFK.136, 137*
St. Pieter (Antwerp): *KFK.51–53*
A/B Sverre (Gothenburg): *KFK.108–110*
Timmer (Delfzijl): *KFK.74*
Unterweser (Bremerhaven): *KUj.1–6*
Valdemarsviks Slifsverv: *KFK.93, 94*
*Varna yards: KFK.17–37*
Vink Boom (Antwerp): *KFK.72, 73*
Yestadts Skepvarv: *KFK.100–103*

Builders unknown: *KFR.50, 262, 439–461, 562, 564–655,*
*669–673, 700–739, 753–912, 973* up

# Minesweepers

*Minesweeper type 1915 and 1916:* **M.61, 85, 132, 136, 502, 504, 507–511, 513, 515, 517, 522, 526, 528–530, 533–535, 538, 545, 546, 550, 557, 560, 566, 572, 575, 581, 582, 584, 589, 598**

These minesweepers all dated back to the First World War and belonged to a successful and reliable type that proved ideal vessels for their role. Initially retained for clearing the numerous minefields which had to be cleared after 1918, they were later converted to tenders for a wide variety of duties. Nearly all of them were, however, again used as minesweepers during the Second World War.

*Displacement:* 515 tons (690 tons full)
*Dimensions:* $183\frac{1}{2}$(pp) $194\frac{1}{2}$(oa) except *M.507, 526, 533–535, 538, 546, 560* $200\frac{3}{4}$(pp) $211\frac{3}{4}$(oa) $\times$ $27\frac{1}{4}$ $\times$ $6\frac{1}{2}/8\frac{1}{2}$ feet
*Machinery:* Two Schulz-Thornycroft boilers (not in *M.538*— pressure 242 lb.); two shafts; reciprocating (VTE) I.H.P. 1,850 = 14 knots, except *M.538* diesel motors, B.H.P. 1,600 = 14 knots
*Bunkers & Radius:* Coal 130/140 tons; 2,000 miles at 14 knots, except *M.507, 526, 533–535, 546, 560* coal 95 tons + O.F. 75 tons; 3,200 miles at 10 knots, and *M.538* O.F. 90 tons; 3,500 miles at 10 knots
*Armament:* Generally one 4.1inch, three 20mm A.A. ($3 \times 1$) guns
*Complement:* 51

**Name** *Pelikan* (ex-*M.28*) **Built by** Seebeckwerft (Geestemünde) **Launched** 6.5.16 **Fate** Experimental vessel, *M.528* (1940); USN 1945

**Name** *Brommy* (ex-*M.50*) **Built by** Seebeckwerft (Geestemünde) **Launched** 19.8.16 **Fate** Tender for MMSs, *M.550* (1940); torpedoed RN surface forces English Channel or bombed Allied aircraft Boulogne 15.6.44

**Name** *Hecht* (ex-*M.60*) **Built by** Seebeckwerft (Geestemünde) **Launched** 28.11.17 **Fate** Fleet tender, *Hille* (1939), *M.560* (1940); Russian 1945

**Name** *M.61* **Built by** Seebeckwerft (Geestemünde)
**Launched** 13.4.18 **Fate** Mined off Netherlands coast 26.7.40

**Name** *Stortebeker* (ex-*M.66*) **Built by** Tecklenborg (Geestemünde)
**Launched** 2.6.17 **Fate** Experimental vessel, *M.566* (1940); USN
1945

**Name** *M.72* **Built by** Bremer Vulkan (Vegesack) **Launched** 20.2.18
**Fate** *M.572* (1940); USN 1945

**Name** *M.75* **Built by** Tecklenborg (Geestemünde)
**Launched** 21.7.17 **Fate** *M.575* (1940); capsized The Sound 2.3.45

**Name** *Nautilis* (ex-*M.81*) **Built by** Seebeckwerft (Geestemünde)
**Launched** 8.9.19 **Fate** Experimental vessel, *M.581* (1940); USN
1945

**Name** *Jagd* (ex-*M.82*) **Built by** Seebeckwerft (Geestemünde)
**Launched** 8.9.19 **Fate** Fleet tender, *M.582* (1940); USN 1945;
scrapped Middlesbrough 21.4.48

**Name** *M.84* **Built by** Atlas Werke (Bremen) **Launched** 10.10.17
**Fate** *M.584* (1940); mined north of Zeeland 3.10.44

**Name** *M.85* **Built by** Nordseewerke (Emden) **Launched** 10.4.18
**Fate** Mined north of Heestermest 1.10.39

**Name** *M.89* **Built by** Tecklenborg (Geestemünde)
**Launched** 11.12.17 **Fate** *M.589* (1940); mined off Netherlands
coast 26.7.40

**Name** *M.98* **Built by** Tecklenborg (Geestemünde)
**Launched** 16.4.18 **Fate** *M.598* (1940); USN 1945

**Name** *M.102* **Built by** Atlas Werke (Bremen) **Launched** 1.6.18
**Fate** *M.502* (1940); USN 1945

**Name** *M.104* **Built by** Neptun Werft (Rostock) **Launched** 27.4.18
**Fate** *M.504* (1940); bombed RAF aircraft Kiel 9.4.45

**Name** *von der Groben* (ex-*M.107*) **Built by** Tecklenborg
(Geestemünde) **Launched** 7.3.18 **Fate** Tender to MMSs, *M.507*
(1940); bombed Allied aircraft Boulogne 15.6.44

**Name** *Delphin* (ex-*M.108*) **Built by** Tecklenborg (Geestemünde)
**Launched** 17.7.18 **Fate** Gunnery school tender, *M.508* (1940);
Russian 1945

**Name** *Sundewall* (ex-*Johann Wittenborg*, ex-*M.109*)
**Built by** Tecklenborg (Geestemünde) **Launched** 7.8.18
**Fate** Surveying vessel, *M.509* (1940); USN 1945

**Name** *M.110* **Built by** Tecklenborg (Geestemünde)
**Launched** 27.8.18 **Fate** *M.510* (1940); USN 1945

**Name** *M.111* **Built by** Tecklenborg (Geestemünde)
**Launched** 17.9.18 **Fate** *M.511* (1940); mined off Kolberg 9.41

**Name** *Acheron* (ex-*M.113*) **Built by** Stülcken (Hamburg)
**Launched** 27.5.19 **Fate** Submarine tender, *M.513* (1940); USN
(1945)

**Name** *Arkona* (ex-*M.115*) **Built by** Atlas Werke (Bremen) **Launched** 12.7.18 **Fate** Experimental vessel, *M.515* (1940); mined west of Fehmarn 22.5.44

**Name** *M.117* **Built by** Atlas Werke (Bremen) **Launched** 20.9.18 **Fate** *M.517* (1940); USN 1945

**Name** *M.122* **Built by** Neptun Werft (Rostock) **Launched** 21.9.18 **Fate** *M.522* (1940); paid-off and scrapped after being bombed Allied aircraft Kiel 20.3.45

**Name** *Alders* (ex-*M.126*) **Built by** Flensburger Schiffsbau **Launched** 21.11.18 **Fate** Tender for MMSs, *M.526* (1940); USN 1945

**Name** *Otto Braun* (ex-*M.129*) **Built by** Reiherstieg (Hamburg) **Launched** 15.1.19 **Fate** Experimental vessel, *M.529* (1940); mined off Kolberg 9.41

**Name** *Fuchs* (ex-*M.130*) **Built by** Reiherstieg (Hamburg) **Launched** 13.2.19 **Fate** Gunnery school tender, *M.530* (1940); Russian 1945

**Name** *M.132* **Built by** Reiherstieg (Hamburg) **Launched** 14.1.19 **Fate** Scuttled 13.11.39 after grounding

**Name** *Wacht* (ex-*M.133*) **Built by** Frerichs (Einswarden) **Launched** 1919 **Fate** *Raule* (1939), *M.533* (1940; lost collision with *R.45* off Dunkerque 9.5.42

*"M" Class sweepers and R-Boats carrying British troops to Heligoland after the German surrender.*

**Name** *Frauenlob* (ex-*M.134*) **Built by** Frerichs (Einswarden)
**Launched** 28.7.19 **Fate** Station tender, *Jungingden* (1939) tender
for MMSs, *M.534* (1940); bombed Allied aircraft Bergen 5.41,
salved and paid-off 27.9.43, USN 1945

**Name** *Gazelle* (ex-*M.135*) **Built by** Frerichs (Einswarden)
**Launched** 15.3.19 **Fate** Fleet tender, *M.535* (1940); Russian 1945

**Name** *Havel* (ex-*M.136*) **Built by** Frerichs (Einswarden)
**Launched** 1919 **Fate** Submarine tender, *M.136* (1940); mined off
Netherlands coast 26.7.40

**Name** *Nettelbeck* (ex-*Zieten*, ex-*M.138*) **Built by** Tecklenborg
(Geestemünde) **Launched** 17.2.19 **Fate** Tender for MMSs, *M.538*
(1940); scuttled Konigsberg after being bombed Russian aircraft
1944.

**Name** *M.145* **Built by** Neptun Werft (Rostock) **Launched** 22.5.19
**Fate** *M.545* (1940); USN 1945

**Name** *Von Der Lippe* (ex-*Taku*, ex-*M.146*) **Built by** Flensburger
Schiffsbau **Launched** 21.12.18 **Fate** Tender for MMSs, *M.546*
(1940); bombed Allied aircraft Boulogne 7.6.44

**Name** *M.157* **Built by** Nordseewerke (Emden) **Launched** 9.4.19
**Fate** *M.557* (1940); foundered off Rugen 23.12.41

## *Minesweeper type* 1935 : **M.1–260**

The design of these vessels generally followed that of minesweepers of the First World War, but they were some 30 feet
longer, oil-fired, and a little faster. When fitted for minelaying
they could stow thirty mines and their displacement increased
by some 60 tons. As they, and subsequent classes of minesweepers, were frequently pressed into service as escort
vessels their gun armament received more attention than was
demanded by their primary role, and was reinforced by the
addition of about six 20mm A.A. (6 × 1) guns during the war.
Cycloidal propellers were fitted in *M.1* and *M.2* only.

*Displacement:* 772 tons (874 tons full load up to M.24), 775 tons
    (878 tons full load from M.25 up)
*Dimensions:* 216½(pp) 224½(oa) × 27¼ × 7/8½ feet
*Machinery:* Two Wagner or Lamont boilers (pressure 808 lb.);
    two shafts; reciprocating (VTE) I.H.P. 3,500 = 18¼ knots
*Bunkers & Radius:* O.F. 143 tons; 5,000 miles at 10 knots
*Armament:* Two 4.1inch A.A. (2 × 1), two 37mm A.A. (2 × 1)
    guns
*Complement:* 104

**Name** *M.1* **Built by** C. Stülcken (Hamburg) **Launched** 5.3.37
**Fate** Bombed Allied aircraft Nordbyfjord 12.1.45

**Name** *M.2* **Built by** C. Stülcken (Hamburg) **Launched** 20.5.37
**Fate** Rocket fire of RAF aircraft Fedjefjord 11.3.45

**Name** *M.3* **Built by** C. Stülcken (Hamburg) **Launched** 28.9.37
**Fate** Russian *T.901* (1945)

**Name** *M.4* **Built by** Oderwerke (Stettin) **Launched** 16.10.37
**Fate** USN (1945), French (1947); scrapped

**Name** *M.5* **Built by** Oderwerke (Stettin) **Launched** 16.10.37
**Fate** Mined north-west of Christiansand 18.6.40

**Name** *M.6* **Built by** Oderwerke (Stettin) **Launched** 8.1.38
**Fate** Mined off Lorient 30.11.41

**Name** *M.7* **Built by** Flender Werft (Lübeck) **Launched** 29.9.37
**Fate** Russian *T.902* (1945)

**Name** *M.8* **Built by** Flender Werft (Lübeck) **Launched** 29.9.37
**Fate** Torpedoed RN MTBs off Hook of Holland 14.5.43

**Name** *M.9* **Built by** Flender Werft (Lübeck) **Launched** 16.11.37
**Fate** USN (1945), French *Somme* (1947); scrapped 1955

**Name** *M.10* **Built by** C. Stülcken (Hamburg) **Launched** 9.8.38
**Fate** Gunfire RN surface forces off Lorient 14.3.44

**Name** *M.11* **Built by** Oderwerke (Stettin) **Launched** 23.8.38
**Fate** Mined south-west of Norway 6.6.40

**Name** *M.12* **Built by** Flender Werft (Lübeck) **Launched** 6.8.38
**Fate** USN (1945), French (1947); scrapped

**Name** *M.13* **Built by** C. Stülcken (Hamburg) **Launched** 28.2.39
**Fate** Mined Gironde estuary 31.5.44

**Name** *M.14* **Built by** C. Stülcken (Hamburg) **Launched** 25.4.39
**Fate** Mined off Swinemünde 3.5.45

**Name** *M.15* **Built by** C. Stülcken (Hamburg) **Launched** 4.9.39
**Fate** Bombed Allied aircraft Kiel 20.3.45

**Name** *M.16* **Built by** C. Stülcken (Hamburg) **Launched** 15.11.39
**Fate** Bombed Allied aircraft Kiel 20.3.45; scrapped

**Name** *M.17* **Built by** Oderwerke (Stettin) **Launched** 29.7.39
**Fate** Russian *T.903* (1945)

**Name** *M.18* **Built by** Oderwerke (Stettin) **Launched** 16.9.39
**Fate** Bombed Allied aircraft Kiel 20.3.45; scrapped

**Name** *M.19* **Built by** Oderwerke (Stettin) **Launched** 28.10.39
**Fate** Bombed Allied aircraft Kiel 20.3.45; scrapped

**Name** *M.20* **Built by** Flender Werft (Lübeck) **Launched** 16.6.39
**Fate** Bombed Russian aircraft Narva Bay 20.7.44

**Name** *M.21* **Built by** Flender Werft (Lübeck) **Launched** 6.9.39
**Fate** USN (1945), French (1947); scrapped

**Name** *M.22* **Built by** Flender Werft (Lübeck) **Launched** 20.3.40
**Fate** Scuttled Kiel Canal 7.5.45

**Name** *M.23* **Built by** Flender Werft (Lübeck) **Launched** 11.7.40
**Fate** Mined off Tallin 7.41, salved; RN (1945)

M.1 *and her sister* M.2 *were fitted with Voith-Schneider cycloidal propellers for greater manoeuvrability. In other respects the design followed that of World War I types already in service.* (Drüppel)

**Name** *M.24* **Built by** Flender Werft (Lübeck) **Launched** 12.10.40
**Fate** USN (1945), French *Ailette* (1947); W. German *Wespe* (1963)

**Name** *M.25* **Built by** C. Stülcken (Hamburg) **Launched** 19.3.40
**Fate** Scuttled French Atlantic port 9.44

**Name** *M.26* **Built by** C. Stülcken (Hamburg) **Launched** 21.5.40
**Fate** Bombed Allied aircraft Bay of Biscay 15.5.42

**Name** *M.27* **Built by** C. Stülcken (Hamburg) **Launched** 20.11.40
**Fate** Mined Gironde Estuary 11.8.44

*General Arrangement of the 1935* M.25 *group of sweepers.*

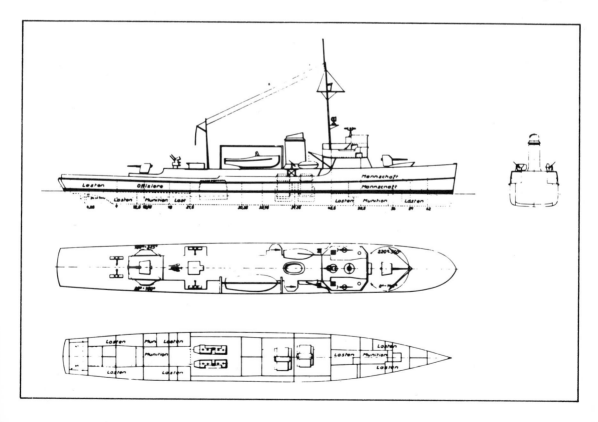

**Name** *M.28* **Built by** C. Stülcken (Hamburg) **Launched** 29.7.40
**Fate** RN (1945), French *Meuse* (1947); scrapped Blyth 3.5.48

**Name** *M.29* **Built by** Oderwerke (Stettin) **Launched** 18.5.40
**Fate** Russian *T.904* (1945)

**Name** *M.30* **Built by** Oderwerke (Stettin) **Launched** 1.6.40
**Fate** Russian *T.905* (1945)

**Name** *M.31* **Built by** Oderwerke (Stettin) **Launched** 13.7.40
**Fate** Torpedoed Russian MTB north of Norway 21.10.44

**Name** *M.32* **Built by** Oderwerke (Stettin) **Launched** 24.8.40
**Fate** USN (1945); scrapped Ghent 1950

**Name** *M.33* **Built by** Lübecker Maschinenbau **Launched** 1.4.42
**Fate** USN (1945); scrapped Ghent 1950

**Name** *M.34* **Built by** Lübecker Maschinenbau **Launched** 7.8.42
**Fate** Russian *T.906* (1945)

**Name** *M.35* **Built by** Schichau (Königsberg) **Launched** 9.11.40
**Fate** USN (1945), French *Bapaume* (1947); scrapped 1950

**Name** *M.36* **Built by** Schichau (Königsberg) **Launched** 21.12.40
**Fate** Bombed Allied aircraft Great Belt 4.5.45

**Name** *M.37* **Built by** Oderwerke (Stettin) **Launched** 12.10.40
**Fate** Torpedoed Russian MTBs Narva Bay 4.6.44

**Name** *M.38* **Built by** Atlas Werke (Bremen) **Launched** 28.2.41
**Fate** RN (1945), French *Oise* (1945); scrapped 1955

**Name** *M.39* **Built by** Atlas Werke (Bremen) **Launched** 8.8.41
**Fate** Torpedoed RN MTB north-west of Ouistreham 24.5.44

**Name** *M.40–80* **Fate** Cancelled

**Name** *M.81* **Built by** Lübecker Maschinenbau **Launched** 20.12.40
**Fate** USN (1945), French *Laffaux* (1947); W. German *Hummel* (1963)

**Name** *M.82* **Built by** Lübecker Maschinenbau **Launched** 23.3.41
**Fate** RN (1945); scrapped Blyth 3.5.48

**Name** *M.83* **Built by** Lübecker Maschinenbau **Launched** 5.6.41
**Fate** Gunfire RN destroyer *Ashanti* and Polish *Piorun* off Cherbourg 14.6.44

**Name** *M.84* **Built by** Lübecker Maschinenbau **Launched** 3.9.41
**Fate** Scuttled Le Havre 11.8.44

**Name** *M.85* **Built by** Nordseewerke (Emden) **Launched** 6.12.41
**Fate** RN (1945), French *Yser* (1947); W. German *Brummer* (1963)

**Name** *M.86–100* **Fate** Cancelled

**Name** *M.101* **Built by** Rickmers Werft (Bremerhaven)
**Launched** 15.3.41 **Fate** Lost by collision west of Namsos 23.11.42

**Name** *M.102* **Built by** Rickmers Werft (Bremerhaven)
**Launched** 1.8.41 **Fate** RN (1945); scrapped Blyth 24.5.48

**Name** *M.103* **Built by** Rickmers Werft (Bremerhaven)
**Launched** 3.12.41 **Fate** Bombed Allied aircraft Ems estuary 15.6.44

M.104 *had the tall funnel typical of the old sweepers dating from World War I. She was renumbered* M.504 *in 1940.* (Drüppel)

**Name** *M.104* **Built by** Rickmers Werft (Bremerhaven) **Launched** 1.4.42 **Fate** RN (1945); scrapped Grays 10.5.48

**Name** *M.105–130* **Fate** Cancelled

**Name** *M.131* **Built by** Lindenau (Memel) **Launched** 20.12.41 **Fate** RN (1945); scrapped Blyth 24.5.48

**Name** *M.132* **Built by** Reiherstieg (Hamburg) **Launched** 7.4.41 **Fate** Torpedoed RN submarine off Eggeroy 20.9.44

**Name** *M.133* **Built by** Reiherstieg (Hamburg) **Launched** 3.8.42 **Fate** Written off as a constructive total loss 14.6.44; scuttled St. Malo 1.8.44

**Name** *M.134–150* **Fate** Cancelled

**Name** *M.151* **Built by** Oderwerke (Stettin) **Launched** 19.10.40 **Fate** Russian *T.907* (1945)

**Name** *M.152* **Built by** Oderwerke (Stettin) **Launched** 16.11.40 **Fate** Mined off Gironde estuary 23.7.43

**Name** *M.153* **Built by** Oderwerke (Stettin) **Launched** 4.1.41 **Fate** Gunfire RN and RNN coastal forces off Ushant 10.7.43

**Name** *M.154* **Built by** Oderwerke (Stettin) **Launched** 3.5.41 **Fate** USN (1945), mercantile

**Name** *M.155* **Built by** Oderwerke (Stettin) **Launched** 19.7.41 **Fate** Russian *T.908* (1945)

**Name** *M.156* **Built by** Oderwerke (Stettin) **Launched** 4.10.41 **Fate** Bombed Allied aircraft L'Abervracht 6.2.44

**Name** *M.157–200* **Fate** Cancelled

**Name** *M.201* **Built by** Neptun Werft (Rostock) **Launched** 18.5.40 **Fate** RN (1945); scrapped Grays, 10.5.48

**Name** *M.202* **Built by** Neptun Werft (Rostock) **Launched** 29.9.40 **Fate** USN (1945), French *Craonne* (1947); scrapped 1950

**Name** *M.203* **Built by** Neptun Werft (Rostock) **Launched** 29.9.40 **Fate** Russian *T.909* (1945)

**Name** *M.204* **Built by** Neptun Werft (Rostock) **Launched** 21.12.40 **Fate** Russian *T.901* (1945)

**Name** *M.205* **Built by** Neptun Werft (Rostock) **Launched** 3.5.41 **Fate** USN (1945), French *Belfort* (1947), W. German *Biene* (1963)

**Name** *M.206* **Built by** Neptun Werft (Rostock) **Launched** 5.5.41 **Fate** Scuttled St. Malo 14.8.44

**Name** *M.207–250* **Fate** Cancelled

**Name** *M.251* **Built by** Deutsche Werft (Hamburg) **Launched** 12.7.40 **Fate** USN (1945), French *Péronne* (1947); scrapped 1950

**Name** *M.252* **Built by** Deutsche Werft (Hamburg) **Launched** 27.9.40 **Fate** USN (1945), French *Ancre* (1947); scrapped 1955

**Name** *M.253* **Built by** Deutsche Werft (Hamburg) **Launched** 23.11.40 **Fate** USN (1945), French *Vimy* (1947); W. German *Bremse* (1963)

**Name** *M.254* **Built by** Deutsche Werft (Hamburg) **Launched** 17.2.41 **Fate** Russian *T.911* (1945)

**Name** *M.255* **Built by** Deutsche Werft (Hamburg) **Launched** 1.4.41 **Fate** Russian *T.912* (1945)

**Name** *M.256* **Built by** Deutsche Werft (Hamburg) **Launched** 31.5.41 **Fate** Lost 5.42, salved; Russian *T.913* (1945)

**Name** *M.257–260* **Fate** Cancelled

## Minesweeper type 1940: **M.261–501**

The war need of the German Navy to conserve stocks of oil fuel resulted in these vessels reverting to coal-firing. The earlier units had their forward 4.1inch gun replaced by light A.A. guns, and the later units were so completed. The final armament in the majority comprised a single 37mm and a single 20mm A.A. guns before the bridge; two single 20mm A.A. guns in the bridge wings; a single 20mm A.A. gun abaft the funnel; a quadruple 20mm A.A. mounting at the after end of the superstructure; and the 4.1inch A.A. gun on the quarterdeck. Fifteen vessels of this series were fitted with two single torpedo tubes on the fo'c'sle for training purposes, but these were not permanently shipped and were carried, or not, as required.

*The torpedo recovery vessel TS.4 was actually a unit of the 1940 M.261 group of sweepers. Note the torpedo-tubes on the forecastle and the derrick aft for recovering the 16 torpedoes carried. She served in the Federal German Navy from 1951 to 1963. (Drüppel)*

*Displacement:* 637 tons (775 tons full)
*Dimensions:* 189(pp) 204½(oa) × 28 × 7/9½ feet
*Machinery:* Two Marine boilers (pressure 232 lb.); two shafts; reciprocating (VTE) with Bauer-Wach exhaust turbine, S.H.P. 2,400 = 16¾ knots
*Bunkers & Radius:* Coal 162 tons; 4,000 miles at 10 knots
*Armament:* Two except *TS boats* one 4.1inch A.A. (1/2 × 1), six 20mm A.A. (1 × 4 and 2 × 1) guns; two 21inch (2 × 1) T.T. in *TS boats* only
*Complement:* 76

**Name** *M.261* **Built by** Atlas Werke (Bremen) **Launched** 10.4.42 **Fate** RN (1945), RNN (1947); scrapped

**Name** *M.262* **Built by** Atlas Werke (Bremen) **Launched** 25.6.42 **Fate** Scuttled Bordeaux 25.8.44

**Name** *M.263* **Built by** Atlas Werke (Bremen) **Launched** 17.12.42 **Fate** Gunfire RN surface forces north of Ile d'Yeu 6.8.44

**Name** *M.264* **Built by** Atlas Werke (Bremen) **Launched** 19.5.43 **Fate** Bombed Allied aircraft west of Heligoland 18.7.44

**Name** *M.265* **Built by** Atlas Werke (Bremen) **Launched** 21.9.43 **Fate** Russian *T.914* (1945)

**Name** *M.266* **Built by** Atlas Werke (Bremen) **Launched** 18.3.44 **Fate** Bombed 8th USAAF aircraft Kiel F.26.8.44, salved; bombed USAA aircraft Kiel 11.3.45

**Name** *M.267* **Built by** Atlas Werke (Bremen) **Launched** 13.6.44 **Fate** Russian *T.915* (1945)

**Name** *M.268–270* **Built by** Atlas Werke (Bremen) **Fate** Cancelled

**Name** *M.271* **Built by** Rickmers Werft (Bremerhaven) **Launched** 1942 **Fate** Bombed Pauillac 5.8.44

**Name** *M.272* **Built by** Rickers Werft (Bremerhaven) **Launched** 1942 **Fate** RN (1945), RNN (1947)

**Name** *M.273* **Built by** Rickmers Werft (Bremerhaven) **Launched** 1943 **Fate** Gunfire RN surface forces off Egersund 12.1.45

**Name** *M.274* **Built by** Rickmers Werft (Bremerhaven) **Launched** 1943 **Fate** Scuttled Schelde estuary 5.9.44

**Name** *M.275* **Built by** Rickmers Werft (Bremerhaven)
**Launched** 25.5.43 **Fate** RN (1945), French (1947); discarded 1948

**Name** *M.276* **Built by** Rickmers Werft (Bremerhaven)
**Launched** 1943 **Fate** Scuttled Schelde estuary 5.9.44

**Name** *M.277* **Built by** Rickmers Werft (Bremerhaven)
**Launched** 1943 **Fate** RN (1945), French (1947)

**Name** *M.278* (ex-*TS.4*) **Built by** Rickmers Werft (Bremerhaven)
**Launched** 25.1.44 **Fate** USN (1945), German *M.202* (1951),
*Seestern* (1960)

**Name** *M.279* (ex-*TS.9*) **Built by** Rickmers Werft (Bremerhaven)
**Launched** 4.7.44 **Fate** Russian *T.916* (1947)

**Name** *M.280* (ex-*TS.14*) **Built by** Rickmers Werft (Bremerhaven)
**Launched** 1944 **Fate** Scrapped incomplete 5.45

**Name** *M.281–290* **Built by** Rickmers Werft (Bremerhaven)
**Fate** Cancelled

**Name** *M.291* **Built by** Lindenau (Memel) **Launched** 27.3.43
**Fate** Russian *T.917* (1947)

**Name** *M.292* **Built by** Lindenau (Memel) **Launched** 19.6.43
**Fate** Bombed Allied aircraft Gironde estuary 21.8.44

**Name** *M.293* **Built by** Lindenau (Memel) **Launched** 1943
**Fate** Rocket fire RAF aircraft (18 Sqn.) Kattegat 2.5.45

**Name** *M.294* **Built by** Lindenau (Memel) **Launched** 4.3.44
**Fate** USN (1945), German *M.201* (1951), *Seepferd* (1960)

**Name** *M.295* **Built by** Lindenau (Memel) **Launched** 1944
**Fate** Scuttled incomplete Gdynia 1945, salved and Polish *Panna
Wodna*

**Name** *M.296* **Built by** Lindenau (Memel) **Fate** Destroyed on slip
23.3.45

**Name** *M.297* (ex-*TS.15*) **Built by** Lindenau (Memel) **Fate** Scrapped
incomplete 1945

**Name** *M.298–300* **Built by** Lindenau (Memel) **Fate** Cancelled

**Name** *M.301* **Built by** Unterweser (Bremerhaven) **Launched** 9.4.41
**Fate** Rocket fire RAF aircraft (18 Sqn.) Skagerrak 4.5.45

**Name** *M.302* **Built by** Unterweser (Bremerhaven) **Launched** 26.7.41
**Fate** RN (1945), RNN (1947)

**Name** *M.303* **Built by** Unterweser (Bremerhaven)
**Launched** 29.12.41 **Fate** Torpedoed Russian MTB off Kiberg
11.10.44

**Name** *M.304* **Built by** Unterweser (Bremerhaven)
**Launched** 30.4.42 **Fate** Scuttled Bordeaux 25.8.44

**Name** *M.305* **Built by** Unterweser (Bremerhaven)
**Launched** 20.10.42 **Fate** Foundered off Brustertort 17.1.45

**Name** *M.306* **Built by** Unterweser (Bremerhaven)
**Launched** 19.12.42 **Fate** RN (1945), RNN (1947)

**Name** *M.307* **Built by** Unterweser (Bremerhaven)
**Launched** 16.6.43 **Fate** Bombed Allied aircraft north of
Spiekeroog 21.7.44

**Name** *M.308–320* **Built by** Unterweser (Bremerhaven)
**Fate** Cancelled

**Name** *M.321* **Built by** Oderwerke (Stettin) **Launched** 29.3.41
**Fate** RN (1945), scrapped

**Name** *M.322* **Built by** Oderwerke (Stettin) **Launched** 31.5.41
**Fate** RN (1945), RNN (1947); scrapped Denmark 1953

**Name** *M.323* **Built by** Oderwerke (Stettin) **Launched** 9.8.41
**Fate** RN (1945)

**Name** *M.324* **Built by** Oderwerke (Stettin) **Launched** 20.9.41
**Fate** Russian *T.918* (1945)

**Name** *M.325* **Built by** Oderwerke (Stettin) **Launched** 31.10.42
**Fate** Bombed Allied aircraft Pauillac 5.8.44

**Name** *M.326* **Built by** Oderwerke (Stettin) **Launched** 30.1.43
**Fate** RN (1945), RNN (1947)

**Name** *M.327* **Built by** Oderwerke (Stettin) **Launched** 12.6.43
**Fate** RN (1945), scrapped

**Name** *M.328* **Built by** Oderwerke (Stettin) **Launched** 12.6.43
**Fate** USN (1947), Italian *Antilope* (1949)

**Name** *M.329* **Built by** Lübecker Maschinenbau **Launched** 27.5.43
**Fate** Bombed USAAF aircraft Wilhelmshaven 30.3.45

**Name** *M.330* **Built by** Lübecker Maschinenbau **Launched** 7.2.44
**Fate** Russian *T.919* (1945)

**Name** *M.331–340* **Built by** Lübecker Maschinenbau
**Fate** Cancelled

**Name** *M.341* **Built by** Neptun Werft (Rostock) **Launched** 10.6.41
**Fate** Russian *T.920* (1947)

**Name** *M.342* **Built by** Neptun Werft (Rostock) **Launched** 11.6.41
**Fate** Russian *T.921* (1947)

**Name** *M.343* **Built by** Neptun Werft (Rostock) **Launched** 6.12.41
**Fate** Gunfire RN destroyer *Ashanti* and Polish *Piorun* off
Brittany 14.6.44; scuttled St. Malo 6.8.44

**Name** *M.344* **Built by** Neptun Werft (Rostock) **Launched** 13.12.41
**Fate** Scuttled French Atlantic port 9.44

**Name** *M.345* **Built by** Neptun Werft (Rostock) **Launched** 27.6.42
**Fate** Bombed Allied aircraft French Atlantic port 18.5.43

**Name** *M.346* **Built by** Neptun Werft (Rostock) **Launched** 27.6.42
**Fate** Torpedoed Russian submarine *S.51* Tanafjord 17.7.43

**Name** *M.347* **Built by** Neptun Werft (Rostock) **Launched** 7.11.42
**Fate** Torpedoed and cannon fire of RAF aircraft north-west of
Schiermonnikoog 25.8.44

**Name** *M.348* **Built by** Neptun Werft (Rostock) **Launched** 7.11.42
**Fate** Russian *T.922* (1945)

**Name** *M.349–360* **Built by** Neptun Werft (Rostock)
**Fate** Cancelled

**Name** *M.361* **Built by** Schichau (Königsberg) **Launched** 5.3.41
**Fate** RN (1945), scrapped

**Name** *M.362* **Built by** Schichau (Königsberg) **Launched** 1.4.41
**Fate** RN (1945), RNN (1947); scrapped Denmark 1952

**Name** *M.363* **Built by** Schichau (Königsberg) **Launched** 31.5.41
**Fate** Scuttled Bordeaux 25.8.44

**Name** *M.364* **Built by** Schichau (Königsberg) **Launched** 9.8.41
**Fate** RN (1945), RNN (1947)

**Name** *M.365* **Built by** Schichau (Königsberg) **Launched** 25.7.42
**Fate** RN (1945), RNN (1947)

**Name** *M.366* **Built by** Schichau (Königsberg) **Launched** 5.9.42
**Fate** Bombed Allied aircraft St. Nazaire 8.8.44

**Name** *M.367* **Built by** Schichau (Königsberg) **Launched** 23.12.42
**Fate** Bombed Allied aircraft St. Nazaire 8.8.44

**Name** *M.368* **Built by** Schichau (Königsberg) **Launched** 15.2.43
**Fate** Lost by collision south of Norway 15.4.45

**Name** *M.369* **Built by** Schichau (Königsberg) **Launched** 18.6.43
**Fate** Russian *T.923* (1947)

**Name** *M.370* **Built by** Schichau (Königsberg) **Launched** 17.7.43
**Fate** Bombed Allied aircraft off Royan 12.8.44

**Name** *M.371* (ex-*TS.1*) **Built by** Schichau (Königsberg)
**Launched** 31.7.43 **Fate** USN (1945)

**Name** *M.372* (ex-*TS.3*) **Built by** Schichau (Königsberg)
**Launched** 25.9.43 **Fate** Bombed Allied aircraft off Swinemünde
12.5.44

**Name** *M.373* (ex-*TS.5*) **Built by** Schichau (Königsberg)
**Launched** 30.11.43 **Fate** USN (1945)

**Name** *M.374* (ex-*TS.6*) **Built by** Schichau (Königsberg)
**Launched** 18.12.43 **Fate** USN (1945); scrapped Ghent (1950)

**Name** *M.375* (ex-*TS.8*) **Built by** Schichau (Königsberg)
**Launched** 10.3.44 **Fate** USN (1945)

**Name** *M.376* (ex-*TS.10*) **Built by** Schichau (Königsberg)
**Launched** 19.4.44 **Fate** Bombed Russian aircraft off Hela 11.4.45

**Name** *M.377* (ex-*TS.11*) **Built by** Schichau (Königsberg)
**Launched** 27.6.44 **Fate** Russian *T.924* (1947)

**Name** *M.378* (ex-*TS.13*) **Built by** Schichau (Königsberg)
**Launched** 1944 **Fate** Scrapped incomplete Rostock 4.45

**Name** *M.379* **Built by** Schichau (Königsberg) **Fate** Destroyed
incomplete on slip

**Name** *M.380* **Built by** Schichau (Königsberg) **Fate** Destroyed
incomplete on slip

**Name** *M.381* **Built by** Elsflether Werft **Launched** 15.2.41
**Fate** Torpedoed RN submarine *Venturer* off Christiansand
12.2.45

**Name** *M.382* **Built by** Elsflether Werft **Launched** 28.6.41
**Fate** Mined north of Molde 31.1.45

**Name** *M.383* **Built by** Elsflether Werft **Launched** 22.11.41
**Fate** Rocket fire of Allied aircraft north of Langeoog 13.8.44

**Name** *M.384* **Built by** Elsflether Werft **Launched** 12.9.42
**Fate** Scuttled Nantes 11.8.44

**Name** *M.385* **Built by** Elsflether Werft **Launched** 1943
**Fate** Gunfire RN cruiser *Mauritius* north of Les Sables d'Olonne 15.8.44

**Name** *M.386* **Built by** Elsflether Werft **Launched** 1.7.43
**Fate** Russian *T.925* (1945)

**Name** *M.387* (ex-*TS.2*) **Built by** Elsflether Werft **Launched** 1943
**Fate** Scuttled Lübeck 2.5.45

**Name** *M.388* (ex-*TS.7*) **Built by** Elsflether Werft **Launched** 22.4.44
**Fate** USN (1945), German *M.203* (1951); *Seehund* (1956)

**Name** *M.389* (ex-*TS.12*) **Built by** Elsflether Werft **Launched** 22.7.44
**Fate** USN (1945)

**Name** *M.390–400* **Built by** Elsflether Werft **Fate** Scrapped incomplete or cancelled

**Name** *M.401* **Built by** Rotterdam D.D. **Launched** 4.4.42
**Fate** Russian *T.926* (1945)

**Name** *M.402* **Built by** Rotterdam D.D. **Launched** 4.4.42
**Fate** Bombed Allied aircraft Boulogne 15.6.44

**Name** *M.403* **Built by** Rotterdam D.D. **Launched** 15.9.42
**Fate** Bombed Allied aircraft south-west of Gothenburg 19.4.45

**Name** *M.404* **Built by** Rotterdam D.D. **Launched** 14.10.42
**Fate** USN (1945), French (1945)

**Name** *M.405* **Built by** Rotterdam D.D. **Launched** 1942
**Fate** Russian *T.927* (1945)

**Name** *M.406* **Built by** Rotterdam D.D. **Launched** 30.12.42
**Fate** Russian *T.928* (1945)

**Name** *M.407* **Built by** Rotterdam D.D. **Launched** 1943
**Fate** Russian *T.929* (1945)

**Name** *M.408* **Built by** Rotterdam D.D. **Launched** 1943
**Fate** USN (1945), French (1948)

**Name** *M.409–410* **Built by** Rotterdam D.D. **Fate** Cancelled

**Name** *M.411* **Built by** De Schelde (Flushing) **Launched** 22.8.42
**Fate** Russian *T.930* (1945)

**Name** *M.412* **Built by** De Schelde (Flushing) **Launched** 6.9.42
**Fate** Blown-up Granville 9.3.45 following stranding

**Name** *M.413* **Built by** De Schelde (Flushing) **Launched** 1942
**Fate** Bombed Russian aircraft Narva Bay 21.7.44

**Name** *M.414* **Built by** De Schelde (Flushing) **Launched** 9.11.42
**Fate** Torpedoed Allied aircraft west of Texel 17.5.43

**Name** *M.415* **Built by** De Schelde (Flushing) **Launched** 16.1.43
**Fate** Russian *T.931* (1947)

**Name** *M.416* **Built by** De Schelde (Flushing) **Launched** 1943
**Fate** Gunfire of RN destroyer south of Norway 12.11.44

**Name** *M.417–420* **Built by** De Schelde (Flushing) **Fate** Cancelled

**Name** *M.421* **Built by** Wilton-Fijenoord (Schiedam)
**Launched** 29.11.41 **Fate** Mined off Kolberg 13.2.45

**Name** *M.422* **Built by** Wilton-Fijenoord (Schiedam) **Launched** 1942
**Fate** Bombed RAF aircraft off St. Malo 4.8.44

**Name** *M.423* **Built by** Wilton-Fijenoord (Schiedam)
**Launched** 18.10.42 **Fate** Russian *T.923* (1946)

**Name** *M.424* **Built by** Wilton-Fijenoord (Schiedam)
**Launched** 18.10.42 **Fate** Bombed Allied aircraft St. Malo 5.8.44;
salved 7.46 and RN; French (1948)

**Name** *M.425* **Built by** Wilton-Fijenoord (Schiedam)
**Launched** 18.10.42 **Fate** Russian *T.933* (1947)

**Name** *M.426* **Built by** Wilton-Fijenoord (Schiedam)
**Launched** 18.10.42 **Fate** Bombed Allied aircraft east of Skagens
12.9.44

**Name** *M.427* **Built by** Wilton-Fijenoord (Schiedam)
**Launched** 18.10.42 **Fate** Gunfire RN destroyer Rekkefjord
13.11.44

**Name** *M.428* **Built by** Wilton-Fijenoord (Schiedam)
**Launched** 18.10.42 **Fate** Bombed Allied aircraft St. Nazaire
8.8.44

**Name** *M.429–430* **Built by** Wilton-Fijenoord (Schiedam)
**Fate** Cancelled

**Name** *M.431* **Built by** Netherlands Dock & Sbdg. (Amsterdam)
**Launched** 7.3.43 **Fate** Russian *T.934* (1945)

**Name** *M.432* **Built by** Netherlands Dock & Sbdg. (Amsterdam)
**Launched** 7.3.42 **Fate** USN (1945), French (1945), *Suippe* (1947);
discarded 1953

**Name** *M.433* **Built by** Netherlands Dock & Sbdg. (Amsterdam)
**Launched** 11.4.42 **Fate** Bombed Allied aircraft Vegafjord 27.10.44

**Name** *M.434* **Built by** Netherlands Dock & Sbdg. (Amsterdam)
**Launched** 11.4.42 **Fate** USN (1945), French (1945)

**Name** *M.435* **Built by** Netherlands Dock & Sbdg. (Amsterdam)
**Launched** 27.6.42 **Fate** Bombed Allied aircraft north of Ameland
14.5.44

**Name** *M.436* **Built by** Netherlands Dock & Sbdg. (Amsterdam)
**Launched** 27.6.42 **Fate** RN (1945), RNN (1947)

**Name** *M.437* **Built by** Netherlands Dock & Sbdg. (Amsterdam)
**Launched** 27.6.42 **Fate** Russian *T.935* (1945)

**Name** *M.438* **Built by** Netherlands Dock & Sbdg. (Amsterdam)
**Launched** 27.6.42 **Fate** Bombed Allied aircraft St. Nazaire 8.8.44

**Name** *M.439–440* **Built by** Netherlands Dock & Sbdg.
(Amsterdam) **Fate** Cancelled

**Name** *M.441* **Built by** P. Smit (Rotterdam) **Launched** 19.6.42
**Fate** USN (1945), German *M.205* (1952), *Seelöwe* (1956)

**Name** *M.442* **Built by** P. Smit (Rotterdam) **Launched** 1942
**Fate** USN (1945), French *Marne* (1947); scrapped 1953

**Name** *M.443* **Built by** P. Smit (Rotterdam) **Launched** 15.9.42
**Fate** Russian *T.936* (1946)

**Name** *M.444* **Built by** P. Smit (Rotterdam) **Launched** 30.11.42
**Fate** Bombed Allied aircraft and mined off Brest 14.8.44

**Name** *M.445* **Built by** P. Smit (Rotterdam) **Launched** 12.12.42
**Fate** Bombed USAAF aircraft Hamburg 31.12.44

**Name** *M.446* **Built by** P. Smit (Rotterdam) **Launched** 3.2.43
**Fate** Russian *T.937* (1947)

**Name** *M.477–450* **Built by** P. Smit (Rotterdam) **Fate** Cancelled

**Name** *M.451* **Built by** Gusto Werft (Schiedam) **Launched** 24.12.41
**Fate** Wrecked off Helsinki 31.1.44

**Name** *M.452* **Built by** Gusto Werft (Schiedam) **Launched** 19.12.42
**Fate** USN (1945), French (1945), *Aisne* (1947); scrapped 1949

**Name** *M.453* **Built by** Gusto Werft (Schiedam) **Launched** 15.12.42
**Fate** USN (1945); scrapped Ghent 1949

**Name** *M.454* **Built by** Gusto Werft (Schiedam) **Launched** 1943
**Fate** USN (1945), French (1945)

**Name** *M.455* **Built by** Gusto Werft (Schiedam) **Launched** 7.12.42
**Fate** Bombed Allied aircraft Cuxhaven 4.45, salved

**Name** *M.456* **Built by** Gusto Werft (Schiedam) **Launched** 3.3.43
**Fate** Russian *T.938* (1947)

**Name** *M.457–458* **Built by** Gusto Werft (Schiedam)
**Fate** Cancelled

**Name** *M.459* **Built by** Netherlands Dock & Sbdg. (Amsterdam)
**Launched** 1942 **Fate** Bombed Russian aircraft Narva Bay 10.4.44

**Name** *M.460* **Built by** Netherlands Dock & Sbdg. (Amsterdam)
**Launched** 31.7.42 **Fate** USN (1945), German *M.204* (1951),
*Seeigel* (1956)

**Name** *M.461* **Built by** Netherlands Dock & Sbdg. (Amsterdam)
**Launched** 24.10.42 **Fate** Russian *T.939* (1945)

**Name** *M.462* **Built by** Netherlands Dock & Sbdg. (Amsterdam)
**Launched** 27.1.43 **Fate** Bombed Allied aircraft north of Skagens
12.9.44

**Name** *M.463* **Built by** Netherlands Dock & Sbdg. (Amsterdam)
**Launched** 1943 **Fate** Scuttled Bordeaux 25.8.44

**Name** *M.464–466* **Built by** Netherlands Dock & Sbdg.
(Amsterdam) **Fate** Cancelled

**Name** *M.467* **Built by** Van der Giessen (Krimpen) **Launched** 9.1.42
**Fate** Russian *T.940* (1945)

**Name** *M.468* **Built by** Van der Giessen (Krimpen) **Launched** 9.7.42
**Fate** Torpedoed Russian MTB west of Namsos 12.8.44

**Name** *M.469* **Built by** Van der Giessen (Krimpen) **Launched** 9.7.42
**Fate** Torpedoed RN MTB north-west of Vlieland 4.7.44

**Name** *M.470* **Built by** Van der Giessen (Krimpen)
**Launched** 21.10.42 **Fate** Russian *T.941* (1947)

**Name** *M.471* **Built by** Van der Giessen (Krimpen)
**Launched** 21.10.42 **Fate** Bombed Allied aircraft Den Helder
25.9.44

**Name** *M.472–474* **Built by** Van der Giessen (Krimpen)
**Fate** Cancelled

**Name** *M.475* **Built by** J. & K. Smit (Kinderdijk) **Launched** 29.8.42
**Fate** USN (1945), French (1945)

**Name** *M.476* **Built by** J. & K. Smit (Kinderdijk) **Launched** 3.10.42
USN (1945), French (1947)

**Name** *M.477–482* **Built by** J. & K. Smit (Kinderdijk)
**Fate** Cancelled

**Name** *M.483* **Built by** Boele's (Slikkerveer) **Launched** 16.5.42
**Fate** Mined English Channel 15.6.43

**Name** *M.484* **Built by** Boele's (Slikkerveer) **Launched** 25.8.42
**Fate** Russian *T.942* (1945)

**Name** *M.485* **Built by** Boele's (Slikkerveer) **Fate** Cancelled

**Name** *M.486* **Built by** Verschure (Amsterdam) **Launched** 1942
**Fate** Gunfire RN cruiser *Bellona*, destroyers *Ashanti* and *Tartar*
and RCN *Haida* and *Huron* off Ile d'Yeu 6.8.44

**Name** *M.487–488* **Built by** Verschure (Amsterdam) **Fate** Cancelled

**Name** *M.489* **Built by** L. Smit (Kinderdijk) **Launched** 28.8.42
**Fate** Torpedoed RN MTB off Mosterhavn 23.12.44

**Name** *M.490–494* **Built by** L. Smith (Kinderdijk) **Fate** Cancelled

**Name** *M.495* **Built by** Gebr. Pot (Bolnes) **Launched** 4.9.42
**Fate** USN (1945), French (1947)

**Name** *M.496* **Built by** Gebr. Pot (Bolnes) **Launched** 12.1.43
**Fate** Russian *T.943* (1947)

**Name** *M.497–501* **Built by** Gebr. Pot (Bolnes) **Fate** Cancelled

## *Minesweeper type 1943:* **M.601–886, 1001–1050**

These vessels were designed, in addition to minesweeping, to
act as escort or torpedo recovery vessels. For the former role
the forward 4.1inch gun was re-introduced and the hull
lengthened some 20 feet to accommodate it. They could be
equipped for minelaying and stow twenty-four mines for this
purpose.

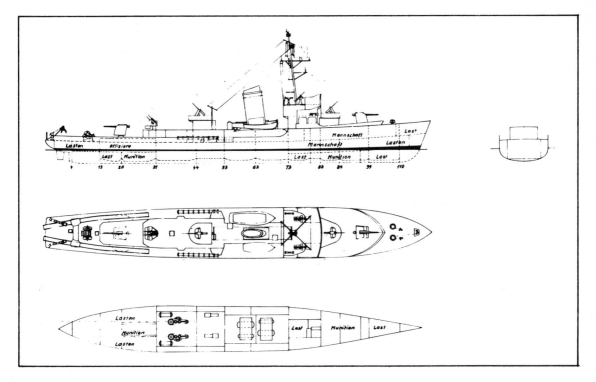

*Displacement:* 668 tons (821 tons full)
*Dimensions:* 207(pp) 224(oa) × 29½ × 6½/8½ feet
*Machinery:* Two Marine boilers (pressure 232 lb.); two shafts;
   reciprocating (VTE) with Bauer-Wach exhaust turbine, I.H.P.
   2,400 = 16½ knots
*Bunkers & Radius:* Coal 136 tons; 3,600 miles at 10 knots
*Armament:* Two 4.1inch A.A. (2 × 1), two 37mm A.A. (2 × 1),
   eight 20mm A.A. (1 × 4 and 4 × 1) guns
*Complement:* 107

*General Arrangement of the
1943* M.601 *group.*

**Name** *M.601* **Built by** Neptun Werft (Rostock) **Launched** 31.8.44
**Fate** RN (1945); scrapped Middlesbrough 20.4.48

**Name** *M.602* **Built by** Neptun Werft (Rostock) **Launched** 21.10.44
**Fate** RN (1945)

**Name** *M.603* **Built by** Neptun Werft (Rostock) **Launched** 2.11.44
**Fate** RN (1945)

**Name** *M.604* **Built by** Neptun Werft (Rostock) **Launched** 10.11.44
**Fate** RN (1945); scrapped Tyne 28.3.48

**Name** *M.605* **Built by** Neptun Werft (Rostock) **Launched** 13.12.44
**Fate** RN (1945)

**Name** *M.606* **Built by** Neptun Werft (Rostock) **Launched** 20.12.44
**Fate** USN (1945); scrapped Ghent 1950

**Name** *M.607* **Built by** Neptun Werft (Rostock) **Launched** 30.12.44
**Fate** USN (1945), mercantile *Hörhum* (1948), *Christian Ivers*
(1960), *Hanne Scarlet* (1953), *Salvatore Lauro* (1962)

*M.608 was one of the last sweepers to be completed and became a passenger ferry in 1948.* (Drüppel)

**Name** *M.608* **Built by** Neptun Werft (Rostock) **Launched** 20.1.45
**Fate** USN (1945), mercantile *Amrum* (1948), *Harald Ivers* (1950), *Lili Scarlet* (1953), *Elena P.* (1964)

**Name** *M.609* **Built by** Neptun Werft (Rostock) **Launched** 29.1.45
**Fate** USN (1945); scrapped Dunston 17.2.48

**Name** *M.610* **Built by** Neptun Werft (Rostock) **Launched** 27.2.45
**Fate** USN (1945); scrapped Ghent 1950

**Name** *M.611* **Built by** Neptun Werft (Rostock) **Launched** 12.3.45
**Fate** USN (1945), mercantile *Wangerooge* (1958), German *M.206* (1952), *Seeschlange* (1956)

**Name** *M.612* **Built by** Neptun Werft (Rostock) **Launched** 23.3.45
**Fate** RN (1945)

**Name** *M.613–616* **Built by** Neptun Werft (Rostock)
**Launched** 1945 **Fate** Scrapped incomplete Rostock 1945

**Name** *M.617–633* **Built by** Neptun Werft (Rostock)
**Fate** Scrapped on slip

**Name** *M.634–666* **Built by** Neptun Werft (Rostock) **Fate** Cancelled

**Name** *M.667–800* **Built by** Neptun Werft (Rostock) **Fate** Cancelled

**Name** *M.801* **Built by** Schichau (Königsberg) **Launched** 9.9.44
**Fate** USN (1945), Italian *Gazzella* (ex-*B.3*—1949)

**Name** *M.802* **Built by** Schichau (Königsberg) **Launched** 29.9.44
**Fate** Bombed USAAF aircraft Kiel 3.4.45

**Name** *M.803* **Built by** Schichau (Königsberg) **Launched** 19.10.44
**Fate** USN (1945), Italian *Diano* (ex-*B.2*—1949)

**Name** *M.804* **Built by** Schichau (Königsberg) **Launched** 1.11.44
**Fate** Bombed USAAF aircraft Kiel 11.3.45

**Name** *M.805* **Built by** Schichau (Königsberg) **Launched** 9.11.44
**Fate** Bombed USAAF aircraft Kiel 11.3.45

**Name** *M.806* **Built by** Schichau (Königsberg) **Launched** 21.11.44
**Fate** RN (1945); scrapped Tyne 28.3.48

**Name** *M.807* **Built by** Schichau (Königsberg) **Launched** 13.1.45
**Fate** Towed incomplete to Rostock 1.45

**Name** *M.808* **Built by** Schichau (Könisberg) **Launched** 1945
**Fate** Towed incomplete to Rostock 1.45

**Name** *M.809–813* **Built by** Schichau (Königsberg) **Fate** Scrapped
incomplete

**Name** *M.814–816* **Built by** Schichau (Königsberg) **Fate** Scrapped
on slip

**Name** *M.817–1000* **Built by** Schichau (Königsberg) **Fate** Cancelled

**Name** *M.1001–1050* **Built by** Korneuburg Werft (Vienna)
**Fate** Cancelled

## *Ex-RNeth.N minesweepers:* **M.551–553**

*Displacement:* 460 tons (585 tons full)
*Dimensions:* 183(wl) 186(oa) × 25½ × 6½/7¼ feet
*Machinery:* Two Yarrow boilers; two-shaft; reciprocating
   (VTE) I.H.P. 1,600 = 15½ knots
*Bunkers & Radius:* O.F. 110 tons; 2,350 miles at 11 knots
*Armament:* One 3inch A.A., four 20mm A.A. (1 × 2 and 2 × 1)
   guns, fitted for minelaying
*Complement:* 59

**Name** *M.551* (ex-*Peter Florisz*) **Built by** P. Smit (Rotterdam)
**Launched** 11.5.37 **Fate** Scuttled Enkhuizen 14.5.40, salved and
German; retroceded 1945

**Name** *M.552* (ex-*Abraham van der Hulst*) **Built by** Werft Gusto
(Schiedam) **Launched** 31.5.37 **Fate** Scuttled Ijsselmeer 14.5.40,
salved and German; retroceded 1945

**Name** *M.553* (ex-*Willem van Ewijk* (*ii*) ) **Built by** P. Smit
(Rotterdam) **Launched** 18.4.40 **Fate** Mined Baltic 21.4.44; salved
20.7.44, retroceded 1945 and scrapped

## *Ex-RDN minesweepers:* **MA.1–6**

*Displacement:* 274 tons (305 tons full)
*Dimensions:* 169(pp) 176½(oa) × 20¾ × 6½/7¼ feet
*Machinery:* One Thornycroft boiler; one-shaft geared turbines,
   S.H.P. 2,200 = 19 knots
*Bunkers:* O.F. 30 tons
*Armament:* Two 3inch (2 × 1), four 20mm A.A. (4 × 1), four
   8mm A.A. (2 × 2) guns, fitted for minelaying
*Complement:* 47

**Name** *M.A.1* (ex-*Sölöven*) **Built by** Naval Dockyard (Copenhagen) **Launched** 3.12.38 **Fate** Scuttled Korsor 29.8.43, salved and German, *Vs.61* (1944); retroceded 1945

**Name** *MA.2* (ex-*Söbjörnen*) **Built by** Naval Dockyard (Copenhagen) **Launched** 16.2.39 **Fate** Scuttled Copenhagen 29.8.43, salved and German; scrapped 1945

**Name** *MA.3* (ex-*Söulven*) **Built by** Naval Dockyard (Copenhagen) **Launched** 1939 **Fate** Scuttled Copenhagen 29.8.43, salved and German; scrapped 1945

**Name** *MA.4* (ex-*Söridderen*) **Built by** Naval Dockyard (Copenhagen) **Launched** 11.4.42 **Fate** Scuttled Korsor 29.8.43, salved and German, *Vs.62* (1944); retroceded 1945

**Name** *MA.5* (ex-*Söhesten*) **Built by** Naval Dockyard (Copenhagen) **Launched** 30.4.42 **Fate** Scuttled Kalundborg 29.8.43, salved and German, *Vs.63* (1944); retroceded 1945

**Name** *MA.6* (ex-*Söhunden*) **Built by** Naval Dockyard (Copenhagen) **Launched** 16.5.42 **Fate** Scuttled Kogebucht 29.8.43, salved and German, *Vs.64* (1945); retroceded 1945

## *Auxiliary minesweepers:* SPERRBRECHER A–C

**Name** *A* See *Sperrbrecher III*

**Name** *B* (ex-mercantile *Ingrid Horn*) **Gross tonnage and year built** 4,006/27 **Commissioned** 17.5.40 **Fate** *Sperrbrecher 25* (1941), target ship (1941); bombed Allied aircraft Kiel 24.7.44, salved and scrapped

**Name** *C* (*ii*) (ex-mercantile *Waldtraut Horn*) **Gross tonnage and year built** 3,995/28 **Commissioned** 17.5.40 **Fate** *Sperrbrecher 24* (1941); paid-off 20.11.42, Russian 1946

## *Auxiliary minesweepers:* SPERRBRECHER I–XII

**Name** *I* (ex-mercantile *Bahia Camarones*) **Gross tonnage and year built** 8,551/18 **Commissioned** 2.10.39 **Fate** Returned 30.7.40; gunfire RN cruisers off Egeray 12.1.45

**Name** *II* (ex-mercantile *Karl Leonhardt*) **Gross tonnage and year built** 6,042/13 **Commissioned** 30.9.39 **Fate** Returned 7.40; scuttled Skagerrak 16.3.46

**Name** *III* (ex-mercantile *Robert Bornhofen*) **Gross tonnage and year built** 6,643/19 **Commissioned** 30.8.39 **Fate** *Sperrbrecher A* (19  ), *Sperrbrecher 14* (19  ), target ship (1941); mined off North Cape 12.9.42

**Name** *IV* (ex-mercantile *Oakland*) **Gross tonnage and year built** 6,757/29 **Commissioned** 16.9.39 **Fate** *Sperrbrecher 4* (1940); bombed Allied aircraft Brest 27.8.44, salved and mercantile *Alain LD* (1950)

**Name** *V* (ex-mercantile *Schwanheim*) **Gross tonnage and year
built** 5,339/35 **Commissioned** 4.10.39 **Fate** *Sperrbrecher 5* (1940);
burnt-out Royan 13.8.44 after bombed Allied aircraft

**Name** *VI* (ex-mercantile *Magdeburg*) **Gross tonnage and year
built** 6,128/35 **Commissioned** 5.10.39 *Sperrbrecher 6* (1940);
scuttled Royan 13.8.44 after bombed Allied aircraft, salved and
scrapped

**Name** *VII* (ex-mercantile *Sauerland*) **Gross tonnage and year
built** 7,087/28 **Commissioned** 11.9.39 **Fate** *Sperrbrecher 7* (1940);
torpedoed RN cruiser *Diadem* off La Pallice 12.8.44

**Name** *VIII* (ex-mercantile Neckar) **Gross tonnage and year
built** 8,417/27 **Commissioned** 4.10.39 **Fate** *Sperrbrecher 8* (1940);
abandoned Brest 28.8.44 after bombed Allied aircraft

**Name** *IX* (ex-mercantile *Lünenburg*) **Gross tonnage and year
built** 5,828/14 **Commissioned** 15.9.39 **Fate** *Sperrbrecher 9* (1940);
scuttled La Pallice 1.7.44, salved 1948 and scrapped

**Name** *X* (ex-mercantile *Vigo*) **Gross tonnage and year built** 7,358/22
**Commissioned** 28.9.39 **Fate** *Sperrbrecher 10* (1941); mined off
Jutland coast 7.3.44

**Name** *XI* (ex-mercantile *Petropolis*) **Gross tonnage and year
built** 4,845/11 **Commissioned** 28.9.39 **Fate** Returned 4.8.40;
beached Juelssard (Elbe) 5.45 after bombed Allied aircraft
29.4.45, scrapped 1946

**Name** *XII* (ex-mercantile *Stolzenfels*) **Gross tonnage and year
built** 7,512/15 **Commissioned** 28.9.39 **Fate** *Sperrbrecher 12* (1940);
mined off Schiermonnikoog 1.8.40

## *Auxiliary minesweepers:* **SPERRBRECHER 1–39**

**Name** *1* (ex-mercantile *Saar*) **Gross tonnage and year
Built** 3,261/35 **Commissioned** 30.7.40 **Fate** Bombed Allied aircraft
Brest 24.8.44

**Name** *2* (ex-mercantile *Athen*) **Gross tonnage and year
built** 4,450/36 **Commissioned** 30.7.40 **Fate** Mined Boulogne 22.9.42,
salved, mercantile *General Brusilov* (1946), *Warynski* (1947)

**Name** *3* (ex-mercantile *Belgrad*) **Gross tonnage and year
built** 4,418/37 **Commissioned** 15.8.40 **Fate** Scuttled Gironde
estuary 25/4/45, salved 1948 and mercantile **Nicole Schiaffino**
(1950)

**Name** *4* to *10* **Fate** See *Sperrbrecher IV–X*

**Name** *11* (ex-mercantile *Belgrano*) **Gross tonnage and year
built** 6,095/36 **Commissioned** 17.5.41 **Fate** Mined Flensburg
4.1.45, salved 1946 and scrapped U.K. 1947/8

**Name** *12* **Fate** See *Sperrbrecher XII*

*The auxiliary mine destructor vessel* Sperrbrecher No. 13. (Drüppel)

**Name** *13* (ex-mercantile *Minerva*) **Gross tonnage and year built** 2,446/39 **Commissioned** 9.40 **Fate** Returned 1948

**Name** *14* (i) **Fate** See *Sperrbrecher III*

**Name** *14* (ii) (ex-mercantile *Bockenheim*) **Gross tonnage and year built** 7,019/29 **Commissioned** 1.1.41 **Fate** Expanded as block-ship Basseins (Gironde) 25.8.44

**Name** *15* (i) (ex-mercantile *Kongsfjord*) **Gross tonnage and year built** 4,103/37 **Commissioned** 1.1.41 **Fate** Decoy *Gonzenheim* (1941); gunfire of RN battleship *Nelson* and auxiliary cruiser *Esperance Bay* North Atlantic 4.6.41

**Name** *15* (ii) (ex-mercantile *Taronga*) **Gross tonnage and year built** 7,003/34 **Commissioned** 2.42 **Fate** Bombed Allied aircraft Hamburg 8.6.42, salved 1943 and target ship, returned 1945

**Name** *16* (ex-mercantile **Tulane**) **Gross tonnage and year built** 5,487/40 **Commissioned** 16.11.40 **Fate** Bombed Allied aircraft La Pallice 16.9.42, salved, scuttled La Pallice 10.8.44, salved and returned 1946

**Name** *17* (ex-mercantile *Templar*) **Gross tonnage and year built** 6,728/29 **Commissioned** 23.11.40 **Fate** Returned 1945, *Katering* (1962)

**Name** *18* (ex-mercantile *Schürbek*) **Gross tonnage and year built** 2,448/30 **Commissioned** 31.12.40 **Fate** Scrapped 1948

**Name** *19* (ex-mercantile *Rostock*) **Gross tonnage and year built** 2,542/22 **Commissioned** 20.5.41 **Fate** Hospital ship *Rostock* (1944); captured RN *MTB.696* and *713* off Lorient 16.9.44, mercantile *St. Maurice* (1944), *Azur* (1955), *Monte Pellegrino* (1957), *Marhonda* (1964)

**Name** *20* (ex-mercantile *Kolente*) **Gross tonnage and year built** 3,723/33 **Commissioned** 25.9.41 **Fate** Scuttled Nantes 8.44, salved and mercantile *Saint Michel* (1947), *Taipooan* (1955); scrapped Hong Kong 12.63

**Name** *21* (ex-mercantile *Nestor*) **Gross tonnage and year built** 2,446/39 **Commissioned** 10.41 **Fate** Mined Gironde estuary 14.6.43

**Name** *22* (ex-mercantile *Zeus*) **Gross tonnage and year built** 2,500/39 **Commissioned** 4.8.40 **Fate** Returned 1947

**Name** *23* (ex-mercantile *Reyniersz\**) **Gross tonnage and year built** 4,399/42 **Commissioned** 15.8.42 **Fate** Mined Kiel Bay 18.5.45, salved 1951 and scrapped 10.52

**Name** *24* and *25* **Fate** See *Sperrbrecher C* and *B*

**Name** *26* (ex-mercantile *Hermes\**) **Gross tonnage and year built** 2,503/44 **Fate** Bombed Allied aircraft Elbe estuary 29.8.44, salved 1944 and mercantile *Empire Dove* (1949), *Pozarica* (1953), *Bluefin* (1964)

**Name** *27* (ex-mercantile *H. C. Horn*) **Gross tonnage and year built** 4,132/32 **Commissioned** 1941 **Fate** Scuttled Skagerrak 26.5.45

**Name** *28* (ex-mercantile *Tamo*) **Gross tonnage and year built** 5,340/41 **Commissioned** 13.10.43 **Fate** Returned 1947, *Vasilio* (1963)

**Name** *29* (ex-mercantile *Algol*) **Gross tonnage and year built** 7,228/40 **Commissioned** 1943 **Fate** Returned 1945, *Alhena* (1947)

**Name** *30* (ex-mercantile *Eilbek\**) **Gross tonnage and year built** 3,013/42 **Fate** Bombed Allied aircraft while building and lost incomplete Hamburg 4.11.44

**Name** *31* (i) (ex-mercantile *Schwan*) **Gross tonnage and year built** 1,311/38 **Commissioned** 1.10.40 **Fate** *Sperrbrecher 131* (1941), mercantile *Weltonwald* (1946), *Rhineland* (1949), *Herriesbrook* (1956), *Inyoni* (1957)

**Name** *31* (ii) (ex-mercantile *Saturn\**) **Gross tonnage and year built** 2,446 **Fate** Returned incomplete 1945, mercantile *Sarpedon* (1947)

**Name** *32* (i) (ex-*V.102,* ex-mercantile *Cressida*) **Gross tonnage** 1,046/39 **Commissioned** 20.6.40 **Fate** *Sperrbrecher 132* (1941), mercantile *Elsenburgh* (1947), *Gernik* (1962); foundered off Scarpanto 23.12.63

**Name** *32* (ii) (ex-mercantile *Mur*) **Gross tonnage and year built** 3,290/39 **Commissioned** 1942 **Fate** French experimental vessel *Ile d'Oleron* (1945)

**Name** *33* (i) (ex-*V.103,* ex-mercantile *Silvia*) **Gross tonnage and year built** 1,049/38 **Commissioned** 1.10.40 **Fate** *Sperrbrecher 133* (1941); paid-off 1941 and scrapped

**Name** *33* (ii) (ex-mercantile *Drau*) **Gross tonnage and year built** 3,200/43 **Commissioned** 1944 **Fate** Scuttled French Atlantic port 1944, salved and mercantile *Sunni* (1948), *Tendefjell* (1949), *Cebu* (1951)

**Name** *34* (ex-*V.104,* ex-mercantile *Falke*) **Gross tonnage and year built** 997/09 **Commissioned** 10.12.40 **Fate** *Sperrbrecher 134* (1941); bombed Allied aircraft off Ile de Groix 8.8.44, salved and scrapped

**Name** *35* (ex-*V.105*, ex-mercantile *Adolph Kirsten*) **Gross tonnage and year built** 995/27 **Commissioned** 10.12.40 **Fate** Bombed Allied aircraft Brest/St. Malo 8.8.44 or 25.8.44, salved and scrapped

**Name** *36* (ex-mercantile *Eider*) **Gross tonnage and year built** 3,288/37 **Commissioned** 1941 **Fate** Target ship *Eider* (1942); exploded Wilhelmshaven 12.4.45 after bombed Allied aircraft, salved and scuttled North Sea 15.10.46

**Name** *37* (i) (ex-*V.107*, ex-mercantile *Botilla Russ*) **Gross tonnage and year built** 996/22 **Commissioned** 10.12.40 **Fate** *Sperrbrecher 137* (1941); mined off St. Nazaire 28/1/44

**Name** *37* (ii) (ex-mercantile *Capo Lena*) **Gross tonnage and year built** 4,820/21 **Commissioned** 1943 **Fate** Scuttled St. Nazaire 18.8.44, salved and scrapped

**Name** *38* (ex-*V.108*, ex-mercantile *Porjus*) **Gross tonnage and year built** 764/37 **Fate** Lost collision m.v. *Tilsit* Brunsbüttelkoorg 1.12.40; salved and *Sperrbrecher 133*, returned incomplete and mercantile *Kronsberg* (1950)

**Name** *39* (ex-*V.109*, ex-mercantile *Flamingo*) **Gross tonnage and year built** 975/09 **Commissioned** 12.40 **Fate** *Sperrbrecher 139* (1942); mined west of Lindesnes 17.2.45

## *Auxiliary minesweepers:* SPERRBRECHER 60–66, 68–71, 74, 75, 91 *and* 92

**Name** *60* (ex-mercantile *Elster*) **Gross tonnage and year built** 1,136/22 **Commissioned** 27.3.41 **Fate** *Sperrbrecher 160* (1942); mined off Netherlands coast 16.8.42

**Name** *61* (ex-mercantile *Iris*) **Gross tonnage and year built** 1,078/35 **Commissioned** 17.5.41 **Fate** *Sperrbrecher 161* (1942); mined Schiermonnikoog 4.7.42

**Name** *62* (ex-mercantile *Delia*) **Gross tonnage and year built** 1,297/29 **Commissioned** 1941 **Fate** *Sperrbrecher 162* (1942); bombed Allied aircraft Brest 25.8.44, salved and scrapped

**Name** *63* (ex-mercantile *Friesland*) **Gross tonnage and year built** 1,029/04 **Commissioned** 25.9.41 **Fate** *Sperrbrecher 163* (1942); mined North Sea 20.3.44

**Name** *64* (ex-mercantile *Bitsch*) **Gross tonnage and year built** 1,172/13 **Commissioned** 2.7.41 **Fate** *Sperrbrecher 164* (1942); mined Schiermonnikoog 2.9.42

**Name** *65* (ex-mercantile *Gebweiler*) **Gross tonnage and year built** 1,481/08 **Commissioned** 15.10.41 **Fate** *Sperrbrecher 165* (1942); mined east of Gjedser Odde 7.7.43

**Name** *66* (ex-mercantile *Schirmeck*) **Gross tonnage and year built** 1,592/05 **Commissioned** 1.4.42 **Fate** *Sperrbrecher 166* (1942); sabotaged Copenhagen 15.11.44, salved and scrapped

**Name** *68* (ex-mercantile *Flora*) **Gross tonnage and year built** 1,248/39 **Commissioned** 11.10.41 **Fate** *Sperrbrecher 168* (1942); lost unknown cause St. Nazaire 9.44, salved and mercantile *Port Navalo* (1947), *Flachsee* (1955); lost Collision s.s. *Canuk Trader* off Varne L/V 11.2.63

**Name** *69* (ex-mercantile *Ceres*) **Gross tonnage and year built** 1,078/36 **Commissioned** 27.6.41 **Fate** *Sperrbrecher 169* (1942); mined Baltic 19/11/42

**Name** *70* (ex-mercantile *Maria S. Müller*) **Gross tonnage and year built** 1,598/36 **Commissioned** 21.10.41 **Fate** *Sperrbrecher 170* (1942); mined off Ostend 7.8.42

**Name** *71* (ex-mercantile *Jason*) **Gross tonnage and year built** 1,025/35 **Commissioned** 1939 **Fate** Mined off Dragorrinne 16/7/40, salved and *Sperrbrecher 171* (1941); mined north-west of Calais 20.2.42

**Name** *74* (ex-mercantile *Tindelfjell*) **Gross tonnage and year built** 1,337/36 **Commissioned** 23.4.41 **Fate** *Sperrbrecher 174* (1941); mined or bombed Allied aircraft, Dunkirk 28.5.42 or 25.8.42

**Name** *75* (ex-mercantile *Baden*) **Gross tonnage and year built** 1,392/37 **Commissioned** 1941 **Fate** *Sperrbrecher 175* (1942); paid-off La Pallice 8.9.44, returned 1945

**Name** *91* (ex-mercantile *Motor I*) **Gross tonnage** 986 **Commissioned** 8.8.41 **Fate** *Sperrbrecher 191* (1941); mined west of Otschakov 1.7.42

**Name** *92* (ex-mercantile *Kepler*) **Gross tonnage** 800 **Commissioned** 1941 **Fate** *Sperrbrecher 192* (1941), abandoned on Danube 5.45

## *Auxiliary minesweepers:* **SPERRBRECHER 102–105, 120–123, 131–139, 141–150, 152–158, 160–195, 199, 201–205, 212**

**Name** *102* (ex-mercantile *Condor*) **Gross tonnage and year built** 889/22 **Commissioned** 1943 **Fate** Torpedoed R.N. submarine Hubert Gat 20.4.44

**Name** *103* (ex-mercantile *Roes*) **Gross tonnage and year built** 1,530/28 **Commissioned** 1942 **Fate** Russian (1943)

**Name** *104* (ex-mercantile *Martha*) **Gross tonnage and year built** 546/20 **Commissioned** 1942 **Fate** Russian (1945)

**Name** *105* (ex-mercantile *Prinz Willem V\**) **Gross tonnage and year built** 1,525/43 **Commissioned** 1943 **Fate** Expended as blockship New Waterway 5.10.44, salved 1947 and revroceded

**Name** *120* (ex-mercantile *Aar*) **Gross tonnage and year built** 1,350/39 **Commissioned** 7.5.43 **Fate** Bombed Allied aircraft Hamburg 17.1.45, salved and mercantile *Rene* (1945); wrecked Casablanca 13.11.48

**Name** *121* (ex-mercantile *Cap Sim*) **Gross tonnage and year built** 1,906/29 **Commissioned** 25.9.41 **Fate** Paid-off 5.9.44, returned 1945, *Sudani* (1954)

**Name** *122* (ex-mercantile *Cap Hadid*) **Gross tonnage and year built** 1,733/38 **Commissioned** 25.9.41 **Fate** Scuttled St. Nazaire or Gironde 25.8.44, salved and returned 1946, *Cap Bon* (1953)

**Name** *123* (ex-mercantile *Sparta*) **Gross tonnage and year built** 1,724/27 **Commissioned** 1940 **Fate** Burnt-out Tripoli 7.41 after bombed RAF aircraft, salved, bombed Allied aircraft Oreglia 5.45, salved and returned 1947, *Ariel* (1959)

**Name** *131* to *135* **Fate** See *Sperrbrecher 31–35*

**Name** *136* (ex-*V.106*, ex-mercantile *Phoenix*) **Gross tonnage and year built** 25.9.41 **Fate** Mined off St. Nazaire 20.11.42, or beached Memel 22.11.44

**Name** *137* **Fate** See *Sperrbrecher 37*

**Name** *138* (ex-mercantile *Friedrich Harl*) **Gross tonnage and year built** 1,262/38 **Commissioned** 1942 **Fate** Mined north of Schiermonnikoog 23.12.42

**Name** *139* **Fate** See *Sperrbrecher 39*

**Name** *141* (ex-*NS.1*, ex-mercantile *Lies*) **Gross tonnage and year built** 465/40 **Commissioned** 11.41 **Fate** Mined off Ostend 31.3.44

**Name** *142* (ex-*NS.2*, ex-mercantile *Westerbroek*) **Gross tonnage and year built** 499/41 **Commissioned** 1942 **Fate** Mined off Ostend 15.9.42

**Name** *143* (ex-*NS.3*, ex-mercantile *Lola*) **Gross tonnage and year built** 498/40 **Commissioned** 11.41 **Fate** Mined off Nieuport 9.10.42

**Name** *144* (ex-*NS.4*, ex-mercantile *Beljerland*) **Gross tonnage and year built** 387/39 **Commissioned** 11.41 **Fate** Mined near Dieppe 12.2.42 or 12.12.42

**Name** *145* (ex-*NS.5*, ex-mercantile *Import*) **Gross tonnage and year built** 395/39 **Commissioned** 1942 **Fate** Returned 1945, *Notus* (1959) *Marika* (1959)

Sperrbrecher No. 141. (Drüppel)

**Name** *146* (ex-*NS.6*, ex-mercantile *Havik*) **Gross tonage and year built** 479/38 **Commissioned** 1942 **Fate** Bombed Allied aircraft Pauillac 4.8.44, salved 1945 and mercantile *Enseigne Yves Bignon* (1949), *Holdendrecht* (1950), *Paul M.* (1952)

**Name** *147* (ex-*N.S.7*, ex-mercantile *Raket*) **Gross tonnage and year built** 482/36 **Commissioned** 1942 **Fate** Mined off Hook of Holland 27.5.42

**Name** *148* (ex-*NS.8*, ex-mercantile *Strijpe*) **Gross tonnage and year built** 544/41 **Commissioned** 1942 **Fate** Returned 1946, *Vassiliki* (1962)

**Name** *149* (ex-*NS.9*, ex-mercantile *Goote*) **Gross tonnage and year built** 544/40 **Commissioned** 1942 **Fate** Mined south-east of Dan Helder 28.12.42

**Name** *150* (ex-*N.S.10*, ex-mercantile *Viriato*) **Gross tonnage and year built** 750/40 **Commissioned** 1942 **Fate** Bombed Allied aircraft north of Ameland 29.5.42

**Name** *152* (ex-mercantile *Fauna*) **Gross tonnage and year built** 1,248/40 **Commissioned** 16.8.42 **Fate** Bombed Allied aircraft Bremen 18.8.44, salved and returned 1948, *Apostolos K* (1962)

**Name** *153* (ex-mercantile *Tantalus*) **Gross tonnage and year built** 1,543/40 **Commissioned** 16.8.43 **Fate** Mined off Brest 27.8.44, salved and Russian 1946

**Name** *154* (ex-mercantile *Eilenau*) **Gross tonnage and year built** 1,011/43 **Commissioned** 1944 **Fate** Mercantile *Markelo* (1948), *Sigvald II* (1962)

**Name** *155* (ex-mercantile *Tanger*) **Gross tonnage and year built** 1,497/42 **Fate** Scuttled Antwerp 1944, salved and mercantile *Ardea* (1947), *Falco* (1954), *Labrador* (1956)

**Name** *156* (ex-mercantile *Konsul A. Sartori**) **Gross tonnage and year built** 1,606/43 **Fate** Completed mercantile *Tachira* (1946), *Mexico* (1955), *Warigi* (1962)

**Name** *157* (ex-mercantile *Tellus*) **Gross tonnage and year built** 1,495/40 **Commissioned** 1944 **Fate** Beached Les Sables d'Olonne, or bombed Allied aircraft Brest, 15.8.44

**Name** *158* (ex-mercantile *Titan*) **Gross tonnage and year built** 1,106/43 **Fate** Completed mercantile *Lyngaa* (1947), *Ile Sainte Marie* (1949), *Fridiotis* (1961)

**Name** *160* to *166* **Fate** See *Sperrbrecher 60–66*

**Name** *167* (ex-mercantile *Malmedy*) **Gross tonnage and year built** 1,506/01 **Commissioned** 6.5.42 **Fate** Mined North Sea 1.45

**Name** *168* to *171* **Fate** See *Sperrbrecher 68–71*

**Name** *172* (ex-mercantile *Ophelia*) **Gross tonnage and year built** 1,446/35 **Commissioned** 1942 **Fate** Mercantile *Wensleydale* (1948), *Fred Borchardt* (1949)

**Name** *173* (ex-mercantile *Westland*) **Gross tonnage and year built** 1,258/26 **Commissioned** 31.1.42 **Fate** Mined north of Ameland 25.5.43

**Name** *174* and *175* **Fate** See *Sperrbrecher 74* and *75*

**Name** *176* (ex-mercantile *Valeria*) **Gross tonnage and year built** 1,450/37 **Commissioned** 16.5.42 **Fate** Mined, or bombed Allied aircraft, south of Heligoland 29.8.44

**Name** *177* (ex-mercantile *Kepler*) **Gross tonnage and year built** 1,236/25 **Commissioned** 4.42 **Fate** Returned and *Olbers* (1946), *Barbara B* (1958)

**Name** *178* (ex-mercantile *Gauss*) **Gross tonnage and year built** 1,236/25 **Commissioned** 19.8.42 **Fate** Gunfire RN destroyers off Dieppe 12.12.42

**Name** *179* (ex-mercantile *Prins Willem IV\**) **Gross tonnage and year built** 1,535/40 **Fate** Bombed while building Hamburg. Allied aircraft 31.12.44, and construction abandoned, returned 1945

**Name** *180* (ex-mercantile *Midas\**) **Gross tonnage and year built** 1,747/41 **Commissioned** 16.8.43 **Fate** Bombed Allied aircraft Brest 25.8.44, salved 1947 and returned, *Hector* (1949)

**Name** *181* (ex-mercantile *Atlas\**) **Gross tonnage and year built** 1,747/42 **Commissioned** 9.11.43 **Fate** Beached Stadlandet 6.6.44 after bombed Allied aircraft, salved 1946 and mercantile *Bravo* (1952)

**Name** *182* (ex-mercantile *Andromeda\**) **Gross tonnage and year built** 1,606/43 **Fate** Completed mercantile *Nueva Esparta* (1946), *Port Paix* (1955), *Sinaloa* (1957)

**Name** *183* (ex-mercantile *Quack*) **Gross tonnage and year built** 560/40 **Commissioned** 2.4.41 **Fate** Mined off Dunkerque 23.6.42, salved and mercantile *Hyke Sophia* (1956), *Cinzia* (1958)

**Name** *184* (ex-mercantile *Bernisse*) **Gross tonnage and year built** 560/41 **Commissioned** 2.4.41 **Fate** Burnt-out Nantes 16.9.43 after bombed Allied aircraft

**Name** *185* (ex-mercantile *Hansburg,\**ex-*Alca*) **Gross tonnage and year built** 1,424/42 **Commissioned** 1.7.43 **Fate** Bombed R.A.F. aircraft Wilhelmshaven 30.3.45, salved and mercantile *Heidberg* (1950), *Melanie* (1960), *Rohrbach* (1962), *St. Jacob* (1965)

**Name** *186* (ex-mercantile *Kirsten (i),* ex-*Delia\**) **Gross tonnage and year built** 1,790/43 **Fate** Completed mercantile *Marguerite* (1949)

**Name** *187* (ex-mercantile *Almeria\**) **Gross tonnage and year built** 1,812/43 **Fate** Scuttled incomplete Antwerp 9.44, mercantile *Escaut* (1949), *Alegrita* (1958), *Aleppo* (1958), *Nissos Serifos* (1964)

**Name** *188* (ex-mercantile *Kirsten (ii)\**) **Gross tonnage and year built** 1,700/40 **Fate** Lost incomplete unknown cause in tow North Sea 8.44

**Name** *189* (ex-mercantile *Bacchus\**) **Gross tonnage and year built** 1,625/44 **Fate** Completed mercantile *Falcon* (1946), *Vera Cruz* (1955)

**Name** *190* (ex-mercantile *Kilwa*) **Gross tonnage and year built** 1,110/42 **Commissioned** 1942 **Fate** Sabotaged Svendborg 8.11.44, salved and mercantile *Kilwa* (1946), *Levensau* (1955)

**Name** *191* to *192* **Fate** See *Sperrbrecher 91* and *92*

**Name** *193* (ex-mercantile *Albrecht Dürer*) **Gross tonnage and year built** 570/25 **Commissioned** 26.6.43 **Fate** Bombed Allied aircraft Sulina 10.4.44

**Name** *194* (ex-mercantile *Potemkin*) **Gross tonnage** 800 **Commissioned** 1943 **Fate** Gunfire—Braila 24.8.44

**Name** *195* (ex-mercantile *Santa Rita*) **Gross tonnage and year built** 5,191/08 **Commissioned** 1943 **Fate** Scuttled Constanta 25.8.44

**Name** *199* (ex-*MFP.199*) **Gross tonnage and year built** 220/42 **Commissioned** 16.6.42 **Fate** USN 1947

**Name** *201* (ex-*NF.3*, ex-mercantile *Zaanland*) **Commissioned** 1940 **Fate** Not known

**Name** *202* (ex-*NF.1*, ex-mercantile *Weser*) **Commissioned** 1940 **Fate** Paid-off 14.8.42

**Name** *203* (ex-*NF.2*, ex-mercantile *Zeeland*) **Gross tonnage and year built** 200/03 **Commissioned** 1940 **Fate** Training ship *Heidje*, mercantile *Antje* (1954)

**Name** *204* (ex-*NF.4*, ex-mercantile *Deutschland*) **Gross tonnage** 361 **Commissioned** 1940 **Fate** Returned 1945

**Name** *205* (ex-*NF.5*, ex-mercantile *Ermland*) **Commissioned** 1940 **Fate** Not known

**Name** *212* (ex-*MFP.212*) **Gross tonnage and year built** 220/42 **Commissioned** 5.42 **Fate** RN (1947): mined Weser estuary 1949

## *Auxiliary minesweeper :* **SPERRBRECHER**

**Name** (ex-mercantile *Arcturus*) **Gross tonnage and year built** 204/97 **Commissioned** 1941 **Fate** Lost unknown cause South of Aalesund 11.43

## *Minesweepers :* **KSB.1–27**

*Displacement:* 1,588 tons (1,724 tons full)
*Dimensions:* $249\frac{1}{4}$ (pp) $274\frac{1}{2}$ (oa) × 36 × $9\frac{1}{4}$/$10\frac{1}{2}$ feet
*Machinery:* Two boilers; one-shaft; reciprocating (VTE) and exhaust turbine I.H.P. 1,350 = $12\frac{1}{2}$ knots
*Bunkers & Radius:* Coal 160 tons; 500 miles
*Armament:* Two 4.1inch (2 × 1), four 37mm A.A. (2 × 2), eight 20mm A.A. (4 × 2) guns
*Complement:* 127
*Notes:* All cancelled

## *Trawlers:* **KUj.1**

The bulk of trawlers employed by the German Navy were requisitioned from the fishing fleets, but a small class of naval trawlers were also put in hand which largely followed mercantile practice and were coal-fired.

*Displacement:* 830 tons (970 tons full)
*Dimensions:* 181(pp) $192\frac{1}{2}$(oa) $\times$ $27\frac{1}{2}$ $\times$ $11\frac{1}{2}/14\frac{1}{2}$ feet
*Machinery:* Two boilers; one-shaft; reciprocating (VTE) with exhaust turbine I.H.P. 850 = $12\frac{3}{4}$ knots
*Bunkers & Radius:* Coal 193 tons; 4,700 miles at $12\frac{1}{2}$ knots
*Armament:* One 3.5inch A.A., one 37mm A.A., nine 20mm A.A. (2 × 4 and 1 × 1) guns
*Complement:* 61
*Notes:* Built 1944–5. *KUj.13* was lost in 1943; *KUj.1, 5, 7–10, 14–16, 21, 22 & 25,* were lost 1944; *KUj.17–20* construction abandoned; *KUj.26–40* projected; *KUj.41* and *42* were cancelled, *KUj.3* and *4* were allocated to the Russian Navy, while at least five (*KUj.2, 11, 12, 23 & 24*) passed into commercial ownership

*The naval trawler* KUj.12. (Drüppel)

*The auxiliary netlayer* Uranus. (Drüppel)

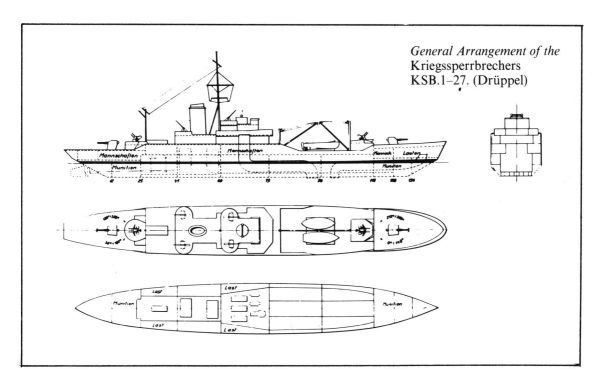

*General Arrangement of the*
Kriegssperrbrechers
KSB.1–27. (Drüppel)

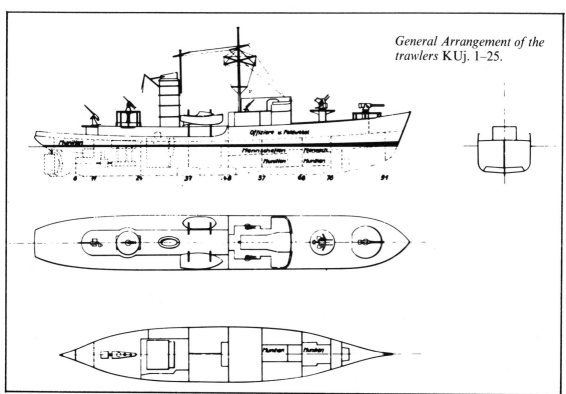

*General Arrangement of the*
*trawlers* KUj. 1–25.

# Minelayers

### Minelayer: **BREMSE**

*Displacement:* 1,435 tons (1,870 tons full)
*Dimensions:* 318¼(pp) 341¼(oa) × 31¼ × 9¼/12 feet
*Machinery:* Two shafts; four M.A.N. diesel motors (two per
shaft) B.H.P. 26,000 = 27 knots
*Bunkers & Radius:* O.F. 333 tons; 8,000 miles at 19 knots
*Armament:* Four 5inch (4 × 1), eight 20mm A.A. (4 × 2) guns:
three-hundred and fifty mines
*Complement:* 192
*Notes:* Largely an experimental vessel in which half the diesel
installation later fitted to the armoured ship *Deutschland*
underwent trial. Was also used as a gunnery training ship

**Name** *Bremse* **Built by** Naval Dockyard (Wilhelmshaven)
**Launched** 24.1.31 **Fate** Gunfire RN cruisers *Aurora* and *Nigeria*
west of Murmen 6.9.41

*The gunnery training ship*
Bremse *was also used as a*
*minelayer.* (Drüppel)

### Minelayer: **BRUMMER (i)**

*Displacement:* 2,410 tons (3,010 tons full)
*Dimensions:* 354¼(pp) 370¾(oa) × 44¼ × 10½/14 feet
*Machinery:* Two Wagner boilers (pressure 1,028 lb.); two shafts;
Wagner geared turbines, S.H.P. 8,000 = 20 knots

*Bunkers & Radius:* O.F. 450 tons; 2,400 miles at 15 knots
*Armament:* Four 4.1inch A.A. (2 × 2), two 3.5inch A.A. (2 × 1),
    four 37mm A.A. (2 × 2) guns; four-hundred and fifty mines
*Complement:* 182 (+ 480 when used as a training ship)
*Notes:* Also employed as a cadet or gunnery training ship, and
    experimental vessel for new marks of guns and mountings

**Name** *Brummer (i)* **Built by** AG Weser (Bremen) **Launched** 29.5.35
**Fate** Torpedoed RN submarine *Sterlet* Kattegat 14.4.40

*The* Brummer (i) *was also
used as a combined minelayer
and gunnery training ship.*
(Drüppel)

# *Minelayers:* **EIGHT projected**

Considerable importance was attached to mine warfare in
the German Navy, and all destroyers, torpedo boats and
submarines were equipped for this task, and provision was
made so that most other surface vessels could be fitted if
required. These vessels were enlarged *Brummers*, with speed
considerably increased, but still insufficient to conduct lays in
enemy waters as they could not outstrip scouting and flotilla
vessels that might be brought in to intercept them. The second
unit of this class was also to serve as a gunnery training ship,
and shipped an alternative main armament, while the two
final units doubled as training ships. An opening was cut in
the counter for the Hein mat method of aircraft recovery.

*Displacement:* 5,450 tons (6,240 tons full)
*Dimensions:* 475¾(pp) 495½(oa) × 53¼ × 15½/17¾ feet
*Machinery:* Four Wagner boilers (pressure 1,028 lb.); two shafts;
geared turbines, S.H.P. 40,000 = 28 knots
*Bunkers & Radius:* O.F. 720 tons; 3,000 miles at 19 knots
*Armament:* Eight 4.1inch A.A. (4 × 2) except *"B"* four 5inch
(4 × 1), eight 37mm A.A. (2 × 2 and 4 × 1), two 20mm
A.A. (2 × 1) guns; 320/400 mines
*Complement:* 320

**Name** *"A"* **Built by** Seebeckwerft (Bremerhaven) **Fate** Cancelled

**Name** *"B"* **Built by** Howaldts Werke (Hamburg) **Fate** Cancelled

**Name** *"C"* **Built by** Deutsche Werft (Hamburg) **Fate** Cancelled

**Name** *"D"* **Built by** Howaldts Werke (Hamburg) **Fate** Cancelled

**Name** *"E"* **Built by** Howaldts Werke (Hamburg) **Fate** Cancelled

**Name** *"F"* **Built by** Howaldts Werke (Hamburg) **Fate** Cancelled

**Name** *"G"* **Built by** Deutsche Werft (Hamburg) **Fate** Cancelled

**Name** *"H"* **Built by** Deutsche Werft (Hamburg) **Fate** Cancelled

## *Ex-RNN Minelayer:* **BRUMMER (ii)**

*Displacement:* 1,596 tons (1,924 tons full)
*Dimensions:* 304(pp) 318¼(oa) × 37¾ × 11¾/18¾ feet
*Machinery:* Three boilers; two-shaft; De Laval geared turbines,
S.H.P. 6,000 = 21 knots and diesel-electric drive for cruising
*Bunkers & Radius:* O.F. 200 tons; 3,000 miles at 14 knots
*Armament:* Four 4.7inch (4 × 1), one 3inch A.A., two 37mm
A.A. (1 × 2), four 20mm A.A. (4 × 1) guns, 280 mines
*Complement:* 168

**Name** *Albatross* (ex-*Olav Tryggvason*) **Built by** Naval Dockyard
(Horten) **Launched** 1932 **Fate** *Brummer* (*ii*) (1941); bombed
USAAF aircraft Kiel 3.4.45

*The former Norwegian
minelayer* Olav Tryggvason
*was first named* Albatros *to
commemorate the torpedo boat
which she sank in 1940, but in
1941 she became the second*
Brummer.

# *Ex-RDN minelayer:* **LOSSEN**

*Displacement:* 640 tons
*Dimensions:* 149¼(pp) × 28 × 10 feet
*Machinery:* Reciprocating (VTE) I.H.P. 900 = 12 knots
*Bunkers:* Coal 44 tons
*Armament:* Two 3inch (2 × 1), two 8mm A.A. (2 × 1) guns,
    one hundred and seventy-five mines
*Complement:* 61

# *ExRNN minelayers:* **GLOMMEN** *and* **LAUGEN**

*Displacement:* 335 tons
*Dimensions:* 137¾(pp) × 28 × 6¼ feet
*Machinery:* Two-shaft; reciprocating I.H.P. 170 = 9½ knots
*Bunkers:* Coal 21 tons
*Armament:* Two 3inch (2 × 1) guns, fifty mines
*Complement 39*

# *Ex-mercantile minelayer:* **NYMPHE·**

*Displacement:* 480 tons (507 tons full)
*Dimensions:* 182¾(pp) 191½(oa) × 24¼ × 7½ feet
*Machinery:* Two Schulz boilers; two-shaft; reciprocating (VTE)
    I.H.P. 1,800 = 16½ knots
*Bunkers & Radius:* O.F.; 2,000 miles at 14 knots
*Complement:* 50

# *Ex-RIt.N minelayer:* **KEHRWIEDER**

*Displacement:* 539 tons
*Dimensions:* 182(pp) 192(oa) × 23½ × 7 feet
*Machinery:* Two Schulz boilers; two-shaft; reciprocating (VTE)
    I.H.P. 1,600 = 14 knots
*Bunkers & Radius:* Coal 125 tons; 2,000 miles at 14 knots
*Armament:* Two 4inch (2 × 1) guns, mines
*Complement:* 49

# *Ex-RIt.N minelayer:* **LAURANA**

*Displacement:* 113 tons
*Dimensions:* 95¼(pp) × 21¼ × 4½ feet

*Machinery:* One Yarrow boiler; two shafts; reciprocating (VTE)
   I.H.P. 280 = 11 knots
*Bunkers:* Coal
*Armament:* One 3inch gun, mines
*Complement:* 27

## *Ex-RYN minelayer:* **DRACHE**

*Displacement:* 1,870 tons
*Dimensions:* 249½(pp) × 42¾ × 11½ feet
*Machinery:* Two-shafts, M.A.N. diesel motors, B.H.P. 3,260 =
   15 knots
*Bunkers:* O.F.
*Armament:* Two 4.1inch A.A. (2 × 1), six 20mm A.A. (6 × 1)
   guns, four hundred mines, one aircraft
*Complement:* Not known
*Notes:* Former seaplane carrier able to stow ten aircraft

## *Ex-RNN minelayers:* **KAMERUN** *and* **TOGO**

*Displacement:* 320 tons
*Dimensions:* 167(pp) × 23 × 6 feet
*Machinery:* One boiler; two-shafts; reciprocating (VTE) I.H.P.
   900 = 13½ knots
*Bunkers:* O.F.
*Armament:* One 40mm A.A., two 12.7mm A.A. (2 × 1) guns,
   mines
*Complement:* 23
*Notes:* Former minesweepers

*The fighter-direction ship* Togo
*had a large array of radar
aerials. She had previously
been a disguised raider.*
(Drüppel)

# Ex-RIt.N minelayer: **FASANA**

*Displacement:* 531 tons
*Dimensions:* 192(pp) × 32 × $5\frac{3}{4}$ feet
*Machinery:* Two shafts; Fiat diesel motors, B.H.P. 700 =
  10 knots
*Bunkers:* O.F. 20 tons
*Armament:* One 3inch gun, fifty-four mines
*Complement:* Not known

**Name** *Lossen* (ex-*Lossen*) **Built by** Not known **Launched** Not
known **Fate** Scuttled Copenhagen 29.8.43, salved and German;
mercantile *Wismar* (194?)

**Name** *Glommen* (ex-*Glommen*) **Built by** Akers Mek. Verksted
(Oslo) **Launched** 1917 **Fate** Lost off Norway 1944

**Name** *Laugen* (ex-*Laugen*) **Built by** Akers Mek. Verksted (Oslo)
**Launched** 1917 **Fate** Retroceded 1945

**Name** *Nymphe* (ex-mercantile *La Nymphe*, ex-*M.42*)
**Built by** Bremer Vulkan (Vegesack) **Launched** 1916

**Name** *Kehrweider* (ex-*Crotone*, ex-*M.120*) **Built by** Neptun Werft
(Rostovk) **Fate** Scuttled Spezzia 9.9.43, salved and German;
bombed Allied aircraft Spezzia 1945 and burnt-out

**Name** *Làurana* (ex-*MF.131*) **Built by** Granz-Danubius
**Launched** 1919 **Fate** Bombed Allied aircraft Trieste 20.2.45

**Name** *Drache* (ex-*Zmaj*) **Built by** Deutsche Werft (Hamburg)
**Launched** 1929 **Fate** Bombed Allied aircraft off Samos 22.12.43

**Name** *Kamerun* (ex-*Rauma*) **Built by** Nylands Verksted (Oslo)
**Launched** 1939 **Fate** Retroceded 1945

**Name** *Togo* (ex-*Otra*) **Built by** Nylands Verksted (Oslo)
**Launched** 5.8.39 **Fate** Retroceded 1945

**Name** *Fasana* **Built by** (Castellammare) **Launched** 1926
**Fate** Tagliamento 2.5.44 and burnt-out; salved

# Auxiliary minelayers

*Adjutant* one 60mm, two 20mm A.A. guns; twenty mines; *Brandenburg*
three 4.1inch (3 × 1), eight 3.5inch A.A. (8 × 1), four 20mm A.A.
guns; *Cobra* two 3.5inch A.A. (2 × 1), one 37mm A.A. guns; one
hundred and eighty mines; *Doggerbank* one 4.1inch, two 20mm A.A.
(2 × 1) guns; two hundred and eighty mines; *Cyrnos* two hundred and
twenty mines; *Dietrich von Bern* one hundred and twenty mines; *Elsass*
two 3.5inch A.A. (2 × 1), ten 20mm A.A. (1 × 4 and 6 × 1) guns;
two hundred and eighty mines; *Hansestadt Danzig* (i) two 3.5inch A.A.
(2 × 1), four 37mm A.A. (4 × 1), six 20mm A.A. (6 × 1) guns; three
hundred and sixty mines; *Hansestadt Danzig* (ii) two 37mm A.A. (2 × 1)
guns; one hundred and eighty mines; *Helgoland* three hundred and

twenty mines; *Juminda* two 20mm A.A. (2 × 1) guns; eighty mines; *Jupiter* eighty mines; *Kiebitz* three 3.6inch A. A., twenty-six 20mm A.A. ( × 4 and × 1) guns; two hundred and fifty mines; *Romania* four 20mm A.A. (4 × 1) guns; eighty mines; *San Giorgio* four 20mm A.A. (4 × 1) guns; eighteen mines; *Schwerin* two 3.5inch A.A. (2 × 1), six 20mm A.A. (6 × 1) guns; two hundred and eighty mines; *Skagerrak* four 20mm A.A. (4 × 1) guns; one hundred and eighty mines; *Konigin Luise* two 3.5inch A.A. (2 × 1), one 37mm A.A., two 20mm A.A. (2 × 1) guns; two hundred and forty mines; *Kuckuck* two 3inch (2 × 1), four 20mm A.A. (4 × 1) guns; two hundred mines; *Linz* two 4.1inch A.A. (2 × 1), two 37mm A.A. (2 × 1), fourteen 20mm A.A. ( × 4 and × 1) guns; three hundred and forty mines; *Lothringen* two 3.5inch A.A. (2 × 1) guns; two hundred and forty mines; *Marienburg* three hundred mines; *Niedersaschen* two 4.1inch A.A. (2 × 1), two 69mm A.A. (2 × 1), twelve 20mm A.A. (12 × 1) guns; two hundred and sixty mines; *Oldenburg* two 37mm A.A. (2 × 1), fourteen 20mm A.A. ( × 4 and × 1) guns; one hundred and forty-four mines; *Ostmark* two 3.5inch A.A. (2 × 1), fourteen 20mm A.A. (2 × 4 and 6 × 1) guns; two hundred and forty mines; *Pommern* two 4.1inch A.A. (2 × 1), twelve 20mm A.A. (12 × 1) guns; two hundred and sixty mines; *Preussen* two 3.5inch A.A. (2 × 1) guns; four hundred mines; *Pruth* two 20mm A.A. (2 × 1) guns; *Roland* two 3.5inch A.A. (2 × 1), one 37mm A.A., two 20mm A.A. (2 × 1) guns; *Tannenburg* three 5.9inch (3 × 1), four 37mm A.A. (4 × 1), six 20mm A.A. (6 × 1) guns; four hundred and sixty mines; *Theresia Wallner* two 20mm A.A. (2 × 1) guns; thirty mines; *Tronje* two 20mm A.A. (2 × 1) guns; thirty mines; *Ulm* two hundred mines.

**Name** *Adjutant* (ex-mercantile *Pol IX*) **Gross tonnage and year built** 354/37 **Fate** Gunfire auxiliary cruiser *Komet* 1.7.41

**Name** *Alexandra* (ex-mercantile) **Gross tonnage and year built** 90/90 **Fate** Retroceded mercantile *Rudnik* (1948); scrapped 1964

**Name** *Barbara* (ex-mercantile *St. Denis*) **Gross tonnage and year built** 2,435/08 **Fate** Accommodation ship *Skorpion* (1945); scrapped 1949

**Name** *Brandenburg* (ex-mercantile *Kita*) **Gross tonnage and year built** 3,894/36 **Fate** Torpedoed RN submarine off Capreira 21.9.43

**Name** *Bulgaria* (ex-mercantile) **Gross tonnage and year built** 1,108/94 **Fate** Torpedoed RN submarine South of Amorgos 8.10.43

**Name** *Cobra* (ex-mercantile) **Gross tonnage and year built** 2,131/26 **Fate** Bombed Allied aircraft Schiedam 27.8.43

**Name** *Cyrnos* (ex-mercantile) **Gross tonnage and year built** 2,406/29 **Fate** *SG.13* (1943), A.A. escort (1944); retroceded 1945

**Name** *Dietrich von Bern* (ex-mercantile *Mazara*) **Gross tonnage and year built** 984/34 **Fate** Bombed British aircraft Genoa 12.8.44

**Name** *Deutschland\**(ex-mercantile) **Gross tonnage and year
built** 2,972/09 **Fate** *Stralsund* (1940); mercantile *Orion* (1945),
*Aniva* (1948)

**Name** *Doggerbank* (ex-mercantile *Speybank*) **Gross tonnage and year
built** 5,154/26 **Fate** Torpedoed German submarine *U.43* North
Atlantic 4.3.43

**Name** *Elsass* (ex-mercantile *Côte d'Azur*) **Gross tonnage and year
built** 3,047/30 **Fate** Mined east of Samso 3.1.45

**Name** *Hansestadt Danzig (i)* (ex-mercantile) **Gross tonnage and
year built** 2,430/26 **Fate** Mined off Olandsund 9.7.41

**Name** *Nansestadt Danzig (ii)* (ex-mercantile *Peter Wessel*)
**Gross tonnage and year built** 1,415/37 **Fate** Retroceded 1945

**Name** *Helgoland* (ex-mercantile) **Gross tonnage and year built** 2,947/39
2,947/39 **Fate** Accommodation ship (1944); scrapped U.K. 1947

**Name** *Juminda* (ex-mercantile *Betta No. 5*) **Gross tonnage and year
built** 475/94 **Fate** Torpedoed RN MTB's off San Stefano 20.9.43
**Name** *Jupiter*

**Name** *Kaiser\**(ex-mercantile) **Gross tonnage and year built** 1,911/05
**Fate** Mercantile *Beniowski* (1946)

**Name** *Kiebitz* (ex-*Ramb III*, ex-mercantile) **Gross tonnage and year
built** 3,667/38 **Fate** Bombed American aircraft Fiume 5.11.44; salved
and Yugoslavian Navy *Galeb* (1950)

**Name** *Königin Luise* (ex-mercantile) **Gross tonnage and year
built** 2,399/34 **Fate** Mined off Helsinki 25.9.41

**Name** *Kuckuck* (ex-mercantile *Ramb III* ) **Gross tonnage and
year built** 3,667/38 **Fate** Bombed Allied aircraft Fiume 5.11.43,
salved and scuttled Trieste 1.5.45, salved and Yugoslav training
ship *Galeb* (1950)

**Name** *Linz* (ex-mercantile) **Gross tonnage and year built** 3,374/40
**Fate** Mercantile *Empire Wansbeck* (1945)

**Name** *Lothringen\** (ex-mercantile *London*) **Gross tonnage and
year built** 2,434/41 **Fate** Retroceded 1945

**Name** *Marienburg* (ex-mercantile) **Gross tonnage and year
built** 6,200/39 **Fate** Completed mercantile *Lensovjet* (1953)

**Name** *Niedersachsen* (ex-mercantile *Acqui* ) **Gross tonnage and
year built** 1,794/34 **Fate** Torpedoed RN submarine off Toulon
15.2.44

**Name** *Oldenburg* (ex-mercantile *Garigliono*) **Year built** 1934
**Fate** Retroceded 1945

**Name** *Ostmark* (ex-mercantile *Côte d'Argent* ) **Gross tonnage
and year built** 3,047/32 **Fate** Bombed Allied aircraft West of
Anholt 21.4.45

**Name** *Passat* (ex-mercantile *Storstad*) **Gross tonnage and year
built** 8,998/26 **Fate** Wreck scuttled Nantes 11.8.44 after bombed
British aircraft Pauillac   .9.42; salved and scrapped 1948

*The auxiliary minelayer*
Niedersachsen. (Drüppel)

**Name** *Pommern* (ex-mercantile *Bélain d'Esnambuc)* **Gross tonnage and year built** 2,956/39 **Fate** *SG.12* (1943); mined south of San Remo 5.10.43

**Name** *Preussen\** (ex-mercantile) **Gross tonnage and year built** 2,529/26 **Fate** Mined off Olandsund 9.7.41

**Name** *Pruth* (ex-mercantile) **Fate** Scuttled Black Sea 14.9.43

**Name** *Roland* (ex-mercantile) **Gross tonnage and year built** 2,436/27 **Fate** Mined off Narva Bay 21.4.44

**Name** *Romania* (ex-mercantile) **Gross tonnage and year built** 364/14 **Fate** Bombed Allied aircraft Constanta 12.5.44

**Name** *San Giorgio* (ex-mercantile) **Gross tonnage and year built** 3,152/04 **Fate** Wrecked Punta delle Mestre 12.2.44; salved and scrapped 1946/7

**Name** *Schwerin* (ex-mercantile) **Gross tonnage and year built** 3,133/26 **Fate** Russian 1945

**Name** *Skagerrak* (ex-mercantile) **Gross tonnage and year built** 1,281/39 **Fate** Torpedoed RN submarine, or bombed Allied aircraft, off Egero 20.1.44

**Name** *Tannenberg* (ex-mercantile) **Gross tonnage and year built** 5,504/35 **Fate** Mined off Olandsund 9.7.41

**Name** *Theresia Wallner* (ex-mercantile *Antigono*) **Fate** Mined off Ozchakov 25.10.41

**Name** *Tronje* (ex-mercantile) **Fate** Mined off Moldova 29.8.44

**Name** *Ulm* (ex-mercantile) **Gross tonnage and year built** 3,071/38 **Fate** *Sciff 11* (1941); gunfire RN destroyers 29.8.42. *Marne, Martin* and *Onslaught* south-east of Bear Island 29.8.42

**Name** *Versailles* (ex-mercantile) **Gross tonnage and year built** 2,156/19 **Fate** Paid-off 1942

**Name** *Westmark* (ex-mercantile *Djebel-Dèra*) **Gross tonnage and year built** 2,835/30 **Fate** *SG.8* (1953); scuttled Marseilles 22.8.44

**Name** *Wullenwever* (ex-mercantile *Rouen*) **Gross tonnage and year built** 1,882/12 **Fate** Mined Baltic 25.4.43; salved 1945 and scrapped 1946

**Name** *Zeus* (ex-mercantile *Francesco Morosini)* **Gross tonnage and year built** 2,423/28 **Fate** Bombed Allied aircraft Gulf of Salonika 30.10.44

# Coast Defence Ships

## Ex-RNN coast defence ships: **NYMPHE** and **THETIS**

*Displacement:* 3,858 tons
*Dimensions:* 279(pp) 304(oa) × 48½ × 16½/17¾ feet
*Machinery:* Three cylindrical boilers, 2-shaft reciprocating
    (VTE) I.H.P. 4,500 = 17 knots
*Bunkers:* Coal 550 tons
*Protection:* Main belt 4(ends)–7(amid) inches, bulkheads 8
    inches, main deck 2 inches, C.T. 6 inches
*Armament:* Seven 4.1inch A.A. (7 × 1), two 40mm A.A. (2 × 1),
    nine 20mm A.A. (2 × 4 and 1 × 1) guns
*Notes:* Former coast defence ships re-armed as heavy A.A.
    batteries

**Name** *Nymphe* (ex-*Tordenskjold*) **Built by** Armstrong Hawthorn
Leslie **Launched** 3.97 **Fate** German heavy A.A. battery (1940);
bombed RAF aircraft and beached Svolvaer 1945, salved and
scrapped 1948

**Name** *Thetis* (ex-*Harald Haarfagre*) **Built by** Armstrong
Hawthorn Leslie **Launched** 4.1.97 **Fate** German heavy A.A.
battery (1940); retroceded RNN 1946

*The AA ship* Thetis *was an
ex-Norwegian coast defence
battleship. Other conversions
included old German and
Dutch warships.* (Drüppel)

## Ex-RNeth.N cruiser: **NIOBE**

*Displacement:* 3,512 tons
*Dimensions:* 310¾(pp) × 48½ × 17¾ feet
*Machinery:* Twelve Yarrow boilers, 2-shaft reciprocating (VTE-cyl. 33″:49″:74″ × 29″ stroke) I.H.P. 9,750 = 20 knots
*Bunkers & Radius:* Coal 1,000 tons; 4,500 miles at 9¾ knots
*Protection:* Belt 6 inches, bulkheads 6 inches, main deck 2¼ inches, C.T. 4 inches
*Armament:* Six 4.1inch A.A. (6 × 1), four 40mm A.A. (4 × 1), sixteen 20mm A.A. (4 × 4) guns
*Notes:* Former armoured cruiser, which had been relegated to training, re-armed as heavy A.A. battery

## Ex-RNeth.N coast defence ship: **ARIADNE**

*Displacement:* 4,560 tons
*Dimensions:* 317(oa) × 50 × 19 feet
*Machinery:* Six Yarrow boilers, 2-shaft reciprocating (VTE) I.H.P. 6,300 = 16 knots
*Bunkers & Radius:* Coal 830 tons; 4,100 miles at 9¾ knots
*Protection:* Main belt 4(ends)–6(amid) inches, bulkheads 6 inches, main deck 2 inches, E.R. gratings 4¾ inches, C.T. 9¾ inches
*Armament:* Six 4.1inch A.A. (6 × 1), four 37mm A.A. (2 × 2), sixteen 20mm A.A. (4 × 4) guns
*Notes:* Former coast defence ship, which had been partially disarmed and relegated to training, re-armed as heavy A.A. battery

## Ex-RNeth.N coast defence ship: **UNDINE**

*Displacement:* 4,445 tons
*Dimensions:* 316¾(pp) 321(oa) × 50 × 18¾ feet
*Machinery:* Six Yarrow boilers, 2-shaft reciprocating (VTE) I.H.P. 6,400 = 16½ knots
*Bunkers & Radius:* Coal 610 tons; 3,300 miles at 10 knots
*Protection:* Main belt 4(ends)–6(amid) inches, bulkheads 6 inches, deck 2 inches, C.T. 7¾ inches
*Armament:* Six 4.1inch A.A. (6 × 1), four 40mm A.A. (4 × 1), sixteen 20mm A.A. (4 × 4) guns
*Notes:* Former coast defence ship re-armed as heavy A.A. battery.

## Ex-RDN coast defence ship: **ADLER**

*Displacement:* 3,500 tons
*Dimensions:* 275(pp) × 51 × 16½ feet
*Machinery:* Six Thornycroft boilers, 2-shaft reciprocating (VTE) I.H.P. 5,400 = 16 knots
*Bunkers & Radius:* Coal 265 tons; 1,050 miles at 14¾ knots

*Protection:* Main belt 6(ends)–7(amid) inches, bulkheads 7 inches, main deck 2¼(flat amid)–3(curved ends) inches. Turrets 7 inches, casemates 6 inches, C.T.7 inches

*Armament:* Two 9.4inch (2 × 1), four 5.9inch (4 × 1), eight 3inch (8 × 1), two 1-pounder (2 × 1), four 20mm A.A. (4 × 1), two 8mm A.A. (2 × 1) guns, four 18inch (4 × 1—fixed fwd, port and stbd, and aft—submerged) T.T.

*Complement:* 275

*Notes:* Former coast defence ship used for harbour service

## Ex-RDN coast defence ship: **NORDLAND**

*Displacement:* 3,800 tons (4,320 tons full)

*Dimensions:* 285½(pp) 295¼(oa) × 53½ × 15¾/16½ feet

*Machinery:* Four Yarrow (two oil and two coal-fired), 2-shaft reciprocating (VTE) I.H.P. 5,400 = 16 knots

*Bunkers & Radius:* O.F. 240 tons and coal 250 tons; 5,000 miles at 10 knots

*Protection:* Belt 6(ends)–7/7¾(amid) inches, bulkheads 6½ inches, deck 2¼(amid)–2½(ends) inches, Gunshields ½(sides and crowns)–1¾(faces) inches, C.T. 6¾ inches and tube 4 inches

*Armament:* Three 5.9inch (3 × 1), seven 20mm A.A. (1 × 4 and 3 × 1) guns

*Notes:* Former coast defence ship whose original armament includes ten 5.9inch (10 × 1), two 6-pounder A.A. (2 × 1), ten 20mm A.A. (10 × 1), fourteen 8mm A.A. (14 × 1) guns, two 17.7inch (fixed port and stbd—submerged) T.T., and complement 365. Partially disarmed for harbour service

**Name** *Niobe* (ex-*Gelderland*) **Built by** Fijenoord (Schiedam) **Launched** 28.9.98 **Fate** German heavy A.A. battery (1942), bombed and torpedoed Russian aircraft Kotka 16.7.44, salved 1948 and scrapped

**Name** *Ariadne* (ex-*Ijmuiden,* ex-*Hertog Hendrik*) **Built by** Netherlands Shipbuilding (Amsterdam) **Launched** 6.02 **Fate** Scuttled 5.40, salved and German heavy A.A. battery (1942); retroceded RNeth.N 1945

**Name** *Undine* (ex-*Vliereede,* ex-*Jacob van Heemskerck*) **Built by** Netherlands Shipbuilding (Amsterdam) **Launched** 12.9.06 **Fate** Scuttled 5.40, salved and German heavy A.A. battery (1942), *Neptunus* (1944); retroceded RNeth.N 1945

**Name** *Adler* (ex-*Peder Skram*) **Built by** Naval D.Y. (Copenhagen) **Launched** 2.5.08 **Fate** Scuttled Copenhagen 29.8.43, salved and German heavy A.A. battery (1944); bombed Allied aircraft Friedrichsort 1945, salved and scrapped Odense 1949

**Name** *Nordland* (ex-*Niels Juel*) **Built by** Naval D.Y. (Copenhagen) **Launched** 7.18 **Fate** Beached Isefjord after being bombed German aircraft 29.8.43, salved and German training ship (1944); bombed Allied aircraft Eckenforder 3.5.45, salved and scrapped 1952

# Auxiliary Vessels

## Ex-RYN light cruiser: **NIOBE**

*Displacement:* 2,370 tons
*Dimensions:* 328(pp) 341¼(ao) × 38¾ × 16/17¼ feet
*Machinery:* Five Schulz-Thornycroft boilers, 2-shaft reciprocating
  (VTE) I.H.P. 8,000 = 21 knots
*Bunkers & Radius:* Coal 580 tons; 4,000 miles at 10 knots
*Protection:* Main deck ¾(ends)–2(amid)–3½(E.R. glacis) inches,
  C.T. 2¾–3¼ inches
*Armament:* Six 3.4inch D.P. (6 × 1), four 20mm A.A. (4 × 1)
  guns
*Notes:* Captured and served successively in the RIt.N, the short-
  lived Croatian Navy, and finally the German Navy

## Light cruisers: **AMAZONE** and **MEDUSA**

*Displacement:* 2,608 tons
*Dimensions:* 328(pp) 341¼(oa) × 38¾ × 16½/17¾ feet
*Machinery:* Nine Marine boilers, 2-shaft reciprocating (VTE)
  I.H.P. 8,000 = 21½ knots
*Bunkers & Radius:* Coal 580 tons; 4,000 miles at 12 knots
*Protection:* Main deck ¾(ends)–2(amid) inches, C.T. 2¾–3½ inches
*Armament:* Six 4.1inch A.A. (6 × 1), five 40mm A.A. (5 × 1),
  four 20mm A.A. (1 × 4) guns
*Notes: Amazone* disarmed as accommodation ship. Machinery
  details are as originally fitted and were considerably reduced in
  power in *Medusa* and probably in *Amazone.* Removed from
  effective list 31.3.31 and 27.3.29 respectively

## Light cruiser: **ARCONA**

*Displacement:* 2,656 tons
*Dimensions:* 328(pp) 342½(oa) × 40¼ × 16½/17¾ feet
*Machinery:* Nine Marine boilers, 2-shaft reciprocating (VTE)
  I.H.P. 8,500 = 21½ knots

*Bunkers & Radius:* Coal 710 tons; 4,500 miles at 12 knots
*Protection:* Main deck ¾(ends)–2(amid) inches, C.T. 2¾–3¼ inches
*Armament:* Four 4.1inch A.A. (5 × 1), four 40mm A.A. (4 × 1),
 sixteen 20mm A.A. (4 × 4) guns
*Notes:* Machinery details are as originally fitted and power was
 later reduced by at least a half. Removed from effective list
 15.1.30

**Name** *Niobe* (ex-*Znaim*, ex-*Cattaro*, ex-*Dalmacija*, ex-*Niobe*)
**Built by** AG Weser (Bremen) **Launched** 18.7.99 **Fate** Torpedoed
RN MTBs *226* and *228* off Adria 22.12.43

**Name** *Amazone* **Built by** Germania Werft (Kiel)
**Fate** Accommodation ship; scrapped Hamburg 1954

**Name** *Medusa* **Built by** AG Weser (Bremen)
**Fate** Heavy A.A. battery; scuttled Wilhelmshaven 6.5.45, salved
and scrapped 1948

**Name** *Arcona* **Built by** AG Weser (Bremen) **Launched** 22.10.02
**Fate** Heavy A.A. battery; scuttled Wilhelmshaven 6.5.45, salved
and scrapped

## *Auxiliary cruiser:* ORION

*Displacement:* 15,000 tons (7,021 t.g.)
*Dimensions:* 463½(pp) 485½(oa) × 61 × 27d. feet
*Machinery:* 1-shaft geared turbines S.H.P. 6,200 = 14 knots
*Bunkers & Radius:* O.F.; 35,000 miles at 10 knots
*Armament:* Six 5.9inch (6 × 1), one 75mm, four 37mm A.A.
 (2 × 2), four 20mm A.A. (4 × 1) guns, six 21inch T.T.
 (2 × 3), two hundred and twenty-eight mines, two aircraft
*Complement:* 377

## *Auxiliary cruisers:* ATLANTIS *and* PINGUIN

*Displacement:* 17,000 tons (7,862 t.g.—*Atlantis*) 17,600 tons
 (7,766 t.g.—*Pinguin*)
*Dimensions:* 485½ *Pinguin,* 488 *Atlantis* (pp) 508½(oa) × 61¼ ×
 31d. feet
*Machinery:* 1-shaft 6-cyl. M.A.N. diesel motors (two per shaft)
 B.H.P. 6,400 = 16 knots
*Bunkers & Radius:* O.F.; 60,000 miles at 10 knots
*Armament:* Six 5.9inch (6 × 1), one 75mm, two 37mm A.A.
 (1 × 2), two 20mm A.A. (2 × 1) guns, four 21inch (2 × 2) T.T.,
 four hundred and twenty mines, two aircraft
*Complement:* 350 (*Atlantis*) or 420 (*Pinguin*)
*Notes:* The 5.9inch guns in the *Atlantis* were removed from the
 battleship *Schlesien*

## *Auxiliary cruiser:* **WIDDER**

*Displacement:* 16,000 tons (7,851 t.g.)
*Dimensions:* 477(pp) 498¾(oa) × 63 × 28¼d. feet
*Machinery:* 1-shaft geared turbines S.H.P. 6,200 = 14 knots
*Bunkers & Radius:* O.F.; 34,000 miles at 9 knots
*Armament:* Six 5.9inch (6 × 1), one 75mm, four 37mm A.A.
    (2 × 2), two 20mm A.A. (2 × 1) guns, four 21-inch (2 × 2)
    T.T., sixty mines, two aircraft
*Complement:* 363
*Notes:* The 5.9inch guns were removed from the battleship
    *Schleswig-Holstein*

## *Auxiliary cruiser:* **THOR**

*Displacement:* 10,000 tons (3,862 t.g.)
*Dimensions:* 379¾(pp) 400¼(oa) × 54¾ × 23¾d. feet
*Machinery:* 1-shaft A.E.G. geared turbines S.H.P. 6,500 = 18
    knots
*Bunkers & Radius:* O.F.; 40,000 miles at 10 knots
*Armament:* Six 5.9inch (6 × 1), one 60mm, two 37mm A.A.
    (1 × 2), two 20mm A.A. (2 × 1) guns, two 21inch (2 × 1) T.T.,
    three hundred mines, two aircraft
*Complement:* 345
*Notes:* The 5.9inch guns were removed from the battleship
    *Schlesien*

## *Auxiliary cruiser:* **STIER**

*Displacement:* 11,000 tons (4,778 t.g.)
*Dimensions:* 408½(pp) 439¾(oa) × 56½ × 21¼d. feet
*Machinery:* 1-shaft 7-cyl. diesel B.H.P. 2,785 = 14 knots
*Bunkers & Radius:* O.F.; 60,000 miles at 10 knots
*Armament:* Six 5.9inch (6 × 1), two 37mm A.A. (2 × 1), four
    20mm A.A. (4 × 1) guns, two 21inch (fixed and sub.) T.T.,
    thirty-five mines, two aircraft
*Complement: 324*

## *Auxiliary cruiser:* **KOMET**

*Displacement:* 7,500 tons (3,287 t.g.)
*Dimensions:* 358¾(pp) 377¼(oa) × 50¼ × 20d. feet
*Machinery:* 1-shaft 6-cyl. M.A.N. diesel motors (two per shaft)
    B.H.P. 3,100 = 16 knots
*Bunkers & Radius:* O.F.; 51,000 miles at 10 knots

*Armament:* Six 5.9inch (6 × 1), one 60mm, one 37mm A.A.,
two 20mm A.A. (2 × 1) guns, six 21inch (all fixed—four above
w.l. and two sub.) T.T., twenty-five mines, two aircraft, one
MTB (fitted to carry twenty-five mines)
*Complement:* 270
*Notes:* Light A.A. augmented by addition of two 37mm (2 × 1)
guns and complement increased to 521 in 1942

## *Auxiliary cruiser:* **KORMORAN**

*Displacement:* 19,000 tons (8,736 t.g.)
*Dimensions:* 515(pp) × 538(oa) × $66\frac{1}{4}$ × $30\frac{1}{2}$d. feet
*Machinery:* 2-shaft 9-cyl. diesel-electric motors (two per shaft)
B.H.P. 16,720 = 18 knots
*Bunkers & Radius:* O.F.; 84,500 miles at 10 knots
*Armament:* Six 5.9inch (6 × 1), four 37mm A.A. (2 × 2), four
20mm A.A. (4 × 1) guns, four 21inch (2 × 2) T.T., four
hundred and twenty mines, two aircraft, one MTB (fitted to
carry thirty mines
*Complement:* 400

**Name** *HS.1 Orion* (ex-mercantile *Kurmark*) **Built by** Blom & Voss
(Hamburg) **Launched** 27.3.30 **Fate** Repair ship (1942), training
ship *Hektor* (1944); bombed Russian aircraft Swinemunde
4.5.45

**Name** *HS.2 Atlantis* (ex-mercantile *Goldenfels*) **Built by** Bremer
Vulcan (Vegesack) **Launched** 31.5.37 **Fate** Gunfire RN Cruiser
*Devonshire* off Ascension 23.11.41

**Name** *HS.3 Widder* (ex-mercantile *Neumark*) **Built by** Howaldts
Werke (Kiel)/Blohm & Voss (Hamburg) **Launched** 21.12.29
**Fate** Repair ship (1941); mercantile *Ulysses* (1945), *Fechenheim*
(1953)

**Name** *HS.4 Thor* (ex-mercantile *Santa Cruz*) **Built by** Deutsche
Werft **Launched** 16.3.38 **Fate** Lost by fire Yokohama 30.11.42

**Name** *HS.5 Pinguin* (ex-mercantile *Kandefels*) **Built by** AG Wesser
(Bremen)/M.A.N. **Launched** 12.11.36 **Fate** Gunfire RN cruiser
*Cornwall* north of Seychelles 8.5.41

**Name** *HS.6 Stier* (ex-mercantile *Cairo*) **Built by** Germania Werft
(Kiel) **Launched** 7.10.36 **Fate** Gunfire mercantile *Stephen Hopkins*
east of Bahia 27.9.42

**Name** *HS.7 Komet* (ex-mercantile *Ems*) **Built by** AG Wesser
(Bremen)/M.A.N. **Launched** 16.1.37 **Fate** Torpedoed RN
*MTB.236* off C. de la Hague 14.11.42

**Name** *HS.8 Komoran* (ex-mercantile *Steiermark*) **Built by**
Germania Werft (Kiel) **Launched** 15.9.38 **Fate** Gunfire RAN
cruiser *Sydney* off Sharks Bay 19.11.41

## Auxiliary cruiser: **MICHEL**

*Displacement:* 11,000 tons (4,740 t.g.)
*Dimensions:* 433(oa) × 55 × 24¼d. feet
*Machinery:* 1-shaft diesel B.H.P. 6,650 = 16 knots
*Bunkers & Radius:* O.F.; 60,000 miles at 10 knots
*Armament:* Six 5.9inch (6 × 1), one 4.1inch A.A., four 37mm
    A.A. (2 × 2) four 20mm A.A. (4 × 1) buns, four 21inch
    (2 × 2) T.T., mines, two aircraft, one MTB (fitted to carry
    thirty mines
*Complement:* 400

## Auxiliary cruiser: **CORONEL**

*Displacement:* 11,000 tons (5,024 t.g.)
*Dimensions:* 418¼(pp) 439¾(oa) × 58¾ × 21¼d. feet
*Machinery:* 1-shaft 8-cyl. diesel motors B.H.P. 5,450 = 16 knots
*Bunkers:* O.F.
*Armament:* Six 5.9inch (6 × 1), six 40mm A.A. (6 × 1), eight
    20mm A.A. (2 × 4) guns, two 21inch (fixed and sub.) T.T.,
    mines, four aircraft
*Complement:* 350

## Auxiliary cruiser: **HANSA**

*Displacement:* 9,144 tons gross
*Dimensions:* 483(pp) 507(oa) × 31¼d. feet
*Machinery:* 2-shaft 6-cyl. B. & W. diesel motors B.H.P. 12,000 =
    18 knots
*Bunkers & Radius:* O.F.; 65,000 miles at 15 knots
*Armament:* Eight 5.9inch (8 × 1), one 75mm, three 40mm A.A.
    (3 × 1) guns, four 21inch (all fixed—two above w.l. and two
    sub.) T.T., one hundred and fifty mines, aircraft and catapult
*Notes:* Light A.A. increased by eight 37mm (4 × 2) and thirty
    20mm (6 × 4 and 6 × 1) guns in 1942

**Name** *HS.9 Michel* (ex-mercantile *Bonn,* ex-*Bielsko*) **Built by**
Danziger Werft **Launched** 4.39 **Fate** Torpedoed USN submarine
*Tarpon* south of Yokohama 17.10.43 Damaged RAF aircraft;
cruise cancelled Dunkirk 15.2.43

**Name** *HS.10 Coronel* (ex-mercantile *Togo*) **Built by** Bremer
Vulkan (Vegesack) **Launched** 1938 Fighter direction ship *Togo*
(1944); mercantile *Svalbard* (1947). Unfinished

**Name** *HS.00 Hansa* (ex-mercantile *Meersburg,* ex-*Glengarry*)
**Built by** Burmeister & Wain **Launched** 1939 **Fate** Training ship
(1943); mercantile *Empire Humber* (1945), *Glengarry* (1946)

*The auxiliary anti-submarine vessel* Uj.2104 *was a converted whale catcher.* (Drüppel)

*The auxiliary patrol vessel* Vp.1610 *was armed with an ex-French Army 75-mm field gun.*

# Ferries and Transports

## *Siebel ferry:* **SF**

*Displacement:* 143 tons
*Dimensions:* 106(oa) × 48¼ × 6 feet
*Machinery:* Two-shaft diesel motors (two per shaft), B.H.P. 640
    = 7½ knots
*Bunkers & Radius:* O.F. 3¼ tons; 350 miles
*Armament:* One 40mm A.A., two 20mm A.A. (2 × 1) guns
    ten lorries of 60t. d.w.
*Notes:* Built 1940–1 as Army transport ferry for U.K. invasion

## *Transport ferry* (*types A, B and C*): **MFP.1–626**

*Displacement:* 200 tons
*Dimensions:* 163½(oa) × 21¾ × 6 feet
*Machinery:* Three-shaft Deutz diesel motors, B.H.P. 505 =
    10¼ knots
*Bunkers & Radius:* O.F. 5 tons; 1,000 miles at 7½ knots
*Armament:* One 3.5inch, one 37mm A.A., two 20mm A.A. (2 × 1)
    guns, 150t. d.w.
*Complement:* 21
*Notes:* Built 1942–4

*Siebel ferry* No. 015.
(Drüppel)

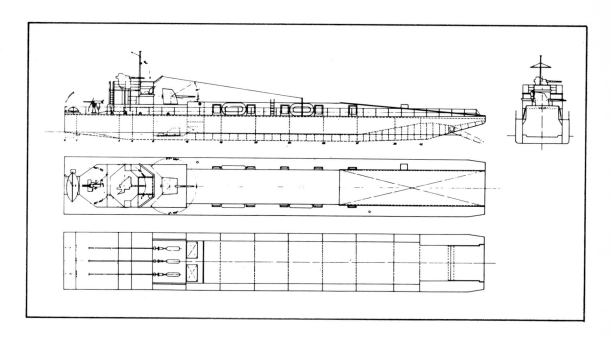

## Transport ferry (type D): **MFP.627–2000**

*General Arrangement of the D Type* MFP.

*Displacement:* 280 tons
*Dimensions:* $163\frac{1}{2}$(oa) × $21\frac{3}{4}$ × $8\frac{3}{4}$ feet
*Machinery:* Three-shaft Deutz diesel motors, B.H.P. 505 = 8 knots
*Bunkers & Radius:* O.F. 5 tons; 940 miles at $6\frac{1}{2}$ knots
*Armament:* One 3.5inch, one 37mm A.A., two 20mm A.A. (1 × 2) guns, 170t. d.w.
*Complement:* 21
*Notes:* Built 1942–4

*The transport ferry* MFP.121. (Drüppel)

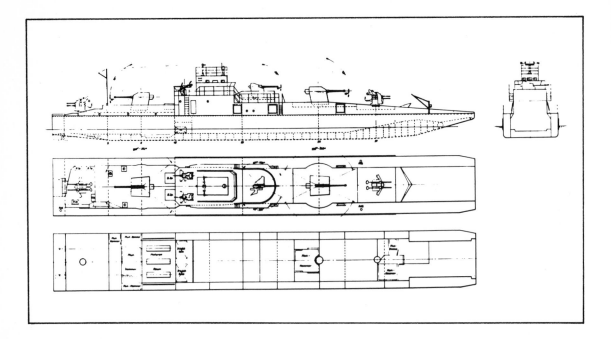

Above: *General Arrangement
of the* AFP, *converted from the
normal D Type* MFP.

Right: *Artillery ferry
AFP.83.* (Drüppel)

## Transport ferry (gun): *AFP.1–120*

*Displacement:* 280 tons
*Dimensions:* $163\frac{1}{2}$(oa) × $21\frac{3}{4}$ × $8\frac{3}{4}$ feet
*Machinery:* Three-shaft Deutz diesel motors, B.H.P. 505 =
    8 knots
*Bunkers & Radius:* O.F. 5 tons; 940 miles at $6\frac{1}{2}$ knots
*Armament:* two 4.1inch (2 × 1), two 37mm A.A. (2 × 1), eight
    20mm A.A. (2 × 4) guns, 170t. d.w.
*Complement:* 65
*Notes:* Built 1942–4 and were converted from *MFP (type D)*

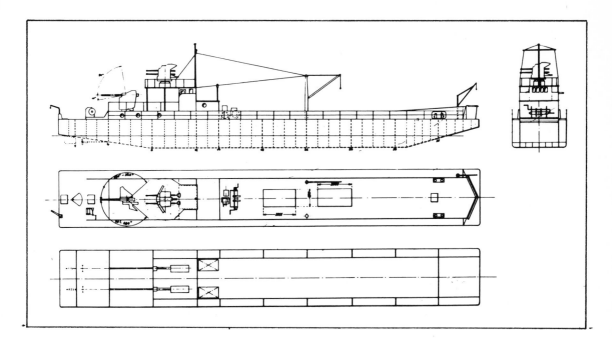

Above: *General Arrangement of the* MNL *or naval supply lighter.*

Left: *Transport* LT.1. (Drüppel)

## Supply lighter (*type II*): **MNL**

*Displacement:* 154 tons
*Dimensions:* 131¼(oa) × 27 × 6 feet
*Machinery:* three-shaft Deutz diesel motors, B.H.P. 505 = 10 knots
*Bunkers & Radius:* O.F. 3½ tons; 500 miles
*Armament:* One 37mm A.A., four 20mm A.A. (1 × 4) guns, 170t. d.w.
*Complement:* 13
*Notes:* Built 1942–4

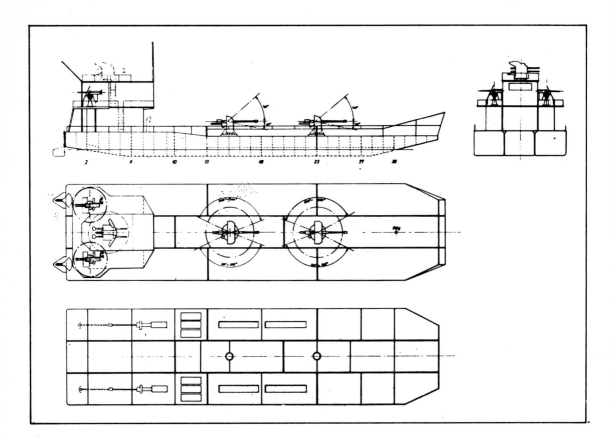

*General Arrangement of the MAL or artillery lighter.*

# Supply lighter (gun—type II): **MAL**

*Displacement:* 185 tons
*Dimensions:* 116½(oa) × 28¼ × 6 feet
*Machinery:* Two-shaft Deutz diesel motors, B.H.P. 270 = 8 knots
*Bunkers & Radius:* O.F. 4½ tons; 500 miles
*Armament:* Two 3inch (2 × 1), six 20mm A.A. (1 × 4 and 1 × 2) guns, one 3.4inch mortar
*Complement:* 28
*Notes:* Built 1942–4

# Transports: **KT.1–54**

*Displacement:* 700 tons
*Dimensions:* 206¾(pp) 223(oa) × 36 × 13 feet
*Machinery:* boilers, two-shaft reciprocating (VTE) and exhaust turbine, I.H.P. 2,400 = 14½ knots
*Bunkers:* Coal 160 tons
*Armament:* Four 20mm A.A. (1 × 4) guns
*Complement:* 37
*Notes:* Built 1941–2

# Submarine Depot Ships

As German submarines operated from well-equipped fixed bases they were served by relatively few depot ships, and these of small size. There was little apparent need for them except that their mobility enabled them to establish a temporary base at short notice for particular operations if shore base facilities did not exist.

The first depot ship, the diesel-engined *Saar*, was authorised in 1934 and was rapidly advanced to serve the Type I submarines then under construction. Compared with foreign contemporaries she was much smaller and primarily afforded command facilities for the attached flotillas and accommodation for the submarine crews.

No fewer than five mercantile conversions were completed in 1938: four from vessels extant (*Donau, Weichsel, Isar,* and *Lech*) and one from a vessel under construction (*Erwin Wassner*). Again, none of these vessels was of large size—generally approximating the *Saar* in dimensions—except the vessel taken over on the stocks which was slightly over 5,000 tons and was the sole unit powered by geared turbines, the other four having reciprocating machinery.

War construction was limited to three further vessels, all expansions of the *Saar* design, but still less than 5,000 tons. The first pair (*Wilhelm Bauer* and *Waldemar Kophamel*) were diesel-engined, while the final unit (*Otto Wunsche*) adopted geared turbines, and all were fast vessels able to steam at over 20 knots. Further units of the latter class were planned but the programme was not implemented as a small number of mercantile acquisitions met war requirements.

From 1940 the German Navy was able to establish major submarine bases in Norway and French Atlantic ports to supplement the principal home bases, and these former—with direct access to the open sea—were more advantageously placed for submarine deployment against Allied trade. The bulk of the operational submarine fleet worked from these bases, under a single centralised system of command. A training command was established in the Baltic which, until the closing stages of the war, was relatively safe for submarines working-up.

**Name** *Donau* (ex-mercantile *Nicea*) **Built by** Flender Werft (Lübeck) **Launched** 1922 **Fate** Internal explosion Flensburg 14.6.45

**Name** *Weichsel* (ex-mercantile *Syra*) **Built by** Howaldts Werke (Kiel) **Launched** 1923 **Fate** RN *Royal Rupert* (1945), Russian *Donetz* (1947)

**Name** *Isar* (ex-mercantile *Puma*) **Built by** Bremer Vulkan (Vegesack) **Launched** 1930 **Fate** Russian *Nyeman* (1946), mercantile *Artsa* (1949)

**Name** *Lech* (ex-mercantile *Panther*) **Built by** Bremer Vulkan (Vegesack) **Launched** 1930 **Fate** USN (1945), mercantile *Mare Ligure* (1948)

## Depot ship: **DONAU**

*Displacement:* 4,620 tons
*Dimensions:* $287\frac{1}{2}$(pp) $318\frac{1}{4}$(oa) × $41\frac{3}{4}$ × $14/17\frac{3}{4}$ feet
*Machinery:* Two Lamont boilers, one-shaft reciprocating (VTE)
    I.H.P. 1,800 = 12 knots
*Bunkers & Radius:* O.F. 240 tons
*Armament:* Four 20mm A.A. (4 × 1) guns
*Complement:* 216
*Notes:* Converted by Oderwerke (Stettin) 1938

## Depot ship: **WEICHSEL**

*Displacement:* 3,974 tons (5,200 tons full)
*Dimensions:* $309\frac{1}{4}$(pp) 351(oa) × $44\frac{1}{4}$ × $13\frac{1}{2}/17\frac{3}{4}$ feet
*Machinery:* Two boilers, one-shaft reciprocating (VTE) I.H.P.
    2,000 = 12 knots
*Bunkers & Radius:* Coal 540 tons
*Armament:* Four 20mm A.A. (4 × 1) guns
*Complement:* 222
*Notes:* Converted by Oderwerke (Stettin) 1938

## Depot ships: **ISAR** and **LECH**

*Displacement:* 3,850 tons (4,560 tons full)
*Dimensions:* 315(pp) $341\frac{1}{4}$(oa) × $45\frac{1}{4}$ × $15\frac{1}{2}/17\frac{1}{2}$ feet
*Machinery:* Three Scotch boilers, one-shaft reciprocating (VTE)
    I.H.P. 1,900 = 14 knots
*Bunkers & Radius:* O.F. 295 tons

*Armament:* Two 3.5inch A.A. (2 × 1), four 37mm A.A. (2 × 2),
   four 20mm A.A. (4 × 1) guns
*Complement:* 198
*Notes:* Converted by Schichau (Königsberg) and Oderwerke
   (Stettin) respectively 1938

## Depot ship: **SAAR**

*Displacement:* 2,710 tons (3,250 tons full)
*Dimensions:* 311¾(wl) 331¼(oa) × 44¼ × 14/15 feet
*Machinery:* Two-shafts, M.A.N. diesel motors, B.H.P. 4,800 =
   18 knots
*Bunkers & Radius:* O.F. 336 tons (9,400 miles at 13 knots)
*Armament:* Three 4.1inch A.A. (3 × 1), twenty-four 20mm A.A.
   (4 × 4 and 4 × 2) guns
*Complement:* 451
*Notes:* Twin 20mm were later replaced by single 40mm guns

**Name** *Saar* **Built by** Germania Werft (Kiel) **Launched** 5.4.34
**Fate** USN (1945), French *Gustave Zede* (1947)

**Name** *Erwin Wassner* (ex-mercantile *Gran Canaria*)
**Built by** Deutsche Werft (Hamburg) **Launched** 29.1.38
**Fate** Bombed Allied aircraft Kiel 24.7.44

**Name** *Wilhelm Bauer* **Built by** Naval Dockyard (Wilhelmshaven)
**Launched** 20.12.38 **Fate** Bombed Travemünde 8/4/45, salved
and scrapped 1950/1

**Name** *Waldemar Kophamel* **Built by** Naval Dockyard
(Wilhelmshaven) **Launched** 15.5.39 **Fate** Bombed Allied aircraft
Gdynia 18.12.44; salved 1949/51 and Russian *Kuban*

**Name** *Otto Wunsche* **Built by** Naval Dockyard (Wilhelmshaven)
**Launched** 23.5.40 **Fate** Russian *Paisherd* (1946)

## Depot ship: **ERWIN WASSNER**

*Displacement:* 5,150 tons (6,080 tons full)
*Dimensions:* 370¾(pp) 403½(oa) × 54¾ × 17/18¼ feet
*Machinery:* Two Lamont boilers, one-shaft A.E.G. geared
   turbines, S.H.P. 6,750 = 19½ knots
*Bunkers & Radius:* O.F. 748 tons (8,000 miles at 13 knots)
*Armament:* Four 37mm A.A. (2 × 2), six 20mm A.A. (6 × 1)
   guns
*Complement:* 229 + 67
*Notes:* Converted while building

## *Depot ships:* **WILHELM BAUER** and **WALDEMAR KOPHAMEL**

*Displacement:* 4,700 tons (5,600 tons full)
*Dimensions:* 413½(pp) 436¼(oa) × 52½ × 14/16 feet
*Machinery:* Two-shaft M.A.N. diesel motors (two per shaft),
   B.H.P. 12,400 = 20 knots
*Bunkers & Radius:* O.F. 650 tons (9,000 miles at 15 knots)
*Armament:* Four 4.1inch A.A. (2 × 2), one 40mm A.A., two
   37mm A.A. (1 × 2), twelve 20mm A.A. (3 × 4) guns
*Complement:* 289 + 423

## *Depot ship:* **OTTO WUNSCHE**

*Displacement:* 5,000 tons (5,900 tons full)
*Dimensions:* 433(pp) 456(oa) × 52½ × 14¾/16¾ feet
*Machinery:* Two shafts, M.A.N. diesel motors (two per shaft),
   B.H.P. 13,800 = 21½ knots
*Bunkers & Radius:* O.F.
*Armament:* Two 4.1inch A.A. (2 × 1), one 40mm A.A., two
   37mm A.A. (1 × 2), twelve 20mm A.A. (3 × 4) guns
*Complement:* 310 + 440

# Survey Vessels and Yachts

## Surveying vessel: **METEOR**

*Displacement:* 1,200 tons
*Dimensions:* 219¾(pp) 233(oa) × 33½ × 9¼/11¾ feet
*Machinery:* Two-shaft M.A.N. diesel motors, B.H.P. 2,200
 = 14½ knots
*Bunkers & Radius:* O.F. 440 tons; 10,000 miles at 9 knots
*Armament:* One 3.5inch, two 20mm A.A. (2 × 1) guns
*Complement:* 138

## Yacht: **GRILLE**

*Displacement:* 2,560 tons (3,430 tons full)
*Dimensions:* 377¼(pp) 443(oa) × 44¼ × 11¼/13¾ feet
*Machinery:* Four Benson boilers (pressure 1,175 lb.), two-shaft
 Blohm & Voss geared turbines, S.H.P. 22,000 = 26 knots
*Bunkers & Radius:* O.F. 1,030 tons; 9,500 miles at 19 knots
*Armament:* Three 3.5inch (3 × 1), four 37mm A.A. (2 × 2),
 four 20mm A.A. (4 × 1) guns
*Complement:* 248

## Yacht: **HELA**

*Displacement:* 2,315 tons (2,500 tons full)
*Dimensions* 303½ (pp) 320(oa) × 40¼ × 11½/13 feet
*Machinery:* Two-shaft M.A.N. diesel motors (two per shaft),
 B.H.P. 6,360 = 19 knots
*Bunkers & Radius:* O.F. 224 tons; 10,000 miles at 15 knots
*Armament:* Two 4.1inch (2 × 1), one 37mm A.A., two 20mm
 A.A. (1 × 2) guns
*Complement:* 244

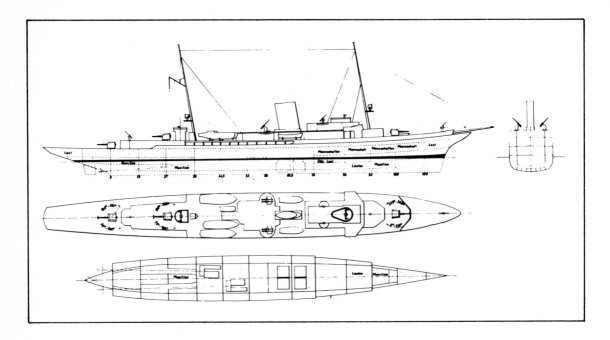

*General Arrangement of the*
*State Yacht* Grille.

## Surveying vessel: **Ersatz METEOR**

*Displacement:* 3,040 tons (3,361 tons full)
*Dimensions:* 308½(pp) 338(oa) × 50¼ × 13/15 feet
*Machinery:* Two-shaft M.A.N. diesel motors (two per shaft),
   B.H.P. 8,300 = 20 knots
*Bunkers & Radius:* O.F. 626 tons; 24,000 miles at 12 knots
*Armament:* Three 4.1inch (3 × 1), four 37mm A.A. (2 × 2) guns
*Complement:* 259

**Name** *Meteor* **Built by** Naval Dockyard (Danzig) **Launched** 18.1.15
**Fate** Russian *Ekvator* (1946)

**Name** *Grille* **Built by** Blohm & Voss (Hamburg)
**Launched** 15.12.34 **Fate** RN (1945), mercantile; scrapped
Bodenstown (N.J.) 17.8.51

**Name** *Hela* **Built by** Stulcken (Hamburg) **Launched** 29.12.38
**Fate** Russian *Angara* (1946)

**Name** Ersatz *Meteor* **Built by** Stulcken (Hamburg)
**Launched** 15.1.40 **Fate** Scrapped incomplete

# BIBLIOGRAPHY

AMERICAN SOCIETY OF NAVAL ENGINEERS, Transactions of
  (Washington, D.C.).
BATTLE OF THE ATLANTIC, The (H.M. Stationery Office—1946).
Brassey's NAVAL ANNUAL (London).
COMPRESSED AIR MAGAZINE (London).
DEUTSCHE FLOTTE 1848–1945 (G. Kroschel & A. L. Evers—1963).
DEUTSCHEN U-BOOTE 1906–1945, Die (B. Herzog—1959).
DEUTSCHEN U-BOOTE 1939–1945, Die (O. Mielke—1963).
ENGINEER (London).
FLOTTES DE COMBAT, Les (H. Le Masson).
GERMAN SUBMARINE WAR 1914–1918, The (R. H. Gibson &
  M. Prendergast—1931).
GOLDEN HORSESHOE, The (T. Robertson—1955).
K-MEN (C. D. Dekker—1955).
LAUGHING COW, The (J. Metzler—1955).
MARINE NEWS, Journal of the World Ship Society (Kendal).
MOTOR SHIP (London).
ROYAL INSTITUTION OF NAVAL ARCHITECTS, Transactions of
  (London).
SCHIFFE DER DEUTSCHEN KRIEGSMARINE & LUFTWAFFE 1939–1945
  (E. Gröner—1954).
SHIPBUILDING & SHIPPING RECORD (LONDON).
SOCIETY OF NAVAL ARCHITECTS & MARINE ENGINEERS,
  Transations of (New York).
SOMMERGIBILI ITALIANI, I (Ufficio Storico della Marine Militaire—
  1963).
SWASTIKA AT SEA (C. D. Dekker—1953).
U-BOATS AT WAR (H. Busch—1956).
U-BOAT 977 (H. Schaeffer—1952).
UNITED STATES NAVAL INSTITUTE, Transactions of (Annapolis).
UNITED STATES SUBMARINE LOSSES—WORLD WAR II (U.S. Navy—
  1963).
WARSHIPS OF WORLD WAR II (H. T. Lenton & J. J. Colledge—
  1963).
Weyer's FLOTTEN TASCHENBUCH (A. Bredt).
WILL NOT WE FEAR (C. E. T. Warren & J. Benson—1961).